OVER THE RANGE

Photographed at Promontory, Utah, in 2007, the curving panel toward the rear of Union Pacific 119's tender (coal car) shows the colorful and ornate artwork incorporated into American locomotives in the Victorian era.

OVER THE RANGE

A History of the Promontory
Summit Route of the Pacific Railroad

Richard V. Francaviglia

UTAH STATE UNIVERSITY PRESS
LOGAN, UTAH

Copyright ©2008 Utah State University Press

Published by Utah State University Press
An imprint of University Press of Colorado
245 Century Circle, Suite 202
Louisville, Colorado 80027

 ASSOCIATION of UNIVERSITY PRESSES   The University Press of Colorado is a proud member of
the Association of University Presses.

The University Press of Colorado is a cooperative publishing enterprise supported, in part,
by Adams State University, Colorado State University, Fort Lewis College, Metropolitan State
University of Denver, University of Colorado, University of Northern Colorado, University of
Wyoming, Utah State University, and Western Colorado University.

∞ This paper meets the requirements of the ANSI/NISO Z39.48–1992 (Permanence of
Paper).

ISBN: 978-0-87421-705-6 (cloth)
ISBN: 978-1-60732-778-3 (paperback)
ISBN: 978-0-87421-706-3 (e-book)

Library of Congress Cataloging-in-Publication Data

Francaviglia, Richard V.
  Over the range : a history of the Promontory summit route of the Pacific / Richard V.
Francaviglia.
       p. cm.
  Includes bibliographical references and index.
  ISBN 978-0-87421-705-6 (cloth : alk. paper) – ISBN 978-1-60732-778-3 (pbk : alk. paper) –
ISBN 978-0-87421-706-3 (e-book)
  1. Pacific railroads. 2. Railroads–West (U.S.)–History. 3. Union Pacific Railway Company. 4.
Central Pacific Railroad Company–History. 5. Railroads–History. I. Title.
  HE2763.F73 2008
  385.3'120979242–dc22
                         2008025853

To
DAVID F. MYRICK,
historian and author, whose books on
the railroads of the American West
continue to inspire

Contents

Acknowledgments

In telling the story of how the area around Promontory Summit developed in relation to the railroad, I not only traveled to the Golden Spike National Historic Site numerous times, but also conducted historical research in archives and through interviews. Both were very pleasant experiences. Promontory Summit and its environs are fascinating but so, too, are the individuals and groups who care about its history. Many kind people helped me in this endeavor to tell Promontory's story, and I would be remiss if I did not thank them here. First and foremost is Robert (Bob) Spude, of the National Park Service, who sought out my services for this project. Bob knew me in my role as a historical resources consultant and professor at the University of Texas at Arlington. However, he also knew about my love of railroad history and my love for the Great Basin, the subject of two of my recent books. More to the point, though, he provided me a weeklong introduction to the site in July 2005, after which he sent box after box of files to our university so that I could begin work on the project. Bob introduced me to the enthusiastic, knowledgeable, and helpful staff at the Golden Spike National Historic Site at Promontory Summit. Superintendent Maggie Johnson, who passed away before this book could be published, was a joy to work with and will be missed by all. My contacts at the visitors' center, including acting superintendent Tammy Benson, lead park ranger Valerie Steffen, historical archaeologist Melissa Cobern, and archaeologist Bret Guisto, kindly shared information and helped me make numerous local contacts who I later interviewed. These included Delone Glover of Brigham City, and Merlin and Doris Larsen, whose ranch lies along the east slope of the Promontory Mountains. Bob Spude also introduced me to Michael Polk and his able staff of archaeologists and historians at Sagebrush Consultants in Ogden, Utah. They proved to be extremely helpful as I consulted Promontory line materials that Michael had collected since the early 1980s. Wendy Simmons Johnson at Sagebrush Consultants kindly provided a wonderful photograph from her personal family collection. Michael personally provided me valuable information as I spent several days at his office in Ogden, and for that I am especially grateful. The staff at the Box Elder County Courthouse in Brigham City were especially helpful in locating historic maps of the old railroad right of way.

Over the years, I have developed a number of excellent historical contacts in this region. These include Noel Carmack of Utah State University in Logan; Michael (Mike) Landon of the archives of the Church of Jesus Christ of Latter-day Saints in Salt Lake City; Phil Notarianni, director of the Utah State Historical Society; and Utah railroad authority Don Strack of Centerville. At the Nevada Historical Society archives in Reno, Eric Moody was also quite helpful. Outside the region, associates like Jim Ackerman of the Newberry Library in Chicago, and Peter Blodgett of the Huntington Library in San Marino, California, were extremely helpful. Peter put me in touch with Huntington staff member Dixie Dillon, who helped me gain access to a crucial document that shed new light on the Mormons' role in surveying the railroad in Promontory and vicinity. Helpful, too, was the staff at the DeGolyer Library, Southern Methodist University, including Anne Peterson and Cynthia Franco. The staff at the Denver Public Library helped me gain access to their treasure trove of historical photographs. In Sacramento at the western terminus of the original Pacific Railroad, the California State Railroad Museum (CSRM) staff also provided numerous materials. In particular, CSRM Curator of History & Technology Kyle Wyatt shared his expertise with me on several occasions. At the Union Pacific Museum in Council Bluffs, Iowa, John Bromley was especially helpful. So, too, were the staff members at the University of Iowa in Iowa City, which houses a considerable collection of Union Pacific materials. At the National Archives in College Park, Maryland, fellow geographer and railroad historian Richard Smith helped me gain access to numerous unpublished maps. David Myrick, the dean of western railroad historians, kindly answered my questions about Promontory despite the fact that he was "wrapping up" two books on other railroads in the Intermountain West at the time. Another former SP employee, Lynn Farrar, also helped point me to historic source material. A new associate, John Masters of Wichita, Kansas, provided valuable information on the 1903 Curved Dash Oldsmobile— one of the very first automobiles to travel through Promontory.

Several colleagues and associates at my university also assisted immeasurably. These include Ben Huseman, of UT Arlington's Special Collections, who—along with other staff members—provided numerous maps from our extensive cartographic collections. UT Arlington graduate Nate Kogan kindly provided a copy of a Mormon mural featuring a painting of the golden spike ceremony at the 1964–1965 New York World's Fair. Ann Jennings, secretary at the Center for Greater Southwestern Studies and the History of Cartography was my right-hand person from the beginning to the conclusion of this project. In addition to typing the original and many revised drafts of the manuscript, Ann made travel arrangements, secured materials, and kept track of paperwork on this multi-year grant-funded project. Without her help, the help of the other people mentioned above, and some I've probably missed mentioning, this book could not have been written.

Introduction

In the 1890s, travel writers faced a daunting task: spectacular west-ern sights often tempted them to write fanciful, exaggerated prose for the public. One writer, Stanley Wood, claimed that he had resisted that temptation when he wrote the popular book *Over the Range to the Golden Gate*.[1] As Wood put it in his preface, "No attempt will be made at 'fine writing'; every effort will be made to state just such facts as the traveler would like to know, and to state these facts in clear and explicit language." Like Stanley Wood, I hope to share new facts about a por-tion of the same transcontinental railroad line that he traversed as he went "Over the Range," which is to say, across the Rocky Mountains to the Pacific. However, unlike Wood, I shall dwell in considerable detail on just one portion of the first transcontinental railroad, the section over Promontory Summit. And unlike Wood, I must admit to having an emotional attachment to the area under discussion. The countryside in the vicinity of Promontory, with its abrupt mountains, dazzling salt flats, and sweeping vistas, is as enchanting as it is interesting. Hopefully, that admission will enable readers to understand why I will provide some personal aesthetic insights, as well as facts, about this part of the Great Basin.

In the process of traveling over the Promontory Range on his fact-finding mission, Stanley Wood made some insightful comments about the countryside travelers saw on the famed transcontinental railroad. As it turns out, Wood's 1904 edition would be the last to make this claim as the mainline of the transcontinental railroad soon bypassed the site of Promontory Summit, where history was made as the rails were joined on May 10, 1869. Most people traveling through this area by rail after 1904 merely mentioned that Promontory Summit, lying north of the stretch of the railroad that ran directly across the Great Salt Lake, was now bypassed and forlorn. That desolation, however, should not deter the serious historian, tourist, or naturalist. Truth is, the area around Promontory Summit is special in terms of both its natural and cultural history, and it is time to share that richness.

As Stanley Wood did, I make many remarks on the landscape along the route. I also share insights about what remains of the present ghost railroad line. My task, however, was a bit more difficult than Wood's for several reasons. First, Wood had fewer sources to consult. He read and summarized some contemporary reports, then integrated them into a lively travelogue. Second, Wood wrote about the present: everything he needed was right in front of him as he traveled, whereas I had to dig for information about what happened in the past along the route over Promontory Summit. Third, because the railroad line over Promontory became part of the Southern Pacific, researchers face an additional burden: About a century ago, the great fire in San Francisco, which resulted from the April 1906 earthquake, destroyed almost all of the company's records. Although that is a factor affecting all histories of the Southern Pacific's railroad activities, on Promontory I faced yet another challenge: for several reasons, the line over Promontory Summit was among the least photographed of the Southern Pacific's lines. Why? Although Promontory was on everyone's lips in 1869, interest faded quickly as writers turned their pens, and photographers pointed their cameras, to other more interesting phenomena—for example, the spectacular snowsheds in the Sierra, or the part of the line through Weber Canyon.

To most people, Promontory was about as bleak a place as can be imagined. Naturally, there was little interest in it aside from what happened there on May 10, 1869. As many people pointed out, the entire railroad line ran through rather inhospitable country for dozens of miles on either side of Promontory Summit. There were few amenities, and only rudimentary services, along much of the line from Corinne, Utah, westward into Nevada. Lastly, with the opening of the Lucin Cutoff in 1904, the Promontory line and Promontory itself faded into obscurity until the mid-twentieth century witnessed the rise of interest in history. At that time, paved roads gave a new generation of Western history buffs and tourists easy access to Promontory and other sites associated with the Old West. For these and many other reasons, the story of the line over Promontory has been difficult to decipher.

There are, however, several bright spots for the researcher and reader. Due to that increasing interest in history, which gathered steam during the Great Depression and began to reach a fever pitch after World War II, the experience at Promontory is one of the most documented subjects in the American West. First, we have at our disposal nearly one hundred books dealing with the building and completion of the transcontinental railroad. Some are better than others, but most highlight the importance of what happened here in 1869. Among the best of these is David Haward Bain's *Empire Express: Building the First Transcontinental Railroad.*[2] The typical book about the transcontinental railroad emphasizes what occurred from Omaha to California, culminating with the driving of the Golden Spike at Promontory Summit in May 1869. The book you are about to read, however, focuses on the section of the transcontinental railroad in the vicinity of Promontory—specifically about fifty miles on either side of Promontory Summit—and it continues in time well *after* that memorable event in 1869.

Second, since the passage of the National Historic Preservation Act of 1966, which coincided with growing interest in commemorating the centennial of the driving of the golden spike, numerous government agencies have sponsored reports on the archaeological and historical resources around Promontory Summit. Among them is the United States Department of Interior, for the site itself became part of our national heritage to be protected and interpreted after the National Park Service acquired it. This book is different because it brings together two separate types of literature—popular history-based, and cultural resource-based. Moreover, it will bring two normally separate disciplines (history and geography) together as it places the line over Promontory Summit in the context of a broad period of history, ca. 1820 to the early twenty-first century. Doing this requires using as many primary sources as possible. Add to this the wealth of information now on the Web sites of organizations like the Central Pacific Railroad Photographic History discussion group, and the Web sites of the National Park Service and the California State Railway Museum, and the resource picture brightens considerably.

Yet another bright spot is the availability of rich and varied collections of maps. Some, like David Rumsey's collection, are online, while others must be visited. Many maps that are closely associated with the transcontinental railroad at Promontory have never been studied carefully. These maps reveal the development of Promontory Summit's place in history. As historian Andrew M. Modelski noted, railroads and modern American mapping techniques were closely associated.[3] The advent of the railroads stimulated mapmaking along many fronts. In the early nineteenth century, a number of promoters of water and rail transportation were, in fact, also surveyors and mapmakers. The close relationship between railroads and commercial cartography was evident by the 1870s, when publishers like Rand McNally & Co. rose to prominence as purveyors of railroad-related maps. Various levels of government have also had a long relationship with railroad maps. Railroad routes often appear on county maps—as in the case of Box Elder County, Utah, through which the railroad line over Promontory Summit runs. Actually, federal maps showing projected travel routes often predated even the formation of counties, which began about 1850. By the early-to-mid 1850s, federal railroad surveys produced highly detailed maps of projected routes that were proposed for railroads in the western United States. The line over Promontory Summit was among these.

In addition to commercial and government maps, the railroads themselves prepared many maps; some were made to help the railroads claim the best routes, while others were of completed lines. The latter were created for purposes of operating and promoting the lines that the railroads had built. These maps, among others, will be employed to tell the story of this railroad. Of the many governmental maps, those by the Interstate Commerce Commission (ICC) from around 1916 contain a wealth of information about trackage, buildings, and other important features. All government railroad maps remind us that a close, and sometimes contentious, relationship has existed between public authorities and privately owned transportation companies that serve the public. All of these maps were once tools of a growing empire, but now are tools of the historian.

This book, then, tells Promontory's story in historic and geographic context using words, photographs, and maps. It differs from other published works because it tells the story of Promontory for almost two centuries rather than one big day—May 10, 1869—in the life of the community. It therefore also tells the story about how the railroad affected the surrounding countryside, and how it operated over a long period— seventy-three years—from 1869 to 1942. Moreover, it also relates the activities at Promontory, and elsewhere, that led to the creation of the Golden Spike National Historic Site, one of the nation's most important transportation-related properties, and a crown jewel of western American history.

Chapter 1

Envisioning Promontory
(1820–1850)

In the early 1800s, when the words rail road began to be heard in the United States, much of the area west of St. Louis and east of Spanish California was terra incognita for most Americans. At that time, the term rail road (or, somewhat later, railroad) referred to any method of transport that relied on rails laid horizontal to the ground and upon which wheeled vehicles could roll. At this early date, the rails were wooden, but might also be made of iron. Horses or mules likely provided the power to haul cars over such a railroad. By around 1820, however, people began to envision railroads in a more modern way: the rails would be lengths of iron, or perhaps sheet metal, strapped onto wood stringers, and the power would be steam. Although most of the early railroad development occurred in England, this new form of transport had especially strong advocates in the United States, where distances were vast and resources seemingly unlimited. By the mid to late 1820s, even before a railroad was built in the United States, a few visionaries actually believed that this iron road would take the westward moving nation to the Pacific Ocean.[1] Fairly primitive and not especially dependable railroad technology did not dampen their enthusiasm. The fact that Mexico and Britain claimed much of this country west of the Rocky Mountains did not deter their ambitions. After all, intrepid explorers were constantly bringing back encouraging reports about the opportunities and resources in this far western frontier.

One of these explorers was John Charles Frémont, who made his way westward into the area around the Great Salt Lake in the summer of 1843. At this time, Frémont was far from American soil as he moved along a poorly defined boundary between Mexico and Britain. His goal was to find better routes of travel for the people who hoped to settle the Oregon country of northwestern North America—an area claimed by Britain but highly desired by would-be settlers from the westward-expanding United States. But Frémont also had an ulterior motive that was part of a larger agenda of national expansion—to help claim this portion of the North American West for the United States.

Unbeknownst to Frémont and his exploring party at this time, the huge desolate region they now entered was an area of interior drainage: About a quarter-million square miles in size, this region was peculiar in that none of the rain or snow that falls here reaches the sea. As the Frémont party gazed across the area, they saw tall, snow-covered mountains (most of which ran in a north-south direction), broad slopes covered with grasses and desert brush, and vast valley bottoms covered either by sheets of water like the Great Salt Lake or, more commonly, glistening flats of salt. Fascinated by the landscape here, Frémont became obsessed with figuring out what lay in this huge area that would soon be called the Intermountain West.

Frémont knew, and acknowledged, that many others had traveled into portions of this region long before he arrived. These visitors included early Spanish explorers in the 1770s and mountain men and trappers who searched for beaver pelts here in the 1820s and 1830s. Frémont also knew that the area was not only remote but poorly mapped. In fact, one of his missions was to map a large portion of the area that was claimed, but essentially unoccupied, by Mexico. Less than a year later, Frémont confirmed something he had deduced from earlier explorers. In early 1844, he proved to his satisfaction that the region's streams and lakes had no outlet to the sea. Frémont coined the term *Great Basin* for this region of mountains, desert playas (dry lakes), marshy areas, and scattered lakes. These water bodies were remnants of much larger (and deeper) lakes that had occupied almost half the surface area during the last ice age. That cooler and wetter period had ended just about 10,000 years ago when the climate became warmer and drier. By the mid-1840s, American pioneers trekking to the Oregon country traversed a portion of this area. Most of them, too, considered it a desolate place; getting through it was the dues they had to pay in order to reach a fabled land—the lush green valleys and fir-clad mountains of the Pacific Northwest. Thankfully, Britain gave up claims to this area without firing a shot, but Mexico was not easy to intimidate. The maps by German-born master cartographer Charles Preuss, that resulted from Frémont's reconnaissances in extreme northern Mexico, helped set the stage for the United States taking the region after the bloody, but relatively short,

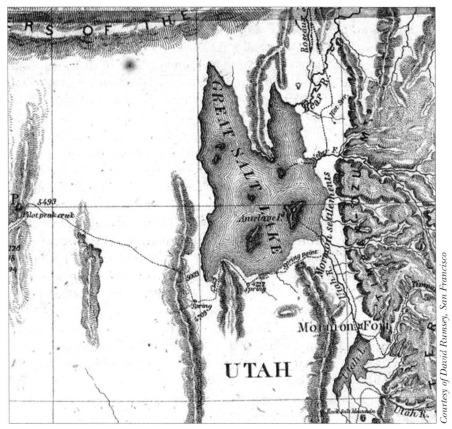

FIG. 1–1
Detail from *Map of Oregon and Upper California . . . .* by John Charles Frémont (Charles Preuss, cartographer), 1848.

U.S.-Mexican War of 1846–48. In that war, Mexico lost about half its territory, almost a million square miles of land that included the Great Basin. There was intense interest in this area as Americans wanted to know more about the region they had just acquired and that Frémont knew so much about.

Frémont's maps were a perfect source for such information. Under the direction of Preuss, Frémont's expedition of 1844 had mapped as much of the region as they could. By 1848, the Frémont-Preuss map summarizing the state of knowledge about the entire Interior West was published, and it helped the American public visualize the Great Salt Lake and environs (fig. 1–1). On this map, their notations stated that the Great Basin was sparsely inhabited by "miserable" Indians—by which they meant that the native peoples had little in the way of possessions— and they lived a difficult life in a region of marginal resources. The map

7

also showed "Mormon settlements" which were of intense interest to Americans as the Mormons were said to be building a "New Jerusalem" in the desert near the Great Salt Lake.

The Mormons played (and still play) a major role in this part of the West, and their claims here predate the United States' victory over Mexico in 1848. In fact, well *before* the U.S.-Mexican War began, the area was eyed by the Mormons, or members of the Church of Jesus Christ of Latter-day Saints. The Mormons knew about, and used, the best maps they could find. With earlier maps prepared by Frémont and S. A. Mitchell in hand, the Mormons arrived at the eastern edge of the Great Salt Lake in July 1847. Led by Brigham Young, the Mormons had fled persecution in the Middle West and now sought a place where they could settle and worship unmolested. The Mormons believed that they had left the United States, which had betrayed them by refusing to protect them from mobs. Upon their arrival in Utah, the Latter-day Saints now had the entire region pretty much to themselves—or so they thought. The Indians offered little resistance at first, and the main battle the Saints would have to fight was the physical environment. However, shortly after the Mormons developed their first community (Great Salt Lake City) and began spreading into the Great Basin, gold was discovered in California. That discovery, in February 1848, reshaped the new nation. Although the U.S.-Mexican War was just about to end, and the entire area would soon become part of the United States, few, including the Mormons, could anticipate the effect that the Gold Rush would have on the interior North American West. In 1849, thousands of people found their way to California, either by sea or by land. Some of those who crossed overland entered Utah east of the Great Salt Lake, on the Mormon Trail, circled north to avoid the forbidding Salt Lake Desert, and continued southwestward to follow the Humboldt River Valley in what would later (in 1864) become the state of Nevada. The Gold Rush of 1849 was yet another event in history that brought calls for better— which is to say, faster and safer—forms of travel from the settled eastern United States to the Pacific Coast. By this time, about 1850, it was well understood that the most desirable way to travel on land was by rail.

The opening of the Great Basin to Anglo-American settlement coincided with growing federal interest in the Intermountain West. Most of the federal expeditions to the area, in fact, were both military and scientific in nature. This was the age of what historian William Goetzman calls the "soldier-scientist." The relatively young discipline of geology was one of their skills, and it helped the nation open the West to development. Less than ten years after Frémont's initial exploration of the area, and at just the time that Congress was being lobbied to support the

Photo by author

FIG. 1–2
The Great Salt Lake—one of the West's most prominent landmarks—
was also an obstacle to east-west traffic in Utah.

exploration of a railroad route, a team of geological and topographical researchers found themselves on the shore of the Great Salt Lake—a huge inland sea that was among the West's signature landmarks (fig. 1–2). This expedition, like many at the time, focused on resources that could speed the area's development and sustain a railroad as part of the process. The expedition, charged to learn more about the area around the lake, including its mineral resources, vegetation, and climate, was led by Captain Howard Stansbury, for whom Stansbury Point and the Stansbury Mountains are named. As tensions began to mount between the Mormons and the federal government over who would control the region, some saw Stansbury's presence as a way for the United States to increase its visibility on the Mormons' doorstep. Stansbury was wise enough, however, to employ Mormons as part of his survey team. It was, in fact, Stansbury, who helped put the area around the Promontory Mountains on the map, as it were. In a remarkable reconnaissance under difficult conditions, Stansbury helped demystify the unusual geography of this enigmatic lake, into which one particularly prominent feature— the brooding Promontory Mountains—extended.

As seen on Frémont's 1848 *Map of Oregon and Upper California*, the Promontory Mountains are easily the most significant landmark in the northern part of the Great Salt Lake, a long peninsula separating Bear

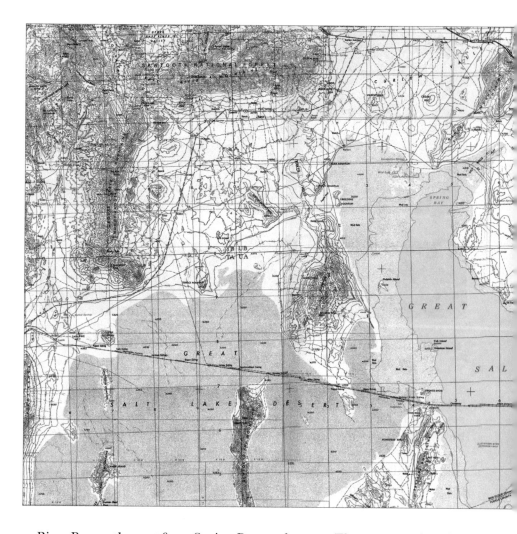

River Bay on the east from Spring Bay on the west. These mountains also continue northward, becoming more fragmented as they rise above the surrounding countryside. Delineated in more detail on a modern map at a much larger scale (fig. 1–3), the mountains are still the most apparent feature at the northern end of the lake. That increased detail is a result of technology that enables the accurate depiction of the topography, vegetation, and other features of the environment.

To today's airline passenger gazing down from an altitude of 36,000 feet, the Promontory Mountains appear as stark and forbidding as they did in Frémont's time (fig. 1–4) In this northeastward-looking air view taken in December 2006, the mountains separate the waters of Spring Bay and the northwestern end of the Great Salt Lake (lower left) from the shallow margins of Bear River Bay (center right). The mantle of windblown snow

FIG. 1–3
Modern (1987) topographical
map of the area adjacent to
the north end of the Great
Salt Lake.

and the mountain's steep-sided canyons accentuate Promontory's harsh character in this view. This was, and still is, a place where nature dominates. The average airline passenger looking down on this scene would have no idea that this was the place where history was made in 1869. To the untrained eye, it looks much like other beautiful, if bleak, scenery that passes below a jet airliner traveling at about 400 miles per hour.

To imaginative observers on foot (or horseback) in the 1840s and 1850s, though, the silhouette of the Promontory Mountains looked like a huge whale nosing its way into the Great Salt Lake. The nose of these mountains makes contact with the lakeshore at a place that would soon be called Promontory Point. Travelers would also have noted an island, named Fremont Island after the famed explorer, toward which the whale appeared to be diving. Although these mountains are easy to imagine

Photo by author

FIG. 1–4
December, 2006, aerial photograph of the north end of the
Promontory Range (*center*) and a portion of the Great Salt Lake
near Spring Bay (*lower left*) and edges of Bear River Bay (*center right*).
View looks north-northeast from airliner at 32,000 feet altitude.

as one huge, dark-colored whale, they are quite complex. Divided into
two separate mountain ranges—the Promontory Range and the North
Promontory Mountains—the mountains seem to be *two* cavorting whales;
that is, the smaller Northern Promontory Mountains seem to be chas-
ing the bigger Promontory Range southward into the lake. Where the
tail of the Promontory Range and the nose of the North Promontory
Range meet, there is a lower, relatively smooth, valley-like swale. Called
Promontory Summit, this area is the lowest—and hence easiest—place
to cross over the Promontory Range. Much like a pass between the two
separate ranges, this is where history was made in 1869.

The name of Promontory Summit deserves some interpretation.
According to the dictionary definition, the word *promontory* signifies a
high point of land or rock projecting into the sea or other water beyond
the line of coast, a headland. It can also be a bluff, or part of a plateau,
overlooking a lowland. Note that *two* factors are present in these defi-
nitions: a promontory is a *landmark* that towers above the surrounding
land and, according to the first definition, is actually a *point* of land that
juts out into a body of water. The very concept of a promontory, then,
is closely tied to a *place* that is both a landmark and very specific in location. The term *Promontory Point*, where the mountains actually reach the

lake, is, in a sense, redundant; after all, a promontory *is* a point. As an astute writer observed in the early 1870s, the name Promontory Point "... appears a strange bit of tautology."[2] In this case, however, it is understandable, for the mountains themselves *are* the promontory (that is, the high land that rises abruptly to form a landmark). Promontory Point, then, is the place where the southern end (or tip) of the Promontory Mountains meets the Great Salt Lake. Promontory Summit, on the other hand, is that location within the Promontory Mountain range(s) where a route of travel can cross the range at the lowest point to avoid strenuous mountain climbing. The term *summit* here refers to the elevation of the mountain pass, while the highest point in the range would be, and is, called the peak. In the Promontory Mountains, the summit or pass lies at about 4,909 feet (1,496 meters) above sea level, while the peak stands at about 7,760 feet (2,365 meters). As seen on a map showing the area's general topography (fig. 1–5), the Promontory Mountains are the most prominent topographic feature in this area.

There are, however, many important geographic features from the Wasatch Mountains westward all the way to the western edge of the Great Salt Lake Desert. Leaving Brigham City and vicinity and skirting the northeast edge of the Great Salt Lake, one first arrives at the aptly-named Little Mountain after crossing the Bear River Valley (fig. 1–6). Like most of the mountains in this area, Little Mountain is a block of sedimentary rocks originally laid down in a marine environment but now high and dry—a result of faulting resulting from the stretching of the western North American continent. Little Mountain provides a hint of the uplifted topography that is so characteristic of the Great Basin. Geologists use the terms *horst* and *graben* for such topography, a horst being an uplifted block of terrain and a graben being the lowered valley adjacent to it.[3] Continuing westward, one encounters the Blue Spring Hills, and then crosses Blue Creek, which is at the southern edge of the Blue Creek Valley and its northern extension, Howell Valley. Lying west of here is the Promontory Range, which so impressed Stansbury.

Westward of Promontory, the land descends in a sweeping arc just northeast of Spring Bay. This is called the Hansel Valley, which is bordered on the west by the Hansel Mountains and on the east by the North Promontory Mountains. West and north of this range, one finds the broad Curlew Valley, which reaches, at its southern edge, the north shore of the Great Salt Lake and the large salt flats. Farther west from the Curlew Valley, the land rises again into the Baker Hills and Hogup Mountains. Still continuing westward, there is a broad swale called the Sink of Dove Creek. West of this swale, the Matlin Mountains rise, as do Red Dome and the Terrace Mountains. These prominent features

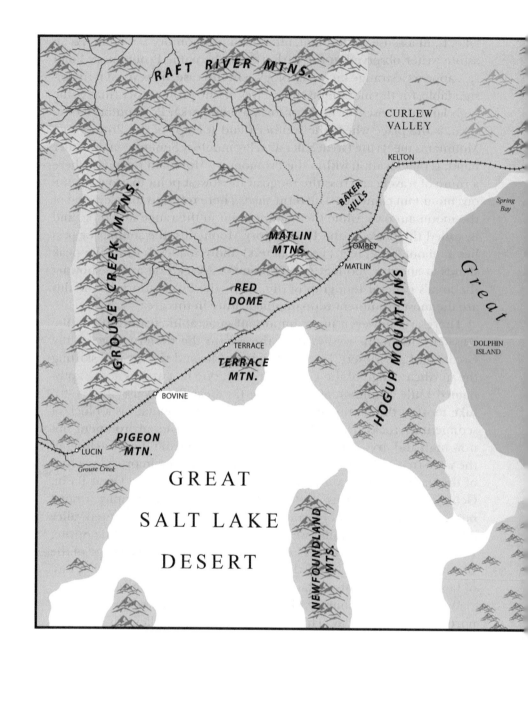

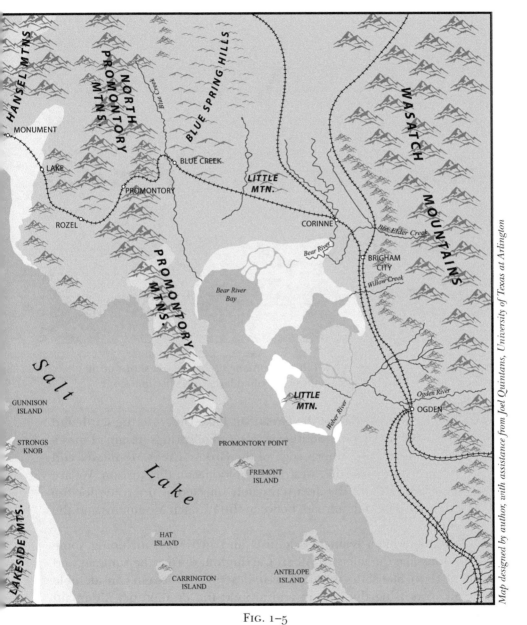

Map designed by author, with assistance from Joel Quintans, University of Texas at Arlington

FIG. 1–5
A stylized map of the area west of the Wasatch Mountains shows the
prominence of the Great Salt Lake and the Promontory Mountains.

Fig. 1–6
West of the Bear River, Little Mountain rises near the shore of the
Great Salt Lake. It is composed of tilted layers of dense limestone.

provide a stunning view of the Great Salt Lake Desert to the south and
the Great Salt Lake to the southeast. A series of springs sustained travelers at Lucin, at the southern edge of the Grouse Creek Mountains and
the Muddy Range. Farther west, Nevada looms on the horizon. We are
concerned here with the area ultimately selected as the route for the
first transcontinental railroad, between the Wasatch Mountains and the
Nevada state line.

Working with a team of scientists and surveyors, including some
Mormons like the talented Albert Carrington, during the summer and
fall of 1849, Stansbury was the first to describe the area in considerable
detail. Traversing the area in and around the Promontory Mountain
Range, Stansbury was primarily concerned with the physical environment. As a geologist, he was especially impressed with the variety of
rocks that undergirded the spectacular landscape here. Of the southern
Promontory Mountains, for example, Stansbury noted that "[t]he rocks
were porphyry, gneiss, dark slaty shales, and metamorphic sandstone."
However, he also noted that "[a]fter proceeding some miles to the
north, dark limestones with white marble veins occurred, alternating
with clayey shales." Being interested in the topography, Stansbury also

FIG. 1–7
The earliest published image of the north end of the Promontory
Mountains looking northwest toward Spring Bay, from Stansbury's
Exploration of the Valley of the Great Salt Lake (1852).

commented on "lofty escarpments" in these mountains.[4] Those escarpments were, at least in part, due to faulting. As in all areas of mountain building, the Promontory Range and vicinity has many fault lines.
These faults tend to run in a north-south direction. Covered by sedi-
ments, most are not visible; however, lines (or scarps) can be detected in
the countryside where the topography on one side is at a different elevation or position than the other. These faults are one indication that
Promontory is earthquake country. Earthquakes, however, have been
widely spaced in time and variable in magnitude. The mountains in this
area did not rise quickly but rather in many small jolts that only lifted
them inches at a time over millions of years.

In his famous report on the area surrounding the Great Salt Lake,
Stansbury's team sketched what may be the first drawing of the site where
the transcontinental railroad would ultimately run. Positioning themselves toward the end of the peninsula that comprises the Promontory
Mountains, they looked northward, surrounded on three sides by water.
Stansbury's "View Looking North West from Promontory Point . . ." (fig.
1–7) reveals the rugged backbone of the Promontory Mountains, and, in
the distance, the hills rising from the Curlew Valley at the northern end
of the lake. It was here, over the low summit between this southern range
of the Promontory Mountains and its continuation northward—just out

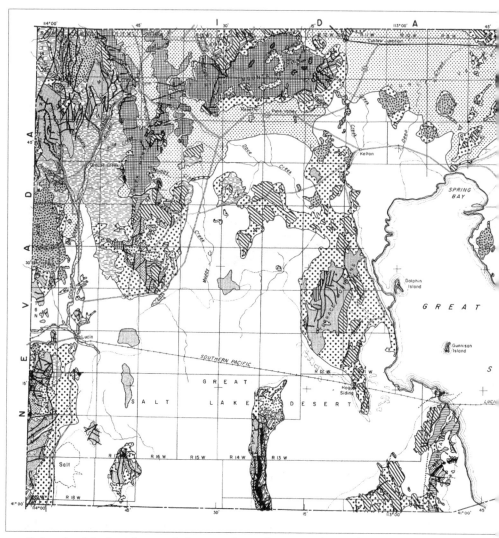

of view in this sketch—and thence along the sweeping edge of the lake's
Spring Bay (seen in the background of the sketch), where the transcontinental railroad would be built about two decades later.

Stansbury also knew that the mountains here displayed vast slices of
earth history. The geology of the area (fig. 1–8) reveals the Promontory
Mountains' connection to the region's long geological history. On their
dark and contorted slopes, the Promontory Mountains did indeed represent powerful geological forces and vast amounts of "deep" time—
that is, time measured in millions of years. These mountains consist, for
the most part, of sedimentary rocks precipitated in ancient seas some
250 million years ago. Over time, the precipitated lime hardened into
dense limestone. Then, through various episodes of crustal movement,

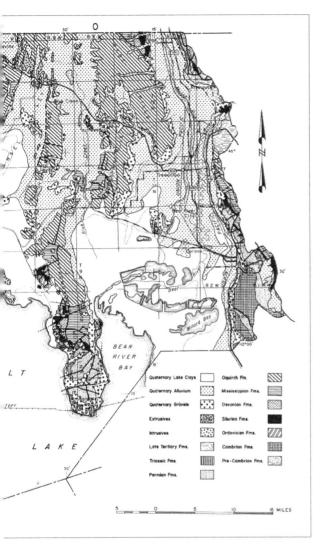

FIG. 1–8
Geological map of Box Elder County, Utah, from Hellmut H. Doelling, *Geology and Mineral Resources of Box Elder County, Utah* (1980).

those limestone layers began to be pushed upward to become dry land. As part of the Great Basin province, these mountains of strata were then faulted, or broken, so that the uplifted mass was no longer one smooth, horizontal set of layers, but rather huge angular chunks of terrain.

The Promontory Mountains represent a slice of time—an originally water-deposited environment, now frozen in stone, set about a mile above sea level. These mountains consist of about 2,600 feet of Mississippian age limestones that are uniformly crystallized and nearly black in color. On top of these lie the resistant, cliff-forming Lodgepole formation, about 430 feet thick, which is, in turn, topped by the Deseret limestone that also contains some siltstone and sandstone. One of the region's characteristic rocks, the Great Blue limestone, is dark gray to

FIG. 1–9
Outcroppings of dense gray-colored limestone on the east flank of
the Promontory Mountains often feature bands of white limestone.

blue. It crops out in the North Promontory Mountains, where it forms
rough, grayish ledges (fig. 1–9).[5] As it turned out, Promontory was a
good name for the mountains because their tough, erosion-resistant
limestones form such spectacular prominences.

The Promontory Mountains are even more spectacular because they
rise from the Great Salt Lake and the lowlands adjacent to it. That
low-lying area, filled with America's largest salty inland lake (ca. 1,700
square miles), contains more than a remnant of a much-larger Lake
Bonneville. It is, in part, the dumping ground of fine material washed
down from the mountains over millions of years. In this area, which is
typical basin and range country, the mountains rise like islands above
the salt flats. Like most of the mountain ranges in this geological province, the Promontory Range is aligned rather close to north-south.
Glimpsed from an airplane or seen on a relief map, these mountains
seem like a herd of caterpillars marching in a north-south direction, as
one imaginative observer put it. Between these ranges are long valleys.
Some, like those flanking the Promontory Range, are filled with salty
lake waters. Most, however, are like the Curlew Valley, with dry salt beds
at the southern edge. Those many large, salty areas in northwestern

Photo by author

FIG. 1–10
Lake terraces from ancient Lake Bonneville, Promontory
Mountains, Box Elder County, Utah.

Utah are remnants of former lakes that existed in the fairly recent geological past. This cooler, wetter period lasted from about two million years ago to about 10,000 years ago, when the lake levels began to drop. Visible on many of the mountainsides in this area are distinctive lake terraces (fig. 1–10); these represent ancient beaches or shorelines when the lake levels were higher. The bench-like terraces are common on the flanks of the Promontory Range, which witnessed the slow receding of these waters. To many casual observers, these perfectly level terraces look man-made. To those who know the area's past, however, they reveal a fascinating story of wetter times followed by increasing aridity that left miles of beaches high and dry.

Among the prominent topographic features west of Promontory is Monument Point, or Monument Rock. This resistant geological feature stands above the plain of the Great Salt Lake at the northeastern end of Spring Bay. Monument is an appropriate name for this mass of dark-colored limestone and marl. The dictionary defines a monument as "a memorial stone or building erected in remembrance of a person or event." Its name and meaning to native peoples is not known, but early Anglo-American travelers were impressed enough by its prominence and sepulcher-like form that it became a landmark for them by the early 1850s. By the next decade, as we shall see, Monument Rock would feature in the surveying and building of the transcontinental railroad.

As the scientists and surveyors moved through this area in Stansbury's time, they also were aware of fairly recent volcanic activity. In arid and semi-arid areas like this, the results of volcanic action can be visible for thousands of years because the vegetation is so sparse. Numerous basaltic buttes are visible in the broad, gently sloping Curlew Valley west of the Promontory Range and south of the Raft River Mountains. These may be the eroded remnants of a much larger lava flow, and their dark gray to brownish-black rock shows the characteristic columnar jointing of basalt.[6] Like most basaltic flows, these suggest relatively peaceful explosions. However, some of the volcanoes closer to the Hansel Valley had evidently exploded violently (some, perhaps, under a portion of Lake Bonneville), spewing clouds that left deep deposits of volcanic ash that can still be seen in places. At Monument Point, for example, geologists identified a "superb exposure of Hansel Valley ash . . . where wave-cut bluffs expose the marl section on both sides of the point and the ash forms a thin brown layer that can be traced for considerable distance."[7] Some commercially valuable rocks and minerals occur in the Promontory region, too. In the Raft River Mountains, for example, deposits of marble and sandstone yield distinctive building stone. These mountains also contain small deposits of precious metals, notably silver.

About twenty-five miles to the east of the Promontory Mountains, the spectacular Wasatch Mountains rise to around 10,000 feet above sea level, in effect, dwarfing the topography near the lower Promontory Range. Composed of sedimentary and other lifted and faulted rocks, the Wasatch Mountains represent the eastern margin of the Great Basin and the westernmost margin of the Rocky Mountain chain. In between the Wasatch Mountains and the Promontory Mountains lies a wide alluvial valley, through which the Bear River runs to meet the Great Salt Lake. Along with the well-watered slopes of the Wasatch Mountains, this valley was recognized even in Stansbury's time as a superb location to grow crops of many types, including fruit trees. This alluvial land at the base of the well-watered Wasatch Mountains is still among Utah's richest farming areas.

Like the explorers and the early Mormons, the non-Mormons who filed into the Great Basin near the Great Salt Lake were well aware that the region was home to native peoples. Stansbury caught glimpses of these native inhabitants, whom he called "Shoshonee Indians." On Wednesday, October 24, 1849, Stansbury noted that his exploring party arrived at a brackish spring just west of the mountains, "where there had been a camp of Indians the night before." Stansbury believed that the Indians fled the site when they heard "the report of some guns that had been discharged in our camp." Even at that relatively early date, the Indians knew they were easy prey to firearm-wielding whites. When Stansbury reached this hastily abandoned campsite, he found numerous things of interest, including "[a] quantity of some species of seeds they had been beating out [which] lay in small heaps around . . . ." He also "found an old water-bottle . . . ingeniously woven of a sort of sedge-grass, coated inside with the gum of the mountain pine, by which it was rendered perfectly water-tight." Stansbury and his men later found "some similarly shaped vessels, and made of the same material, that would hold nearly two gallons."[8] The word *ingeniously* confirms that Stansbury recognized and appreciated the Indians' survival skills.

In exploring this area, Stansbury also described a "Utah digger" Indian man and his wife and child. Stansbury noted that the family was dressed in the style common to the Indians here. The man, for example, was ". . . quite naked, except [for] an old breech-cloth and a tattered pair of moccasins." Stansbury noted that "[h]is wife was in the same condition precisely, minus the moccasins, with a small buckskin strap over her shoulders in the form of a loop, in which, with its little arms clasped around its mother's neck, sat a female child, four or five years old, without any clothing whatever."[9] Given the modesty of Anglo-Americans during this early Victorian era, the fact that Indians were semi-clothed, as the whites put it, was not only "proof" of their lack of proper morals, but also proof that they were culturally impoverished. Like many travelers, Stansbury noted that the Indians appreciated some cloth that he gave them to cover themselves. Stansbury no doubt felt some relief that he could help improve their moral and material situation. At this time, it would not have occurred to Stansbury and other white travelers that the Indians had lived here for a very long time without their help. The Indians had arrived about 13,000 years earlier to become the Paleo-Indians of the Clovis period. During this time, about 12,000 to 9,000 B.C., the Indians commonly lived at sites at the ancient shorelines of the retreating lakes. It is tempting to think that the Indians survived for at least ten thousand years here in much the same condition, but changes did occur.

Evidence exists in many places of early Native Americans, usually where habitations existed. In addition to temporary brush shelters, Native Americans occupied rock shelters and caves near the Promontory Mountains. A rock shelter on the east side of Blue Spring Hill yielded stone chips, a mano, and scrap bone. Artifacts found at a cave site included projectile points, animal bones, potsherds, and grinding stones. At Salt Creek Marsh, archaeologists found two indi-cations of human settlement—obsidian flakes and fire-cracked rock.[10] From this type of evidence, archaeologists divide the area's long prehis-tory into three periods.

Over several thousand years, the Paleo-Indian peoples' culture evolved. By about 9,000 B.C., their lifestyle had developed around the large mammals that roamed the area. They hunted now-extinct game, including bison, camels, ground sloths, and mammoths in what arche-ologists call the Bonneville Period (ca. 9,000 to 7,500 B.C.). By the time the Pleistocene lakes were in full retreat, the environment was changing and becoming more diverse. More effective food harvesting and the use of spear-throwers occurred during the Wendover Period (ca. 7,500 to 4,000 B.C.). Bow and arrow hunting became common toward the end of the next period, 4,000 B.C. to 500 A.D., the Black Rock Period. In the Formative Period, from about 400 A.D. to 1,300 A.D., the practice of horticulture began and pottery was made. Because European American discoverers often named things found in the environment, it should come as no surprise that a portion of this life-style in Utah is called the Frémont Culture (named after the Frémont River, which was, in turn, named in honor of explorer John Charles Frémont). During this period, horticulture declined and hunting and gathering increased. A common pottery type from this period is called "Promontory Gray[ware]" after its development in the vicinity of the Promontory Mountains. By around 1,200 A.D., ancestors of the mod-ern-day Numic-language-speaking Shoshone Indians began to arrive, and the Frémont Culture peoples left. Today's Shoshone Indians, par-ticularly the Northwest Band, are the descendants of these new arrivals. They are, in fact, the peoples that Frémont and other explorers like Stansbury encountered here (fig. 1–11).[11]

Given the early explorers' interest in both natural and cultural his-tory, they believed many of these Indian peoples had regressed from the people who had built the pueblo communities of the Southwest. This was not true, but it helped explain the gap they perceived between what they called "civilized" and "primitive" Indians. Moreover, one senses in the writings of explorers, an urgency to modernize the Indians' behav-ior (and beliefs) and describe them quickly before they inevitably van-ished in the face of progress; this was a common theme as the Indians were susceptible to diseases and constantly besieged by would-be settlers anxious to use their resources and appropriate their land. Being part of the advance guard of civilization, however, most of the newly arrived European Americans believed that the native peoples in this area were living on borrowed time and held them in low regard. To a European

Courtesy of Mae Timbimboo Parry

Fig. 1–11
Northwestern Shoshone mother and
daughters: Phoebe (in cradleboard),
Towange (mother of the children,
Zudu pu chee, and Goo seep.

American culture emphasizing material progress, the native peoples of
the Great Basin seemed not only impoverished, but also especially primitive. The local Indians near the Great Salt Lake were semi-nomadic
and seemed to exist on the edge of starvation. To the horror of the
European Americans, the Indians harvested grubs and even the larvae
of flies that swarmed at the edges of the lakes in the Great Basin. Most
of the Indians lived in brush shelters and some lived in caves. Moreover,
they often moved from place to place as they hunted small game or for-
aged for seeds and nuts. Anglo-Americans called the Indians here "digger" Indians. Although regarded as negative and insensitive today, this
term reveals that the Anglo-Americans marveled at the Indians' ability
to subsist on things dug from the ground. At the same time, Anglo-
Americans disdained the Indians for not practicing agriculture that
could free them from a seemingly hand-to-mouth, dismal existence.

For their part, the Indians were superbly adapted to live under
skies that brought little precipitation and periods of intense heat or

bone-numbing cold. Widely spaced plants covered their landscape, but it impressed the typical explorer as *completely* barren. This was especially true of the low-lying areas near salt lakes or dry lake beds, such as the country at the northwestern edge of the Great Salt Lake. However, studied more carefully, most of the area was not barren, but sparsely vegetated. The Indians here, most of whom were part of the Shoshone tribe or nation, knew the area's landscapes and resources far better than the new arrivals did. Consequently, the white people who moved through the area, and even the settlers who stayed here, often learned about local edible plants and herbal remedies from the Indians. One example is "squaw" or "Indian" tea, now called "Mormon" tea.

Despite their better knowledge of the area, the Indians were at a disadvantage as their numbers were small and their resources relatively scarce. Unlike the Anglo-Americans, who brought livestock to tend and seeds to harvest as crops, the Indian lifestyle largely depended on local flora and fauna. When conditions were better elsewhere, the Indians simply moved to those places. The Anglo-Americans, however, had a different perspective that was difficult to reconcile with that of the Indians. The Anglo-Americans not only hoped to settle the land permanently, they also *claimed* the land upon which they wanted to settle. With their greater numbers, better weapons, will to settle, and desire to own land, the Anglo-Americans were on a collision course with the native inhabitants, whose numbers dwindled through warfare, disease, and famine. By the mid-1850s, the region's Indians were in frequent conflict with the whites. Although the Indians won a few of these battles, they would ultimately lose the war to control the entire area. The Indians who survived did so by adapting to the newcomers, avoiding conflict, and ultimately becoming more closely connected to the new economy that offered some stability in a physical—and now cultural—environment that was in constant flux.

By 1861, the United States government produced a map showing the location of the different bands of Indians in the Utah Superintendency. On it, the Indian population in today's Box Elder County is divided between the "N.W. Bands [of] Shoshonies" and the "Goshoots." Located in the northern part were the Shoshone, whose territory on the map includes portions of the northern Wasatch Mountains. On this map, the Shoshone inhabited the little settlement called "Ogden Hole" (northeast of present-day Ogden), the Promontory Mountains, and much of the country comprising the northwest corner of the Great Salt Lake. At a point near the mountains at the west edge of the lake, however, a dividing line runs east and west. South of this line, and the Shoshone territory north of it, the Goshute (or, as their name is sometimes written,

Gosiute, or Goshoot) are shown as occupying the area of today's south-western Box Elder County. In reality, though, much of the area of the "Lake Desert" (as it is called on the map) was likely very lightly populated and perhaps not as tightly defined as the Superintendency claimed. In fact, the Goshutes and Shoshones were closely related; they spoke the same language and intermarried. Although this remarkable map is so worn in places that it is difficult to read, and would have been even more difficult to reproduce here, it does substantiate the presence of native peoples in and around Promontory. Those names "Shoshonies" and "Goshoots" on the map suggest that the Indians' territories were recognized. With time, and the pressures of development, all of the Indian tribes here were relocated to reservations of villages farther from Promontory, leaving far fewer of them in this area.[12] For example, the Northwest Shoshone Indians were moved to Washakie, Utah, and the Goshutes to the area west of the Great Salt Lake. Those actions were controversial, but they did spare many Indians from violence.

Not all Anglo-Americans in the area near the Promontory Mountains were anxious to fight the Indians. The Mormons—who claimed that the Indians were descendants of the Lost Tribes of Israel who had migrated to the Americas about 2,500 years ago—originally hoped to accommodate and convert the Indians to their Christian religion. That worked to some degree, but even this ideological belief was not sufficient to avoid bloodshed, as the warfare that occurred here tragically confirms. That, however, was in the early to-mid-1850s. By the mid-1860s, Indian conflict had considerably died down in this part of Utah, unlike in the area along the Union Pacific line farther east. Whereas that westward-building railroad faced considerable resistance in surveying and building its railroad line across the Great Plains of Nebraska Territory, the Indians in western Utah and Nevada were far more peaceful at the time the transcontinental railroad was built through the area.

As early as the 1850s, when scientists and surveyors like Stansbury tramped across this area, that beautiful farmland along the Wasatch Front contrasted with the desolation found in the area near, and west of, the Promontory Mountains. In fact, much of western Utah is arid or semi-arid, and its desert and steppe (grassland) vegetation is classified as the type that grows in "cold" deserts. The winters here, in other words, are fairly severe, with occasional temperatures well below zero. During cold spells, even the daytime highs may be well below freezing for weeks, and the nighttime temperatures can fall to minus 10 degrees for a week or more at a time. During cold snaps, when the air is still, ice fogs can occur. The Indian term for this frosty, foggy weather is "pogonip." But

Photo by author

FIG. 1–12

Great Basin Sage (*Artemisia tridentata*), a distinctive plant seen here near Promontory Summit, was important to Native Americans and also served as fuel for Anglo-Americans. Note the woody trunk of this mature plant.

the varied topography here is always a factor in the weather. Sometimes as the pogonip settles close to the ground, leaving the valleys ice-box cold, the mountaintops are bathed in warm sunshine.

To understand this area, we should recall that the relationship between land and water in both space and time defines everything here. The Promontory Range is both mountain and peninsula. Other mountain ranges isolated from land by water are islands rising from the Great Salt Lake. Even the swale between the Promontory Range and the North Promontory Mountains was once covered with water, meaning that in Pleistocene times the Promontory Range was also an island. Today, this area is well above lake level, and covered with grasses and shrub-like vegetation. Note, too, that the more thickly vegetated areas on the map are at the higher elevations. In the Promontory area, those green (i.e., forested) areas consist of juniper and pinyon pine trees. These higher areas receive more moisture than the lowlands.

Adapted to grow in these cold semi-arid lands, the sagebrush (*Artemesia tridentata*) (fig. 1–12) thrive in the middle elevations, along with grasses and pinyon pine in the higher elevations. West of Promontory is real desert. This is especially apparent in the area embracing the northern arm of the Great Salt Lake, a broad low-lying area of the Curlew Valley where the transcontinental railroad was ultimately constructed; this remains some of the most desolate country in the entire Intermountain West, especially where the fluctuating lake levels in historic times left saline soils in their wake. Low shrubs such as greasewood, which John Charles Frémont discovered in the mid 1840s, cover this area.[13] In the broad saline and alkali plains north of the Great Salt Lake, greasewood (*Sarcobatus*) dominates, but one can also find other desert plants such as shadscale (*Atriplex confertifolia*) here. These, too, were new plants to scientists who traversed the area in the 1850s.

Early travelers to the Great Basin noted the importance of the sparse vegetation. Writing in 1849 with Frémont's report in hand, American mapmaker S. Augustus Mitchell noted that "[t]he wild sage is the only wood; it grows of large size, being often one foot in diameter, and from six to eight feet high." Mitchell added that sagebrush "serves for fuel . . . and for some sort of covering for the feet and lets of the miserable inhabitants in cold weather." Sagebrush served one additional purpose for the native peoples, namely "[i]t is also the material of which they construct their diminutive wigwams."[14] In using the term *wigwam*, Mitchell revealed his eastern United States roots. In the Great Basin, such brush shelters are often called "wickiups." In using the term *miserable* for the native peoples here, Mitchell revealed his prejudices and his belief in material progress as the measure of a culture.

Consider in more detail the varied vegetation communities—called ecoregions today—found near the Promontory Mountains. A map of these ecoregions adjoining Promontory (fig. 1–13) reveals that they are correlated with altitude or elevation and other factors, such as proximity to the Great Salt Lake. Generally, much of the area is arid or semi-arid in appearance, but there are two exceptions. Because the mountains intercept the moisture moving into the area and are cooler, pinyon pine and juniper trees often grow here. This is apparent in higher slopes of the Promontory Mountains, on which woodland and shrub vegetation are found. Ironically, although the lowest portions of the area possess the driest, hottest climate, they may be relatively wet places because all snowmelt and runoff from the mountains winds up there. These areas adjacent to the Great Salt Lake possess typical wetlands vegetation of

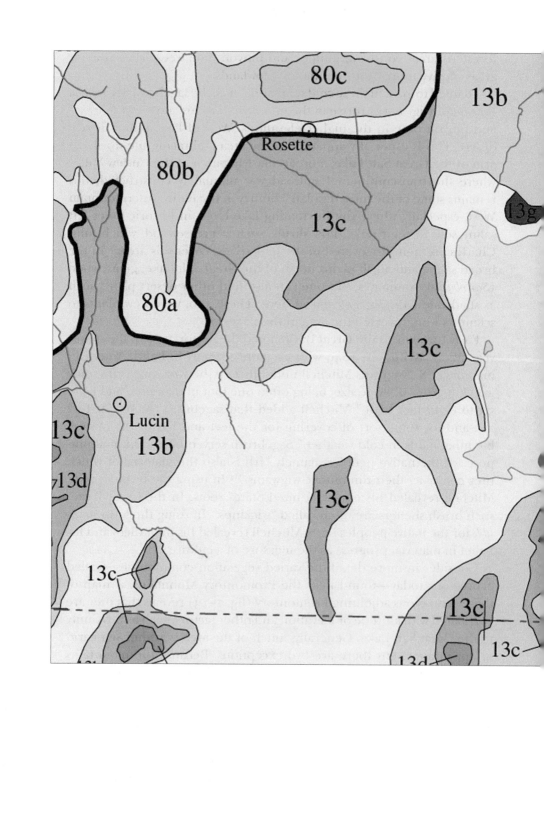

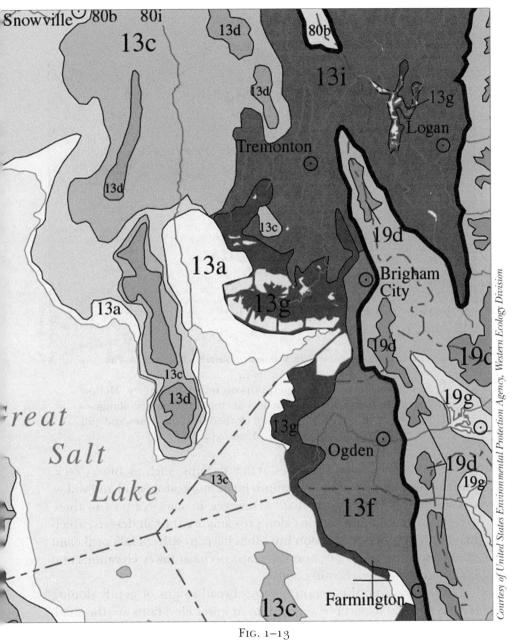

FIG. 1–13

Detail of *Ecoregions of Utah Map* showing area at the north end of the
Great Salt Lake. See text for explanation of numbered areas.

Photo by author

FIG. 1–14
Viewed from grass and sagebrush-covered Promontory Hollow (foreground), the higher reaches of the Promontory Range—especially on the north slopes—are clothed in scrub pines and still retain creases of snow in this May 10, 2008 photo.

reeds and rushes. Along the freshwater streams, such as Blue Creek, one can find lush riparian vegetation, including cottonwood and willow trees in places (13g on the map). However, in stark contrast to these green marshlands and ribbons along streams are the salt deserts, which may seem devoid of vegetation but often have growths of salicornia and salt grass. These areas (13a on the map) occur at lower elevations and have poorly drained, clay-like soils.

Mostly, however, the region features broad swaths of gently sloping terrain covered by scrubby vegetation. At lower elevations are the shadscale-dominated saline basins (13b on the map), where shadscale, winter fat, and greasewood plants thrive. In terms of elevation, these areas generally lie below the sagebrush basins and slopes (13c on the map), Here, usually on well-drained slopes, the Great Basin sagebrush dominates the landscape with its characteristic silvery bluish-green color. Promontory Summit, at an elevation around 4,800 feet, is a typical sagebrush-covered landscape. Sagebrush may reach heights of six or

FIG. 1–15
"Valley Between Promontory Range and Rock Butte—Camp No. 2 G. S. Lake," from Stansbury's *Exploration of the Valley of the Great Salt Lake* (1852).

seven feet in this area. Soils in this zone tend to be less saline, and better drained than soils in the shadscale and desert salt plains. The presence of sagebrush usually indicates conditions in which grasses can also thrive. Usually, sagebrush-covered areas contain grasses, though they may be easy to overlook. In a few places, usually those elevated, well-drained areas at the bases of mountains where fires triggered by lightening may occur, broader swaths of grass may be found. At the higher elevations near Promontory, at about 6,000 to 8,000 feet above sea level, one finds areas of scrubby pine trees (13d on the map). In the highest elevations near Promontory, including the Raft River and Wasatch mountains above 9,000 feet, one finds tall pine and fir trees in dense forests (80b and 80c on the map).

The landscape around Promontory, then, is far from uniform. From the sagebrush- and grass-covered slopes at Promontory Summit, one can gaze up into the higher elevations of the Promontory Range and see pinyon pines and junipers (fig. 1–14), while a glance out to the Great Salt Lake reveals sweeping vistas of more sagebrush, and, at lower elevations, shadscale-covered terrain and finally, rimming the lake itself, fairly sterile salt flats. And yet, at a place like Locomotive Springs, a patch of green reveals the reeds and sedges of dense wetland vegetation that today, as in Stansbury's time, attracts, and provides sanctuary for, waterfowl (fig. 1–15). These environmental distinctions are important. Although some might consider the environment of Promontory to be monotonous, it is actually quite varied. Moreover, despite centuries of use by humans, it remains an important mosaic of habitats worthy of careful development and protection.

This area in the nineteenth century was actually a remarkable habitat that sustained Indian populations who had learned its secrets. Not surprisingly, however, it was here that early pioneers left vivid descriptions of a God-forsaken place unfit for human habitation. That, of course, was not quite true, as the Shoshone Indians found enough to subsist on here as they moved from place to place. But land is always judged by one's experiences with other, more familiar, places, and to most westward-moving European Americans, this was no more than a very desolate place to get across—quickly. For their part, though, the Mormons embraced the challenge of settling this area, for it resembled the landscape they had read about in the Bible. Shortly after their arrival, they named the river flowing from Utah Lake into the Great Salt Lake the Jordan River—named after, of course, its counterpart in the Holy Land—the River Jordan. It is the landscape near Promontory, stretching for hundreds of miles in all directions, that the Mormons considered their promised land. Like that fabled land, it, too, could blossom as the rose—provided enough concerted energy was expended irrigating land and tending crops.

Like other European Americans arriving in this area, the Mormons first relied on the assessments of earlier authorities. By the mid-1840s, in fact, two specific sources of information spread the word about the suitability of the Great Basin for settlement. The first, of course, was John Charles Frémont's widely read report, which characterized the bottom lands in the portion of the region adjacent to the Bear River as being "extensive; water excellent; timber sufficient; the soil good, and well adapted to the grains and grass suited to such an elevated region."[15] Frémont's report noted other well-watered areas but characterized much of the region as sterile and covered with sand. Still, it suggested that Americans could make a go of it here, provided they knew the land and its resources.

The second source of information was Lansford Hastings's briefly popular *Emigrant's Guide to Oregon and California* (1845). Hastings described the entire region between the Wasatch Range and Sierra Nevada using a broad brush that also characterized the section of it near Promontory: "about one third of the whole section," he wrote "is susceptible to cultivation, while about two thirds, including the arable lands, are well suited to grazing purposes . . ." At this point, it seems that Hastings had accounted for the entire (or three-thirds of the) area. However, throwing mathematical accuracy to the winds, he decided to add a sarcastic comment about "the remaining third, [which] for extraordinary fruitfulness, and entire destitution, of all fecundity, can be surpassed only by some portions of Oregon, which are seldom if ever surpassed in worthlessness."[16]

Being farmers, many of the early travelers here evaluated the land in terms of its agricultural potential. They realized that the landscape from the base of the Wasatch to the western edge of the Great Salt Lake was quite diverse. With Stansbury's report in hand, they could see that the land near the Wasatch consisted of a series of old lake terraces that stood above broad alluvial plains. This well-drained area possessed great potential for agriculture. This is broadly called the Wasatch Front, and the Mormons would turn it into a well cultivated Eden where crops and fruit trees thrived. Farther west, the land leveled off toward the forbidding Great Salt Lake. The area adjacent to the Bear River (near present-day Corinne) was especially fertile; the soils were fine, and water was always available. They quickly learned that, as one gets closer to the Great Salt Lake, the soils in this area became increasingly alkaline, and the area could only serve as marginal grazing lands. The Promontory Range was the next major feature they encountered, and it rises high enough to possess well-drained soils. Water, however, is scarce in this range; only a few springs were known. Westward from Promontory, the land spreads out in a broad plain at the edge of the Great Salt Lake. For miles, the plain here consists of a powdery alkaline soil that was once the bottom of the lake during wetter times. The soil is good enough to sustain crops only well above this lake plain. Although this was, in fact, one of the bleakest portions of the Interior West, it would later become the area selected for the transcontinental railroad.

Most travelers who encountered the Promontory Mountains in the 1850s found them to be quite desolate. Despite their bleakness, they were undeniably fascinating to those who looked at them a bit more carefully. This was a land of seemingly bare—some called them naked—hills and mountains where the bedrock geology was exposed. During the last half of the nineteenth century, the American public became more interested in geology; that helps explain why even government reports like Stansbury's were read with interest by the reading public. As they learned from reports and first-hand observation, the area near Promontory was not only of scientific interest, but also somewhat mysterious. It was a land of mirages made all the more apparent by the Great Salt Lake, whose blue waters and white salt flats frequently played tricks on both eye and mind. The mystical connection becomes more apparent when we recall that during this period the Great Salt Lake was often compared with a lake in the Bible—the Dead Sea. Like the legendary Dead Sea, the Great Salt Lake is a body of saline water in a desert land. It is, however, far less salty and dead than its Middle Eastern counterpart.

The area also appealed to the romantic early Victorian imagination in search of the sublime, and the Promontory Range was particularly fascinating. Travel writer Franklin Langworthy penned one of the more detailed and romantic descriptions on Promontory in the early 1850s:

A LONG PROMONTORY

September 1st.—Sunday.—Still pursuing our course, at the base of the mountain, which rises like a wall of naked rocks on our right. Towards the northern end of the lake, I perceived that a high mountain promontory makes out from the shore, in a direction nearly south, almost dividing the lake into two parts. This promontory cuts off the prospect, so that we can see only the sheet of water between it and the eastern shore. This sheet varies in width from five to twenty-five miles. At the city we can see past the southern extremity of the cape, and obtain a view of the broad expanse beyond it. The lake is there of such extent, that the sun seems, at setting, to sink beneath its briny waves.[17]

With its flaming sunsets and spectacular vistas, the Great Salt Lake had special appeal to the romantic mindset in Victorian times. That stunning inland sea and its stark adjacent mountain ranges, like the Promontory Range, therefore, must be considered in the context of the human history unfolding here in the 1850s and early 1860s. In addition to the romantic descriptions of travelers and adventurers, the area also presented considerable economic potential. By this time, two very different kinds of economic activities were occurring in Utah Territory. The first—agriculturally-based settlement by the Mormons—was strong in the Salt Lake City area but had also spread into other parts of the region, including small parts of what would soon become Nevada. However, Nevada was consciously pursuing a different path—the development of precious metals including silver and gold that the Mormons were now instructed to avoid. This second type of enterprise, mining, would thrive in the rich mountains of the Great Basin—even in Utah, where the Oquirrh and Wasatch mountains and other ranges yielded precious metals. Gentiles (non-Mormons) developed most of these mining, but they were located well south of the Promontory Mountains.

The Mormons' aversion to quick wealth was based on church doctrine, reaffirmed after some Latter-day Saints developed gold fever following the discovery of gold at Sutter's Mill in California; Mormons, in fact, were among the first who actually found that gold. By the early

1850s, church President Brigham Young realized that precious metals might distract Mormons from building up Zion in the Intermountain West, but that did not mean that the Mormons were backward. On the contrary: As early as 1852, Young advocated the railroad as a force that could help the Mormons meet the challenge of "the gathering"—that is, bringing Saints to Zion to practice their religion in these "last" (or latter) days. Railroads, then, were of interest to everyone in Utah Territory—miners, farmers, merchants, Mormons—but it would take considerably more time, and more maneuvering, before the iron horse was ready to arrive in the Great Basin and scale the Promontory Mountains.

Chapter 2

IN THE PATH OF HISTORY
(1850–1868)

The report of Stansbury's 1849 expedition, published in 1852, helped the federal government and the Mormons better understand a portion of early Utah Territory. By that time, this area was being eyed as one of many places through which a transcontinental railroad might run. After all, railroad technology had also improved over the last two decades, generating confidence in the idea of a railroad spanning the entire continent. Private business interests had long speculated about such a railroad, and now official interest was growing. Originally slow to act, the United States Congress now took a serious interest in the project. Railroads had proven themselves the most efficient and safest mode of overland travel, and politicians began to get on board, so to speak. By 1852, Congress authorized extensive surveys to determine the best routes for a railroad to reach the Pacific coast. The big question was: Where would this railroad run?

It is here that we should consult maps of the period to better understand how Promontory worked its way into the popular consciousness. During the growing discussion and then debate about where the railroad would run, several interest groups figure prominently. Consider again the Mormons' interest in bringing a railroad to Utah Territory. Despite President Young's astute acquisition and use of maps, he could not consult every map containing future railroad routes. Maps, though, were essential. They held the key to how the selection of Promontory as the ultimate meeting point of the first transcontinental railroad would unfold. That drama was part of the broader mapping of the entire West after about 1850.

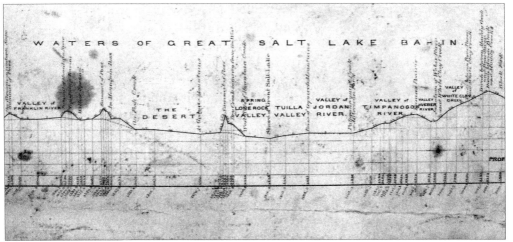

FIG. 2–1

Profile of the topography in the area from the Wasatch Mountains (*right*) across the Great Salt Lake Valley (*center*), to the mountains of eastern Nevada (*left*), from *Explorations and Surveys for Rail Road Routes from the Mississippi River to the Pacific Ocean . . .* (1855).

In the early 1850s, the route that the Pacific Railroad would take was unknown. Asa Whitney's vision for the railroad to the Pacific showed *three* destinations on the Pacific coast—*San Diego* (by way of a southerly route); *San Francisco* (via a central route); and the *Seattle/Puget Sound* area (by a northern route). Significantly, Whitney's route to San Francisco crossed the Wasatch Mountains and dropped into the Great Basin in the immediate vicinity of Great Salt Lake City, as it was then called, and thence westward along the *south* side of the Great Salt Lake.[1] The topographic profile of this route (fig. 2–1) revealed very easy going for the railroad south of the lake. Even the Springs or Stansbury Mountains could be skirted around their north edge, thus maintaining an easy grade throughout the entire area.[2] Brigham Young assumed the railroad would take this route, but the actual route was far from certain. In fact, the geography of the Interior West was still relatively sketchy, as maps of the period reveal.

The issue of where the railroad should run in the West perplexed the federal government as much as it did entrepreneurs. Given the strong regional interests in the East, it is not surprising that Southerners advocated a southern route, Middle Westerners preferred a direct route to San Francisco through Utah Territory, and people from New England and the Upper Middle West preferred a route to Oregon Territory. In

1853, Congress authorized the Pacific Railroad Surveys, which resulted in six major expeditions. To stimulate the process of surveying and mapping the prospective railroad routes, Congress appropriated $150,000. This enabled the Army's Corps of Topographical Engineers to conduct the work, which, in addition to surveying, included gathering information on the geology, climate, vegetation, and animal life along the routes. This, of course, was required for reasons other than pure science or aesthetics. Those mineral and biotic resources could encourage mining, farming, and ranching. They could also help support considerable freight and passenger traffic on railroads.

The southernmost Pacific Railroad survey was made along the 32nd and 35th parallels, and the northernmost along the 47th and 49th parallels. These ultimately led to the construction of the Southern Pacific and Santa Fe to the south (ca. 1879–1883) and the Northern Pacific and Great Northern to the north (1876–1886). However, the middle or central route through the West was surveyed along three parallels—the 38th, 39th, and 41st. Those three surveys were crucial in determining the ultimate route, but considerable politicking and maneuvering would occur over about a dozen years before the route of the first transcontinental railroad, through Utah, was finally determined. That may sound like a long time, but as the dates above suggest, the first railroad through Utah and Nevada would be built earliest, and completed in 1869, more than another dozen years *before* the railroads along the southern and northern routes. Although there would be other last spike ceremonies in the 1880s, none was more important than the first—an honor that would go to Utah Territory.

The main problem was how to integrate the fragmented maps appearing in the varied railroad surveys for that was key to comparing the routes and determining which was best. That, too, would require maps. In his *Memoir to accompany the Map of the Territory of the United States from the Mississippi River to the Pacific Ocean* [U.S. Serial Set 801], topographer Gouverneur K. Warren identified the need to bring together individual maps from numerous surveys, the goal being to create a single map of the entire American West. This was in 1857, when the individual maps used to create the master map were so diverse, and so fragmentary, that it proved difficult to construct an accurate map. By 1858, however, Warren realized his vision as his map rolled off the presses. Warren hoped that travelers and would-be entrepreneurs would consult his map, and he was not disappointed. Called *Map of the Territory of the United States From the Mississippi River to the Pacific Ocean . . . to accompany the Reports for the Explorations for a Railroad Route*, it became one of the most popular maps of the period (fig. 2–2).

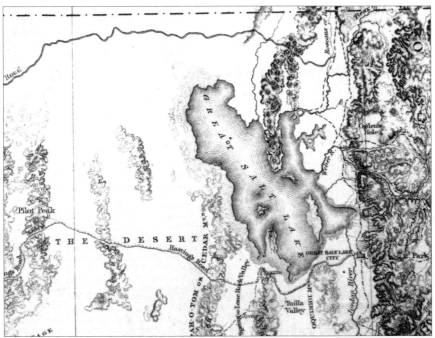

Courtesy of Cartographic and Architectural Records Section, National Archives, College Park

FIG. 2–2

Detail from the *Sketch Exhibiting the Routes between Fort Laramie and the Great Salt Lake* (1858) shows two prominent travel routes—one north, the other south—around the Great Salt Lake.

Like most maps, it relied on multiple sources. The map's cartouche proclaims that it was "based on surveys and compiled by G. K. Warren, Lieutenant of the Topographical Engineers, and prepared under the direction of Bvt. Major W. H. Emory." On this map, two routes cross Utah close to the Great Salt Lake. One route—the Hastings Road—heads westward from Great Salt Lake City. This road to California skirted the southern edge of the huge lake, worked its way around the spurs of the mountains, and then headed westward toward Pilot Peak. The second route, called the Emigrant Road, ran north around the lake from the vicinity of Bear River, west around the northern end of the Promontory Mountains, then headed roughly west-southwest on a meandering path until it reached the Humboldt River in present-day Nevada.[3] Like all maps of this period, it is not as accurate as we demand today. Note, for example, that the Salt Lake Cutoff actually crossed into a portion of Idaho to meet the main emigrant road coming out of City of Rocks before reaching Nevada.

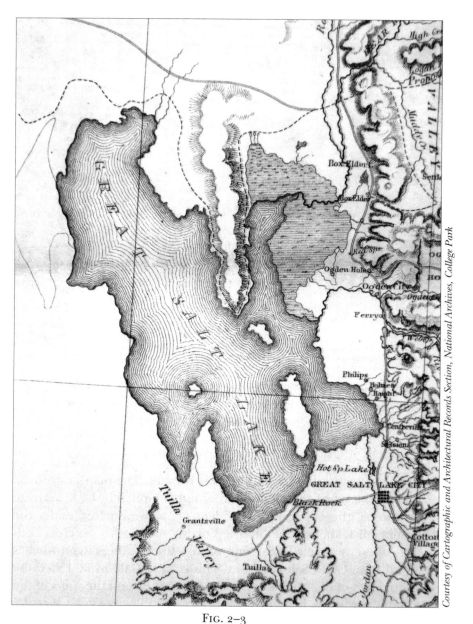

FIG. 2-3

Detail of the Great Salt Lake on *Map From Great Salt Lake to the Humboldt Mountains* in *Explorations and Surveys for a Rail Road Route from the Mississippi River to the Pacific Ocean* (1855) shows proposed railroad line running around south edge of the lake.

Other routes could take the traveler to the vicinity of the Great Salt Lake, as shown on the *Sketch Exhibiting the Routes between Fort Laramie and the Great Salt Lake* (fig. 2–3). Based on explorations by John C. Frémont, H. Stansbury, E. G. Beckwith, F. T. Bryan, and F. W. Lander, the map shows existing "routes practicable for wagons" and "routes explored but generally not practicable for wagons without improvement" (shown as hatched lines). The latter was a warning much like those on today's maps—"suitable for four-wheel drive vehicles only." As the map shows, there were several wagon roads, in varying condition, to the Wasatch Front from Wyoming. Two reached Salt Lake City from Fort Bridger via Echo Creek. Still another route—the Pacific Wagon Road—was proposed to run from the Green River over Martin's Pass to the Wasatch Front, where it headed directly west, skirting the northern end of the Promontory Range. On the eastern side of the Great Salt Lake, a series of routes threaded their way down the canyons of the Wasatch or via Ogden's Hole—a large, amphitheatre-like valley northeast of present-day Ogden (not the same as the village of Ogden Hole shown west of the city). But this map, too, is inaccurate. There were really only three viable wagon roads into Salt Lake City from the east in 1858, two of them were forks of the Echo Canyon route—over Big and Little Mountain to descend Emigration Canyon and the Golden Pass route down Parley's Canyon—the third was down the Malad and Bear from Fort Hall. These are shown on the map, as is a road through Ogden's Hole that I do not think existed as a wagon road any farther east than Ogden's Hole.

When they finally reached the western slopes of the Wasatch Range, travelers had to make a decision that faced anyone wanting to continue traveling westward: How to get around the Great Salt Lake? That huge body of water, beautifully articulated with ripple-like curving lines mirroring the shorelines, reveals a swampy area of marshland at the northeast edge of the lake that would present problems to travelers. On this map, there were only two ways to get around the lake—going southward to the vicinity of Salt Lake City, or going northward. The latter choice required travelers to traverse that large area of marshy land that posed a major obstacle to wagons. By avoiding the marshiest land, the traveler got around the northeastern edge of the Great Salt Lake, then turned westward to face the Promontory Range, which appears on the map as a formidable obstacle, though it is unnamed.[4]

Brigham Young sought maps that could better inform him about the region, and that included official maps of Utah Territory prepared by the federal government. One impressive map—*Explorations and Surveys for a Rail Road Route from the Mississippi River to the Pacific Ocean—Route Near the 41st Parallel, Map No. 1, From the Valley of the Green River to the*

Great Salt Lake (fig. 2–4)—clearly shows the proposed line running westward as it crosses the Green River in what would later become the state of Wyoming. Then, when the proposed railroad line reaches the Black Fork, it turns southwest to Fort Bridger, and from there, follows a twisting course down Sheep Rock Cañon of the Weber River, by which it reaches the Wasatch Front. At Lower Cañon, however, instead of going toward Ogden City, this proposed rail line turns sharply south, heading toward Salt Lake City. As it reaches the Salt Lake Valley proper, it turns southwestward, crossing the Jordan River and passing the far northwestern edge of the city. This route pleased the Mormons greatly, for the growth of their church depended on good transportation. From there, the proposed railroad runs due southwest. Upon reaching the northern edge of the Oquirrh Mountains, it hugs the southern edge of the Great Salt Lake, then curves northwestward again.[5]

On the second map in this series—*From the Great Salt Lake to the Humboldt Mountains* (fig. 2–5)—the route around the south end of the Great Salt Lake takes nearly the same course. Past the city, this route heads northwestward to skirt the northern end of the O-Na-Kui (Stansbury) Mountains, runs across the Spring or Lone Rock Valley (now Skull Valley), crosses a pass in the northern Cedar Mountains (or Pah-o-tom Range), heads southwestward into "The Desert," then goes north to skirt the north end of the Humboldt Mountains before it reaches the Humboldt River.[6] At this time, the route that the transcontinental railroad would follow in this area was not determined. However, the survey's topographer, E. W. Egloffstein, clearly preferred a route around the southern side of the Great Salt Lake.

The map that accompanied the survey's report attracted considerable interest. North of the Great Salt Lake on Egloffstein's map, the Shoshones, or Shoshonee Indians, are prominent; so is the unnamed [Promontory] mountain range jutting into the Great Salt Lake. Just east of those mountains, the map shows and names Bear River Bay, while Spring Bay and Gunnison Island are indicated north and west of the range. Of transportation routes here, Egloffstein shows only the Emigrant Road. In contrast, the area south of the Great Salt Lake appears to be much more promising for a future transcontinental railroad line. Toward "The Desert"—that forbidding area of salt flats west of the Great Salt Lake, Egloffstein shows the "Proposed Rail Road" route that passed Great Salt Lake City skirting the southern edge of the lake. The railroad's projected route meanders a bit, then curves southwest where it joins another line on the map. Labeled as a "Route Believed to be Practicable for a Railroad," it runs even farther south of the lake, rising over the southern spurs of the O-Na-Kui (Stansbury) and the Cedar

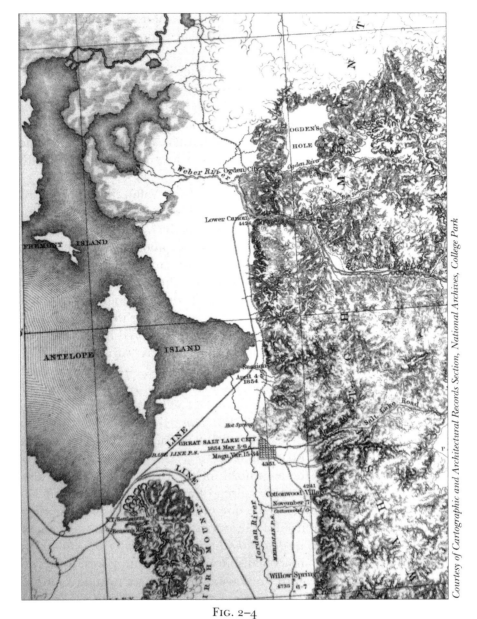

FIG. 2-4
Detail from *Map 1 From the Valley of Green River to the Great Salt Lake*
shows projected railroad lines running south of the Great Salt Lake.
From *Explorations and Surveys for a Rail Road Route from the Mississippi
River to the Pacific Ocean* (1855).

mountains.[7] At this time, the Mormons had explored alternative routes to California through what was still Indian country—as Egloffstein's map makes quite clear.

How strongly did maps of the mid 1850s advocate a railroad route around the southern end of the Great Salt Lake rather than around the northern end of the lake near Promontory? On the *Skeleton Map Exhibiting the Route Explored by Capt. J. W. Gunnison* (fig. 2–6), Egloffstein shows the traverses made with a possible railroad route in mind. The term *skeleton* here is appropriate, as the map does not show all the details of the topography, only the bare bones, so to speak.

On the map, one route runs into the Utah Valley, then northward toward the Great Salt Lake, where it heads west along the southern shore of the lake. From there, it runs straight west to the Humboldt Mountains, where it heads north into the Humboldt River Valley. The second route, west of the lake, is farther south and unfinished; Captain John W. Gunnison, who explored the area in the early 1850s, advocated this route. Both routes followed a rugged route through the Wasatch Mountains, but the persistence of the latter on maps was a tribute, perhaps, to the memory of Gunnison, who was massacred by Indians near Sevier Lake in 1853. The "proof" of this map was "corrected in [the] office [of the] P[acific].R.R. Surveys Feb. 10, 1855"—and it endorsed a still more southerly route through western Utah. Tellingly, the title of the map, on its verso, is *St. Louis, via Great Salt Lake. To Benecia, Cal.— Explorations and Survey for a Pacific R.R. between—1854 Capts. Gunnison and Beckwith,* and is boldly labeled "P.R.R. Routes"—that is, projected routes for a Pacific Rail Road—in red.[8]

By the early 1860s, the area north of the Great Salt Lake was also eyed as a possible locale for a railroad line. There was a long precedent for travel here, and, in fact, one of the routes that took travelers westward into Nevada around the north end of the lake was named for Stansbury. An official *Map of the Territory and Military Department of Utah (1860)* (fig. 2–7) shows Stansbury's route running west from the Wasatch near Logan toward the Promontory Range, turning south at the base of the Promontory Mountains and running all the way around them by way of Promontory Point. From there, the route runs north along the west side of the Promontory Range, which is indicated by a series of hachure lines.

Stansbury's route then skirts the northern edge of the Great Salt Lake, runs around the southern edge of the Red Dome Mountains (not shown) and joins up with Hastings' Road just east of Pilot Peak, where a series of springs revived weary travelers.[9] The federal government prepared many of these maps, but others were by private map

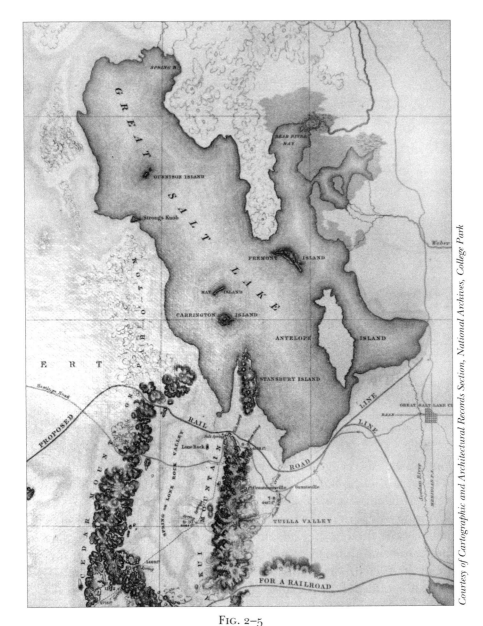

FIG. 2–5

Detail from Great Salt Lake on *Map From the Great Salt Lake to the Humboldt Mountains* in *Explorations and Surveys for a Rail Road Route from the Mississippi River to the Pacific Ocean* (1855) shows proposed railroad line running around south edge of the lake.

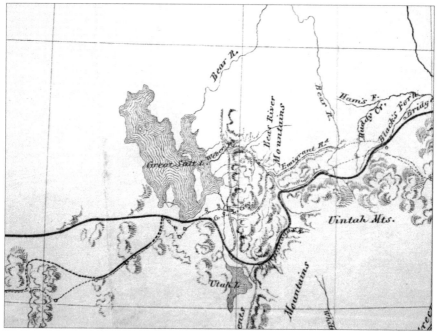

FIG. 2–6

Detail of the area adjacent to the Great Salt Lake on the *Skeleton Map Exhibiting the Route Explored by Captain J. W. Gunnison* (1855) reveals the official preference for a railroad line around south edge of the Great Salt Lake at this time.

companies. All recognized the centrality of Salt Lake City, which was both territorial capital (and still is the state capital) and the Mormons' New Jerusalem—as an 1852 German map called it.

During this period, the Latter-day Saints were honing their own map-making skills though they remained dependent on government maps to show projected railroad routes. They developed industries and sought the most efficient ways to dispatch information and ship goods. To that end, they built telegraph lines that linked them with the rest of the world and provided speedy communication between their far-flung villages. The Mormons' efforts continued into the 1860s, but other telegraph systems from outside Utah also reached the territory. Thus, the Mormons used a combination of their own and others' telegraph lines. As president of the Mormon Church, Young expressed an interest in *any* form of transportation, and this sometimes took an odd turn. An interesting telegraph message revealing Young's transportation concerns was located recently in the Church Archives: Under the title "Camels —," the Pacific Telegraph Company dispatch out of Austin, Nevada, on

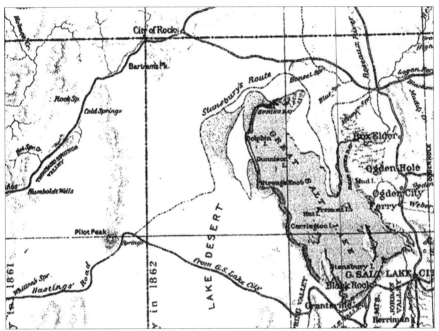

FIG. 2–7

Detail of the area west of the Great Salt Lake from the official *Map of the Territory and Military Department of Utah* (1860) shows Hastings' Road (south) and Stansbury's Route (north) of the lake.

August 27, 1861, was addressed directly "To the Hon. Brigham Young." The message noted: "I am informed that the camels are owned by some frenchmen [*sic*] in Virginia [City] they are now transporting Salt from Humboldt [Nevada] to that place —." Signed only by "operator," it was sent "free" to Young—no doubt in response to an earlier inquiry.[10] For his part, President Young had his hands full with many pressing issues, including reorganizing his Saints in Utah to maintain self-sufficiency now that the United States had taken control of the territorial government in Salt Lake City. Federal troops were recalled to participate in the American Civil War in the East but were soon replaced by Patrick Connor and the California Volunteers. That war would help Nevada become the Silver State in 1864 and provide silver to the coffers of the Union, a cause that the Mormons—most of whom were originally Northerners—generally supported, but did not actually engage in because building Zion was their top priority.

Shortly after the start of the Civil War, the Mormons received good news about the Interior West's position in the national communication network. On October 24, 1861, H. W. Carpenter, president of the California State Telegraph Company, telegraphed Mormon President Brigham Young with an important message. "That which was so long a hope," Carpenter began, "is now a reality." Carpenter was referring to the completion of the Transatlantic Telegraph line from coast to coast. In congratulating Young on this "auspicious event," Carpenter added, "[m]ay it frame a bond of perpetual union and friendship between the people of Utah and the people of California."[11] By this, Carpenter no doubt meant Mormons and non-Mormons.

Another message that same day, sent from San Francisco to Salt Lake City, gave an indication of the events underway. Anticipating the language used later at Promontory Summit, the message of 1861 noted that "[w]e join you in rejoicing over the event of the link between the Pacific & Atlantic—The importance of which will be better realized in the future." This statement was prophetic in several ways. In a general sense, it recognized the importance of communication in creating the American West as we know it. In particular, the "better realized" part of the telegram meant only one thing: the railroad, which would indeed reach Utah "in the future." The Mormons, who were a part of this rapidly developing western drama, knew that transportation would facilitate the growth of their church. They were especially familiar with all the railroad routes surveyed in the 1850s; now they craved closure on the issue. The Mormons were interested in the Pacific Railroad Act, which in 1862 authorized the survey and ultimate construction of one transcontinental railroad. The telegraph message about the telegraph system linking East and West hinted at the event that would occur eight years later—the actual joining of the rails in Utah to complete the first transcontinental railroad. In the meantime, however, Carpenter and his crew in California added: "we have just been drinking [to] the health of Prest. Young—with all the Honors."[12] When one recalls that Brigham Young was said to be fond of an occasional stout lager—in moderation, of course—this statement was not as irreverent as it sounds today.

That this message was sent by telegraph is a reminder that communication and transportation work hand in hand. Invented in the 1830s, the telegraph consisted of three basic components—a *transmitter* connected to a *receiver* by *wires* carrying a low-voltage electric current. The receiver was originally a needle that pointed to particular letters; however, Morse code, with its familiar dots and dashes, proved that an arrangement of clicks was a faster way to receive messages over the wire. By 1858, the first transatlantic telegraph cable was laid, while in the American West, the telegraph's arrival soon thereafter helped spell the end of the fabled Pony Express. Although seemingly separate from railroads, the telegraph was essential to their operations because it enabled messages regarding train movements to be sent in advance of the trains. In fact, the Pacific Railroad Act called for a telegraph and railroad system to be built *simultaneously*. In effect, then, the telegraph helped to lay the groundwork for the railroads' arrival, and the device would be indispensable for their efficient operation.

Brigham Young not only encouraged the development of telegraph lines linking Mormon communities, but he also continued to emphasize the importance of a railroad connection with the outside world. Consider another telegram: In September 1862, church official Heber C. Kimball and Samuel H. Weber telegraphed Mr. E. Creighton, superintendent of the Pacific Telegraph Company in Chicago, on behalf of President Young. In that message, the Mormons informed Creighton that "we take pleasure in informing you that the telegraphic reports of the Proceedings of the Pacific railroad Convention now in session in Chicago, are perused here with deep interest." Never shy about suggesting a route through Utah for such a railroad, they added, "[w]e trust that the Pacific Railroad maybe located on the route that will bring the greatest good to the greatest number & that the work may be speedily accomplished." At that time, Mormon Utah was the most populous location between the Colorado goldfields and the Pacific coast, so the Saints' appeal mentioning population must have resonated with Creighton. However, in order to leave absolutely no doubt as to where the line should run, Kimball and Weber persuasively concluded that "Utah will doubtless, when opportunity offers, add deed to words in so great and useful an enterprize."[13]

Brigham Young's interest in railroads ran quite high, and through a rather remarkable series of events, the Mormon Church would become closely allied with one of the two railroads that ultimately drove the golden spike at Promontory Summit. Having considerable experience with the route from the East to Utah due to the nearly constant migration of Latter-day Saints via handcarts and wagons since 1847, Young knew the route well. Although Young had many LDS associates in northern California, he apparently never envisioned the Saints controlling that area, which was beyond the boundaries of the Mormon state of Deseret.

The American Civil War intervened at a crucial time, and it affected activities in Utah in many ways. First, it necessitated the return of troops in Utah Territory to the eastern states, where much of the war took place. However, the federal government recognized the strategic nature of Utah, and soon re-established a presence here when Fort Douglas opened at Salt Lake City in 1862. Most important, the Union cause and ultimate victory in the war ensured the selection of a central route, rather than a southern route through New Mexico and Arizona. The war had helped military personnel gain considerable surveying skills, as well as experience in building and running railroads. After the war, former military personnel looking for employment often found a ready market for their skills working for the railroads. Many proved perfect for the job. Seasoned by extensive field experience, used to discipline and teamwork, and able to conceptualize western topography as a battleground waiting to be taken, the military topographers tended to work quickly and accurately.

In June of 1862, about a year after the Civil War began, Congress passed several bills, among them the Homestead Act, the creation of the Agriculture Department, and the Pacific Railroad Act. All of these, especially the latter, had an impact on northwestern Utah. The Pacific Railroad Act was a long time in development and represented closure on several issues that were on the minds of legislators (and their constituents) and business interests. The railroads would receive subsidies of cash and land as an incentive to invest in such a risky endeavor. The act was, as railroad historian Wallace D. Farnham put it, "moderately useful to the private groups that sponsored it and ineffective, or worse, for 'the great national road.'" And yet, with its subsequent amendments that further encouraged private interests, the act achieved its purpose of stimulating railroad development. Farnham was no idealist about what really transpired. Writing on the centennial of the act, he concluded that it was "the act of a democracy of abundance and license, wholly consistent with laws that gave valuable lands to citizens who had trespassed upon them, that eased restraints upon bankers who had no funds, that took from Indians land demanded by voters, and that bestowed bankruptcy and stay [that is, enduring] privileges [sic] upon impecunious citizens."[14]

As the two actors in the drama of building the transcontinental railroad, the Union Pacific and Central Pacific Railroads deserve a formal introduction here. Although we tend to think of the nation—and hence the railroads—as expanding westward, the Central Pacific was actually the result of mergers involving California's earliest railroad, the Sacramento Valley, begun in 1852 and completed in 1856. Well before the Civil War (1861–1865), the "Big Four"—Collis P. Huntington, Charles Crocker, Mark Hopkins, and Leland Stanford (an oversimplification, as Crocker's brother was also involved)—recognized California's need for a railroad linking the Golden State with the eastern United States and incorporated the Central Pacific in 1861. As this suggests, the railroad was a private, entrepreneurial effort.

By contrast, the United States Congress chartered the Union Pacific in 1862. With the nation at war with itself, Congress now recognized the need to connect the East Coast and West Coast; the result would be a stronger economy and greater national security. As an incentive, Congress provided subsidies to the Union Pacific and its slightly older western counterpart. The passage of the Pacific Railroad Act assured a central route. That route symbolized the Union's belief that the nation would be reunified after the war. As painted in broad brushstrokes on a map of the nation, the Union Pacific would run from Council Bluffs and Omaha on the Missouri River westward to an as-yet-undetermined meeting point with the Central Pacific. Both roads were to receive land adjacent to their rights of way, as well as cash bonuses, for railroad construction. The Central Pacific, which would build eastward from California, began construction in January of 1863. The Union Pacific began its construction two years later, in 1865, as the war ended. The Central Pacific's earlier start was explained by the fact that it was the first kid on the block, but that kid had a tougher job as it elected to build over the formidable Sierra Nevada mountain range in California.

Both railroads had different personalities too. As the child of capitalists from California's Gold Rush country, the Central Pacific seemed more risk-oriented. It was certainly apt to employ mining-like techniques to assault the granitic Sierra Nevada with pickaxes and gunpowder. Ton for ton, Central Pacific probably built more mileage through granite—including tunnels—than any other railroad. Central Pacific also pioneered the use of non-white labor, notably the Chinese, who both fascinated and disgusted European Americans. Additionally, Central Pacific management was closely linked to the Comstock Silver Rush in Nevada that occurred in the early 1860s. To some, it seemed that Central Pacific's route over Donner Summit was calculated to bring it as close to Virginia City as possible—and why not? That silver-producing area was a major economic force in the American West. For its part, the Union Pacific was more eastern in its demeanor. As the child of a governmental action that offered incentives, its management was a bit more bureaucratic than Central Pacific's. The Union Pacific looked eastward, and it was prone to hire Irish-American workers. Union Pacific was a granger—that is, agriculturally-oriented—railroad, though its extensive coal lands in Wyoming positioned it to become a major user and producer of black diamonds, as coal was commonly called at this time.

We also need to put these two railroads in the context of geopolitics. With the onset of the Civil War, the nation was nearly torn in two, but even during that conflict, the Union was resolved to not only build the Pacific Railroad, but to build it in a location that could unite the country and the West. Logically, the central route was advocated by President Lincoln, and mandated by Congress, to run from the Missouri River at Council Bluffs to the new capital of California at Sacramento, and ultimately, beyond to the San Francisco Bay area. The *central* in the name Central Pacific was significant. As one of the participants in a central route, the railroad would occupy a central position that could help unify the entire westward-moving nation after the war. Similarly, the symbolism of the word *union* in Union Pacific meant that the line would help unify the nation as well as belong to a union of regional interests by building westward into the Intermountain West. Other studies have covered the creation and early development of both the Central Pacific and the Union Pacific Railroads.[15] However, we need to keep in mind that Central Pacific as a corporation formed in the *West* to achieve part of the national goal, as well as view Union Pacific as its *eastern* counterpart that would do much the same thing. We should also remember that the two railroads would bring somewhat different corporate philosophies together—or rather face-to-face—in their mutual goal of spanning the West with an iron road. Ultimately, both railroads would put Promontory on the map.

From the perspective of Promontory, the role of these two railroads in politics *within* the Intermountain West is especially interesting. If it is likely that the close gold and silver rush connections of financiers in California and Nevada helped shape the thinking of Central Pacific Railroad's entrepreneurs, including the Big Four, then it is also likely that their association with easy riches put off Brigham Young. Understandably, Young developed a very close relationship with the Omaha-based Union Pacific rather than the Central Pacific, based out of Sacramento and San Francisco. At this time, Utahns and Californians had little regard for each other, and it is not surprising that the Central Pacific and the Mormons had little to do with each other, at least at first. By contrast, the attention showered on Young by the Union Pacific was noteworthy. On September 9, 1863, the Union Pacific contacted Young by telegraph, informing him that they were "about making Union Pacific a board of directors for a permanent organization." The railroad then asked Young a question that must have delighted the Mormon leader: "[W]ill you serve as one of the said board?"[16] When the Union Pacific reported that they "[b]roke ground today amid great rejoicing—Cannon flags banquets speeches & illumination of [the] City" of Omaha, they telegraphed Young that "Nebraska shakes hands with Utah In the great national undertaking—Your name will be Toasted—at the banquet tonight." Young must have felt an added sense of appreciation and accomplishment at this recognition.[17]

The Mormons also had a much closer relationship to the Union Pacific for another, more down-to-earth, reason: the railroad needed help in grading its line, and the Mormons could provide it. The Union Pacific seems to have been very shrewd in this matter. Inasmuch as the railroad agreed to pay the Saints to configure its grade, it played on Young's relatively weak position: he needed money as much or more than the railroad did. This meant that, in effect, the Union Pacific could barter with Young. This arrangement, while at times disconcerting to Young, actually played to his hand because the Union Pacific was the most direct route to get European Mormon converts into Utah. Then, too, the Union Pacific knew that Young envisioned developing rail lines elsewhere in Utah, and would entice him to take rails and equipment in lieu of funds. The Union Pacific also paid Young in company stock, which explains the fact that the Mormon Church ultimately became one of the major stockholders in the Union Pacific. Rather than do what most business leaders might have done—sue the Union Pacific for failure to pay—Young brilliantly parlayed this arrangement to the Mormons' lasting advantage. Young's patience proved wise as he received many lasting benefits by, in effect, becoming a creditor to this westward-building railroad.

Upon its arrival in Utah in early 1868, the Union Pacific contracted the Mormons to grade its right of way. Brigham Young insisted on this arrangement; rather than employing the Mormon workers individually, the Union Pacific contracted with Young and the Church officials. The *Deseret Evening News* of May 21, 1868, reported that ". . . there is money for the job for those who are industrious and prudent . . . ." This call for workers came at a good time for both the Church and the workers because "at the present time . . . there is such a scarcity of money and a consequent slackness of labor."[18] Two days later, Young reported on his contract with the Union Pacific as "a God-send." Young observed that "[t]here is much indebtedness among the people, and the Territory is drained of money," adding that "this contract affords opportunity for turning labor into that money, with which those here can pay each other and import needed machinery, and such useful articles as we cannot yet produce. . . ."[19] As a letter in the *Millennial Star* put it, by earning money for railroad construction, the Mormons could "keep the money so earned in the midst of Israel."[20]

The record suggests that Brigham Young hoped to use the available Mormon labor as an incentive to get the line built to Salt Lake City. As early as April 25, 1864, Union Pacific correspondence reveals that the railroad's survey to Great Salt Lake City from Green River had a Mormon connection. The Union Pacific board of directors noted that "President Young has volunteered to furnish your party and Transportation for your work."[21]

Truth be told, Young favored the Union Pacific for yet another reason. He was apprehensive about the Central Pacific. When the church mentioned that Utah should be on the route of the transcontinental railroad, the Saints actually meant that the railroad should go through Salt Lake City. Many observers, including the Mormons, figured that the Pacific railroad would come straight across the desert west of Salt Lake City and run directly into the Mormon city, which was also the territorial capital. That, of course, would have put, and kept, Promontory out of the picture. One of the unresolved items, however, was where the railroad would tackle the rugged Wasatch Range. By the early 1860s, the railroad surveyors had determined that a route through the mountains near Ogden would be most practicable. Rather than having much to do with Promontory, the topography of the Wasatch Range was the issue. Weber Canyon, east of Ogden, was the best way through the Wasatch Mountains. Although Ogden was situated almost fifty miles north of Salt Lake City and the Pacific Railroad was now determined to build through Weber Canyon, this was fine with the Mormons, who understood that the steep narrow canyons east of Salt Lake City were not practicable for railroad routes. Understanding this, the Saints figured that the railroad would simply curve south from Ogden, run to Salt Lake City, and then head directly west.

At this time, many road and railroad surveyors had military training, and many military and ex-military personnel used their considerable expertise to develop the railroads. Veterans also readily found work in railroad survey projects. One of these former officers was the legendary Grenville Dodge. As the chief engineer of the Union Pacific, Dodge had a similar vision of preparing a highly accurate map that would facilitate the building of the railroad. As Dodge somewhat immodestly put it to General Easton on January 14 of 1866: "I have about completed the map I have been so long in the making, and it is probably the best that has ever been gotten Union Pacific of the country embraced in my command." According to Dodge, this map (fig. 2–8) showed as much detail as possible: "It has all the roads, mountains, rivers, military posts, mining districts, & c. with all the distances."[22]

Dodge later reflected on the political context in which he created this map. He noted that "[t]he Government had gotten so economical"— his word for cheap—"that they did not even want to pay for a map but as soon as they saw the map they were not only willing to pay for the copies I asked for, but they had to print a very large number of them—every officer of the Government wanted them." As Dodge bragged: "They were the standard maps for all the country west of the Missouri, to the California State line until that country was mapped from Government surveys."[23] In other words, Dodge's map did what Warren's map had done about a decade earlier. As a cartographic historian recently observed, "There can be little doubt that the 1866 Dodge map . . . is a critical synthetic map in the tradition of the 1857 Warren map."[24]

Let us take a closer look at Dodge's map in regard to possible railroad routes in the vicinity of the Great Salt Lake for it can help us understand how contested the selection of a route west of the Wasatch Range would become. At first glance, Dodge's map seems to only show existing mail routes traversed by horse-drawn wagons. Listed first in the table showing distances is the Overland Mail Route. This route begins at Fort Leavenworth, travels west through numerous forts to Great Salt Lake City (1206 miles), continues around the southern edge of the lake westward into Nevada, over the Humboldt Mountains, then southwest, as the Overland Mail Route did, all the way to California.[25] In addition to these two roads running west from Salt Lake City—one north of the Great Salt Lake and one south of it, Dodge's map also shows "Stansbury's Route" as a red line consisting of dashes. Looking more closely, however, one can also barely make out dashed lines penciled in as a seeming afterthought by Dodge. In reality, these seemingly insignificant unnamed dashed lines are the most important, for they indicate possible routes of the transcontinental railroads. Tellingly, one runs westward from Salt Lake City to the Humboldt River, the other runs north from Ogden City, then westward over the Promontory Range, continuing generally southwest (directly under the words "Stansbury's Route") to the Humboldt River. Whereas one line would serve Salt Lake City, the other would miss it by well over fifty miles. Naturally, the former line most pleased Brigham Young, who envisioned Great Salt Lake City astride that more southerly line. Ultimately, however, Congress selected the path that partly followed Stansbury's route as the route of the Pacific Railroad—a decision that finally put Promontory on the map.

By the mid-1860s, it was widely known that the Central Pacific would build across north central Nevada following the Humboldt River, and that the Union Pacific would follow Nebraska's Platte River on its way toward Utah Territory. However, speculation was running high about just where the two lines would meet. In 1864, C. H. Lubrecht & Co. of New York published *The American Continent Topographical and Railroad Map* (fig. 2–9). As with many such maps of this period, it clearly shows the "Proposed Central Pacific R.R." running southwest from Wyoming directly into Salt Lake City, then west-northwest to Nevada after skirting

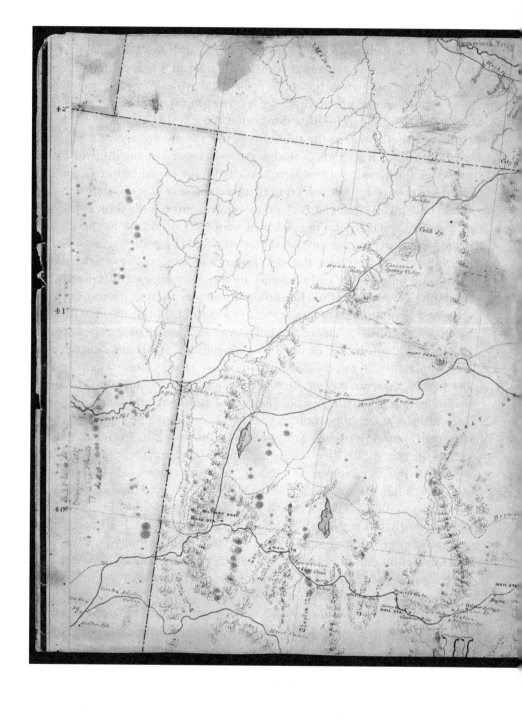

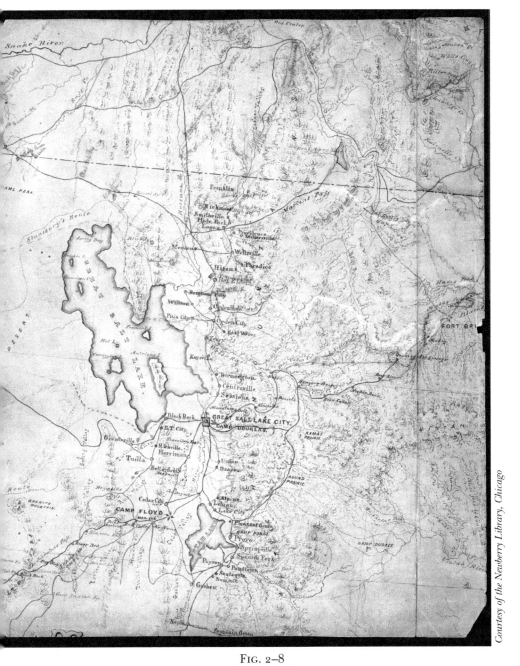

FIG. 2–8

Detail of a portion of the Intermountain West on map by Grenville
Dodge showing roads and projected railroad routes (1866).

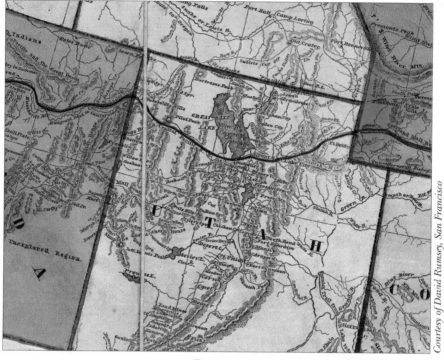

FIG. 2–9
Detail of *The American Continent Topographical and Railroad Map*
showing projected railroad south of the Great Salt Lake (1864).

the southern edge of the Great Salt Lake. On this map, the only indication of a travel route near Promontory is "Lander's Cut Off" which traverses the area north of the Promontory Mountains, then reaches City of Rocks in southern Idaho.[26] In its December 9, 1865, issue, *The Pittsburgh Gazette* featured an article on "The Union Pacific Railroad" in which it noted the vagueness of the route—especially that portion across the eastern Great Basin. As the *Gazette* put it, ". . . parties of engineers have been engaged in surveying the Spanish Fork and the country west from Salt Lake to the valley of the Humboldt. . . ." among other areas. However, it quickly added that, "No choice of the line across this wide stretch of territory has been determined on [*sic*] as yet; but the determination is to find the one offering the largest advantages."[27]

Despite increasing mention of "Promontory" as a place through which the Pacific Railroad would pass, many observers still considered Salt Lake City the most logical choice. For example, an interesting map in Samuel Bowles's popular travel book *Across the Continent* (1865) clearly shows the "Route of Central Pacific R.R." coming down the Wasatch Front near Salt Lake City and running around the *south* shore of the lake, thence to the Humboldt River in the recently created state of Nevada.[28] This, of course, was the route that the Mormons preferred.

After considerable fieldwork and other calculations, however, engineer Samuel Reed recommended that the Union Pacific railroad go around the north end of the lake. Still, that recommendation needed to be based on the kind of solid surveying that Union Pacific's chief engineer demanded. Accordingly, Reed's general initial survey was supplemented by a more detailed survey of the route over Promontory Summit. To Reed, the Promontory Mountains were not insurmountable even by the Union Pacific standards that favored relatively low grades. This proved a revelation. More important, though, was the fact that the Central Pacific heard about Reed's reconnaissance and was galvanized into surveying Promontory. After all, the quicker the Central Pacific surveyed, graded, and laid track across the Great Basin, the quicker it could get into, and beyond, the Wasatch Mountains. The railroads' reasoning was simple: the farther they got, the more lucrative the payments by Congress would be. Central Pacific surveyors were the first to successfully survey a specific route over the Promontory Range in 1867 under the direction of Samuel Skerry Montague, topographical engineer. Central Pacific surveyor Butler Ives moved eastward and located a feasible way over the Promontory Range at an "inclined pass" that would later be called Promontory Summit. For its part, Union Pacific had much the same goal, namely, to build as far west as possible, hopefully across much of the Great Basin—certainly to the Humboldt River. The trick was to survey as much of the route as possible and get it graded quickly.

On other maps of the period 1866–67, Promontory Summit was soon clearly shown as the chosen route. Consider, for example, [W. J.] Keeler's *Map of the U. S. Territories [and] Pacific R.R. Routes Mineral Lands and Indian Reservations 1867*[29] (fig. 2–10). It shows the C.P.R.R. line running over the route that would ultimately be used. Keeler's work reminds us how powerful a map can be. A map not only shows what exists but can also influence what *will* exist in the future. Keeler soon published this information to a nation anxious to see the Pacific Railroad become a reality. In 1867, the public glimpsed the route of the Pacific Railroad on Keeler's *National Map of the Territory of the United States from the Mississippi River to the Pacific Ocean.* This map was "Compiled from authorized explorations of Pacific Rail Road Routes, Public Surveys, and other reliable data from the Departments of the Government at Washington, D.C." On Keeler's popular map, the Pacific Railroad's two major components— Central Pacific and Union Pacific—are shown in the standard ladder symbol, that is, as twin parallel lines containing equally spaced lines crossing them at right angles. A closer reading of the map reveals that

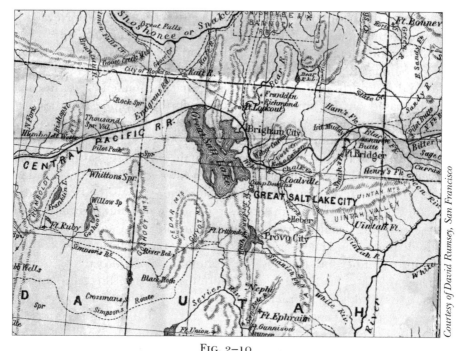

FIG. 2–10

Portion of W. J. Keeler's *Map of the U.S. Territories [and] Pacific R.R. Routes . . .* (1867) shows the transcontinental railroad running north of the Great Salt Lake and over the unnamed Promontory Range.

Courtesy of David Ramsey, San Francisco

this railroad symbol, colored in blue for added emphasis, indicates "Rail Roads in Progress" while the bolder symbol featuring alternate "rungs" of the ladder symbol in black, and over-colored in red, indicates "Rail Roads completed." By the time the weather warmed in June of 1867, Butler Ives had returned, surveyed much of the area for the Central Pacific, and effectively mapped the route over Promontory Summit.

On Keeler's 1867 *National Map of the Territory of the United States from the Mississippi River to the Pacific Ocean*, the route of the Central Pacific is shown as running around the north end of the Great Salt Lake and across an unnamed mountain range indicated by the familiar hachures. Derived from the French word *hacher* (to chop up or hash something), these straight lines symbolized the downhill slope of the mountainsides. The range they depict is, of course, the Promontory Mountains. To the east of these mountains, the line curves south to Ogden, where it then heads east into Weber Canyon and beyond Ft. Bridger into "Dakota Territory" (the western portion of which would become part of Wyoming in 1868). Only in the vicinity of Sulphur Creek and Bridger Pass, which lie far out in Wyoming, is the name "Union Pacific" indicated on Keeler's map. Significantly, Keeler names each railroad twice. He likely assumed that their meeting point would be about halfway between Sacramento and Omaha—perhaps near the Green River in today's Wyoming.[30] That would have put the Central Pacific well into territory that Union Pacific assumed to be its own.

The year 1868 was crucial for both railroads—and for Promontory. On Keeler's map, the blue lines were speculative in at least two senses. They indicated the selected route generally, although slight deviations in the actual route could, and would, occur. Moreover, the question of exactly where the railroads would meet was still unknown. That two-hundred-plus-mile stretch of railroad over both the Promontory Range and the Wasatch Range was not indicated as belonging to any particular railroad, and with good reason: The actual point at which they would meet was not only undetermined but also hotly debated.

Before long, many voiced opposition to the route west of Salt Lake City, including the railroads themselves. The unthinkable had materialized: Ogden, rather than Salt Lake City, would be the only Utah city on the Pacific Railroad. A route that would bypass Utah's economic and spiritual center in favor of Ogden would be nothing less than a snub to both the Mormons and the territorial capital. One could understand why the Central Pacific favored a route that bypassed Salt Lake City, for they did not have a close relationship with the Latter-day Saints. For its part, though, the Union Pacific had to face a reality despite their closeness to the Mormons. Despite the fact that it would miss Salt Lake City, a route through Nevada's Humboldt River Valley connecting with Weber Canyon would be the shortest possible. That route, however, would not run at the lowest elevation along the edge of the Great Salt Lake, but rather *over* that pass or "saddle" in the rugged Promontory Mountains northwest of Ogden. The Mormons were unsuccessful in lobbying for a change in the northern routing which, although straightest for the railroad, would be less advantageous to the Saints' interests.

If the Mormons had had their way, Promontory would never have become a household word. By March 30, 1868, however, the handwriting was on the wall regarding the route's selection. Union Pacific's Grenville Dodge wrote J. Blickensderfer directing him to "put parties on location north and south of [the] lake when they can be freed from work east of Lake." He then soberly added, "But everything indicates that for Grades, distances, water, work, and to avoid the Desert on Mud Flats the north line is best." At this time, mention was made of Promontory Point, which was virtually due west of Ogden and seemed like a feature the railroad could curve around. To reach it, the railroad would have to take a snaking route north to the base of the Promontory

Range, then south around Monument Point, then north again to curve around the northwest edge of the lake. That, however, was easier said than done. As surveyors discovered, the chief problem with Promontory Point was getting there: it would require pilings across a portion of the lake, on a fill.[31] Still, evidence suggests that Union Pacific hoped to go around the northern end of the Great Salt Lake at lake level, in effect hugging the north shore rather than going over the range. That was the route mapped by Stansbury (fig. 2–7), and it was almost perfectly level. Dodge's 1866 map (fig. 2–8) has a route right across Bear River Bay to Promontory Point, yet another indication of Union Pacific's penchant for a water-level route wherever possible.

Yet, the decision to build the railroad in the vicinity of Promontory—the exact route was far from certain at that time—still seemed rather counterintuitive. Railroads not only like to traverse straight and level lines, but they also know that serving population centers can be quite lucrative. Both the Central Pacific and the Union Pacific recognized the desirability of serving Salt Lake City, and both had surveyed a southern route. However, even though it meant missing the biggest city in the entire region and receiving less in subsidies that the government would pay per mile of railroad constructed, the math always worked out in favor of the northern route. As Dodge put it in August of 1868, the route north of the Great Salt Lake "was shorter by 76 miles, had less ascent and descent, less elevation to overcome, less curvature, and the total cost was $2,500,000 less." With the Bear River and perhaps Blue Creek in mind, Dodge also claimed that the resources adjacent to the northern route were better, with "more running water, more timber, and better land for agriculture and grazing." To lessen the disappointment to Young and the Mormons, presumably, Dodge stated that the Union Pacific planned to build a branchline south to Salt Lake City.[32] As an astute political leader, Young saw the handwriting on the wall. Still, he continued to advocate the southern route for months thereafter—even when it was a lost cause.

With the northern route chosen by both railroads, the exact line over Promontory Summit was still uncertain. After all, *several* northern options were possible. One route might run around the far northern edge of the Promontory Range. Although this would offer a more level route, it would add considerable mileage. Then, again, one might run the line around the southern edge of the Promontory Range, in effect skirting the lakeshore and touching that now-important landmark, Promontory Point. Although that route would follow the old Stansbury route and be a "water level" route, it would also add considerable mileage, and, as we have seen, present construction obstacles. Lastly, one could go over the range. By tackling the fairly rugged eastern slopes of the Promontory Mountains, one could cut out a 2.21 percent grade for the railroad, gain the pass at the summit, and then engineer the right of way down the western slope of the range, reaching Monument Point on a more reasonable 1.6 percent grade. This would be the shortest, and best, route.

As late as September 5, 1868, as both railroads were building toward Utah, Young was unsure about which route would be traversed. He did know that Salt Lake City would have a railroad—even if he had to build it himself. On that date he telegraphed "all the Bishops south of the city" a message imploring them "to send me all the help you possibly can, as quick as possible, to work on the railroad." The reason for the urgency, Young stated, was that "[w]e wish to rush it through to Monument Point, or to this city." Leaving little doubt as to his seriousness, Young noted that "[i]f the teams which have lately come in with the immigration will go to work, I will employ them right away." How *well* would Young pay the work teams? Anticipating this question, perhaps, he concluded, "[t]he pay will be sure, and in money at liberal rates." When Young ordered the telegraph operators to send the message "immediately,"[33] he was already envisioning a web of rail lines in Utah, but had his hands full with other matters. The church was growing rapidly but facing economic pressures as it needed to develop coal and iron mines. Missionary activity had rapidly expanded throughout Europe and from Hawaii to the far islands of the Pacific and even Australia. The church needed the money that the railroad labor would yield, for they had suffered setbacks with locusts and grasshoppers in the spring and summer of 1868. Indigenous to the Great Basin, the locusts had seriously damaged the Saints' crops just as they had soon after the Mormons settled Utah, leading them to the "miracle" of seagulls' intervention. Now, however, the problem was a full-scale invasion of flying locusts—grasshoppers that became migratory and voracious. Of the locust invasion in Utah, Union Pacific's Samuel B. Reed wrote to his wife Jennie on June 14, 1868, noting that "Grass Hoppers distroying thousands of acers [*sic*] of grain Mormons wage war upon them drive them into water ditches then as they pass over some full prepared for the purpose they catch them in sacks and baskets and thus incredulous as it may seem destroy them by the thousands of bushels. . . ."[34] Then, too, political pressure mounted against polygamy and an increasing number of Mormon patriarchs began to fret about federal authorities who would prosecute violators. However, Young and his church officials could only control so much outside of Utah. One of those uncertainties was the exact route that the railroad would take within Utah Territory. That route would be determined in boardrooms far distant from Utah. The result of those deliberations was that Promontory, rather than Salt Lake City, was destined to be on the transcontinental railroad. To understand how Promontory became the most celebrated location in the West in 1869, we need to closely consult the maps wielded by the railroads themselves.

Chapter 3

THE BATTLE OF THE MAPS
(1868)

On New Year's Day of 1868, Central Pacific's Collis Huntington did what he always did on holidays—obsess about business matters. At that time, business and railroad were synonymous to Huntington. Concerned about the slow progress the Central Pacific Railroad was making, Huntington wrote to "Friend Crocker" outlining the turf battle that had been brewing in northwestern Utah, and was about to reach the boiling point. Of the "UNION PACIFIC," as he wrote the name of his nemesis in capital letters for emphasis, Huntington noted that the "one thing that they do understand is the importance of meeting us west of Salt Lake . . . ." That scenario would give Union Pacific the prosperous Wasatch Front with its large population centers and rich farmland. Holiday or not, Huntington was in no mood to allow this to happen. In his characteristically abrasive style, Huntington then chided Crocker, observing that "sometimes I think you do not know the importance of extending the Central Pacific east of the lake to the Wasach [sic] Mountains . . . ." Crocker, of course, certainly understood this, but the ever-impatient Huntington knew that speed was of the essence. Huntington candidly added, "It would be better to have it understood that we were working quietly and building a good road, but I would build the cheapest road that I could and have it accepted by the Commissioners, so [that] it moves on fast . . . ."[1] Later that month, Huntington clarified this in another letter to Crocker: "I would build the road in the cheapest possible manner and then go back and improve it at once, because the Union [Pacific] Company has built the cheapest kind of road."[2]

Huntington had good reason to be concerned, for the route of the Pacific Railroad through northern Utah had now been selected from at least four distinct possibilities—one through Salt Lake City, one running directly west from Weber Canyon and straight across the lake on a trestle, another running northwest out of Weber Canyon and hugging the north shore of the Great Salt Lake, and one running over the Promontory Mountains. The Central Pacific soon learned that its idea of running across the lake would be prohibitive because the lake was found to be deeper than originally thought. The three remaining alternatives appeared, in one form or another, on maps of the period.

With Grenville Dodge in command of its route selection, Union Pacific took a decidedly militaristic approach toward mapping. Dodge wanted the most accurate maps and preferred as much detail as possible. An anecdote about mapping reveals just how serious Dodge was about it. On January 16, 1868, J. E. House wrote to Dodge, apologizing about his sloppy cartography which, of course, Dodge readily spotted. "I am sorry . . ." House began, "that the land map meets your disapproval." After apologizing, House quickly confessed, rationalizing that "I did not give it as much attention as I ought to have done, owing to the fact that Mr. Davis was looking after the details . . . ." Besides, he rather brazenly added to Dodge, "Your letters hurrying the matter up, did not give us much time."[3] Another statement by Dodge reveals his near obsession with the geography along the route, and how insistent he was that his surveyors fully understand the country they were traversing. On May 11, 1868, the lack of knowledge about the countryside surrounding the Great Salt Lake became intolerable to Dodge, who wrote to an engineer lamenting: "We have not got much knowledge of that country." Dodge insisted that the party surveying there had "to *feel* the country." Only after receiving that type of knowledge, Dodge stated, could he confidently "*pour* the *Location* Parties on to that 200 miles and have it ready for work in sixty days after parties commence."[4]

For his part, Huntington and his Central Pacific had a different, and more expedient, approach to mapping. Based partly on geographic knowledge and partly on bluster, the approach it would serve the Central Pacific well as it pushed eastward toward the Union Pacific. Huntington emerges as a shrewd visionary who believed that maps served one major purpose—to help him meet his political objectives. To Huntington, this meant barely satisfying the requirements and doing so ahead of the Union Pacific. By providing less detail, for example, of the topography and exact location of line than Dodge customarily provided, Huntington believed he met the letter, if not the spirit, of the legislation. It also saved him time. To Huntington, then, geography was something to be overcome, while to Dodge it would dictate the character—and ultimate success or failure—of his railroad. As early as 1865, Dodge had speculated about routes that could be traversed by the Pacific Railroad in this area of Utah. One revealing Union Pacific map from 1866 shows the Humboldt Valley of Nevada in considerable detail and projects the line of the "Union Pacific Division" at a scale of 2,000 feet to the inch. This map provides additional evidence that Union Pacific planned to build far into the Intermountain West. In fact, the Union Pacific had surveyed, if hastily, well into Nevada's Humboldt River Valley as early as 1864–65. Thus, while most observers and taxpayers assumed that both railroads would simply survey the route proposed in the Pacific Railroad surveys to a point where they would finally meet, the railroads had other, more ambitious and less disciplined, plans.

The events taking place in eastern Nevada suggested that a more complex scenario was occurring. From the Humboldt River eastward, the route, or rather routes, became more problematic, and that requires a look at maps of the proposed routes in more detail. One route projected to go around the southern edge of Great Salt Lake would directly serve Salt Lake City, and then presumably run northward to Weber Canyon. The second route would take the line around the north side of the Great Salt Lake, and then over the summit or saddle of the Promontory Range. The more mountainous route that bypassed Salt Lake City had won out.

As historian Wallace D. Farnham observed, albeit from a viewpoint sympathetic to the Union Pacific, Central Pacific's Huntington mounted a campaign to hamstring the Union Pacific's survey and construction activities. In Farnham's words, the ferocious competition between the railroads "began with the battle of the maps."[5] Both the Central Pacific and the Union Pacific had prepared maps showing routes through what had now become, in the eyes of journalists and hence the public, the most contested part of the entire transcontinental railroad—its route through northern Utah. The Central Pacific provided a map to Secretary of the Interior Orville Browning that showed that line's route from Nevada's Humboldt Wells (today's Wells) as far east as Monument Point, though Huntington had far more lucrative sites in mind—the Salt Lake Valley, the Wasatch Front, and well into Weber Canyon. His maps soon showed these prizes, if rather vaguely.

According to Farnham, Central Pacific's maps were surprisingly easy to prepare because they were so unclear in places. Nevertheless, they served the purpose of positioning the Central Pacific well into northern Utah. Politically, the Central Pacific appeared to have the edge. It appeared that government officials had rubber-stamped their survey work while frequent inspections burdened the Union Pacific. This caused much consternation at Union Pacific as it suggested favoritism. Relentlessly, Central Pacific cranked out map after map, one of which Farnham considers "one of the curiosities of the campaign" as it contains "simply a jagged line on a vast sheet of paper." Oddly, this Central Pacific map shows none of the topography or hydrology along the proposed route—not even the region's most prominent feature, the Great Salt Lake![6] In fairness to Central Pacific, it should be stated that this map could have overlaid a more detailed map, saving time by not depicting any specific geographical features. Regardless, it was in stark contrast to Union Pacific's more detailed/accurate maps. For its part, the Union Pacific was perplexed when Huntington's schemes were approved *pro forma*, while it seemingly had to battle federal bureaucrats at every turn.

Meanwhile, although the beleaguered Union Pacific was preparing rather accurate maps, confidently grading line, and laying track along the route east of Utah, sections of the Central Pacific's route were legally approved and moving ahead at a much faster clip. To make matters worse for the Union Pacific, Huntington and Crocker finally signed a contract with the Mormons, lured the railroad's workers away, and continued to thwart Union Pacific at every turn. By a congressional decree, the railroads could only survey their routes an additional three hundred miles beyond their completed construction work, and so any obstacle posing a problem for one railroad—for example, Union Pacific's trouble-plagued tunnel construction in Weber Canyon—was greeted with joy by the opposing railroad.

By early summer of 1868, the Union Pacific had decided to run its line nearer the Promontory Mountains and thus found itself in a quandary with Brigham Young. The zealous sermons that Young gave at this time still strongly favored the line running directly west from Salt Lake City, which is to say south of the Great Salt Lake. That route would mean constructing the railroad across miles of salt flats, roughly following the old Hastings trail, at least in part. It also meant ignoring the basic geographic fact that the entire Pacific railway would have to swing about thirty miles out of its way to reach Salt Lake City and go south of the lake—adding at least fifty extra miles. Yet no one, not even the Central Pacific, could deny that Salt Lake City was a lucrative and tempting prize in that it would generate considerable traffic for the railroad. To the dismay of Collis Huntington, the Union Pacific had cultivated the Latter-day Saints very carefully and effectively. Central Pacific correspondence at this time reflects Huntington's paranoia about the Union Pacific's confidence in serving Salt Lake City, for he, too, realized that relying on Mormon support and labor was necessary to bring his project to completion. With the volatile "Mormon Question" still simmering, and considerable anti-Mormon sentiment palpable, going out of the way to serve the Saints was not politically expedient nationally. Yet, that is just what was required locally.

The Union Pacific evidently took two approaches to the more northerly route that would miss Salt Lake City and bring its line closer to the Promontory Mountains, and it is here that the name "Promontory Point" again enters the picture. Railroad historians have long lamented the fact that people often use the wrong placename for the location where the rails finally met on May 10, 1869. Stressing that it is not Promontory Point—it is, of course, properly called Promontory Summit—they bemoan the fact that the public persists in using the name Promontory Point. However, given the reporting at the time and the confusion of routes, the public's misnaming is perfectly understandable. Even Congress itself used the term *Promontory Point* for the meeting point of the railroads in its resolution. Promontory Point itself—that location where the southern tip of the Promontory Mountain Range juts out into the Great Salt Lake—was considered by some to be a viable location for a railroad line around the northern edge of the lake. With this in mind, as noted earlier, Union Pacific explored the possibility of building its line around the north edge of the lake, rather than going over the Promontory Mountains. Union Pacific's reasoning seemed logical enough, as a water-level route would conform to their much-publicized mantra of "no grade over 90 feet" (per mile). There were, however, several problems: the line around the northern shore of the lake would be longer as it was quite sinuous. Moreover, the level of the Great Salt Lake was rising at this time, and the lakeshore itself was notoriously marshy in many places. Surveys also identified many areas of quicksand. Nevertheless, Union Pacific surveyors appear to have made a noble effort to skirt the lake's northern edge and leave the summit to the hawks—and the Central Pacific. After all, if Union Pacific could pull it off, considerable cutting and filling, not to mention steep mountain grades in the Promontory Mountains, could be avoided. Union Pacific dispatches during the summer of 1868, however, reveal that nature had other plans. In telegram after telegram, the difficulty of running the line around Promontory Point became painfully clear.

Three Union Pacific maps reveal much about the railroad's knowledge of western Utah and eastern Nevada during the fall of 1868. All were prepared under the direction of Chief Engineer Dodge, though they naturally involved input from many others. The first, a *Map of Location 11th Hundred Miles U.P.R.R.,* is drawn at a scale of 1 mile to 1 inch, and is dated November, 1868. This map shows the Union Pacific's projected route from the 1000–mile location in Weber Canyon, down into the Wasatch Front at Taylor Mill, through Ogden (a name only) to the northeast edge of the Great Salt Lake (Hot Spring), to the Bear River at Corinne, nearly straight westward to the base of the Little Mountains (near Salt Springs and Mud Beds) to Blue Creek Station [*sic*], then curving upgrade to Promontory Summit to "End of U.P.R.R." at "1085.88 miles," then down along the Union Pacific survey curving northwest to U.P.R.R. 1100 miles, near Station 4099.09. A wonderful vignette shows two surveyors lounging under the pennant/flag. This last page of the folio-style map also contains an inset of alignment of temporary track on the eastern slope of Promontory. Clearly, Union Pacific was on its way over the range.

This map got around, so to speak. In addition to the bound original copy of it at the Union Pacific archives in Council Bluffs, another very similar copy made at the same time, resides in the National Archives. This is a reminder that railroads often produced many copies of the same map. The map reveals those surveyors resting at the end of their labors. Although unnamed, they clearly played a major role in locating the Union Pacific. That pennant suggests victory. It flies above, proudly marking "U.P.R.R. 1100 miles Sta 3968.155 Location Aug. 2nd 1868." The location, about ten miles west of Promontory Summit at the north end of Spring Bay, was significant. Crowned by the pennant, it suggested that Union Pacific was in control here. To get to this point, the Union Pacific was surveying along the edge of the lake plain, passing the "Mud Beds" and "Salt Springs" at the base of the rugged Little Mountains. At this time, Corinne is shown as a blank area, the only information appearing in red as the surveyed railroad route crosses the blue lines of the Bear River. Of Ogden, the surveyors have drawn a series of squares or blocks astride the "Ogden Riv[er]," the railroad route passing at the west side of the fledgling town.[7]

The second map in the series, titled the *Map of Location 12th Hundred Miles U.P.R.R.*, dated December 1868, with a scale 5280:1/12 (fig. 3–1), shows Union Pacific's ambitions far to the west beyond Promontory. The line from about the Nevada-Utah state/territorial line runs arrow-straight eastward for several miles [to north of the present-day Grouse Creek area], curves southeast, then northeast [around the base of the Grouse Creek Mountains?] then south of "Raft River Mountains" [likely today's Muddy Range near Immigrant Pass] to Terrace Pass, then passes just south of "Sink of Duff Creek" [likely today's "Sinks of Dove Creek"], which was possibly named after Union Pacific Railroad official John Duff. If so, this placename, though modified into "Dove," may be the

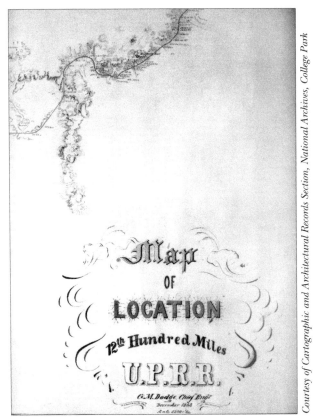

FIG. 3–1
Cartouche of Union Pacific *Map of Location*
for the 12th hundred miles of line surveyed
in 1868 was positioned below the section
showing that railroad running over Red
Dome Summit west of Promontory.

only lasting tribute to the Union Pacific west of Promontory. At any rate, from the sinks of Duff Creek, the line then runs along the southeast edge of the Baker Hills [unnamed] through Red Dome Summit just south of Red Dome Mountain, curving east to Monument Point [just north of North Cape of the Great Salt Lake] to 11th Hundred miles [north edge of the Great Salt Lake].

For our purposes, the section of the area of Promontory (fig. 3–2) is particularly interesting. Reorienting our view from east to west, it shows the Union Pacific Railroad line reaching Blue Creek, then curving westward to assault the mountain range. From this point, the line gains elevation. There is a reason why the line here looks like a worm trying to avoid being put onto a fishhook. In a series of sinuous twists, the proposed

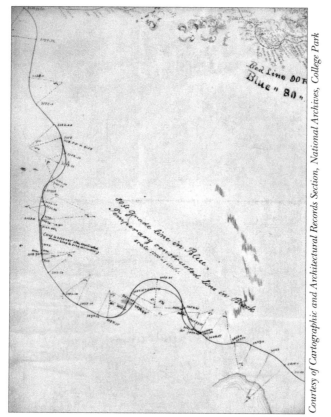

FIG. 3–2
An inset on the Union Pacific *Map of Location*
of the line surveyed over Promontory,
showing the temporarily constructed line.

railroad line works it way up the eastern slopes of the Promontory
Range. An inset on the map gets the railroad over Promontory Summit
at an 80–foot grade (fig. 3–3). Here, unbeknownst to the Union Pacific,
history would be made the following year. Once at Promontory, the railroad followed the east-west trend of the swale.

The last document, a *Map of Location 59.4 Miles of the 13th Hundred
Miles U.P.R.R.*, is dated December 1868 and shows the line from the terminus of location of U.P.R.R. along the Humboldt River several miles
west of Humboldt Wells (Nevada)—today simply called Wells—eastward
through Cedar Pass, Pequop Pass, and Ives Pass [possibly near present-
day Valley Pass Siding] to near present-day Tecoma, which is very close
to today's Utah-Nevada state line. Like Dodge's earlier 1866 map, the

FIG. 3–3
Detail of Union Pacific *Map of Location* showing the two lines surveyed at different gradients.

1868 map reveals Union Pacific's seriousness about running a Pacific Railroad line at least as far west as east-central Nevada. A copy of a similar Union Pacific map, an original on muslin, is also located in the National Archives. One wonders if maps of this type found their way into the hands of the competing railroad, and if so, how that happened. As in all types of high stakes endeavors, espionage is an ever-present possibility and threat. Yet, because copies were sent to the Department of Interior and Congress, secrets were virtually impossible to keep. The two railroad companies were private entities, but by conducting business with the federal government, they were subject to considerable public scrutiny. One can only imagine the intrigue such maps generated in Washington, D.C.

Meanwhile, back in Utah, the cash-strapped Mormons continued to provide surveying and grading expertise and labor to the Union Pacific. Grading could be easy or tough, depending on the topography. The goal was to prepare as level and smooth a roadbed as possible. The typical Mormon grading team included dozens, sometimes hundreds, of men working with picks and shovels. Usually, horse-drawn carts and wagons helped workers move earth or rock out of the way, typically spreading it as fill in the low spots. Information and photographs from this time reveal the difficulty of the work: the Fresno scrapers we normally associate with railroad grading were not widely used until about the 1870s and 1880s. Nevertheless, workers sometimes used horses and mules to pull boards or other objects along to help flatten out the soil. In the very rugged and rocky areas, blasting with explosive dynamite made the work go more rapidly. The Mormons helped the Union Pacific grade extensively in Utah, but these grading contractors still had a great deal of trouble getting paid for their efforts. For their part, the Union Pacific was perennially short of funds and paid the Mormons in promises. This included much of their line in Utah, especially the portion that reached west of the Wasatch and then toward and beyond Promontory. Although the Mormons felt that the Union Pacific was "their" road in that it seemed to be tailored to serve their needs, the relationship was often strained.

Central Pacific kept an eye on its competitor's progress in grading roadbed, impressed by the work the Mormons accomplished. Not surprisingly, Central Pacific approached Mormon leaders about doing similar work. It was not easy at first because Young associated Central Pacific with the northern route. As Governor Stanford wrote Mark Hopkins on June 9, 1868, Brigham Young seemed difficult to convince, but there was hope as Young's son (presumably, Joseph A. Young) was easier to convince. At first, Brigham Young was "cold and close" because "[h]e and every body here was dead set for the Southern rout [sic]." Nevertheless, Stanford's correspondence reveals that "I am inclined to make an arrangement by which Brighams [sic] son shall undertake to furnish the men and to help push the works as we want it and receive so much, conditioned upon the grading being accomplished as we want it."[8] Both railroads no doubt appreciated the sobriety and discipline of the Mormon track graders. As the church-owned *Deseret Evening News* bragged, "As a whole, the conduct of our 'Mormon Boys' is worthy of high commendation, no swearing, no drinking, no quarreling." The paper added that the Union Pacific officials seemed to think well of the Mormons.[9]

Various individuals influential in Mormon congregations, or wards, hired the Mormon roadbed graders under broader contracts. For example, English immigrant Thomas A. Davis recalled that one team grading the Union Pacific consisted of twenty-one workers, many of whom were from Wales. The team, it turned out, was directed by "Some Spanish

Fork people who had taken a large contract and needed some good men." This occurred in Weber Canyon. While there briefly, Thomas noted that his brother John was working for Sharpe & Young, and John invited him to join the Welsh team. Living conditions were rough in these construction camps. Thomas noted that they had to build "a shanty to sleep in," but that one man became sick and had to leave. With the work in Weber Canyon nearly completed, Thomas and his brother left. After working their way down to the Wasatch Front, Thomas rested a day in Willard, then "went to work grading the line at the Hot Springs for Thomas E. Jeremy [?] and his son John." This was tougher work than Thomas expected. As he put it, "[t]he nature of this job was wheelbarrow work, and it was heavy being in heavy alkaline clay and water." Nevertheless, the workers did what was necessary to grade the line here at the northeastern edge of the Great Salt Lake. Thomas noted that "[w]e finished that job before the arrival of the tracklaying force." Upon completing work here, Thomas headed to Promontory.[10] According to Moroni Stone, workers grading the right of way of the Union Pacific's line, including the Big Fill in the vicinity of Promontory, received five dollars per day per man and team, and ten dollars for Sunday work. "These wages," the Ogden newspaper reported fifty years later, "seemed enormous to the frugal pioneers."[11]

The willingness of the church to provide grading crews to the Union Pacific built the Saints' credibility in the eyes of that railroad. That may help explain how one of the Mormon "topographers," James H. Martineau, got the break that enabled him to become one of the West's more important railroad survey engineers. Martineau first mentions the Pacific Railroad in his July 7, 1868, entry titled, "Start on the Union Pacific Survey." In it, Martineau notes that he "received a telegram from Mr. S. B. Reed," superintendent of construction of the Union Pacific Railroad "giving me an offer of employment as an engineer of that road." His first assignment would have involved surveying the railroad's route along the Weber River. However, because Martineau arrived several days late, he received "bad news for me." The Union Pacific had given that job to another engineer, so he hoped he could "get a place as a common hand, if they had any vacancies" farther up river.[12] By July 9, he worked his way from camp to camp along the Union Pacific where he "was instructed in reading the leveling rod and in keeping the level book." Aware of the anti-Mormon attitudes expressed by others around him, Martineau added, "[I]f it were not for the chance to be proficient as an Engineer I would not wish to stay an hour longer."

But things were about to change for Martineau, who would soon find himself surveying for the Union Pacific Railroad in the Great Basin. On

August 7, Martineau reported, "I am appointed Topographer of our party[,] the former incumbent being assigned to duty in S. L. City." Martineau's salary now rose from $45 to $75 per month, even though, in his words, he had "not much to do on the line, only to take a topographical sketch of the line and country as we progress." However, he quickly added, "I have also to make maps, profiles, plans & c. of the line." Of this work, Martineau concluded: "It just suits me."[13] He threw himself into the work with near abandon. Martineau was not only a natural at surveying and mapping, he was also a budding songwriter and poet. Of his work surveying the railroad, Martineau wrote the "Engineer's Song," which could be sung to the tune of "Red, White, & Blue." One stanza of this song cleverly links the surveying of the railroad with the labor that will follow:

> On the side of a precipice, craggy and steep
> The transit directs where the Chinamen shall creep
> And clinging like bats to the steep mountain side,
> They calmly look down on the fierce surging tide.[14]

This suggests that even at this early date, the work of Chinese graders and track layers had entered the folklore. Martineau's song continues, "We run to the westward, beating our line, Till the Central Pacific we finally join." "Finally" is the operative word here, for agreeing where to meet was still in the future. Reminiscences of surveyors like Martineau can help us determine the route surveyed. His song continues, noting the landscape that the surveyors crossed: "The lone desert, so dreary and still/Spreads out from the Lake to the far distant hill;/Its vast bosom glitters with salt, like the snow, But 'onwards' our motto, and onward we go."[15]

By August 15, 1868, a Union Pacific survey crew drove a survey stake into the loamy soil at Promontory Summit. That act started additional surveys and grading. Although Union Pacific had now completed its survey across Promontory Summit, it did so using, in part, the stakes that Central Pacific's Ives had driven there. The Union Pacific surveyors even honored Ives by crediting him with originally locating the pass. To this day, Promontory Summit is unofficially called "Ives's Pass," though the true Ives Pass is located about a hundred miles farther west in Nevada. The Union Pacific survey was under the direction of Frederick Hodge, whose field notes reveal that the crew was outfitted in Salt Lake City.

On August 27, 1868, Grenville Dodge wrote to Thomas C. Durant from Red Dome Pass, which is about thirty-five miles west of Promontory Summit. Here Dodge noted that:

A careful approximate estimate of the six miles of 90 ft. Grade —[?]— Promontory Point which includes the Heavy work before spoken of gives the following quantities

Rock Excavation	68,524	cubic	yards
Earth	63,613	"	"
Embankment	553,000	"	"

The Rock & Earth Excavation nearly all go into Bank as there are deep fills at each cut.

As Dodge concluded, "[t]he grading of the six miles will cost at a Liberal estimate about Seventy Thousand dollars per mile." Dodge then added that he "had some dozen lines run over the Point and three fully Located." For their part, "[t]he C.P.R.R. Co have run as many more and they told me tonight that they should adopt virtually my line." There was, however, one bright spot in assaulting the Promontory Range. "The western slope," as Dodge called it, "is twelve miles of very light work and fifty foot grades." That meant "[t]he entire eighteen miles crossing the Range which includes the heavy work on eastern slope and light work on the western slope will cost [an average of] about 30 000 dollars per mile."[16]

Martineau was part of the feverish Union Pacific surveying of Promontory and vicinity at this time. By August 28, Martineau reported in his diary that "we crossed the Promontory range to day, obtaining a magnificent view of Spring and Bear River Bays, and the islands in the Lake." Cognizant of the competition, Martineau writes, "we passed Stephenson's C.P. Camp and led Hudnutts U.P. Camp. Traveled about 17 miles."[17] The next day, Martineau reported that the survey team "went 27 miles to day to Locomotive Springs, which, like all the springs, almost, of this part of the country, are salty." Here, he observed, "was a camp of C.P. engineers; also Hodges and Maxwell's U.P. parties making in all five engineer camps, making quite a city of tents." Here Martineau wrote a poem, "The Muster Role" about his survey team, or "Engineer party," as he called it. In the poem, he praises Mr. Morris, "a shrewd Engineer," and "transitman Coons, with an eye quick and clear." He also praises "Bob Fulton, our leveler," who "will see his way through." Being sure to mention all members of the survey party, Martineau then noted, "There's Crebus [?]), or [our?] Rodman, and Wykoff, Black Flag, And Scurry [?] and Brown with the chain never lag."[18] Martineau adds his own name as the person "who all our topography do."

On Monday, August 31, Martineau noted that "We started today for Red Dome Pass, where our labors are to begin again." This was among the most barren country that Martineau surveyed. At this location just beyond the northwestern margin of the Great Salt Lake, he noted, "There is no road, at all, and our teams travel slowly." In the broad, sweeping plains beyond Promontory, the landscape of the western Curlew Valley was notoriously barren. Toward the lake, the valley was covered with a whitish powder-like dust consisting of alkali (potassium and/or sodium carbonate) and halite (sodium chloride, or common table salt). In addition to penetrating nostrils and stinging eyes, the salts' high reflectivity further contributed to eyestrain. Describing the conditions west of the Promontory Mountains, Martineau recalled that his party "suffered much from thirst, and from inflammation of the eyes and partial blindness, caused by the intense glare of the sun upon the salt-incrusted plains." He added, "the only remedy to hand was to wear a handkerchief over the face all day."[19]

Water was a problem here too. As Martineau's survey team traveled west, they began to run out of water but found a small stream about "4 miles off" where they obtained water. Martineau also describes setting up camp on Duff Creek on September 1, where the water, "though clear, is horrible, having an indescribable flavor." As if this were not descriptive enough, Martineau concluded that the odor of this water "almost made me think of carrion." By September 4, he moved the camp back nine miles, where the elements soon threw even more challenges at the survey team as "a fearful tempest of wind, rain, thunder and lightning began." The wind was so strong that it "blew down some of our tents, in spite of us."[20] On September 7, because Coons the transitman was sick, Martineau ran the line that day, making a connection eastward with Maxwell and moving back to Red Dome Pass at Duff Creek, where he "found Mr. Blickensderfer, with orders to hurry up as fast as possible." As if to confirm the urgency, Martineau then noted he "found a company of C. P. engineers, camped there, who are locating their line on the same ground." Although both railroad lines had long been in a desperate race to outdo each other, things were coming to a head near Promontory.

The reason for Martineau's haste is found in letters written by Grenville Dodge. On September 2, 1868, Dodge wrote to Thomas C. Durant with the news that "Central Pacific Rail Road have abandoned all surveys east of Monument Point . . . [and] have put all their force locating the one hundred miles west of Monument." As if this were not disconcerting enough, Dodge added that the Central Pacific had "contracted to Bishop West & Benson," who planned to "open work on it next week." Nevertheless, Dodge believed that Monument Point, which "is equidistant from two ends of track & is point to which the filed located maps last spring" would be the point at which Central Pacific intended to meet the Union Pacific. In believing the Central Pacific would "evidently give up everything east of that point," Dodge was sorely mistaken.[21]

Two days later, on September 5, Dodge reported to S. B. Reed that "you are no doubt aware of the Contracting of 100 miles west of Promontory Point by the C.P.R.R. C[o]" to, as he called them, "three Mormon bishops." Dodge regretted the fact that the Central Pacific had "let the work before they had a mile located, while our Location was or nearly all done" before the Union Pacific railroad contracted for grading. Dodge now felt that the railroads might meet either at Toano "or even at Monument Point, if they show energy."[22] This, too, was a miscalculation on Dodge's part.

Realizing that so much was at stake for the Union Pacific galvanized Martineau to survey westward. On September 8, he "climbed a mountain and triangulated all the peaks around." Gazing off to the distant peaks, Martineau got a "grand view" of the countryside. There, he "prayed, when alone, and dedicated all to the Lord."[23] As he reconnoitered the area, Martineau saw many remarkable sights, including mountain sheep. The air must have been clear on that day because he could see distant Pilot Peak in incredible detail. He noted, "Desert Mountain, rising from a salt plain fully 25 miles away to the south, seems to be only a mile or two." After working all night to finish the maps, he sent them via the mail line.

Meanwhile, Huntington seemed to relish the intrigue surrounding the race west of Promontory. Learning from his "usual source" that Dodge now knew that the Central Pacific "had let 100 miles of the grading near [the Great] Salt Lake and who we let it to"—that is, the Mormons—Huntington knew that Thomas Durant, head of the Union Pacific, would *say* he would head there immediately but wouldn't actually do it. Or would he? Huntington was concerned that Durant, whom he called "a great blower, but still a man of great energy and somewhat reckless . . ." might actually go to Utah. Huntington, therefore, urged Governor Stanford to personally go to Utah because "[s]ome one must be there until the roads meet . . . ." Leaving no doubt about who should go to Utah, Huntington added that "[s]ome one of *us* must be there soon after the first of October to take possession of the line when the location is approved . . . ."[24]

On the sixteenth of September, Martineau traveled twenty-five miles and camped with Mr. Bates's Central Pacific party, which he noted was "going to the Red Dome Pass to locate their line there." Of this encounter, Martineau noted that the Central Pacific survey team was so confident that, as he put it, "they are willing to bet [that] their line will reach Ogden before ours." At Surprise or Grouse Creek on September 17, Martineau found Central Pacific Engineer Ives's survey party "camped in a large meadow of several thousand acres of grass, with good water." Here Martineau also "found a split stake holding a letter from Genl Dodge to Morris." Fifteen miles west of that location, on September 18, Martineau reached Tuarno [sic] Pass and, "for the first time since we left Weber, had some good, cold, clear water."[25] Martineau was now in Nevada, hoping that the Union Pacific could grade and lay track fast enough to claim the area as a prize.

The next day, Martineau was "camped at Peuquop [sic] Pass, from the Summit of which I could see the Snowy range of Humbolt [sic] Mountains." At Pequop Pass, he found Dodge's party, including Van Troben, General Dodge's topographer, "and was glad to see him." Although it was mid-September, Martineau noted that the weather was cold and threatened to snow. The next morning, they awoke to find "ice 1/3 of an inch thick" in their tin cups.[26] On September 21, Martineau began running the Union Pacific line *east* from the Summit of Pequop Pass. The next day, he made a map of Hudnutt's line by request of General Dodge, and on September 24, Dodge requested another map "of some 16 miles of Hudnutt's survey, to be sent to Mr. Reed." Martineau notes that Dodge was satisfied with the results, which were completed the next day. On September 30, Martineau "began to alter the line from Grouse Creek east," taking "observations with the sextant, for variation of needle, taking observations on Jupiter and Polaris." By October 5, he "found some U.P. graders at work" on the railroad's grade near the north end of the Ambe mountains, with "the CP lying close by and crossing ours." With supplies running very low, Martineau tried, but failed, to hunt some game. On October 9, he came upon some graders working on the Central Pacific, and also Colonel William Hyde and Arthur Stagner, whom he was happy to see. Here Martineau also "got a quarter of beef, and during the evening ate most of it up, being very hungry." By nightfall, Martineau and the survey team had reached their camp at Terrace Point. They were now within sight of the brooding Promontory Range.

Martineau's recollections confirm that birds and mammals were widely scattered, if not downright scarce at times, in the area west of Promontory. This scarcity made things tough for the advance-guard surveyors. In describing the desert country that he encountered in "locating the line of the railroad about two hundred miles west of Ogden," Martineau noted that "we got out of provisions—had nothing left but a little corn meal and some vinegar—not a morsel besides." As "the boys" in the survey team desperately put it, they were "out of grub," and so "every man except one or two, went out to kill a few rabbits or birds." By day's end, despite the fact that they were armed with pistols, "not a man had seen a rabbit or bird, but each fondly hoped the others had." When Martineau finally returned to camp, the men hoped he had managed to shoot a rabbit or bird, but he, too, came up empty handed. That night, all fifteen men in the survey party were about to mutiny. Luckily, however, Martineau calmed them down and supplies arrived the next day.[27]

Clearly, the two hundred miles centering on the Promontory Range was gaining fame for two seemingly perverse reasons: it was among the most impoverished as well as the most contested on the entire transcontinental railroad. As a surveyor in the employ of the Union Pacific, Martineau was well aware of both factors, not to mention the railroad's (that is, Dodge's) high standards for surveying and mapping.

From his comfortable office that same day, Huntington fired off another letter to Stanford. Now aware that Durant's Union Pacific had been surveying as far west as Nevada, Huntington informed Stanford that "I am not much surprised that Durant should set men at work at Humboldt Wells, as he is a bold, reckless, and, in some things, a foolish man . . . ." However, Huntington left no doubt as to how Stanford should personally confront Durant. As Huntington put it, "you want to look him square in the eye and hold your own and not give him back in the least." Huntington was sure this confrontational approach would intimidate Durant, concluding: "That is the way to deal with him; he is then not dangerous."[28]

For his part, Durant now tried to contract his Mormon workers to grade to far western Utah and eastern Nevada. According to Central Pacific sources, Durant had "doubts at his ability to do the work within the time they [Union Pacific] desire & he dislikes it is said doing work along side of the Benson Farr and West contract."[29] The Central Pacific viewed Durant as irrational, and their correspondence reveals they knew that "Col. Seymour & Gen. Dodge have been laboring with Durant for three days to induce him to come to reason about grading along side of our present work." Central Pacific's George Gray wrote Stanford that, "I told Durant & Genl Dodge that if they offered to withdraw their contractors west of Monument Point I thought there would be more chance for a compromise but as it is I did not see any hope." With the compromise off the table, Gray decided to play even rougher. "Our only hope . . . ," as he put it, "is now to push on the Iron rapidly and occupy any road bed we find east of Humboldt Wells whether graded by Central Pacific or any other party."[30] It was war, and despite even the railroads' concerns about "avoiding double expenses" in constructing the transcontinental railroad, the Union Pacific and Central Pacific would stay locked in battle until Congress threatened to intervene.

On October 10, Martineau's survey team went to Duff (i.e., Dove) Creek, where they "found many camps of men from Cache County at work for the C.P.RR." and where he saw Bishops Hughes, Littlewood, and Maugham. Martineau here confirms that his fellow Mormons from Cache County worked for the Central Pacific west of Promontory. Four days later, on October 14, his survey party reached Locomotive Springs, where they "were serenaded by the Ogden Brass Band, who are grading here." The next day (October 15), after picking up supplies consisting of "sugar, canned fruit, raisins, bottled pickles, dried fruit, fresh peaches, flour, bacon, mackerel, and other things" Martineau's survey team was explicitly ordered to locate a "new line over the Promontory, when we get there." Thus, by fall of 1868, both the Union Pacific and Central Pacific were resolved to go over Promontory Summit side by side, or head to head, if necessary.

In fact, the Union Pacific was pondering yet another survey over Promontory—one that would produce the best rail route for them—as Hudnutt's early survey seemed less than adequate. With the Mormon contractors grading rapidly, however, Central Pacific got the upper hand on Union Pacific west of Promontory. As a letter from Central Pacific's M. A. Carter to George Gray put it on October 12, 1868, "[t]he work from 'Monument Point' to the west end of the line of the one hundred miles let to Benson Farr and West is progressing rapidly . . . [h]aving completed their contracts within the short period of a few weeks to their surprise and that of their principals."[31] From Martineau's diary, it is evident that the Mormon work teams were often identified by the last names of the bishops in charge. From Martineau's diary, it is also clear that Mormons played a major role in getting the railroads over the range. As surveyors and roadbed graders, their performance met or exceeded expectations. Meanwhile, Central Pacific's workforce of Chinese and European Americans worked just as tirelessly.

By November, Central Pacific's Leland Stanford could report to Hopkins that "[t]o day I had a talk with Brigham Young . . . [who] will do our grading west from Ogden to the Promontory and will not make our work secondary to the Union Pacific." Young had both railroads pretty much at his mercy, and promised "[t]hat he will put plenty of men on both lines"—to which Stanford added, "I am satisfied he can do it." By using Young's workers, as the Union Pacific had done, Central Pacific concluded that "[w]e cant [sic] stop the U[nion] Pacific from grading their line, but we can through Young have our own graded and have it to ourselves to lay track on when we can reach it . . . ."[32] As the railroad's correspondence and Martineau's diary entries confirm, the Mormons sometimes worked for the opposing railroads. The fact that they were now essential players in the affairs of *both* railroads underscores Young's entrepreneurial—and political—talents.

As if Martineau's whirlwind surveying was not frantic enough, the next day (October 16) he learned that "Genl. Dodge had sent orders for me to join Hudnutt's party, and help run a line from Locomotive Springs to Portland, Oregon!" The exclamation point in his sentence underscores the boldness of Union Pacific's vision. Martineau's entry squares with other correspondence revealing that the Union Pacific railroad desired to begin a line to the Pacific Northwest even *before* the golden spike was driven. This opportunity gave Martineau much to ponder. Ever in need of hard cash, he agreed that he would do this for two months at $100 per month. In turn, his boss, Morris, agreed, but more than money concerned Martineau. When the time-conscious Martineau also learned that he would have to stay on until the line to the Pacific Northwest was actually *completed*, the homesick Mormon patriarch noted with certainty, "This I would not do." Martineau missed his family as much as he needed the money.

With that issue resolved, Martineau set out to survey Promontory Summit itself more carefully than his predecessor Hudnutt had done. On October 30, he reported, "we have been running several lines over the Promontory, seeking a better one than Hudnutt's if possible." Needless to say, Martineau was understating the situation when he noted that he had "been very busy at my business." By November 7, he noted that he had "spent the week in taking cross section notes of Hudnutt's two lines, one of 80 feet grade per mile, the other 90 feet."[33] The next day (November 9), Martineau noted that he "went on the line, and made estimates of the culverts and masonry required, on both lines." Martineau here confirms that Union Pacific had surveyed two separate routes over Promontory Summit. Later that evening, he reported that he "spent most of the night helping Morris make his estimates of cost of [the] two lines," determining "that the 80 foot grade line would cost $596,000.00 [and] the 90 foot line $549,000.00." With typical thoroughness, Martineau shows how he arrived at these figures using standardized calculations: "The equation used on the U.P. is $50.00 for each degree of (central angle) curvature; $15.00 per foot for length of line; 20 feet rise = 1 mile level road; $75.00 per lineal foot of each culvert from 6 to 12 feet span, 4.50 per lineal foot of box culverts of 2 to 4 feet span."[34] Using these figures, Martineau noted that the "actual cost of road bed for the 80–foot grade is 47,000 *less* than the 90 foot line, but the equation for length throws the balance the other way."[35]

Clearly more confident, Martineau was interested in earning as much money as he could on his own terms. Therefore, it is not surprising that after spending a couple of weeks with his family in Logan, Martineau was back looking for railroad work—this time with the Central Pacific! On November 19, he went to "see Mr. Benson about getting a contract at grading on the C.P.RR." Unable to meet with Benson for several days, Martineau arrived back in camp on November 27, where he personally "talked with Gov. L. Stanford, Prest of C.P.RR. company, who wishes me to help them engineer" their line. It appears that the Central Pacific's hasty surveying had also left some questions unanswered, and Martineau was the man who could set things straight.

To begin this work accurately, Martineau and his team identified and climbed some mountains in early December in order to triangulate for days at a time. "We do this," he wrote, "to connect the triangulations from the west, with that from the east, at Ogden, for the Smithsonian Institution." To triangulate in the mountains at this time of year was risky for several reasons. Bitterly cold winds plagued Martineau, as did fickle weather conditions that piled clouds against the peaks, making it impossible to triangulate. On December 6, the weather cleared, allowing Martineau to continue his work, and to pen one of the most inspirational topographic descriptions ever written in the nineteenth century West. "At length the clouds settled below me," Martineau begins, "leaving me in bright sunshine with the clouds below me like a vast illimitable ocean; the mountain peaks rising through them resembled Islands." This was cheering enough, but "at length a hole appeared in the cloud below through which I could see the earth." Always fascinated by heights—the loftier the better—Martineau noted, "I seemed to be on another planet, and had the strangest feelings, until the cloud cleared away." To leave no doubt that this is *exactly* what a surveyor and mapmaker would most desire, Martineau quickly added, "Below me lay the lake—in fact—hundreds of square miles were spread out like a map."[36]

From this incredible vantage point, Martineau could see much of the western Utah countryside through which the transcontinental railroad would ultimately run; he notes that Ogden, the Great Salt Lake, "Pilot Peak in Nevada, [and] the Raft River Mountains, were all plainly visible." After "taking angles," that is, determining the locations of all the prominent points, Martineau finished after sunset. He adds a hair-raising description of what he did after he finished that mapping, observing "in descending the mountains, in the dark, I slipped, fell[,] rolled, and got to the bottom in all sorts of ways, several times narrowly escaping going over precipices, which I could not see until just on the brink." For several days thereafter, the bruised but elated Martineau continued to climb mountains and "took my angles" to ensure that his engineering surveys were accurate. Some of these ascents were so slippery that one of his companions repeatedly "slipped on the frozen earth and slid down the mountain side some distance." More annoyed than injured, Martineau noted of his companion's downhill distress: "He presented a very comical appearance, sometimes."[37]

Both railroads now recognized Martineau's skills. In December of 1868, he relates, "When I was going to leave the Company, Mr. Morris tried hard to dissuade me, promising me permanent employment by the U.P.R.R. Company if I would stay." Morris knew that Martineau's services were valuable to his competitors and hoped Martineau would stay on. Moreover, Morris paid Martineau the ultimate compliment: Martineau proudly noted that Morris "said I was the best topographer on the whole U.P.R.R. line, which, as I am a Mormon, is considerable praise." Despite this glowing commendation, Martineau decided to return home to the Cache Valley, where his family awaited. In parting from Morris, Martineau notes that "he gave me a recommendation of the best kind, which was endorsed by the principal engineers of the Company . . . ."[38] Upon returning home on December 16, 1868, Martineau began to actively survey numerous towns and section lines in Cache Valley, including Wellsville, Mendon, Hyrum, Paradise, Millville, Providence, and Logan. By late spring in 1869, he began survey work for the Utah Central Railroad, which was the brainchild of Brigham Young, who knew that a rail connection from Salt Lake City to Ogden was essential.

By late 1868 and early 1869, the surveyed route over Promontory Summit was recognized as the approximate location where the transcontinental railroad would run. What mattered now was *which* company's route would be chosen as *the* official route. If Union Pacific felt it was getting a rough deal from the federal bureaucrats that approved or disapproved of maps, it also had other problems during this crucial time. Nature conspired against the Union Pacific through the winter of 1868–1869, for the weather was mild in northern Nevada and northwestern Utah, which was just what Central Pacific needed. Meanwhile, just over the Wasatch Mountains, blizzards raged along Union Pacific's line in Wyoming, stalling roadbed grading and completion of track.

Union Pacific's maps of the period reveal its accomplishments and disappointments. The *Map of the Union Pacific Rail Road and Surveys of 1864, 65, 66, 67, 1868 from Missouri River to Humboldt Wells* by G. M. Dodge, chief engineer, presented a detailed delineation of the topography/hydrology, trails, and, of course, the Union Pacific line. The many years noted on the map represent, in effect, Union Pacific's claims to the region. The Union Pacific map is detailed for a good reason. Dodge's railroad had aggressively surveyed a large portion of this area in its effort to determine the best route for the railroad and its constituents.

The location of the Union Pacific route on maps of the Promontory area deserves scrutiny. The maps reveal that Dodge and his surveyors had selected a line that closely followed one of the early railroad surveys. From an unknown location near Ogden, the Union Pacific line heads north along the east side of the Great Salt Lake, crosses the Bear River as it turns northwestward, then travels almost directly west to the summit of the Promontory Range, where it descends toward the north end of the lake near Locomotive Springs. From that landmark, it runs straight west, crosses the southern spur of the Red Dome Range, then turns southwestward in a nearly straight line to Hot Springs Creek, where it meanders through the mountains on its way to Humboldt Wells. This route is generally close to, but not exactly, the route that the Central Pacific sought. Certainly, however, it was similar enough near the Promontory Range to ensure a battle with the Central Pacific. The line on Dodge's map heads up the southeast face of the Promontory Range where time and circumstances would put the Union Pacific and Central Pacific side-by-side, pickaxe to pickaxe.

The battle to grade as much of the line as quickly as possible with little or no governmental oversight resulted in the railroads surveying— and then grading—parallel roadbeds. As might be expected, this duplicate effort became the source of conversation nationwide and consternation in Washington, D.C. The area adjacent to Promontory Summit became ground zero in that fiasco. The correspondence of railroad officials themselves makes equally interesting, and revealing, reading. In a frantic telegram dated February 16, Union Pacific's S. B. Reed wrote to Thomas C. Durant that he "just returned from Promentory [sic][.]" Reed quickly added that "Ben is moving three hundred rock men on work today[.] Will probably get one hundred from McGees outfit[.] Will commence where both lines are the same[.] Will you order Morris to turn over notes on the line you want built[.] Will see Sharpe & Young to-morrow."[39] Reed's terse message sheds considerable light on how disenchanted the railroads could become with graders who dallied. Speed was of the essence here as the railroads sought to grade as many miles as possible—even though they were now bypassing each other, sometimes within yards of each other. In fact, in several places on the grades to Promontory Summit, the railroads' surveyed grades actually *crossed* each other! But each mile completed equaled money in the railroads' coffers.

As the graders blasted and hacked their way up the east side of the Promontory Range, they drew considerable attention. Up to six

Fig. 3–4
The Central Pacific Railroad's Big Fill at Promontory, 2005.

thousand workers were reportedly toiling away in a scene that was captivating and chaotic. In characteristic Victorian prose, the Salt Lake City
Telegraph described it as "a marvelous view [that] reveals new clusters
of tents, hitherto obscured by some towering mass of grey rock" as one
approaches Promontory. The beholder of this scene "may delight in
vision with the discovery of camps almost innumerable" that were scattered "above the grade, along the grade, remote from the . . . blasting,
carting, shoveling, wheeling, picking, etc." Side by side, often within
yards or even feet of each other, the Central Pacific and Union Pacific
crews labored mightily, pushed to the utmost endurance to be ready for
the track layers rushing upon them now, at such proximity, from front
and rear."[40]

Their handiwork on the east face of the Promontory Range was
remarkable. Within about three months, the face of the range changed
from an austere, steeply sloping natural surface to one scarred by the
cuts and fills that enabled the railroads to gain elevation as if on tilt-
ing ramps. By early to mid-spring of 1869, the range had been transformed from a natural feature into a cultural artifact. On the west side of
Promontory, too, men at work covered the landscape. Although the western grade was gentler, it still required considerable labor. The Mormon
work camp at Cedar Springs was located here, where the view southward
toward the Great Salt Lake presented an awesome panorama.

Courtesy of DeGolyer Library, Southern Methodist University, Dallas

FIG. 3–5
Historic photograph of Union Pacific's trestle east of Promontory
Summit, being crossed by a work train in 1869.

But it is on the southeast side of the mountains that the competition between the two railroads reached its fiercest level. Workers of many nationalities and cultures, including Chinese, Irish, Mormon and Gentile—even about two hundred Paiute Indians—lived and worked for the brief season that would bring Promontory glory. The features they created, including the Big Fill (fig. 3–4) and spindly trestles (fig. 3–5), are legendary. They remain to this day as part of the Golden Spike National Historic Site's interpretive trail. Here, the extensive cutting and filling remain highly visible reminders that railroads seeking the easiest grades and broadest curves do not always get off easily.

Of the many interesting features here, Chinese Arch (until recently called "Chinaman's Arch") (fig. 3–6) is an open-arch formation in the dense gray limestone. Like a Chinese arch, which typically forms the gateway to towns and cities in China (and to Chinatowns in the Americas), Chinese Arch is tall enough to walk through and it helps frame vistas in the landscape. Surprisingly, known historical literature does not comment on this unique feature, at least not by the evocative name that we call it today. Is the name *Chinese Arch* a historical moniker crediting

Photo by author

FIG. 3–6

"Chinese Arch," eastern slope of the Promontory Mountains, Utah, appears to be a natural feature, possibly modified by construction activities in 1869.

the Chinese workers who toiled here, or is it a recent name given by history-conscious people of the twentieth century who recognized the efforts of the Chinese workers? Archaeological work is necessary to verify the claim that a cluster of graves of Chinese workers is located nearby (close to the present highway). Moreover, it was commonly stated that the bodies of Chinese workers who were killed or died of natural causes while building the railroad in Nevada would ideally be shipped home to China, though if and how this worked in Utah is unknown.

Even more perplexing than the naming of Chinese Arch or the actual location of the Chinese cemetery is the location of "Junction City"— the place east of Promontory where the two railroads were supposed to meet. By January 1869, a townsite had been platted in anticipation of being that fabled place. One reporter from *The Deseret News* described it as ". . . the largest and most lively of any of the new towns in this vicinity." Junction City was reportedly located where the railroad lines begin their ascent toward Promontory, which would likely be in the vicinity of Lampo, and "nearly surrounded by grading camps [with] Benson, Farr and West's head quarters a mile or two south west [*sic*]." Junction City was reportedly a tame and orderly place while the community of Dead Fall, about two miles distant, was said to be "notorious for its violence."[41]

The location of these camps remains one of Promontory's many mysteries, and archaeological fieldwork will be needed to find them.[42]

The surveying frenzy that had provided Martineau and others with work not only caused rampant roadbed grading; it also resulted in a stunning set of maps showing the two competitors' positions. The Special Pacific Railroad Commission was empowered to determine exactly what both roads had accomplished. These maps produced by the commission were important, for they clarify what led up to the joining of the rails at Promontory. Although the photographs taken on May 10, 1869, suggest that the Union Pacific and Central Pacific met head-to-head at Promontory, in fact, the tracks of the two railroads originally were some distance apart here. Because the United States Congress now demanded the railroads *meet* here, however, the Union Pacific routed its line closer to the Central Pacific at a point that would become legendary in the history of the West. That, however, only occurred after maps showing the locations of the two routes for the Pacific Railroad from Ogden over to the Summit of Promontory and as far west as the western end of the Great Salt Lake were prepared. These maps could better help federal authorities and Congress comprehend what the railroads had accomplished. Based on the surveys and construction records of the Union Pacific Railroad Company and the Central Pacific Railroad of California (scale 1 inch to 1,000 feet), these maps show the position of the railroads *before* Congress required they meet at Promontory Summit (fig. 3–7).

The Special Pacific Railroad Commission's maps, then, reveal the expended effort and the money spent, in places where the surveys and roadbeds were duplicative. As it turns out, the countryside for about forty miles in either direction from Promontory Summit was the scene of a gargantuan battle between two giants. It also happens that this same eighty miles of contested right of way would ultimately coincide, almost exactly, with what we now call the Promontory Summit line of the Pacific Railroad.

In this regard, the large-scale Special Pacific Railroad Commission map section between Ogden City & Bear River is worth a closer look. It shows the City of Ogden consisting of about two-dozen blocks, and located 1,033 miles from Omaha and 744 miles from Sacramento. West and north from Ogden, the railroad lines diverge considerably, with the Central Pacific farther east. They come much closer together at Hot Springs, running nearly parallel with the Central Pacific still east of the Union Pacific. Continuing west-northwest near Willard City, the lines again diverge, and they are about a mile apart at Brigham City. By the time they reach the Bear River, however, both lines again converge. That is because natural features tend to limit a railroad's options. For

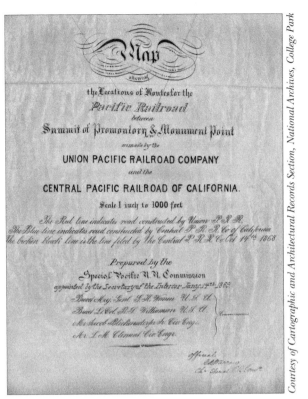

FIG. 3–7
Cartouche of the Special Pacific R.R.
Commission map for a portion of the
railroads' grades, 1869.

example, an ideal or narrow crossing place of a river like the meandering Bear River will find surveyors in closer agreement as to where their routes will run. It is in this area that Corinne would soon thrive.

From this section of the map set, we see a pattern that tends to prevail wherever Union Pacific and Central Pacific competed. Generally, Union Pacific seems to prefer a lower elevation, in many cases hugging the lakeshore, while Central Pacific takes the higher ground, topographically speaking. This likely happened because Union Pacific was obsessive about keeping its grade as nearly level as possible. Meanwhile, the Central Pacific, which had tackled the Sierra Nevada early on, seemed less concerned about grades and curves. To Central Pacific surveyor teams, in fact, surveying much of western Utah must have seemed to be relatively easy work—except in the area around Promontory.[43]

No section of the Special Pacific R.R. Commission's map portfolio was more spectacular than the portion between *Bear River & Summit*

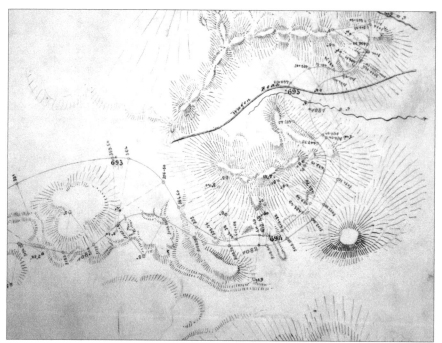

Courtesy of Cartographic and Architectural Records Section, National Archives, College Park

FIG. 3–8

A portion of the Pacific Railroad Commission's map showing both the Central Pacific (blue) and the Union Pacific (red) railroad lines on the steep grade just east of Promontory Summit, 1869.

of Promontory. For the first twenty-one miles, the lines run across fairly "level ground," as the mapmakers called it. This includes the Bear River Plains, and continues through the "mud beds formed by Salt Springs" at the base of the Little Mountains. West of this point, after the lines traverse the desolate "Sage Plain," are the formidable "Mud Flats" and "Salt Marsh." At Salt Springs Point, the Union Pacific and Central Pacific lines cross each other, running fairly parallel though separated by about one hundred feet. They cross again at an unnamed creek actually known (then and now) as Blue Creek. At this point, things change noticeably, for the railroads are about to tackle the Promontory Range (fig. 3–8). For the next seven miles, both railroad lines run upgrade as they scale the east slope of the range. For the first two miles, the Union Pacific line is located slightly higher than the Central Pacific line, but from the point where a creek bed is crossed, the Union Pacific and Central Pacific cross. From there to the summit of Promontory, the Union Pacific is located at a slightly lower elevation, and south, of the Central Pacific line. This portion of the line had the most spectacular cuts, fills, and trestles.[44] It

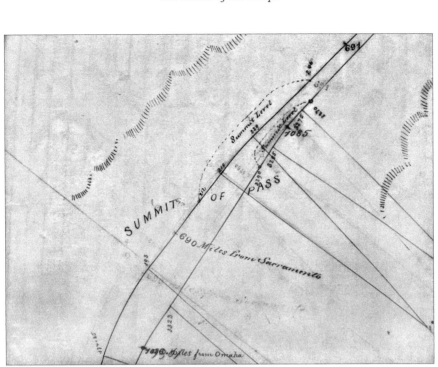

FIG. 3–9

The first map of Promontory Summit seen widely by the public, by the Pacific Railroad Commission, 1869. Central Pacific is shown in blue, Union Pacific in red.

was in this stretch that both railroads speculated about building a tunnel that could avoid the east face of the Promontory Range, but careful surveying proved that would be unnecessary.[45]

The next adjoining map section prepared by the Special Pacific R.R. Commission shows the *Locations and Routes for the Pacific Railroad between the Summit of Promontory & Monument Point.* It, too, offers interesting commentary on the battle between the Union Pacific and the Central Pacific. As on all maps in this series, the lines of the two railroads appear in color—Union Pacific in red, Central Pacific in blue. This section map appears to be the first to publicly show the "Summit of Pass" (fig. 3–9). The map reveals a half-mile swath of land as "Summit Level"—the levelness revealed by the lack of any hachure marks. This summit was, in fact, a fairly broad plain, and it would later prove an ideal location for the two railroads to meet.

At that time, however, it was unknown exactly where the railroads would meet. As on the other maps in the series, the two mapped railroad lines shown here make subtle reference to the battle underway. Next to

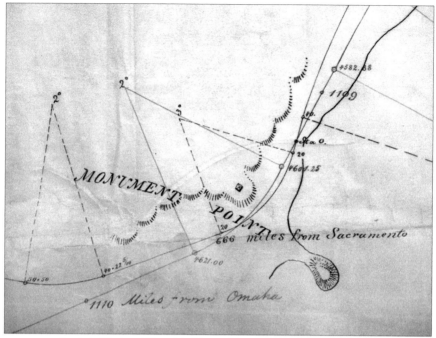

FIG. 3–10

The two competing railroads' locations at Monument Point, Utah, from a map by the Pacific Railroad Commission, 1869. Central Pacific is shown in blue, Union Pacific in red.

the line in red, a point about a half-mile west of the summit reads "1086 miles from Omaha," and a point on the blue line just west of the pass reads "690 miles from Sacramento." Similarly, at Monument Point (fig. 3–10), the Central Pacific mileage is "666 miles from Sacramento," and the Union Pacific is "1110 miles from Omaha." Before grading road-beds, each railroad had to "file"—i.e., officially submit a map to federal authorities. In several areas between Monument Point and Promontory Summit, a "broken black line" shows the "Line filed by the Central P[acific] R.R. Co., Oct. 14th 1868."[46] In reality, though, both railroads became overzealous in those final months, anticipating approval. To add to the public's confusion, names like Monument Point, Promontory, Promontory Point, and Promontory Summit were not easy to differentiate. With the terms *Point* and *Summit* mentioned so prominently and interchangeably, small wonder the public tended to use the term *Promontory Point* for where the railroads would meet!

Also contested was the line west of Monument Point, which is located on the sweeping lake plain west of the Promontory Range. To that end,

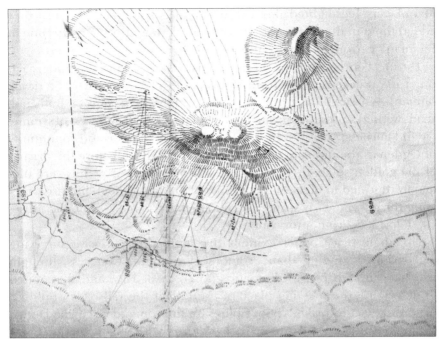

Courtesy of Cartographic and Architectural Records Section, National Archives, College Park
FIG. 3–11
Detail of Pacific Railroad Commission map showing the two competing railroads' grades near Red Dome, Utah. Central Pacific is shown in blue, Union Pacific in red.

another map in the series—*Map Showing the Locations of Routes for the Pacific Railroad . . .*— showing the area from Monument Point to the Summit of Red Dome Pass (fig. 3–11). Drawn at a scale of 1 inch to 1,000 feet, like the map from Promontory Summit to Monument Point, the map reveals how far the two lines diverged in some places. For example, while the Central Pacific ran farther north of the Great Salt Lake in this area, the Union Pacific actually crossed the streams issuing from Locomotive Springs and one called, appropriately enough, "Brackish Springs."

As the surveyed lines neared Red Dome, however, they continued to run closely parallel, crossing each other in a couple of locations. Once again, in rugged country where options were limited, the two railroads crowded each other. This again reminds us that rugged topography tends to reduce options for railroad surveyors and graders. The drawing of Red Dome features beautiful details using the hachure style so common at this time. The language on this map is telling, for "the Red line indicates line located by Union Pacific R.R.," but "the Blue line indicates line located *and constructed* by Central Pacific R.R. Co. of California."

Mapmakers highlighted those words "and constructed" because they added them in the same script, in darker ink. It is clear from this line in the map's cartouche that Central Pacific had the edge here.[47]

During February 1869, the railroads were grading alongside each other in numerous places from Monument to Weber Canyon—a development that caught the full attention of the U.S. Congress. Both railroads wanted a presence in Salt Lake Valley and, in the interest of symmetry and fairness, Congress leaned toward the small Mormon community of Ogden as the ultimate end of each railroad. Even before the driving of the golden spike, then, Union Pacific and Central Pacific were ultimately destined to meet in the vicinity of Ogden, though intense wrangling during the early spring of 1869 dictated a more symbolic, if isolated, locale—Promontory Summit.

No single place better exhibits the railroads' aggressive surveying and roadbed grading than Promontory Summit. Congress, though, had had enough of this dramatic and costly activity, and threatened to determine the meeting place of the rails if the railroads wouldn't. Accordingly, on April 8, 1869, Collis Huntington and Grenville Dodge met in Washington, D.C., in order to determine the final meeting point of their railroads. It must have been a tense meeting indeed, with the determined titans finally chained together and told to make peace. After negotiating much of the night, they reached an agreement that finally put Promontory on the map. Their agreement also added to the perpetual confusion about what to call the place, for the document itself identified "the summit of Promontory Point" as the meeting place! On April 10, however, Congress accepted the location, properly identifying it as "Promontory Summit, at which point the rails shall meet and connect and form one continuous line." Because of the agreement, the Central Pacific crews stopped working at Blue Cut, and Union Pacific halted its construction activities at Monument Point. The goal now was to make the meeting of the rails at Promontory Summit as orderly, and as spectacular, an event as possible.[48]

In this regard, it is worth looking at the Union Pacific's maps of the transect from Humboldt Wells to Ogden in a bit more detail. Tellingly, Grenville Dodge's private copy of the location maps comprising the entire Union Pacific Railroad route end at an unnamed location in the Promontory Range.[49] There, in a masterfully drawn map, the Union Pacific line reaches skyward into the forbidding, rugged Promontory Range—and stops cold. The fact that absolutely nothing is depicted beyond "1085.88 miles" on the map—no former Union Pacific survey, no Central Pacific line—is symbolic. It is almost as if Dodge ended the story not wanting to publicize the outcome: was it just another job to

FIG. 3-12
The sign erected by Central Pacific Railroad commemorates the feat
of laying ten miles of track in one day.

him? Dodge knew, of course, that politics and fortune had kept the
Union Pacific from reaching as far west as Nevada, and possibly beyond.
And yet, that unnamed spot in the Promontory Range would be the
location—perhaps *stage* is a better word—for the singular event of the
nineteenth century, the joining of the rails.

The diaries and internal correspondence of those working for the
railroads reveals some interesting twists on the Promontory story. James
H. Martineau's diary clearly indicates that Union Pacific had now com-
mitted to building over the Promontory Range with more than just the
Omaha-San Francisco Pacific Railroad contracts in mind. As Martineau
makes clear, that was not the only route-related issue concerning Union
Pacific. They were also bound for the Pacific Northwest, and had envisioned a junction close to the Promontory Range to do so. Moreover,
Union Pacific actually hoped to best Central Pacific at its own game, surveying a lower elevation line to central California over the Sierra Nevada
via the Feather River—a route that would later (ca. 1908) become the
Western Pacific.

As the two railroads built toward Promontory, Central Pacific was
full of surprises, including the widely publicized feat of laying ten
miles of track in one day. What seemed like a more or less spontane-
ous result of hard work was actually a carefully orchestrated publicity stunt. The Central Pacific already knew how much track the now
nearly completed Union Pacific had laid in one day. Union Pacific was

now only 9½ miles from Promontory Summit, while Central Pacific conveniently had a gap much longer than that to fill. In anticipating meeting Union Pacific at Promontory, Central Pacific was ready to outshine its competitor in the eyes of the press and the nation. It is clear that the monumental work of building the transcontinental railroad suggested immortality, and Central Pacific wanted that prize in lasting recognition and remembrance.

Getting it required considerable logistical planning and a bit of secrecy. For days, Central Pacific carefully stockpiled all the necessary supplies and equipment at Rozel Flats. Now, in the early morning hours of April 28, with laborers champing at the bit, Central Pacific made its move, or rather staged its show. Carefully coordinated tie-laying crews consisting of Chinese and white workers progressed methodically and rapidly. With the ties now laid, another team quickly dropped rails "at a quick trot," while mostly Irish workers placed tie plates and spiked the rail. They reached the future site of Rozel at noon and continued their animated pace uphill into the Promontory Range using a cut that Union Pacific had made. By evening, they had reached the ten-mile location, which was about two miles west of Promontory Summit. Amid rejoicing, news went out that the feat had been accomplished. A sign erected here declared "10 miles of Track, Laid in One Day, April 28th 1869"[50] (fig. 3–12). It became a landmark for passing trains for at least a generation, until it succumbed to decades of weathering by the blistering sun, freezing precipitation, and strong winds of the Promontory Mountains.

Chapter 4

A MOMENT OF GLORY: PROMONTORY
1869

The joining of the rails ceremony that took place on May 10, 1869, has become part of the nation's folklore and mythology. Most books written about the event treat it as the culmination of the transcontinental railroad, but Promontory's story runs deeper and broader than that. I mean that Promontory should be placed in broader geographical and deeper historical context. The written record enables us to understand how what took place at Promontory compared to what was occurring on the world stage. One observer writing for the *Montana Post* noted that the event marked "the completing of an enterprise fraught with more interest than the tunneling of Mount Cenis or connecting the Red Sea and Mediterranean Sea by the Suez Canal."[1] This is an enthusiastic assessment but also a reminder that the transcontinental railroad was not the only major engineering project undertaken at about this time.

Another report in *The Deseret News* commented that "[a] thousand throbbing hearts impulsively beat to the motion of the trains as the front locomotive of each company led on majestically up to the very verge of the narrow break between the lines."[2] As the trains drew close to each other at a few minutes after noon, Central Pacific President Leland Stanford held aloft a silver-plated maul that would spike the last rail into place. As he did so, Stanford never realized that a controversy would develop as to just how many special ceremonial spikes were actually present—and how many were driven into the special laurel tie. Typically, four spikes would be used to complete such a task, and many historians concur that four were used: two from California of gold (alloyed with copper for strength), one from Nevada that was an alloy of silver, and yet another from Arizona made of a mongrelized mixture of silver, iron, and copper.[3] However, in *Empire Empress*, Haward Bain claims that only three were driven. Recent evidence leads to the conclusion that the second California golden spike may not have been used. Adding to the confusion, others claim that the original golden spike itself has been lost (or stolen) and that the golden spike presented today is not the real spike; and so the controversy rages on the Internet blogs about the numbers and authenticity of the "golden spike[s]." Regardless of these claims, a golden spike *was* driven at Promontory Summit, Utah, on May 10, 1869, though the fact that "there are extant no official or public records of the day's events"—only news dispatches from twenty *different* newspapers—helps explain why uncertainty reigns on this issue.[4] This driving of the ceremonial spikes marked "the Last Act," as Stanford called it, but even how that transpired is not without alternative explanations. The commonly repeated story that the railroad executives missed hitting the spike certainly makes good revisionist sense as the ceremony seemed to include more railroad brass and reporters than track workers.

Well known as the site where the railroads met on that memorable day, Promontory Summit found itself center stage in what some historians consider the most important single event in nineteenth-century western American history. The crowd at Promontory Summit that day was relatively small—perhaps about a thousand souls had gathered. Significantly, only three photographers were on hand to record the event. These included Salt Lake City-based Charles Savage, Central Pacific's guest Alfred Hart, and Union Pacific's guest Andrew J. Russell. That only three photographers were present is ironic because the event on that site marks the time and place of what is perhaps the single most important American photographic image of the nineteenth century—the one in which two locomotives finally meet, pilot to pilot (or as the public put it, cowcatcher to cowcatcher), after years of anticipation.

Virtually everyone who thinks about the joining of the rails at Promontory visualizes the scene in which two locomotives meet amidst a crowd. Consider, though, a photograph taken before that image, but shot from virtually the same perspective (fig. 4-1). Here the locomotives are still some distance apart (a reminder that space and time are interconnected) and the crowd has not yet surged. They stand patiently near the trains, not ready to swarm onto the locomotives. This pose, as it were, is a

FIG. 4-1
A. J. Russell's dramatic photograph, titled "Laying of the Last Rail,"
captures the anticipation of joining east and west on May 10, 1869.

Courtesy of DeGolyer Library, Southern Methodist University, Dallas

remarkable moment in time and the anticipation must have been almost unbearable. We see history, or rather time, seemingly suspended for moments while everyone anticipates what will be a history-making event.

Although many lesser-known photographs of the joining of the rails were taken from different angles that day, the most frequently published images are where we may begin to understand the relationship between the railroad and the place called Promontory. Photographs, like texts, can be deconstructed, that is, analyzed carefully as to the meaning and positioning of the different elements that comprise them. This deconstruction can reveal new insights into photographs we have looked at a thousand times but have never really "seen" for their deeper meanings. Consider, for example, the design composition of the photograph by A. J. Russell shown above. Taken to emphasize the trains arriving from opposite directions, this photograph's symmetry is noteworthy. The photograph's nearly perpendicular angle to the track emphasizes action moving from both right and left. The scene is much like a stage setting, the action on which enters from left and right. Perhaps coincidentally, due to the angle of the sun needed to light the subjects, the photographer looks north with the sun at his back; significantly, this put north "up," so to speak, in the composition. That being the case, east is to the right, and west to the left. The enduring photograph, then, is actually cartographic: it recreates the concept of most maps of the period, which are also oriented north, with east on the right and west on the left. Consider this photographic image a cartographic metaphor for both the meeting of the rails and the mapping of westward expansion.

The photograph's simple composition—all action focuses on the center—is a statement about time as well as space and emphasizes that history is about to be made in a particular place. No more effective device than the tall smoke stacks and sturdy boilers of the most powerful machines traversing the land—the locomotive—could be found anywhere at this time, and the fact that the locomotives were pointed toward each other suggests that a collision of sorts is about to occur.

Next, consider the track upon which the trains in the photo are standing: iron "T" rails laid on wooden crossties. In order for the track to be laid properly, the ground must be first graded, then ties laid, then rails spiked onto them. The Central Pacific grade west of Promontory and the Union Pacific grade east of Promontory drew a lot of attention from journalists. The Union Pacific tended to use hand-hewn "pole" ties while the Central Pacific used more finished-looking sawmill-cut "slab" ties. Note that the track itself is a defining element in this photograph. It stands on a roughly graded roadbed that essentially lifts the trains off the ground. That slightly elevated roadbed separates the railroad track from the natural setting, emphasizing that what is going on here is both an event in history and a symbol of technology.

The photograph portends the future but also documents the unfolding of recent history: Union Pacific trains had reached Ogden two months before the photograph was taken, and the celebration there involved considerable hoopla and was reported in *The Deseret News*. As spring arrived, however, excitement mounted about exactly where the rails would finally meet. Work crews grading right of way for both companies presented quite a spectacle as they went about their business. On the eastern slope of the Promontory Range, the railroad lines were cheek-by-jowl. Reporters on the scene commented on their progress, and many people were astounded that relatively little hostility was exhibited by competing crews. For the most part, the crews consisted of Irish, Anglo (usually Mormon), and Chinese American workers.

Let us look past the people, locomotives, and track in the photograph's middle ground to the wide-open landscape beyond. The place where the rails finally met was not only isolated but bleak. Many people commented on how forlorn it appeared. "This summit ..." as one observer put it, "is a considerable plateau, covered with artemisia, and quietly resting between two mountain combs."⁵ Most everyone at the time knew that Artemisia was the exotic name of common sagebrush, for John Charles Frémont had immortalized that symbol of the Intermountain West in his numerous reports. In terms of its natural topography, the site itself had a symbolic kind of symmetry. The Promontory Mountains, divided here by this plateau-like valley called the summit, witnessed the stitching together of the nation's fabric. That valley, however, appeared desolate, and most observers that day were simply unimpressed with its appearance. Some asked: Could this place have any agricultural potential? An unidentified mail clerk from the East noted that although there was very good grazing land in parts of the area, much of the land hereabouts was, as he put it, "entirely worthless." To him, it was simply "boundless plains white with alkali and mountains covered with sage brush."⁶

Yet, as early as the spring of 1869, some speculated that Promontory itself might have a future, as the soil in the Promontory Summit area was arable. In fact, as a group of "Western men, with a six-mule team, were breaking ground for railroad purposes," a reporter for *The Daily Bee* in Sacramento pondered the upturned soil, which, to his surprise, "looked warm and loose and rich." Intrigued, the reporter asked, "Will this grow good wheat?" One man responded, "Yes," followed by the opinion that "any land that will grow good sagebrush will grow good wheat."⁷ This statement, as people in the Promontory Summit area would later confirm, had a good deal of truth to it. Of Promontory's location, *Crofutt's Trans-Continental Tourist* noted the bench on which the station stands would "doubtless produce vegetables or grain, if it could be irrigated for the sandy soil is largely mixed with loam and the bunch grass and sage-brush grow luxuriantly."⁸

Let us return now to the crowd gathered on that day in 1869. Virtually everyone in Promontory's most famous photograph is looking at the space between the locomotives. However, in other days, they looked away from the railroad activity long enough to ponder Promontory as a unique place. Taking time to explore Promontory's site, the same writer of *Crofutt's Trans-Continental Tourist* noted that "[b]ehind the station at Promontory the hills rise into the dignity of mountains." On one bright spring morning, "[a]fter an hour's toilsome walking through sage-brush and bunch grass, then among sage-brush and rocks until we have attained a height to which that persistent shrub could not attain," the writer entered another, considerably more enchanted, world. Among the rocks at this higher altitude, he found "stunted cedars, tiny, delicate flowers and blooming mosses." Now at the top of the range at an elevation of about 7,500 feet above sea level, the writer found himself and his companions "on the summit of the peak, on a narrow ridge of

Photo by author

FIG. 4–2
The swale between the Promontory Range and North Promontory Mountains would provide an excellent location for a railroad. Note the presence of grasses and sagebrush (2007).

granite . . ." where the view of the Great Salt Lake was superb.[9] This observer had a good eye for vegetation but not for geology: resistant sandstones and dense limestones, not granite, cap the tops of the mountains around Promontory. Nevertheless, the rocks certainly impressed him as being as solid as the rock of ages. Well below him lay the swale where history was made earlier that spring (fig. 4–2).

The challenge of Promontory's position was not its lack of trees, but rather its lack of water. This problem was well known by the time that the rails were joined. The May 13, 1869, *Daily Bee* reported, "Here, at Promontory, there is no water fit for use, and all [that is] consumed by the few inhabitants of the place and by their stock, has to be hauled in wagons a distance of eight miles. . . ." The writer soberly concluded that "the only hope of the place, if it ever becomes a permanent station, will be in finding and leading hither some mountain spring."[10] Man and beast—including the iron horse—needed water, and it was scarce at Promontory Summit.

In the early spring of 1869, when it was still not known exactly where the rails would meet, two fledgling towns—Promontory to the west of the Promontory Mountains, and Junction City to the east—sprang up. However, both became virtually deserted when Promontory Summit was

Photo by author

FIG. 4–3
A wye track permits the turning of a locomotive or train using three switch tracks joined together to form a y-shaped configuration, as seen at Promontory Summit (2007).

decided upon as the meeting place of the rails. Events of mid-spring 1869 determined the future of Promontory Summit as a community. As the railroads surveyed and graded their lines, it became apparent that they would develop all activities in Promontory Summit with reference to the railroad rights of way. At this time, however, the railroads were located several hundred feet apart. In order to connect the tracks, a curving or arching track about a half-mile long was under construction to link both on May 8.

When trains began running to Promontory Summit in 1869, they faced a number of operational challenges imposed by inertia and gravity. Union Pacific was familiar with these challenges. Because Promontory was located at the summit of a steep grade, extra locomotives were often needed to assist those trains. Additionally, because Promontory was the end of the line for each of the railroads, they needed a way to turn loco-motives around for their return trip. Promontory used two of the three possible turnaround methods. The first—and easiest—was to use a wye track such as the Union Pacific had constructed. A wye is a track con-figuration consisting of a switch track that led to a curve with a switch at the end which led in the opposite direction, then met with a third switch track, which led in the opposite direction, back to the first (fig. 4–3).

These sections of track between the switch tracks are called legs. By traveling in this "Y" pattern (actually, more like a slingshot with a leg between the top portions of the Y), a locomotive could be turned around. Wyes are relatively simple to build, but consume a lot of space, and of course, require extra railroad track. Nevertheless, if the legs of a wye are long enough, it is possible to turn an entire train end-for-end on one.

A simpler way to turn a locomotive around involves using a turntable, which consists of a relatively short piece of track (long enough for the longest locomotive) that is mounted on a table-like bridge. Balanced on a center bearing, the bridge can be rotated by means of a sturdy pivot located in the center of a shallow, circular pit. The earliest turntables were "Armstrong," that is, they used manpower to push the table (and locomotive) around 180 degrees. As can be imagined, this is fairly hard work, but, with a properly centered locomotive and good turntable bearings, two men could turn a locomotive weighing up to about 30 tons in a few minutes. Once turned, the locomotive simply moved off the turntable in the opposite direction. Turntables also proved perfect for providing access to locomotive storage and repair tracks. By directing locomotives onto tracks radiating out from them, engines could be serviced or stored in a relatively compact space. Given the round shape of their pits, it was logical for the resulting building nearby to be semicircular in outline, hence the term *roundhouse*. Turntables are more difficult to construct than wyes, but they use far less space and can turn a locomotive more quickly than a wye. Their main shortcoming is their limited length; they cannot turn a full train, only a locomotive.[11]

By the weekend of May 8 and 9, the lines were close enough to each other to be easily joinable. That weekend, Union Pacific built a wye track at the summit. Saturday, May 8, originally envisioned as the day that the rails would be joined, was marred by poor weather—a cold, drizzling rain under a lead-gray sky—that seemed too somber for such an auspicious event. Moreover, even though the telegraphers of both railroads were within about fifty feet of each other, trouble on the westbound train carrying Union Pacific officials at Devil's Gate held up the ceremony. Monday, May 10 dawned clearer, and the event took place amid a crowd of people and cluster of tents immortalized by the photographers.

Most photographs taken that day reveal that Promontory was a typical "tent city," an ephemeral settlement that exuded both optimism and cynicism. The only thing exceptional about Promontory was its strategic position—at the end of both lines. A closer look at photos on May 10 shows that Promontory's tents were oriented along—that is, with their fronts parallel to—the tracks. An early photograph by Alfred A. Hart reveals the Wells, Fargo & Co. tents on one side of the tracks and

Courtesy of the National Park Service

FIG. 4–4
Promontory as tent city, May 1869. Note the signs for various enterprises and the "wall" sides that increase the tents' height and stability.

Union Pacific Railroad ticket office and telegraph tents on the other. Although these tents had begun to spring up in late April and early May 1869 in anticipation of the rails meeting here, they now constituted the small community where history was made. Seventeen tents stood at Promontory on the day the rails met.

Photographer Russell captured a fine image of the Union Pacific track layers ballasting the section of track they laid early on the morning of May 10, but looking beyond that action, one can see three tents facing the tracks. Other photographs of Promontory show that a row of tents had taken shape by the time the crowd had gathered here, and this became the nucleus of the town (fig. 4–4). This arrangement is much like a typical Main Street, but it lines the track. This arrangement is understandable in that predominant forms of transportation, such as roads and canals, tend to dictate the shape of communities. Since the railroads were the reason for the embryonic town's existence, the fact that the tents face the railroads confirms the importance of the Central Pacific and Union Pacific in the affairs of Promontory Summit.

The earliest photographs of Promontory confirm the arrangement of tents in rows facing the railroad tracks, but they were located about 100

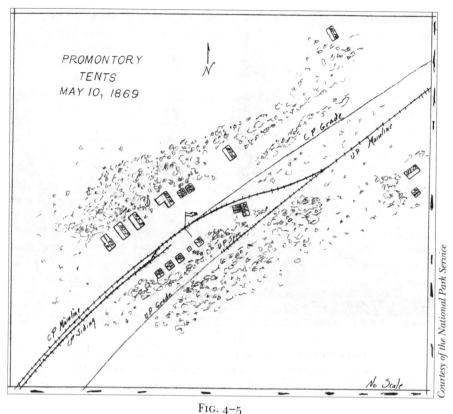

PROMONTORY
TENTS
MAY 10, 1869

Courtesy of the National Park Service

FIG. 4–5

Sketch Map by National Park Service historians showing the railroad lines, tents, and other features at Promontory, May 10, 1869. Note the linearity of the tents, which face the railroad rights-of-way.

feet from the right of way. Although an early property map of Promontory Summit has not been located, the photographs suggest that even in the chaotic month of May 1869 a type of order prevailed. This *linear* arrangement not only characterized early Promontory's morphology: it would persist throughout the town's history. From these photographs and other descriptions, historians F. A. Ketterson (1974), Paul Hedren (1978), and Robert Spude (2005) reconstructed the early town's layout (fig. 4–5). Whereas, the tents faced the railroad and tended to be located close to each other, one tent of the Union Pacific engineers and speculators represented what Spude calls the "site of future Promontory City." That tent was the command center of Union Pacific's activities and became the focal point of the town's early development.

Promontory Summit's other railroad station—if it could be called that—also epitomized the temporary nature and make-do quality of the new community. As recorded by photographer Andrew Russell, the

Courtesy of the National Park Service

Fig. 4–6
Photograph showing the Central Pacific's first station (center)—
really a boxcar outfitted for the purpose—May 1869.

Central Pacific station (fig. 4–6) is nothing more than a boxcar. Still on its trucks, its railroad car heritage was obvious, though the smoke-jack suggests that it could be warmed inside to ward off the high desert chill. Called an "outfit car," this offered a temporary but weather-proof structure. A makeshift set of stairs was located at one end of the car, and it permitted people to enter this "station" in order to conduct railroad business. This station was not much to look at, but was far more comfortable than the Union Pacific's ticket and telegraph office where Charles Savage slept before he took his classic photographs at Promontory Summit on May 10.

In addition to the booming tent town, the railroads' facilities were also a significant part of the infrastructure at Promontory. At first, the railroad facilities also reflected the general confusion here. Even though Congress determined a month earlier (April 10) that the rails would "meet and connect *and form one continuous line*" at Promontory, competition between the railroads nevertheless remained intense. The thorny issue was now which railroad would get the best of things at Promontory Summit. The animosity between Ames's and Huntington's railroads manifested itself in several ways at Promontory in May of 1869. Union Pacific Vice President Durant and others conveyed Ames's orders that "you will make no permanent arrangements for connection" with the Central Pacific, and that they should "change cars only at end of track laid by us—till they pay."[12] Durant was present at the events on May 10 but observers claimed he had a headache and left early. Given the tension simmering here, his headache was understandable. For his part, Dodge informed Ames that when Governor Stanford had "notified us that he would put in a siding on his old grade" at Promontory, Dodge countered by putting in his own siding "before day light and when their workmen arrived in the morning we had it completed, much to their disgust." This delighted Dodge, who ordered that "all transfers should be done opposite our office and opposite our main track." Clearly, Union Pacific wanted a large share of the action at Promontory Summit.

A closer look at the tent city central to this drama reveals that the individual tents were typical of those of the Civil War-era. Most of them were "wall tents"—that is, they had canvas walls, and could be made taller by the addition of wooden side boards. They appear to be similar to "Sutler" tents used by the military to provide dry goods and tobacco. Only one tent, used as the Central Pacific quarters, was an "A" or Wedge tent. Those tents, however, were common in Central Pacific construction camps. The sizes of tents at Promontory varied, although standard military sizes (such as 10 x 16; 12 x 14; 14 x 14; and 14 x 16) were probably used. A business occupying a site of about 16 x 20 in size might pay around $100 for the tent and about $100 in lumber, plus the cost of nails. Tents were easy to find (many were sold by mail order), cheap to buy, easy to erect, and—equally important—easy to move when needed elsewhere. They were also highly versatile. Despite their relative flimsiness, tents could be used to house a remarkable variety of activities. They were, in other words, perfect for boomtowns like Promontory Summit.[13]

The photographs of Promontory reveal a place huddled along the railroad; while wide-open nature surrounds, the throng of people suggests bazaar-like activity. One observer characterized the railroad tent town of Promontory as "thirty tents upon the Great Sahara, sans trees, sans water, sans comfort, sans everything."[14] Everything, that is, except opportunism. Promontory soon gained a reputation as a den of iniquity where con artists swindled travelers. One writer called it "a fearful place composed entirely of open gambling booths and whiskey shops." Here, he noted, "one of our passengers [was] fleeced of all he had by gamblers." Overall, Promontory was not impressive, and most found it unpleasant. Upon leaving the place, the same writer was, as he put it, "[g]lad to get away."[15]

Other observers were not as kind. One writer for the Elko Nevada *Independent* concluded that God must have become more lenient and patient toward sinners "since Sodom and Gomorrah had been destroyed, as recounted in the Bible." Was God now forgetting to destroy such wicked places? "If God weren't," the writer observed, "Promontory would have fallen long ago." This quote is all the more amazing when one considers it was written in October 1869, when Promontory was not quite six months old! Evidently, the writer was none too pleased at what he experienced during the stop here. Leaving little doubt as to what he thought should happen to Promontory, the writer concluded that "[i]t would be a mercy to the public . . . if the cleansing element of fire would sweep the town from the face of the earth."[16]

This made for colorful copy but fate had less spectacular plans for the place. In late May of 1869, a more rational assessment turned out to be pretty much on target: ". . . Promontory City, as it is called, is not likely to become a commercial emporium, while it will have some fame and romantic interest attached to it as the place where the Atlantic and Pacific first embraced."[17] As this sober account concluded, "But a few days since, this point was an almost unsettled waste; now it is the temporary transfer point for freight transported from the extremities of the continent."[18] The amenities here were passable enough: "Of the improvements here," as he called them, "some enterprising soul has erected a large tent, 30 x 70 feet, in which is kept a first class eating house."[19]

Union Pacific's Grenville Dodge described the town's origins as simply as anyone could. At Promontory, as he put it, "neither company had plans for supporting a town at the summit, it just grew there."[20] This suggests a kind of unplanned synergy and opportunism, and that certainly appears to be the case. By mid-May, a row of tents lined the north side of the tracks at Promontory. Some of the businesses here included a branch of the Salt Lake City firm T. D. Brown (General & Commission Merchants) and its likely West Coast counterpart, The California Store; the San Francisco Saloon; a dry goods store operated by J. S. Fyfer; a Chinese laundry operated by Sam Hing and Ah Lee; a cigar shop; the Pacific Hotel; a bakery; barber shops; billiard halls; and other services catering to the largely male crowd. By late May, the town of Promontory City had reached its zenith, about thirty tents.[21] Those Chinese laundry operators offered westbound travelers their first glimpse of Asians. As one group of travelers observed of their first "Chinamen," Sam Hing and Ah Lee had "little huts adorned with signs vouching for 'good washing and good ironing done here.'" Moreover, these travelers also encountered "[a] gang of Chinese laborers, in loose blue muslin garments and peaked parasol hats of straw [who] were grading a new switch at the station."[22]

Promontory City was a one-street town (fig. 4–7). Although originally consisting of tents, a number of these were soon improved. These tents were given façades sided with board and batten lumber, and they represented an investment in the future—however long it might last. This false-front construction was quick and simple. The boards were placed vertically, and where they met a narrow strip of lumber, called

Courtesy of the National Park Service

FIG. 4–7
By mid-1869, Promontory was still a city of tents, but some now had wooden false fronts to enhance their appearance, draw customers, and suggest permanence.

a batten, was nailed in. These façades were all pretense, but they gave an air of permanence and hope. In practice, however, these wooden façades were little better than the tents they concealed from the street. True, they provided some protection from the weather, but their slip-shod construction just as often permitted wind and snow to find their way inside between the cracks.

When a group of Cincinnati travelers described early Promontory, they alluded to the town's "rough characters," as did many observers. However, they also described the one-street town in some detail as consisting of "thirty-six [business] houses in one row, all of which were one-story high and roofed with canvas." The group emphasized that these "houses" were not actually dwellings but rather commercial in nature, "every shanty being occupied for business, the inhabitants sleeping in odd corners and recesses." Among these thirty-six enterprises, they identified a "barber shop, drugstore, saloons, restaurants, fruit stalls, and stores filled with general merchandise."[23] Like all speculators, the operators of these businesses hoped that Promontory would become either a permanent meeting place between Central Pacific and Union Pacific, and/or a major railroad junction point, as the Union Pacific's plans to build a line from here to Oregon were widely rumored and discussed.

The two railroads remained strong competitors even after the events of May 10, but they created a community here despite the tension that hung in the air.[24] In June, for example, Central Pacific's chief engineer Samuel Skerry Montague called for a meeting at Promontory with Dodge. At least two issues needed resolution. The first involved putting an end to the ongoing disputes as to which company owned and operated which trackage. The Central Pacific wanted to make several improvements, including adding a new switch or turnout that would make operations smoother. A second, and related, issue was the need for better cooperation aimed at interconnecting the operations of the two railroads. This was important to the Central Pacific, which wanted to use eastern Utah coal shipped into Promontory by the Union Pacific—an intimation that the days of wood as locomotive fuel were numbered. Then, too, the Central Pacific wanted to build a new 18 x 24 frame ticket and telegraph office. Central Pacific did not plan to build a shop or roundhouse here but evidently envisioned a place where the two railroads could simply interconnect more or less harmoniously. That, too, appears to have become Dodge's goal, for they agreed to better align trackage by straightening out some of the kinks and adding more ballast to ensure that the track stayed level. The railroads hoped these improvements would result in smoother operation, thus saving money and easing the burden on passengers who had to change trains here at Promontory. To better mark the junction, Dodge ordered a stone placed here to be marked as the "junction of the Union Pacific and Central Pacific Railroads, May 10, 1869." This made sense as the whittled laurel tie marking the junction proved so desirable an artifact that souvenir hunters frequently cut sections out of it! Within a month and a half or so of the meeting of the rails, Promontory had secured a unique position in the popular mind as the place where the rails converged. The stone marker would be the first of several monuments aimed at immortalizing the place and the event.[25]

Another easily overlooked item in the historic photos of Promontory is the telegraph line strung high on poles along the railroad right of way. The telegraph was a vital form of communication that operated in conjunction with the railroads at the time. Telegraph poles are the tallest man-made objects in the photos at Promontory. The fact that an American flag flies from an extension added to one symbolizes the importance of the telegraph as well as the national importance of events taking place on the adjacent railroad. As is widely known, the message that the rails were joined was telegraphed around the world on May 10; however, those telegraph lines now needed to be improved as communications increased. Although Central Pacific had originally agreed to let Western Union use its lines, the telegraph company now needed to build a line east from Promontory to its existing lines in the Salt Lake Valley. By August 1869, Western Union had completed its new telegraph line into the valley and assigned a telegrapher to the Central Pacific's new station. Union Pacific, though, had different plans. It contracted with Western Union's rival—the Atlantic Pacific Telegraph Company—whose lines were strung along the Union Pacific line and on poles west of Promontory.[26] This is yet another reminder that both railroads were separate companies with different allegiances and different methods of operating.

Union Pacific's presence at Promontory was always regarded with some misgivings by that railroad. After all, Promontory Summit was simply a place the railroad envisioned going *through*—not terminating at—on its way west. The location was, in fact, a bitter prize given the fact that Union Pacific had hoped to be exchanging passengers and freight with Central Pacific in Nevada. Moreover, in terminating at Promontory, the Union Pacific's last few miles of operation were among the most tortuous and expensive to operate on the entire system. Trains had to "double" the hill—that is, be broken into two separate trains, each taken up the hill by a locomotive. The alternative was double-heading—placing two locomotives on the front of the train. Both of these solutions cost the company time and money. The grade up to Promontory Summit also posed a safety problem. In August of that year, a brakeman was badly injured in a wreck that occurred as his train toiled upgrade, and he later died at Promontory.[27]

Word got around that Promontory was a miserable place. Fearing that its image was suffering, Union Pacific decided to take action at Promontory Summit. Superintendent Hammond ordered several improvements, one of which would diminish the town's image as a place where gamblers preyed on travelers. A wood-frame eating house and hotel opened in September, and it soon became a landmark. The belief was that this facility would be less subject to the shady behavior of the tent city. Hammond also ordered upgraded facilities including a roundhouse and enlarged railroad yard.[28]

That a photograph of two locomotives meeting each other with pilots nearly touching became one of the most arresting images of the nineteenth century was due in part to the nearly magical presence of the iron horse in the American imagination. Both locomotives present—the Union Pacific *No. 119* and the Central Pacific *Jupiter*—were of the classic "American" types whose wheels were arranged in a 4–4–0 configuration. This means that each locomotive had a total of eight wheels—four large driving wheels located under the firebox and a four-wheel leading truck under the front. This front truck swiveled while the drivers were rigidly mounted to the frame. The last number (zero) in the 4–4–0 designation refers to the fact that these locomotives had no wheels under the firebox area toward the rear of the locomotive. The lack of a trailing truck here confirms that these locomotive's fireboxes were relatively light, that is, did not need additional support.

It was symbolic that both locomotives at Promontory were American-type locomotives, for Promontory's ceremony helped immortalize American ingenuity and tenacity. Originally designed in Philadelphia in 1836, the American-type locomotive was named in response to the more twisting or curving track configuration in the United States. That swiveling front truck represented a break from British locomotive design. Then, too, the United States pioneered the use of the prominent pilot (cowcatcher), where livestock more commonly roamed onto unfenced railroad rights of way. Another feature that qualifies as American on these locomotives was the large, box-like headlight, which was illuminated by either tallow or oil. Lastly, these locomotives provided cabs as cover or shelter for their engineers and firemen, whereas in England their counterparts had little protection from the elements.[29]

The American-type 4-4-0 locomotive was not only American in design but also in ornamentation. During the period from about 1855 to 1880, ornately decorated American locomotives reflected the American spirit of promotion. As early as the 1850s, Matthias Baldwin was advised by Henry Campbell that a locomotive's "ugly, clodhopper appearance" would be detrimental to marketing. Homely locomotive decoration, as he put it "would strike people unfavorably." The British commented on how ornate American locomotives had become. For example, not only did American locomotives have cabs to protect engineer and firemen from the elements, those wooden cabs, or "houses" were elaborate. This led the British to call American locomotives "gingerbread peacocks" that glistened with "brass, planished Russia iron" and other shiny metals.[30] By the time the two railroads arrived at Promontory, then, American locomotives had become both functional and beautiful. In the drab, sagebrush-covered landscape, the sight of such gleaming and brilliantly painted locomotives was, and is, simply stunning. It was a matter of almost artistic contrasts, for nature had painted the desert with a palette of soft subtle tones while American railroaders painted their locomotives in bold, bright colors rendered in intricate patterns. One accent, the well-polished brass trim on the locomotives, shone as brightly as the desert sun it reflected.

As seen in a close up photograph taken on May 10, 1869, the Central Pacific *Jupiter* (fig. 4-8) was one of the "Monarchs," as an enthusiastic publicist put it that brought the transcontinental railroad to completion. *Jupiter* was one of four identical locomotives built in 1868 by the Schenectady Locomotive Works of New York. Even under a swarming group of well-wishers, the locomotive's lines are evident. Passenger locomotives like the *Jupiter* had tall driving wheels (the larger diameter the

Courtesy of DeGolyer Library, Southern Methodist University, Dallas

FIG. 4–8
Central Pacific's *Jupiter* (#60), "The Monarch from the West."

driving wheels, the faster the locomotives). These passenger locomotives were usually more brightly colored than freight locomotives, though the *Jupiter* could, and did, haul freight cars on occasion. With its intense blue color accented by crimson and its brass ornamentation, *Jupiter* was absolutely resplendent. Every detail on this locomotive was carefully selected from architectural and artistic motifs. Given the medieval-era Gothic style of the headlight brackets, the Baroque scrollwork on the tender, and the Rococo Revival sandbox, it is easy to see why this loco-motive has been called "the mechanical equivalent of a brass band,"[31] which appears in front of it in this photograph. The name *Jupiter*, a Roman god, was typical in the days when most locomotives had names, not numbers. Technically, even though *Jupiter* also bore the number 60 for recordkeeping purposes, as indicated by its number plate on the boiler front, it was called by its Roman name.

Courtesy of DeGolyer Library, Southern Methodist University, Dallas

FIG. 4–9
Union Pacific Locomotive *No. 119*, "The Monarch from
the East," Promontory, Utah, 1869.

The other "Monarch" photographed that day—Union Pacific's
No. 119—had several features that were signs of things to come (fig.
4–9). Those who gathered at Promontory Summit on May 10, 1869,
could tell, by sense of smell alone, that these two iron horses came
from different stables. Whereas Central Pacific's *Jupiter* burned pun-
gent wood—anything from hardwood and/or pine to sagebrush—the
aroma from Union Pacific's *No. 119* was more acrid, as anyone who
ever smelled the oddly sweet, metallic scent of coal smoke can testify.
Even though the *119* was also built in 1868, it had several features
that would later become common, including its burning of coal, rather
than wood, as fuel. The year 1870 represented a turning point nationwide, as coal would overtake wood as the locomotive fuel of choice.
Coal was a more efficient fuel that burned without scattering flaming embers. That explained *119*'s straight smokestack rather than the

ember-catching (and eye-catching) funnel-shaped stack on wood burn-ers like the *Jupiter*.

Although coal-burning engines could (and did) start fires when hot cinders left the stack and landed on fields or even buildings, wood-burn-ers were far more prone to do so. As a wood-burner, *Jupiter* had a bonnet stack (often erroneously called a balloon stack) because it resembled a popular woman's hat of the period. This was a large funnel-shaped casing containing a deflecting cone, as well as a wire screen cover to trap embers. As a coal-burner, *No. 119* was easier on its surroundings. Nevertheless, even this engine was designed to reduce the likelihood of fires. John Thompson originally introduced the extended smokebox in 1860 as a spark arrestor for coal-burning locomotives. *No. 119*'s extended smoke-box also featured a modification by Isaac H. Congdon, master mechanic of the Union Pacific, who *extended* its smokebox forward about two feet. The theory behind these improvements was that cinders or sparks would burn themselves out in the extended smokebox, though the effective-ness of this claim was debated for years thereafter, well into the 1880s. Ultimately, railroads adopted internal spark suppression controls based on this idea as standard equipment in later locomotives.[32]

Equally significant, too, was the fact that the Union Pacific locomo-tive bore only the number 119 rather than a name. Despite these two features, however, *No. 119* was a truly Victorian-age machine. One of five identical locomotives built for the Union Pacific by Rogers Locomotive Works as numbers 116 through 120, some considered *No. 119* to be a freight engine because it had smaller drivers than *Jupiter*'s. However, *No. 119*'s drivers were certainly "tall" enough—that is, of large enough diameter—to enable its use in passenger service. It was, in fact, an early example of what would later be called a "general purpose" locomotive. Regardless of the type of service in which it was employed, *No. 119* still had plenty of ornamentation. From its cast iron bell stand that simu-lated foliage, a fluted brass dome cover, and walnut cab with touches of Gothic and Italianate styling, *No. 119* was testimony that even freight engines were ornately decorated at this time. If anything, in fact, *No. 119* had an even more ornate paint job than *Jupiter*. Number 119's ten-der featured superbly gilded flourishes on each side of the oval num-ber panel. Two beautiful landscape paintings (both of them different) graced the curving back corners of the tender while each side of the sand dome featured a smaller landscape painting. As railroad historian Jim Wilke astutely observed, walking around this locomotive was like touring an art gallery.[33] We can only conjecture about *No. 119*'s original paint colors, but a similar locomotive also built by Rogers had a wine red tender featuring gilt lettering shaded in green and black.

Courtesy of DeGolyer Library, Southern Methodist University, Dallas

FIG. 4–10
Photograph showing Union Pacific *No. 119* and train (*left*)
and Central Pacific *Jupiter* with the Stanford Special (*right*)
on May 10, 1869.

Passenger cars, too, were beautiful as well as utilitarian. A remarkable photograph taken that day reveals the full sweep of the two trains with few people obscuring them (fig. 4–10). The Stanford Special on the right consisted of the locomotive *Jupiter* and two cars. First in the train was the commissary car, which looked similar to a short baggage or express car. It had one large door on each side for the loading and unloading of goods that needed to be shipped at passenger train speed. In this case, the commissary car probably contained food and supplies for those traveling on the special train. The second car in the train was called Governor Stanford's private car by some, and Crocker's private car by others, but it was more properly known as the Central Pacific's Commissioner's car, or Director's car.[34] Down the track to the left is the Union Pacific train, which consisted of the *No. 119*, an arched-roofed baggage car, and three passenger coaches. It was, in essence, a fairly typical passenger train consist (grouping of cars) for the times.

The photographs discussed so far anticipate that something grand is about to transpire. That climax occurred at about half past noon.

FIG. 4–11
Andrew J. Russell's legendary photograph of "East and West
Shaking Hands at Laying of [the] Last Rail," May 10, 1869.

When these two trains finally pulled toward each other that day, the
rambunctious crowd nearly enveloped the locomotives. The photograph capturing that moment became *the* definitive image of the nineteenth century—the technology of the photographic process capturing
the technology of the railroad (fig. 4–11). Note the men leaning toward
each other, one holding a bottle of spirits, and the other two bottles—
presumably for good measure. Some sources noted that the act of joining the rails was consummated when champagne was poured from one
of the bottles into a glass held by the others. In addition to the yin-
yang (male and female) connotation of this act, where east and west are
united, this act is also a perfect metaphor for national reconciliation.
Sensing that history has been made and distances conquered, others
shake hands to congratulate each other and the nation. The crowd of
people obscures even the track. This, then, is a human moment, much
like the landing of men on the moon almost exactly a century later
("one small step for [a] man, one giant leap for mankind"). The *dominance* of people in this scene is a reminder that all technology is an artifact of humankind.

Those people who took the time to study those railroad passenger cars at Promontory that day were also witnesses to changes in railroad technology. As was the case with the two locomotives present, the

passenger cars reflected a time of transition. In the 1850s and early 1860s, the simple coach was the most common type of passenger car, and it most often had a curved or arched roof that kept rain and sun off passengers. These arched roofs were serviceable enough but required ventilators mounted on the roof to help cool the cars' interiors in summer. Baggage and express cars, too, featured these arched roofs, which were easy to build and relatively strong. At this time, American passenger cars typically rode on two four-wheel trucks. These passenger car trucks were longer than freight car trucks and this helped smooth the ride a bit. The car bodies of both passenger and express/baggage cars were usually of wooden construction, with additional strength provided by metal truss rods under the car and in the car sides, and bolted at car corners and other points of stress.

By the mid 1860s, however, a series of developments began to slowly transform the passenger car. The equipment photographed at Promontory in 1869 beautifully represents this transition. As evident in photographs, some of the passenger and baggage cars have a newer type of roof—the monitor or clerestory. These cars feature a raised section of roof that runs most of the length of the car. In the sides of the raised clerestory section are windows that let in light and that open to help ventilate the car's interior. Although the clerestory roof is somewhat weaker than the simple arched roof, its advantages outweighed that concern; riding in a clerestory-roofed car was a far more pleasant experience. There was also more headroom in the aisle that ran the length of the car under the clerestory section. Viewed from the outside, the clerestory section might end before reaching the car's end platform, or it might gracefully curve downward toward the platform end in either a compound curved "duckbill" or a complete section that reached the very end of the platform in a single graceful curve.

Well before the joining of the rails at Promontory Summit, the Central Pacific railroad was busy experimenting with new passenger car designs. In its August 20, 1868, issue, the Sacramento *Daily Union* reported that "a new passenger car, 'doubled roofed' appeared on the Central Pacific . . . ." The car roof, according to the brief article, "is arranged with a skylight, after the manner of the saloon of the San Francisco steamers, and the car is thus not only perfectly ventilated, but unusually well lighted."[35] About two months later, *The Daily Bee* Local News section reported "a consignment of laurel wood was received per Chrysopolis by the C.P.R.R. Company designed for use in the interior adornment of its passenger cars." In addition, the wood "shall furnish and finish in the elaborate style which has been so admired in similar work in the Pacific Insurance building in San Francisco and on the steamer McPherson and our favorite Capitol, all the panels and mouldings of the first passenger car which shall leave the Capitol of California for the city of New York."[36]

This reminds us that one type of transportation can influence another, and that even architecture may owe a debt to transportation.[37] Rail passenger car design helped set a new standard in travel that is evident today in the interior of most commercial airliners, which usually have a raised or open section running lengthwise. Like rail passengers in the late 1860s, air passengers can sit near (and gaze out of) windows, stow luggage in racks above their seats, and enjoy illumination along the ceiling; they can also stand and walk comfortably in a central aisle that runs the length of the passenger compartment.

The style and detailing of any vehicle, however, is usually a result of the time or era in which it was built. In the Victorian period, the interiors and exteriors of passenger cars became increasingly more elaborate. In addition to ornate cars built in Sacramento, those from the East arrived as the Union Pacific reached Promontory Summit. Under the title "Elaborate Cars," *The Daily Bee* in Sacramento reported that "two passenger cars of most elaborate pattern, style and finish . . . were visited by many to-day, and, as a matter of course, universally admired, for beauty must and will have its admirers." Like the finer homes and commercial buildings of the period, these cars were beautiful as well as functional. Manufactured by Wason Manufacturing Company of Springfield, Massachusetts, they were, as the journalist called it, "replete with the latest improvements . . ." (fig. 4–12). Continuing his description, the article's author noted that "[t]he cars are most substantially built, with solid gearing underneath, and supplied with brakes of formidable purchase." Each car had thirty seats that could accommodate two people; the car, in other words, could seat sixty passengers.

The Wason cars' interiors were similar to the most lavish ones produced by the best car manufacturers. They featured elaborate woodwork of bird's-eye maple, black walnut, and oak, while the exteriors and interiors featured ornate panels "worthy of all commendation." Although the cars' interior and exterior paint colors are not specified, they contrasted nicely "thanks also to how tastily the brush had been applied." Although these cars were "things of beauty and objects of admiration," they had to be comfortable and safe as well. In a telling summary about the cars, the article noted that "[t]hey not only attract the vision, but they convey a very satisfactory idea of comfort and more still, safety."[38]

Despite improvements in passenger service, rail travelers either carried their own food or ate at various meal stops situated several hours apart. Because passengers transferred from one train to another here,

Promontory was a meal stop on the new railroad line connecting East and West. A handbill of the period announced:

> THIS TRAIN STOPS
> 20 MINUTES FOR SUPPER AT THE
> GOLDEN f HOTEL
>
> Promontory Utah
> First Class meals, 50 cents
> The Golden Spike
> Completing the first Trans-continental
> Railroad was driven at this Point May
> 10 1869. Don't fail to treat
> yourself to a first class meal
> at this celebrated point.
> T. G. Brown, Prop.[39]

That meal stop had been a time-honored tradition dating back to the era of stagecoaches and the earliest railroad lines.

In the days and months after the driving of the golden spike, Promontory settled down to a more mundane existence—that of a small railroad town where travelers from two railroads "changed cars." The community was called Promontory by some, and Promontory Summit by others, but some called it Promontory Station. The latter is no doubt a reference to the fact that all passenger trains stopped here. Although gamblers and other rogues still occupied the town, giving it a reputation as a rough place where travelers should beware, vigilante groups helped ease the situation. This represented a concerted effort on the part of both the railroads and a number of outraged citizens, who resented Promontory's evidently well-deserved reputation as a pickpocket's (and swindler's) dream—and a traveler's nightmare. As noted earlier, improvements at the site took place throughout all of this commotion. Promontory also started to take a slightly more permanent form as the Union Pacific completed its depot. This two-story building contained a waiting room, telegraph office, and restaurant where travelers stopped long enough to consume meals. Upstairs were two apartments. Meanwhile, the Central Pacific also built an office in Promontory, which helped to confirm the community's status as a two-railroad town. This condition lasted until November 17, 1869, when it was announced that the official meeting place of the two railroads would be at or near Ogden, about thirty miles distant in the more developed area along the Wasatch Front. The change was official on December 1, 1869, when the Union Pacific employees left town—as did most of the

WASON

MANUFACTURING COMPANY,

ESTABLISHED 1845.

Builders of all descriptions of

RAILWAY CARS,

And Manufacturers of

Car-Wheels and Railway Castings.

Particular attention paid to the shipment of Cars,
and Materials for Cars, to all parts
of the world.

GEORGE C. FISK, President.
H. S. HYDE, Treasurer.
G. T. WASON, Secretary.

SPRINGFIELD, MASS.

FIG. 4–12 Advertisement for the Wason Manufacturing Company shows a Central Pacific passenger car with clerestory roof, elaborate side paneling, and window shutters.

Author's collection

remaining "brigands" who had been playing havoc with immigrants and other souls traveling along the transcontinental railroad. Promontory was now a Central Pacific town.

Changes in rail equipment technology signaled changes along the right of way. For example, when dining cars were introduced, the press noted that ". . . to put on a dining car is to wipe out the railway side inns and thus injure many people" through lost local wages. "But for this" concern about putting people out of work, the paper noted, "all the railroads would be inclined toward them . . . both for the purpose of making time and to please their passengers." The handwriting was now on the dining room wall, however, and the days of the railroad dining stops were numbered. The article concluded that on a dining car, "one gets good food well served and takes his own time to eat, at rates not much if anything higher than the ordinary prices."[40] Just as the railroad had superseded earlier wagon and stage transportation, developments *within* the railroad industry focused on speed and comfort. A train at rest, whether freight or passenger, represents lost revenue and time wasted. By century's end, passengers in dining cars could gaze out the windows at the forlorn station stop at Promontory Summit, a reminder

Courtesy of DeGolyer Library, Southern Methodist University, Dallas

FIG. 4–13
The day before the last rail was laid, Central Pacific's Stanford
Special is seen eastbound at Monument Point (May 9, 1869).

of the march of progress. In the meantime, the meal stop at Promontory
was a part of the daily scene at this otherwise isolated spot.

Promontory was not the only summit along this section of railroad
line. The profile of the completed railroad from the Wasatch Front to
near the Nevada border resembled a roller coaster with high points scattered between long sections with gentle grades. As railroad topographers
knew, all of this particular section of the railroad from Ogden to Lucin
lay between 4,223 and 4,909 feet above sea level. Careful surveying had
assured that only about 600 feet separated the highest and lowest points
on the line. However, in some places, much of those 600 hundred vertical feet of relief were compressed into short distances. That meant
some steep grades in places. Beginning at the Nevada/Utah border, the
line reached Lucin at 4,498.88 feet above sea level, descended a long
grade into the plain of the Great Salt Lake, rose again and leveled off at

milepost 698 (Bovine). From there it undulated through a series of cuts and fills through Terrace (elevation 4,549.78), then continued upgrade to Terrace Pass, where it leveled out at 4,720.41 feet. Afterwards, the line dipped briefly then rose steeply, only to dip again near Red Dome, beyond which it rose again in the vicinity of the Red Dome hills. Then the line began its descent to near Matlin, after which it rose again after crossing Duff Creek on a trestle, then continued up the long grade to Ombey and the summit of Red Dome Pass. From here, the railroad line dropped into miles of rugged badlands through Peplin, reached the lowlands northwest of the Great Salt Lake in the Curlew Valley near Kelton, then gently undulated for miles, seldom varying more than ten feet in elevation, near the geographic landmark called Monument Point. This was a spectacular setting where photographers took several memorable photographs, including one of the *Jupiter* and the Stanford Special, complete with a water car (fig. 4–13). Coupled behind the locomotive, this framed car boxed in a more-or-less watertight compartment that could hold several thousand gallons.

The car enabled the locomotive to travel farther between water stops, a reminder that water towers were still some distance apart as the line was nearing completion. This photograph is remarkable for several reasons. First, it is one of the few action scenes taken in May of 1869. Second, it beautifully reveals the predominantly limestone nature of the landscape and the configuration of one of the line's true landmarks. At this point, the line was ascending toward a small summit about a mile west of Rozel. From here through Bronte, the line continued upgrade west of Promontory, then dipped and rose again to Promontory Summit (elevation 4,909 feet above sea level).

The profile of the railroad grade at Promontory Summit (fig. 4–14a) shows that the nearly level line here required very light cutting and filling. From Promontory, the line began a slight descent, then briefly rose before beginning its steep descent down the east face of the Promontory Range. The profile drawing illustrating just how much work needed to be done along the right of way here (fig. 4–14b) reveals quite a different story than the easy going the railroad encountered at the summit. Here on the grade, the railroads desperately tried to strike a balance between cutting, filling, and maintaining a reasonable grade. The appropriately named Big Fill shows on the profile as a deep, v-shaped defile.

Illustrators who drew such profiles were not the only ones who depicted the engineering work here. Lithographers of the time portrayed railroad grading here as a titanic struggle with limestone, which is shown being blown out in huge blocks (Fig. 4–15) by Chinese and

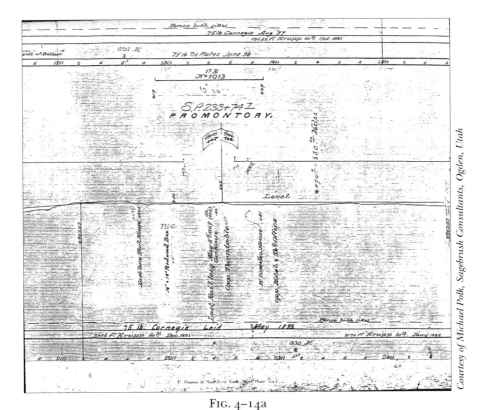

Fig. 4–14a

Portion of the profile chart showing the summit at Promontory
requiring little grading and filling.

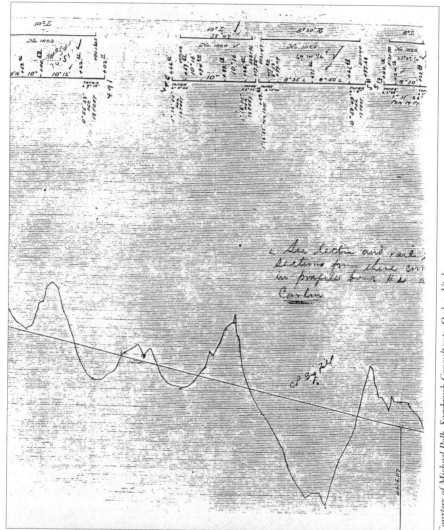

FIG. 4–14b
Portion of the Central Pacific line east of Promontory, on the east slope of the Promontory Range, shows considerable cutting and filling.

Courtesy of the National Park Service

Fig. 4–15
In this dramatized illustration, laborers grading the line up the east slope of the Promontory Range use explosives and plenty of hard labor to get the work done, *Frank Leslie's Illustrated Newspaper,* 1869.

Irish workers. Continuing eastward through Surbon, the grade was still steep but leveled off east of Blue Creek. From here, it rose again for about a half-mile at a spur of land that reaches down toward the lake flats. All the way to Corinne and Bear River, the track gently undulates, but rarely more than a few feet on very gentle grades. In the low-lying areas hereabouts, the track averages about 4,225 feet above sea level. Between Willard and Bonneville, the track undulates about five feet, rising to reach about 4,320 feet at Ogden.[41]

At that time, Ogden was emerging as a major rail center, in part because the Central Pacific had won the battle in reaching the Wasatch Front. Still, for several years (until 1874), the Union Pacific and Central Pacific actually met several miles from Ogden at a location near Hot Springs. Here, a tent town similar to Promontory existed until the railroads finally connected just west of downtown Ogden. With both railroads now meeting in Ogden, the city soon became a major railroad servicing facility.[42]

By the 1870s, the railroad route over Promontory had become a historical curiosity as the location of the driving of the golden spike, or what *The Pacific Tourist* called "the meeting of two railroads." However, it was also famous for another reason. The route provided the visible remnants of the gargantuan battle between Union Pacific and Central Pacific that had riveted the nation's attention a few years earlier. As *The Pacific Tourist* commented, when the train left Blue Creek and a helper locomotive was put on to "assist in pulling us up the hill to Promontory," the scenery soon became more spectacular. Here on the east slope of the Promontory Range, the railroad traverses "some very heavy grades, short curves and deep rocky cuts with fills across ravines," where one could see—as one can today—the right of way of "the old grade of the Union Pacific [which] is crossed and recrossed in several places and is only a short distance away." Paying tribute to the railroads' effort of blasting and filling, *The Pacific Tourist* also commented on "rock cuts where each road expended thousands of dollars, and where [Mormon] Bishop John Sharp, now President of the Utah Central, exploded a mine [*sic*] which lifted the rock from the grade completely out, and gave a clear track after the rubbish was cleared away."[43] We use the term *rubble* (rather than *rubbish*) for such waste rock today, and it actually served an important purpose. Much of it was a source of the "fill" that helped the railroad build its line over rugged ravines along the east slope of the Promontory Range.

For their part, the Mormons were elated about the completion of the line—but not quite elated enough for Brigham Young to attend the ceremony, which, some claimed, he snubbed because the event wasn't occurring at Salt Lake City. The church, however, did send representatives. On May 12, 1869, *The Deseret News* featured an article on "The Celebration yesterday" [*sic*] when "the hour appointed for laying the last nail [*sic*] connecting the U.P. and C.P. lines" arrived and "all classes of citizens seemed to be in earnest in participating in the proceedings." In the article, the Honorable John Taylor, who would succeed Young as president of the Mormon Church, is quoted as saying: "we have now got a highway cast-up on this continent, and we hope to see thousands of Latter-day Saints come on this way to their homes without the slow process of traveling with ox teams"—a sentiment that celebrants reportedly greeted with applause. No doubt recalling the sacrifices that Mormon contractors and their workers had made, Taylor also mentioned, "The laborers who have worked on this magnificent enterprise, may they share in the glory of its consummation" [*sic*].[44]

Speaking of laborers, we should recall that their ethnicity was a likely factor in who was, and who was not, photographed front and center on that eventful day the rails met. Yet, Chinese workers present on May 10 were photographed in several work-related scenes. *The Pacific Tourist* related "a curious incident" associated with "the laying of the last rails" that "has been little noticed hitherto." This happened when "two lengths of rails, 56 feet, had been omitted." The Union Pacific had rails brought up and placed "by Europeans," by which he probably meant Irish and possibly British. The Central Pacific, however, brought up its rails with "the labor being performed by Mongolians." Naturally, the foremen overseeing the work of both crews "were Americans." This *The Pacific Tourist* viewed as highly symbolic. As they put it: "Here, near the center of the Great American Continent, were representatives of Asia, Europe and America—America directing and controlling."[45] Whereas the American press saw an opportunity to emphasize American ingenuity and initiative here—and that should never be forgotten—we are today more prone to recognize the fact that the construction, completion, and operation of the railroad was a multicultural and multinational effort involving peoples from three continents.

We often read about the Chinese presence on the Central Pacific in California because "Crocker's Coolies" had performed such Herculean feats working in the Sierra. However, the Chinese were an essential element throughout the entire Central Pacific system, even in Utah. They lived in tent camps as work progressed from Nevada into Utah Territory, as seen in a photograph taken in 1869 (fig. 4–16). This scene contrasts the tents with the mobile train of workers' larger "bunk" cars that could be hauled to the end of track. The cars here are similar to boxcars, and some of them indeed were. The larger cars more often feature small monitor additions to their roofs for added light and/or ventilation and were specially built to house workers. Boxcars were common for work train service as well as on regular trains because they could carry cargo, such as dry goods and supplies, including explosives, which needed to be kept out of the weather.

Other rolling stock in construction trains at Promontory included a wide range of work cars based, in large part, on the standard freight car designs of the period. Platform cars (or flat cars, as they would later be called) were common. These were the simplest cars of all: an open, flat deck to carry freight that could be used to haul bulky cargoes—such as large crates—and long items, such as telegraph poles or pipes, which were unable to fit into boxcars. Other types of cars were constructed using flat cars as a starting point. These included tank cars, which originally involved placing several vertical wooden tanks or tubs side by side

Courtesy of DeGolyer Library, Southern Methodist University, Dallas

FIG. 4–16
Alfred Hart's photograph, "Chinese [work] Camp . . . at End of
Track" in Nevada, 1869, shows a tent town as well as a Central
Pacific work train with cars housing workers.

on the car; by the 1860s and 1870s, a long cylindrical tank held together
by metal bands or hoops was often mounted horizontally. These tank
cars could carry water and other liquids such as oil. Gondola cars, which
had sides and ends but no roof, carried loads of lumber, sand, or gravel.
Gondolas could be made by putting wooden sides and ends onto flat
cars, though some gondolas were made solely for loads like sand or
gravel, and others had doors (either at the lower portion of the sides or
the car's bottom) through which such loads could be dumped.[46]

The photograph of the work train reveals the desert-like sagebrush
vegetation so common along the Central Pacific right of way—not a tree
in sight. When that train moves farther east toward Promontory, this
tent camp will be forlorn indeed. When the work is completed and the

tents taken down, nature will once again reclaim the site. Yet, the tent camp will not vanish without leaving a trace. Tent posts and spikes will leave impressions, campfires will leave ashes and rings of stone, privies will be filled, and Chinese workers will leave distinctive artifacts that, more than a century later, will be discovered by archaeologists who help tell the story of the work crews.

The Chinese presence here in this part of Utah, while scant today, was once more dominant. In the 1868–1870 period alone, several hundred locations occupied by Chinese could be seen. Most were but temporary construction camps and dugouts, but the people who occupied them were essential to the railroad's operation and construction. In reporting the death of Wah Kee, who had been present during the driving of the golden spike, S. G. Snively wrote in the company newsletter, the *SP Bulletin*, "With the death of Wah Kee, pensioned Chinese interpreter, at Canton, China on June 4 [1926] there passed from the annals of this division a picturesque character." Snively noted that Wah Kee, who had been "employed by the old Central Pacific, was present at the driving of the 'Golden Spike' at Promontory." The article noted that Wah Kee had appeared in the film "Iron Horse," and that his "services as interpreter for his countrymen was of great value to them as well as the Company."[47]

Most people living in the United States in 1869 could probably point to the approximate location of Promontory on a map. Not all of these maps were accurate, as the next map confirms. If, as we recall, it was easy for Central Pacific's detractors to criticize their maps, the railroad must have felt vindicated when the beautiful *Map of the Central P.R.R.— final location of the—from Wadsworth [Nevada] to Ogden* (fig. 4–17) was produced in 1869. After all, it revealed their victory in getting to the Wasatch Front. Prepared by Henry M. Roberts of the Engineer Office of the Military Division of the Pacific and "copied from [the] Latest Data Obtained From Central Pacific R.R. Co.," the map appears to be exquisite in its clarity and simplicity. As the line enters Utah just beyond Tecoma (Nevada), it traverses the territory from Lucin to Ogden, continuing as a vermillion-colored line. Shown are the stations of Bovine, Terrace, Matlin, Kelton, Monument, Rozel, Promontory, and Corinne. In the vicinity of Promontory, likely on the eastern slope of that range, several springs are shown in blue, as is the unnamed Blue Creek.

This map seems confident enough, but trouble mounts as the line runs east of Corinne into what was solidly Union Pacific country until the decision to award Central Pacific the line all the way to the fledgling town of Ogden. There, where Brigham City should be, is the name of Ogden! Just when the folks in Brigham City and Ogden began to

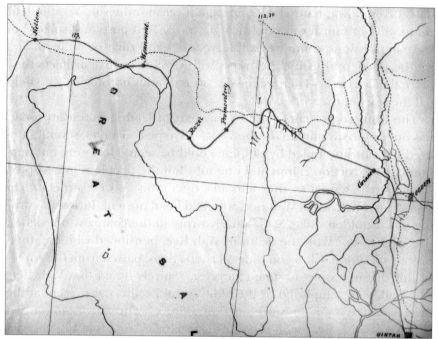

FIG. 4–17

Detail of a map showing the final location of the "Central P[acific] R.R. . . . from Wadsworth [Nevada] to Ogden" was reportedly copied from Central Pacific data but contains several errors in the vicinity of the Wasatch Front.

recover from shock, chagrin, or laughter, those who looked for Ogden found only a town called, with the authority a map usually commands, Uintah. Given its frequent mention as the future junction of the Utah Central and the Union Pacific, the omission of Ogden on this map must have seemed strange indeed to people who knew the area's geography. These errors and omissions must have been even more embarrassing to the Central Pacific when we recall the railroad's own "data" supposedly informed the map. Thankfully, at least, Salt Lake City is properly named and located. This map[48] is a reminder that whereas it is easy to say Ogden is located along the Wasatch Front, it is quite another to actually place it properly—though transposing it with Brigham City is a stretch. Mercifully, few people probably saw this map. Usually, they relied on printed maps produced by the thousands—often in conjunction with articles about the now-completed transcontinental railroad.

Photographs, of course, were especially interesting to the public as they represented the modern technology of freezing time. By closely studying the dozens of photographs taken near Promontory, we can better understand features in the landscape along the right of way. To the Victorian mind, the deep cuts, large fills, and spindly trestles were noteworthy. The Union Pacific Promontory Route trestles, as they are now called, appear to be the work of Mormon contractors John Sharpe (assistant superintendent of public works under LDS President Brigham Young) and Joseph A. Young (son of Young and active overseer of Union Pacific's surveying). Many of the smaller trestles were named "culverts" in the early reports. Although originally designed and built by Union Pacific, it appears that the trestles on the line, which was used by the Central Pacific, were rebuilt by Central Pacific Railroad construction crews in 1872.[49]

Yet, many things apparently eluded photographers who so intently focused their attention on the locomotives and railroad cars, earthwork and grading crews, and even the ramshackle community of Promontory itself. Where, for example, did these crews of pick-swinging and dynamite-wielding workers actually live? Some, we know, lived in the railroads' bunk cars, but others did not—with a few exceptions such as figure 4–16. Looking for pictures of their housing is futile—most are off-camera or out of focus. Historical archaeologist Adrienne Anderson observed that a number of "clusters of what once were habitations are scattered across the entire Promontory range" and that "each cluster is associated with a major construction effort." These clusters, she noted, "appear to reflect individual groups of workers concentrating on a major project" and they "also suggest family or community groups"—possibly Mormon workers, in some cases.[50] In contrast to the Chinese and Irish workers, the Mormons tended to bring their wives and children to the roadbed grading sites, hence the word "family" used by Anderson. Still, life in all work camps along the railroad grades here will benefit from additional research.

Enigmatic, too, are the complete names of the crews who operated the locomotives that met at Promontory on May 10, 1869. The names of the engineers and firemen cannot be determined with certainty despite the examination of thousands of documents. Most secondary sources list them as Sam Bradford (on *No. 119*) and George Booth (on *Jupiter*). However, Ms. Delone Glover of Brigham City mentioned in a December 2005 interview that, when thinking of the events that took place at the joining of the rails, she considers Union Pacific *No. 119* to be "her" locomotive because "Sam Bradford was the engineer that day." Ms. Glover's maiden name was Bradford, and she wondered whether her father's brother (i.e., her uncle) was named Sam—perhaps after the famous locomotive engineer. Not citing a source other than "memory," Ms. Glover stated that the Central Pacific *Jupiter* engineer that day was named Booth—though she could not remember his first name. This information is tantalizing. If correct, it suggests that the names of the crew may have been preserved in oral history—even after almost 140 years—thus substantiating the written record.[51] Tellingly, perhaps, the engineers' names are better preserved than those of the firemen on the locomotives that day. That may be because the engineers mounted the pilots to touch celebratory champagne bottles, while other men climbed all over the locomotives to stand or lean against their warm iron flanks triumphantly.[52]

If the official written record from 1869 does not identify the men in the locomotive cabs, subsequent records do. At least one of the men in the cab of engine *No. 119* on that day was later interviewed. David Lemon, who recalled the event in considerable detail more than fifty years after the fact (1924), noted that he was the fireman on *No. 119*. As a Civil War veteran from Illinois, Lemon had served the Union Pacific in the spring of 1868, and he continued west with the work crews as the railroad construction progressed in Utah Territory. Lemon's job was mundane enough; he fired the locomotives hauling construction material such as ties, rails, and supplies. At Promontory on that auspicious day, Lemon had fired *No. 119* and realized that the iron spike that replaced the golden spike was a truly important artifact. So when the iron spike was driven into the hole after the golden spike had been removed, Lemon kept an eye on it. At an opportune moment, Lemon implored Superintendent H. M. Hoxie to let him remove and keep the iron spike. Because Lemon had helped during Indian raids in Nebraska a year earlier, Hoxie conceded, adding: "Let's go and get that spike for you." That was not the only debt the railroad paid to Lemon. On June 9, 1869, Lemon helped the railroad avoid considerable delay when he personally plugged a bad leak that his engine developed while hauling a train carrying dignitaries eastward over Promontory. Very pleased with Lemon's ingenuity, Central Pacific President Leland Stanford gave him ". . . a whopping big orange."[53] Despite Stanford's gratitude, Lemon's luck with the railroads' top brass was about to run out. When cuts in manpower came later that spring as construction wound down, Lemon was laid off. His last day was June 25, 1869, after which he returned east to pursue other opportunities. As a fascinating postscript, Lemon kept that iron spike for many years, finally donating it "to the library" for posterity—presumably the library at Stanford University, where artifacts from the event were displayed.[54]

We are less fortunate when it comes to knowing the identity of the fireman on Central Pacific's *Jupiter* that day. Of all the information recorded in print, the details of who fired the two starring locomotives seem to have escaped the press, unlike the names of the executives on hand. Few histories fail to mention the top brass who tapped the golden and silver-copper alloy spikes home. The highest-ranking railroad officials at the ceremony included Central Pacific President Leland Stanford, Chief Engineer Samuel Montague, and construction boss, James Strobridge. On Union Pacific's behalf, Vice President Dr. Thomas C. Durant was joined by board chairman Sidney Dillon and Chief Engineer Grenville Dodge. This is yet another reminder that people higher up on the corporate chain are usually given credit (or blame), while the bulk of railroad workers go unrecognized.

Although it is relatively easy to blame the social stratification of the nineteenth century for this oversight, there is another equally plausible answer. Consider again A. J. Russell's classic photograph "joining of tracks, Promontory, Utah"—as this photo was titled in *How we built the Union Pacific Railway and other Railway Papers and Addresses* by Grenville M. Dodge (fig. 4–1). Our eyes are naturally drawn to that spot where the locomotives will meet and where people now begin to congregate. Russell's photograph reveals that the most important people are positioned here, and they are the ones with the greatest authority and power. Even that ersatz flagpole, with its brave individual atop it (and another climbing to get a better look at the event or to keep people from accidentally breaking the telegraph wire connected to the rail) serves to focus our attention toward where the man on the pole is looking—right down into the gap between the trains. At dead center in the composition, a woman in a light-colored hoop skirt stands out prominently as most others here are dressed in dark clothing. She represents civilization and innocence in a scene where men have now come of age by the act of binding the continent with ribbons of iron. The fact that all the women in the picture are evidently clustered there surrounded by men, seems significant as it reaffirms the men's control over social and physical space. Note, also, that the opening made so that the photographer could shoot the scene unobstructed by the crowd is actually funnel-shaped. This opening in the crowd further draws our view toward the point where the crowd and the lines of perspective converge.[55] Most of the rank-and-file workers, unfortunately, were not within this field of view—lost, as it were, to the gaze of people in the future. Significantly, the United States military had a presence that day, as evidenced by the men in uniform who appear in some photographs. They symbolize both the victory of the Union in the war, and the participation of many military veterans in the building of the railroad. Likely, their presence here may have kept the events of May 10, 1869, from becoming a bit too rowdy, or untoward, for such an auspicious event.

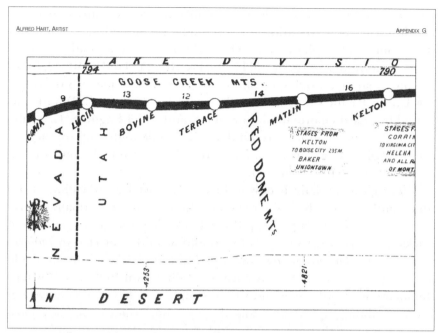

FIG. 4–18a
Detail of the Utah section of the transcontinental railroad on Alfred
A. Hart's map reveals that the line west of Monument Point was
simplified into a nearly straight line.

In 1870, just a year after he gained fame as one of the photographers
who immortalized the events at Promontory, Alfred A. Hart was back
in the public eye. This time, it was a new, illustrated volume called *The
Traveler's Own Book—A Panorama of Overland Travel, from Chicago to San
Francisco* that brought him fame. Hart's easily carried book was "illustrated by fine photo-chromo views" of scenes he had photographed
along the route in 1869. What made *The Traveler's Own Book* even more
interesting, however, was a series of page-sized stylized maps that covered the railroad route. Two of the map sections covered that portion
of the line from the Nevada border over Promontory Summit to Ogden
(fig. 4–18a) (fig. 4–18b).

Several things about Hart's maps are noteworthy. First, in a reminder
that maps often serve to simplify reality and reduce complexity, note
that the 74–mile section of track from Lucin to Monument Point is virtually straight as an arrow. The Red Dome Mountains, while shown on
the map, seem to have had absolutely no effect on the railroad! This is
noteworthy because most detailed descriptions of the line note that the
topography here caused the line to twist and curve while climbing over

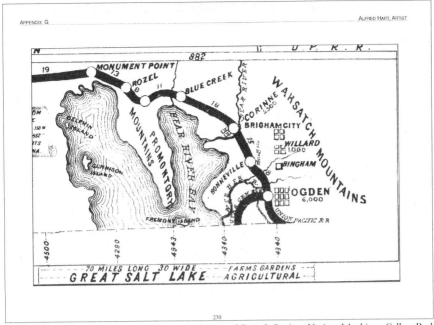

APPENDIX G
ALFRED HART, ARTIST

Courtesy of Cartographic and Architectural Records Section, National Archives, College Park

FIG. 4–18b

The eastern portion of the line over Promontory on Hart's map
shows, but does not name, Promontory Summit.

the summit of Red Dome Pass. Equally odd, perhaps, is that although
Promontory Summit appears as one of the many dots signifying communities or stations, it alone is not actually named! At this time, it is
possible that the public was less familiar with the other places indicated—Lucin, Bovine, Terrace, Matlin, Kelton, Monument Point, and
Rozel west of the Promontory Mountains, and Blue Creek, Corinne,
and Bonneville to the east—and would have known that the unnamed
station here was Promontory Summit. This is plausible because the
Promontory Mountains are indicated on the peninsula jutting southward into the Great Salt Lake, and most people might naturally know
that Promontory Summit is the place indicated by a dot. Actually,
though, it is just as likely that the cartographer ran out of space and
could not find enough room to indicate "Promontory Summit" on this
crowded map.

It is worth noting something else that most travelers reading guidebooks knew at this time, but which is also indicated along the bottom margin of the map. The Great Salt Lake is named along the bottom of the map and designated as "70 miles long and 30 wide." The
country along the base of the "Wahsatch Mountains" east of the Great

Salt Lake is designated as "FARMS GARDEN AGRICULTURAL" land, while the area west of the lake is simply called "DESERT." At this time, the Union Pacific and Central Pacific met near Ogden, where the Utah Central from Salt Lake City also connected with the transcontinental railroad line.

Interestingly, Hart also included a profile of the railroad line at the bottom edge of the map. Varying from 4,253 feet near Lucin to 4,943 in the Promontory Mountains, the line at Ogden shows as 4,340 feet. For some unknown reason, though, Hart's visual profile completely misrepresents Promontory Summit. Instead of being about 600 feet higher in elevation than Ogden, the profile shows Promontory as lower in elevation, since the profile line trends continually upward. Clearly, a person consulting only the map's visual profile without reading the written elevation numbers would assume the railroad is uphill all the way from Lucin to Ogden, a perception that eliminates Promontory Summit just as deftly as it did Red Dome Summit.

Hart's publication reminds us that the joining of the rails was a marketable event. Both railroads realized early on the public relations value of May 10, 1869. So, too, did other enterprising publishers and authors. On August 24, 1869, T. Clapp of Pittsfield, Massachusetts, wrote to H. C. Cram of the Union Pacific to endorse a book project by Dr. John Todd. The book Dr. Todd was writing on "California and the Railroads" would feature photographs of scenes along the line from Omaha to Utah. As a sign of showing his seriousness, and perhaps interested in capitalizing on Central Pacific-Union Pacific competition, Clapp also noted, "I have written to Mr. Huntington." Two days later, however, Clapp wrote Cram another follow-up letter, this one noting that Dr. Todd's "friends have abandoned the idea of illustrating in this way, and think a few woodcuts of the points of interest and scenery will be preferable. . . ." Clapp further noted that the "offices of the road could consider it any object to have a set of photographs put up, that the engraver can select from, and make his estimates, presuming it will be considered a good card for the road."[56] Todd's book, *The Sunset Land; or, The Great Pacific Slope* was published in 1870. It joined the many books of the time that featured Promontory as the place where national, and international, history was made.

Chapter 5

ON THE EARLY MAINLINE
(1869 to 1875)

In one sense, Promontory in 1869 represented a Central Pacific victory. By pushing Union Pacific back from Promontory to the Bear River, and ultimately to Ogden, the federal system rewarded the California rather than Omaha crowd. A Map Showing U.P.R.R. Lands in the Salt Lake District (fig. 5–1) shows "Land withdrawn by [the] letter of May 15 1869 [and] acknowledged . . . May 24, 1869 . . ." reveals the Union Pacific relinquishing the line over Promontory Summit. A written note on the map, apparently made a few years thereafter, mentions that this is a "Diagram of six townships showing [the] line of road+limits and the division line between the two roads, sent to R&R at Salt Lake City, April 22, '72." This map is important as it confirms Union Pacific's withdrawal from the Promontory Summit route. Moreover, one unexplained double set of squares, one inside the other, apparently indicates the site of the short-lived railroad town just a few miles north-northwest of Ogden.[1] The rise of that new town meant the end of Promontory as a meeting point of the Union Pacific and Central Pacific. With that new meeting point of the railroads at the base of the Wasatch, the Central Pacific's wish to reach completely across the entire Great Basin now became a reality. From this point forward, Promontory became a one-railroad town.

By Christmas of 1869, Promontory was just another stop on the Central Pacific mainline from California to Ogden. Now that Central Pacific called all the shots here, it is worth looking at the railroad's operations over the range. At this time, railroads ran at a relatively slow pace. An early Central Pacific handbill of "Rules and Regulations for Employees" states that "Passenger Trains will not run faster than twenty-five miles

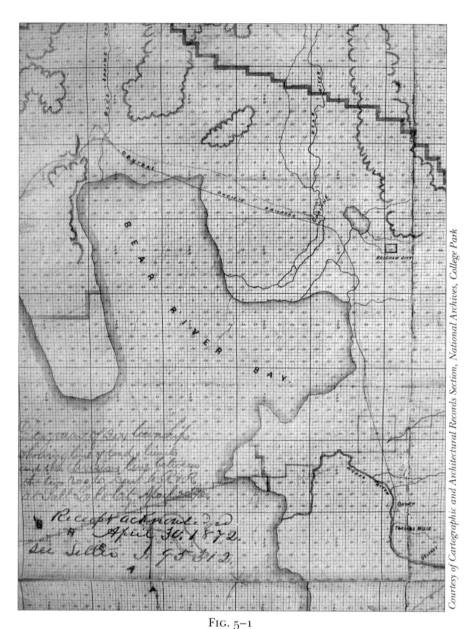

Fig. 5–1

Portion of the Map Showing U.P.R.R. lands in the Salt Lake District (1872) indicates the Central Pacific line over Promontory and a second alignment in that area; also features a large square symbol at the future site of Bonneville (unnamed, double square above "Weber River") which never grew into a major place, despite hopes.

an hour, except on special order, over any part of the road, and Freight Trains will run as near to Time Table as practicable." To prioritize types of service, it was noted that "Through Freight trains will keep entirely out of the way of passenger trains, but will have the right of road over way freight trains"—those freight trains that plod along, picking up and dropping off cars at local stations along the line. These lowly way freights had to ". . . keep entirely out of the way of both Passenger and Through Freight trains." Engineers in all trains were required to "[a]pproach all Stations slowly; pass all Stations carefully, and be sure the switches, by their levers, are seen to be right." In rural areas, enginemen were required to take care to avoid running over livestock, and furthermore that "[t]rains must come to a full stop, if necessary, to avoid doing so." One assumes that mishaps involving pedestrians alongside the tracks also occurred, as one of the rules stated: "Enginemen and Firemen are particularly directed not to throw any wood from the Tender while in motion." However, the scarcity of wood along much of the Central Pacific route was also a factor. This rule evidently resulted from the fact that some of the wood provided as fuel was too large to fit into the fire-box opening and might be tossed off the train in disgust. Such wood, the rules stated, "should be thrown off at the next station" and in the meantime "not be piled on Tenders in such a manner as to be liable to fall off." Presumably, woodcutters chopped the wood into smaller pieces for use in locomotive fireboxes or stoves in railroad buildings. Speaking of the combustibility of wood, the rules further stated that "[d]ampers of [locomotive] ash pans must in all cases be closed while Engines are crossing bridges and passing wood yards." Some of these rules seem obvious today, but evidently resulted from mishaps. One can only imagine what inconvenience or disaster prompted the railroad to state the obvious: "Cars must never be allowed to stand on the Main Track, but must be placed on a siding, and the wheels must be securely blocked."[2]

With its line running all the way across the Great Basin to Ogden, Central Pacific became more dependent on coal for fuel. To its chagrin, Central Pacific territory in Nevada and California was notoriously coal poor, while Union Pacific traversed one of the world's great coalfields. Accordingly, Central Pacific's coal was supplied by Union Pacific, which owned and operated coal mines throughout Wyoming.[3] The coal was brought to Ogden, which occupied a strategic location at the base of the Wasatch Mountains. There it provided fuel for locomotives but was also shipped in gondola cars to coaling stations along the Promontory line well into Nevada.

The Union Pacific's retreat to Ogden from Promontory Summit in December 1869 ensured that the former would become a major

Courtesy of Union Pacific Archives, Council Bluffs

FIG. 5–2

A superb photograph of Ogden (ca. 1885), showing the coordination of activities between Central Pacific and Union Pacific. The eastbound *California Limited* (behind second locomotive at *left*) received passengers who transferred from its Central Pacific counterpart (behind locomotive, *center* of photograph), which had taken the train over Promontory Summit. The Ogden station is between these two trains, which are in turn flanked by other locomotives in the busy railroad yard.

railroad town and service center while Promontory would remain a small community straddling the mainline. At Ogden, Central Pacific and Union Pacific shared some of the same facilities. Central Pacific also had a 1–stall engine house located just northwest of the turntable. It was also here that the trains of the Central Pacific and Union Pacific met the Mormon-built standard gauge Utah Central, colloquially called "Brigham Young's railroad," which was completed from Salt Lake City to Ogden in 1870. Some of the locomotives and rolling stock for Young's standard gauge Utah Central came second hand from the Union Pacific as partial payment for the money the railroad owed the Saints for contracted grading work in 1868–1869. This was another example of Young bartering to obtain what he needed to make Utah, and the Mormons, prosper.

As Brigham Young's brainchild, the Utah Central helped Salt Lake City maintain its lead as Utah's capital city. This Mormon-owned railroad also ensured Ogden's status as a railroad center and "Crossroads of the West" where the Central Pacific, and later, Southern Pacific lines terminated. By 1872, another line, the narrow gauge Utah Northern, extended north from Ogden to the mines and agricultural/grazing lands of southern Idaho paralleling the Central Pacific line to about Brigham City. Ogden, in other words, was the strategic place where the two Utah railroad lines crossed at right angles, and connected with the two major railroads that formed the Pacific Railroad route. For our purposes, these developments further increased the volume of rail traffic over Promontory Summit; however, that once-strategic place was becoming increasingly forlorn as the trains now met, and exchanged passengers, at bustling Ogden (fig. 5–2).

As part of the agreement by which Union Pacific moved its westernmost terminal to Ogden, Central Pacific now ran over the Union Pacific line from Corinne to Ogden, as the proposed Central Pacific roadbed between those two points had never materialized. Central Pacific also inherited the challenges of running trains up and down the east side of the Promontory Range. When it was the end of the line for the Union Pacific and Central Pacific from May to December 1869, Promontory Summit was the place where both railroads needed to turn their locomotives around. With most trains running through town now, however, Central Pacific had less need to turn locomotives here. Nevertheless, it still needed to turn helper locomotives—locomotives added to assist trains upgrade—at Promontory. On the grades leading up to Promontory Summit, helpers were a necessity. American (4–4–0) type locomotives did the job at first, but larger 2–6–0 (Mogul) and 4–6–0 (Ten-Wheeler) locomotives began to appear around 1875. Because these were larger engines, their weight increased accordingly. By the mid-1870s, 30–ton locomotives were common. Once they reached the summit either as helpers added to the front of the train or as pushers helping to boost the train from behind, locomotives had to be turned for the return trip downgrade. "Light" locomotives—those unencumbered by trains—ran to the bottom of the grade at Blue Creek. After being turned at Blue Creek, they again headed upgrade, boosting the next train needing assistance. On the entire line between Ogden and Lucin, there were five turntables. In addition to those at Blue Creek and Promontory, turntables were located at Lake, Kelton, and Terrace. Situated at the bottom of helper grades, most turntables only turned locomotives and did not require large roundhouses for locomotive storage. However, large multi-stalled roundhouses and shops at Ogden and Terrace serviced, stored, and repaired locomotives.

Travelers passing over Promontory Summit, in effect, traversed geological time and could see the results of a geological drama millions of years in the making. Nineteenth-century geologists Arnold Hague and S. F. Emmons observed that the limestone hills or ridges east of Promontory "show a number [of] synclinal and anticlinal folds, with gentle dips, which can be traced from the Promontory Mountains nearly to Bear River." The sedimentary rocks here undulate: The first ridge east of Blue Creek inclines to the east and the second ridge dips westward, then dips under the valley, reappearing west of Corinne as the isolated feature called Little Mountain. The Promontory Mountains form what they described as "a rocky promontory, which divides the two north arms of Salt Lake." The railroad traversed the Promontory Mountains through "a gap in the range," that is "about three miles in a north and south direction" and shows, on both north and south sides of the gap, "the upper terrace-lines of the old lake . . . ." That Old Pliocene lake, as they called it, had once "unquestionably occupied this pass, making the southern part of the range into a huge island." North of the railroad, Hague and Emmons noted that the Promontory Range "is comparatively low, with rounded outlines, the greater part of its surrounding surface being covered with loose soil and grass, and showing but few outcrops." South of the railroad, the Promontory Range was narrower but more rugged, comprised of "dark heavy beds of nearly black limestone . . . ." About four miles south of Promontory Station, though, "the range widens rapidly to the westward," where it becomes about seven miles wide. This portion of the Promontory Range overlies ancient, Archaean rocks consisting of quartzites and mica-bearing schists.[4]

By the time that travelers took the train over Promontory Summit in the early 1870s, a number of the man-made landscape features had become landmarks. Travel guides often highlighted areas where the competing railroads had changed the topography. Impressive cuts and fills, especially, revealed something about the furious competition between the two protagonists. For example, as the train entered "the deep rock cuts as we wind around Promontory Mountain," with "the engine puffing and snorting with its arduous labors," *Crofutt's Trans-Continental Tourist* told tourists to be alert. Just east of Promontory, the publication noted that "[t]he track along here has been changed recently to avoid passing over several high trestle bridges built by the Union Pacific Company when they extended their track to Promontory, and afterwards abandoned by order of Congress, which fixed the junction of the two roads near Ogden." With that story related, and the train reaching the point where "the summit is gained, . . . we arrive at the former terminus of the two Pacific railroads"—Promontory.[5]

Promontory was now on the mainline of a Central Pacific line that ran west from Ogden over the range and along Nevada's Humboldt

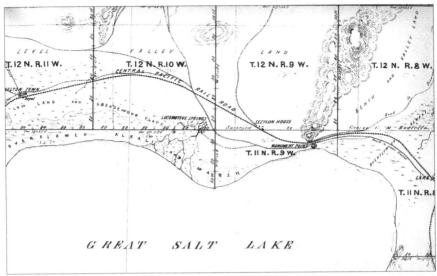

Courtesy of Michael Polk, Sagebrush Consultants, Ogden, Utah

FIG. 5–3

A portion of the *Diagram of the Survey of the Third Standard Parallel North and Exterior Lines in Utah Territory*, 1873, by Joseph Garlinski, depicts the Central Pacific line, and the nature of the lands north of Spring Bay in considerable detail.

River to California. In 1872–1873, Joseph Garlinski produced a remarkable map showing a portion of the route of the railroad in some detail (fig. 5–3). Prepared as a *Diagram of the Survey of the Third Standard Parallel North and Exterior lines in Utah Territory*, the map identifies the railroad itself and shows certain buildings, like section houses, as well as topography and vegetation. South of Kelton, the map indicates "Low Land and Greasewood Flats," while between Monument Point and Lake Station, the railroad crosses a low-lying area covered by overflowed "Alkali and Marsh." The map also reveals that roads, such as the "Road to Lake Station" and "Road to Promontory" existed even at this early date. It also shows the "Underground Aqueducts" running from the mountains to the towns of Terrace and Kelton.[6] Unfortunately, no Garlinski map(s) showing the area around Promontory, or other portions of the line from Ogden to Lucin, have been located to date.

The surveying and construction of the line over Promontory Summit had been so frantic that it took Congress years to figure out exactly what had happened. As a post mortem to 1869, report after report sought to clarify the situation between the Central Pacific and Union Pacific. In 1877, Captain William J. Twining of the Corps of Engineers compiled a detailed report on the Union and Central Pacific Railways for the 44th

Courtesy of the National Park Service

FIG. 5–4
This 1869 photograph of the Union Pacific yard and
main track at Blue Creek shows the large water tank
(*left*, in distance). Note the work train with workers'
bunk cars and boxcars (supply cars) at *right*.

Congressional Session of the United States House of Representatives.
Congress authorized the report in 1876 to address some unanswered
questions. In making the detailed survey, Twining's report identified the
locations of the portions of track for which bonds were set.[7] Later that
year, the Union Pacific's terminus was at MP 1038, "Five miles west of
[the] crossing of Utah Central Railroad." From that point near Ogden
westward—through Bonneville (MP 1043), Brigham (MP 1050),
Corinne (MP 1058), Blue Creek (MP 1077), Promontory (MP 1086),
Monument (MP 1110), Kelton (MP 1125), Matlin (MP 1146), Terrace
(MP 1157), and Lucin (MP 1178)—the railroad line over Promontory
was now in the hands of the Central Pacific.[8] In this same report, Captain
W. H. Heuer provided extensive field notes that included detailed read-
ings of "nearly every curve, bridge, trestle, tunnel, and water tank,
together with numerous culverts and other points noticed on the railroad."[9] Captain James F. Gregory's report covered the portion of the
Central Pacific line "from its eastern terminus at Ogden, Utah, to the
west switch at Battle Mountain, Nevada." There were numerous trestles, bridges, culverts, and water tanks along the section from Ogden
to Lucin. Gregory details the location of every culvert as to type (either
box or open), section post, water tank, bridge (by type), switch (i.e.,
turnout), mile and half-mile post, and trestle.

Steam locomotives consumed tons of wood and coal, but they consumed even larger amounts of water. In the 1870s, locomotive tenders held about 2,000 to 2,500 gallons of water. Water tanks helped quench the thirst of the iron horse and were ideally located about twenty-five miles apart. The earliest water tanks consisted of tubs (open-topped, barrel-like vertical tanks held together with metal hoops) mounted on an elevated framework. Each tub held about 5,000 gallons. When the Union Pacific first began operation to Promontory Summit, there was a tank at Blue Creek[10] (fig. 5–4) but none indicated at Promontory.

Central Pacific very likely used this original Union Pacific water tank at Blue Creek upon taking over this portion of the line in late 1869. Yet, a water source at Promontory remained a problem. Early photos confirm that water cars transported water to Promontory, probably from Indian Springs. Across the Promontory Range, Central Pacific had a four-tub water tank at Rozel, which lies at the foot of the Hansel Mountains; an eight-tub water tank at Kelton in the Curlew Valley; two water tanks, each with four tubs, at Terrace; and a four-tub tank at Lucin at the edge of the Salt Lake Desert.[11] It is noteworthy that each of these locations had a dependable source of water, while Promontory did not. This is not to say that the locations themselves were well-watered, only that dependable sources of water were diverted from higher up the watersheds to those places by redwood aqueducts. Blue Creek also had an aqueduct, though it was evidently the best watered of these locations. Water stops on the line over Promontory were located at Lucin, Terrace, Kelton, Rozel, Blue Creek, and Corinne.[12] The typical Central Pacific water tank house featured a 50,000–gallon, 16–foot diameter water tank mounted in a frame building with slightly tapered or slanted sides. Some, like the tank at Promontory, had straight sides but retained their boxy look (fig. 5–5). These water tank houses, as they were called in railroad records, were 21 feet square at their base, and their shingled roofs peaked at 28 feet tall. They not only presented a more finished appearance but also helped keep the water pipes from freezing because the interior of the building, and hence the piping, could be heated in winter.

Promontory Summit often appeared as a dot on maps of the 1870s. In 1871, W. H. Gamble of Philadelphia produced a beautifully colored lithograph *County Map of Utah and Nevada* prominently featuring the Central Pacific (fig. 5–6). This map is noteworthy because it perpetuates a common error: Promontory is called "Promontory Point." A pocket map titled *Map of the C.P.R.R. and Connecting Lines* (ca. 1874), shows Promontory as well as other stations along the line from Ogden to the Pacific Coast.

FIG. 5–5

Central Pacific water tank house at Promontory had straight wooden sides, an elaborate cupola, and was painted barn red. Note tank spout, barely visible against left side of tank house, and the 1½ story "telegraph office" to the right of the tracks.

On an inset feature called "Distances & Altitudes on C.P.RR," Promontory—at 828 miles from San Francisco at an elevation of 4,905 feet above sea level—is the only locale shown between Toano (Nevada) and Ogden. Tellingly, however, Promontory appears not because of its population, but rather because it was a summit (as were Taono, Cisco, and other locations). Promontory was probably also listed because of its association with recent history. In fact, the map's font shows Promontory as an inconsequential place much like Rozel, Monument, and Matlin. Only Kelton—with its strategic stagecoach line connection to the mining camps of the north—appears in bold letters. Moreover, of the eleven illustrations bordering the map, only the more spectacular points along the line—snow coverings (snow sheds), the Summit of the Sierra, Emigrant Gap, the Palisades along the Humboldt River—are shown. For all its notoriety in 1869, Promontory is not among them.[13]

By the early 1870s, travelers and travel writers commented on Promontory's depot, which continued to serve as a restaurant and store. Photographs of the period (fig. 5–7) show the bustling activity during "train-time" at Promontory's Station, which also served as an eating house. Perhaps equally important was the fact that the Central Pacific built an engine house there with a turntable to turn around helper locomotives. Typical of such places where engines were turned or kept, Promontory also had a water supply consisting of water cars and, possibly, a cistern connected to a water plug. However, Promontory soon had a water tank and sand house. Most sources agree that Promontory's water was always shipped to the summit from Blue Creek in wooden tank

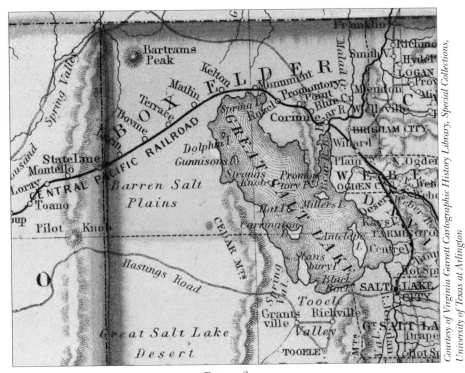

FIG. 5–6

Detail of W. H. Gamble's 1871 *County Map of Utah and Nevada* prominently shows Central Pacific Railroad line and misnames Promontory Summit as "Promontory Point"—a common mistake that persists to the present.

cars, though some suggested that the summit originally had springs that later dried up. The sand house was important indeed. Given the steep grades in the area, sand was necessary to keep locomotives from slipping their drive wheels, that is, help them gain and maintain traction when starting or moving upgrade. At the sand house, workers in the engine servicing area placed fine sand in the sand domes of locomotives. The engineer diverted the sand, when needed, from the sand boxes or sand domes atop locomotive boilers down pipes to the driving wheels.

Because servicing locomotives and maintaining stretches of railroad track require manpower, Promontory also had several homes, or section houses, where railroad employees lived. These were located across the tracks on the north side. Anglo as well as Chinese workers lived in these section houses. By the early 1870s, coal became an increasingly common locomotive fuel; accordingly, coal sheds were constructed. These were located to the west of the depot on the south side of the tracks, the same side of the tracks on which the depot stood. By the 1870s, Promontory

Courtesy of the National Park Service

FIG. 5–7
Train time at Promontory shows the Central Pacific station and eating
house (*left*) and a train containing Central Pacific fruit cars.

had the characteristic "look" of a Central Pacific railroad town. Most
of the railroad buildings were painted in the standard Central Pacific
color, which was apparently similar to boxcar, or perhaps Tuscan, red.

We know a fair amount about Promontory from the written sources
and railroad reports of the era. This is fortunate because virtually nothing from the period ca. 1869–1880 is visible there today. However, underground archaeological investigation confirms many details about the size
and location of structures such as the roundhouse, with its brick foundation revealing a 5–stall structure. Interestingly, some remains of that
building exist today in the form of a barn-like ranch building containing
several recognizable elements, including wooden doors and metal roofing material, some of the latter bearing the stamp "CP RR" (fig. 5–8).

The 1870 census is also helpful in reconstructing the character of
Promontory. The population of Promontory Precinct at this time was
158, about two-thirds (117) of whom were Chinese.[14] Almost everyone

Courtesy of Michael Polk, Sagebrush Consultants, Ogden, Utah
FIG. 5–8
A barn-like shed near Promontory Summit constructed
from wood and corrugated metal salvaged from the
doors and roofing, respectively, of the Central Pacific
roundhouse at Promontory.

in town either worked for the railroad or was in some way dependent
on it. The town of Promontory had only seven residences; the majority
of the population lived in temporary quarters nearby. Most of the towns-
people were men. Only one woman appears in the census: the wife of
hotel operator William Case, whose occupation was listed as "house-
keeper." Among the men enumerated, occupations included one conductor, a steam engineer, three firemen, a car inspector, and a telegraph operator. The latter was extremely important as he received and
transmitted messages. Virtually all of the men in railroad service jobs
were white, but the majority of the town's track worker population was
Chinese; the census shows that twenty-six Chinese track workers occupied two section houses. These railroad-owned houses were utilitarian
places where railroad workers slept and ate meals. Most of the Chinese
employees were responsible for keeping the track in order, and they
answered to a section foreman or section "boss." The other Chinese
man living here was a cook.

Adolph Reeder recalled living in Promontory in the early years. In an
undated, hand-written manuscript, he noted that the town had a population of "about 150 people consisting of between 20 and 30 families
and several single laborers (firemen and section crews)." The majority of engineers and brakemen, he recalled, "were married men with

families." Most of the buildings in town were of lumber construction and were one story, except a two-story section house; there were also several dugouts in which section workers lived. As Reeder recalled, a "Chinese [man] [who] lived in one, sold fire works to children on the fourth of July."[15] The census figures above confirm that over 90% of the population was associated, in one way or another, with the railroad. The remainder (four) consisted of three men who ran a stock farm, and one who listed his occupation as a "quartz miner." The latter must have been a perpetual optimist, for there was relatively little precious metals mineralization nearby—the best hope being a small area on the west side of the Promontory Mountains south of the station, where metals were ultimately mined.[16]

Promontory's Golden Spike Hotel typified the services offered in the days of slow railroad travel, when trains stopped at stations so that passengers could eat meals. The Golden Spike Hotel was said to be the brainchild of T. G. Brown, who opened a general store, saloon, and restaurant that could seat one hundred travelers. Brown originally lived in Corinne but took advantage of opportunities at Promontory when the place was still an important railroad stop. He was quite well connected, and evidently used technology to help his restaurant business thrive. Old-timers recalled Brown's ingenuity: in order to better prepare for serving the westbound passengers, he would rely on someone in Corinne to telegraph the numbers of people who would stop to eat at Promontory. That twenty-eight-mile run would take about an hour and a-half, and Brown's cooks made good use of the time. As if by magic, when the train had finished laboring upgrade to the summit, meals for the proper number would be ready and waiting. Brown became something of a legend. He is said to have bought more than 3,000 acres close to Promontory, where he also was sheriff, postmaster, and operator of the telegraph office. Being an enterprising soul, however, Brown ultimately opened a general store in Corinne when Promontory's fortunes declined.[17]

If railroad officials had any concerns about the volume of railroad traffic that would follow the driving of the golden spike, those concerns did not last long. On May 21,[18] 1869, a Central Pacific Railroad circular noted that freight between Sacramento and its terminus with the Union Pacific could be shipped immediately and that each first-class shipment of one hundred pounds cost $3.25 ($65 per ton), and $45 per ton for second class.[19] In addition to a private excursion that gained much attention for its fast speed (an average of twenty miles per hour over the line) regular trains handled growing numbers of passengers. In early June, for example, about two hundred passengers, many of whom were women and children, journeyed eastward through Promontory aboard the cars.[20] On June 8, 1869, Silver Palace Sleeping Car B left Sacramento for Promontory "with every section taken." Sleeping Car A was scheduled to leave the next day. With new cars on order at the rate of one or two per week, the newspaper reported that "a sleeping car will be attached to every train."[21] That this was no idle promise became apparent when "[a] new Silver Palace sleeping car, to be designated as 'Q'" arrived in December.[22] In early 1870, a train consisting of ten cars—a Pullman sleeper, Pullman commissary, two Silver Palace sleepers, four coaches, a baggage car, and an express car—traversed the line over Promontory Summit.[23]

European observers frequently commented on the openness and flexibility of accommodations in these railroad cars. In the best-selling adventure novel *Around the World in Eighty Days* (1873), French writer Jules Verne's characters travel over the recently completed transcontinental railroad. Upon leaving Sacramento, and heading eastward into the night, Verne's protagonist, Phileas Fogg, travels in a passenger car described as "a sort of long omnibus on eight wheels, and with no compartments in the interior." Verne here draws a fundamental distinction between European and American railway cars. The former often rode on four wheels that were rigidly affixed to the car, as opposed to the swiveling trucks upon which American cars rode. Moreover, the openness of the American car contrasted with the numerous compartments that divided up the typical European passenger car. Verne noted that the American car's interior ". . . was supplied with two rows of seats, perpendicular to the direction of the train on either side of an aisle which conducted to [connected] the front and rear platforms." This, too, differed from European trains, where compartments were usually accessed from doors on the sides of the passenger cars. Verne was thus struck by the way people could move through the typical American train: "These platforms," he wrote, "were found throughout the train, and the passengers were able to pass from one end of the train to the other."

Verne provides an example of how the Pullman cars could be converted into sleeping cars. As Verne put it, when bedtime arrived at around eight o'clock, the car could be "transformed into a dormitory." The conversion was surprisingly simple. "The backs of the seats were thrown back, bedsteads carefully packed were rolled out by an ingenious system, berths were suddenly improvised, and each traveler had soon at his disposition a comfortable bed, protected from curious eyes by thick curtains." Verne was clearly impressed with the quality and design of this train, which ". . . was supplied with saloon cars, balcony cars, restaurants and smoking cars . . . ." With both speed and safety in mind, Fogg and his companion rode the train across the Great Basin and into ". . . Utah, the region of the Great Salt Lake, the singular colony of the Mormons."[24] In writing this description, Verne relied on the voluminous travel literature describing the transcontinental railroad. That his description appeared in one of the world's most popular travel novels reminds one just how readily the transcontinental railroad fit into the Victorian-era imagination.

In 1873, the adventurous Isabella Bird traveled through Promontory describing "the huge Pacific train, with its heavy bell tolling" and the Silver Palace cars she found so comfortable. As Bird noted, the car featured "a luxurious bed three and a half feet wide, with a hair mattress on springs, fine linen sheets, and costly California blankets." The car was, as she put it, "a true Temple of Morpheus"—the Greek god of dreams. It was sumptuous, and its "[f]our silver lamps hanging from the room, and burning low, gave a dreamy light." Moreover, the plush interior had "green and crimson curtains, striped with gold" and a "soft Axminster carpet." Although it was below freezing outside (27 degrees), the inside temperature of the car "was carefully kept at 70." The observant Bird went so far as to describe the train's consist. It "consisted of engine and tender, two baggage cars 45' each, two cars loaded with peaches and grapes, two Silver Palace cars, 60' each, a smoking car, then five ordinary pass[enger] cars, which gave the train a length of 700'." One can imagine this train at night snaking through the curves over Promontory Summit and rolling over the wide open, desolate country of the Curlew Valley, its bright headlight, glowing firebox, illuminated windows, and red marker lights briefly disrupting the nearly funereal solitude and darkness of a chilly night in what would come to be known as the "Great American Desert."

At the other end of the scale from such plush accommodations was the lowly emigrant car. Any rundown or cheaply constructed passenger car was termed an *emigrant car*. Eastern railroads used emigrant cars three decades before the completion of the transcontinental railroad. They reflected a highly culture- and class-stratified society, the premise being that the cars "were so inferior that only emigrants would ride in them." By 1869, anticipating a thriving traffic in emigrants over the transcontinental railroad, Central Pacific's general manager Alban N. Towne oversaw the design of special emigrant cars that would ". . . improve the emigrants' lot by providing supereconomy sleeping cars." Towne's emigrant cars appeared similar to other passenger cars, but had special "Emigrant Car" lettering on the outside and a no-frills setup on the inside. Featuring oak plank interiors, board seats, common cooking stoves, and simple toilet facilities, these cars answered an important need. In April 1869, Central Pacific's Sacramento shops "were busy fitting up twenty-five emigrant sleepers." Extant photographs and plans suggest that Central Pacific's first emigrant cars had simple arched roofs, but those in the 1870s and 1880s featured clerestory roofs.[25] In other words, emigrant cars underwent an evolution similar to other passenger cars, only more economically. Union Pacific also had emigrant cars, and they presumably ran them on the Central Pacific when travelers needed to reach the Pacific Coast. It is also likely that the Union Pacific cars carried a large number of Mormon converts only as far as Ogden (and Salt Lake City).

In the 1870s, evidently before Union Pacific had the opportunity to upgrade its emigrant cars, Scottish writer Robert Louis Stevenson crossed the United States on a trip to San Francisco. At Council Bluffs, Iowa, Stevenson boarded a Union Pacific emigrant train, leaving a lasting record of the dreadful experience in *The Amateur Emigrant* (1879). The last three cars on the long train were reserved for emigrants. To board these cars, families consisting of "women and children" ran toward the very last car; single men were directed toward the next (i.e., middle car of the three), and Chinese to the third car. Stevenson described the typical American railroad passenger car as a "long, narrow wooden box, like a flat roofed Noah's ark, with a stove and a convenience [toilet], one at either end, a passage down the middle, and transverse benches upon either hand." Union Pacific emigrant cars, however, were even more Spartan: "Those [cars] destined for emigrants on the Union Pacific are only remarkable for their extreme plainness, nothing but wood entering in any part into their constitution, and for the usual inefficacy of the lamps, which often went out and shed but a dying glimmer even while they burned." The seats were, in effect, "benches [that] can be made to face each other in pairs, for the backs are reversible." At night, boards could be "laid from bench to bench, making a couch wide enough for two, and long enough for a man of middle height"—provided that the car was not too crowded to permit that option. The cars were shabby enough, but became more intolerable with every mile westward. To make matters worse, the food at way stops was horrible, and Stevenson contracted food poisoning.[26]

Upon changing trains at Ogden, things brightened considerably. Stevenson pointedly compared the cars of the Union Pacific with those of the Central Pacific, noting that the latter "were nearly twice as high, and so proportionately airier; they were freshly varnished, which gave us all a sense of cleanliness as though we had bathed; the seats drew out and joined in the center, so that there was no more need for bed boards; and there was an upper tier of berths which could be closed by day and opened at night." Central Pacific's Alban Towne would have been proud to hear this praise, since he had designed a better car for emigrants than Union Pacific's cars. Still, Stevenson found traveling on the Pacific Railroad emigrant-style wanting. Stevenson observed that the people traveling aboard the cars were a sorry lot, and Americans who boarded the cars were particularly mean to the emigrants. The occupants in the "Chinese car"—who "travel by steam conveyance, yet with such a baggage of old Asiatic thoughts and superstitions as might check the locomotive in its course"—were especially reviled. Why? Sharpening his pen into a stiletto, Stevenson thought it was "because their dexterity and frugality enable them to underbid the lazy, luxurious Caucasian." Unfortunately, in contrast to most traveling writers, Stevenson was so concerned with social commentary that he paid no heed at all to the area around Promontory. As he put it, this "little corner of Utah is soon traversed, and leaves no particular impressions on the mind."[27]

From the very beginning, the problem with the line over Promontory was that it slowed down the traveler, who always craved faster ways to get places. Despite improvements in shipping people and express, some people envisioned methods of travel that would ultimately supersede the railroad itself. Shortly after the completion of the transcontinental railroad, in fact, an inventor in Sacramento demonstrated a contraption consisting of a machine to be suspended below a lighter-than-air balloon. It would, he predicted in 1871, "be able to carry passengers from one place to another at the rate of fifty miles per hour . . . " in order to offer a "style of traveling" whose "greater safety, speed, avoidance of dust, healthiness of route, etc., will cause it to be a powerful opponent of railroads and steamboats."[28] That, of course, would be long into the future. In the meantime, with the completion of the railroad, goods previously shipped by sea now moved westward, and eastward, over Promontory Summit. Despite visionary glimpses at this time, most people realized the train was the fastest way to travel. The passenger trains they rode were likely to have on board at least one travel writer like Isabella Bird or Robert Louis Stevenson, who could help immortalize the railroad line and prepare future travelers for the sights that they would see, and trains they would ride, along the route over Promontory Summit. As opposed to the fictional Phileas Fogg, who traveled west to east, they usually related the experience much as the public envisioned railroad travel, that is, going from east to west. Most writers briefly described Ogden, but also commented on the meeting point between Central Pacific and Union Pacific west of that flourishing town. When *Crofutt's Trans-Continental Tourist* described Union Junction in 1874, it noted that the place "is a station only in name, six miles west of Ogden" but suggested better things were scheduled for the future. That same writer also noted, "the companies propose to jointly erect at this 'junction' ample permanent buildings to accommodate their own interests"—that is, railroad services—"as well as a magnificent building to be called the WASATCH HOTEL." Continuing with a description of what would be a magnificent Victorian-style building, the guide described nearby HOT SPRINGS, which "in cold weather send up a dense cloud of vapor, which is visible for a long distance." Given the sulphurous content, the guide politely warned travelers that "the odor arising from them is very strong, and by no means pleasant for some people to inhale."[29] This junction, then, offered amenities, and the locale had various names, including Bonneville. In describing Bonneville, *Nelson's Pictorial Guide Book of The Central Pacific Railroad* (1871) noted that "The chief feature of interest here is the Hot Springs, whose clouds of vapour rise far away at the foot of the mountains, reminding one of the 'cloud' which protected the Israelites by day on their march through the weary wilderness."[30] If both railroads had had their way, Bonneville City might have blossomed into a spectacular tourist transportation hub, part spa and part bustling railroad terminal. Central Pacific's Huntington certainly hoped so, until Stanford talked him into accepting Young's recommendation that Ogden become the city where the railroads converged. Alas, Bonneville remained what *Crofutt's Trans-Continental Tourist* called "unimportant," adding that the train passes through "fine farming lands, which yield crops of wheat, barley, and corn" in this area of the Wasatch Front. Beyond Willard City and Brigham City, the train reached Corrine, a potentially-Edenic place surrounded by "thousands of acres of land, which require only irrigation to render them productive in the highest degree."[31]

After leaving Corinne, the train skirted the northeastern edge of the Great Salt Lake for about fifteen miles, then dug in to assault the steep grade up to Promontory Summit. Travel writers with vivid imaginations frequently commented on the form and color of the landscape near Promontory Summit. In reference to the dark color of the limestone outcroppings and strata on Promontory, *The Pacific Tourist* described the scene at Quarry as "a side track, with a huge, rocky, black castle on the right and back of it." The use of the term *castle* is quite revealing as many observers of the time fancied seeing the shapes of ancient buildings in the rugged western landscape. *The Pacific Tourist* continued as the train passed beyond Quarry near Little Mountain: "As we pass beyond and look back, an oval-shaped dome rises from its northern end as the turret of a castle."[32] Victorian-era readers expected such imaginative prose, and the scenery along the transcontinental route over Promontory offered plenty of grist for the pulp-era descriptions.

In a handwritten manuscript at the Utah State Historical Society Archives, Thomas A. Davis described his life near Promontory Summit from 1869 to the 1880s. Davis, who had recently arrived there as a ranch hand just before the railroads met, "was denied the priviledge [*sic*] of witnessing that great event by being sent to Willard with some horses to prevent them [from] being stolen." Davis describes his partnership with Mr. John L. Edwards in the cattle ranching business. Through his connection with Edwards, Davis soon "became located on the Promontory, taking up a place of my own, which I homesteaded when I became of age." Marrying Margaret Davis of Willard in 1871, Thomas Davis and his new bride "soon made our home on the place I had located." Here, ". . . on the Promontory in the Summer of 1871, I built a house of old Telegraph poles." Although the poles "were rotted at the bottom," they nevertheless made "a room of 16 by 14 feet," where the Davis family lived until the spring of 1887. During the sixteen years that they lived in the house, Thomas "built a kitchen at the back made of square Rail Road ties."

This was typical of the cobbled together materials many pioneers used in this part of the West, where timber was scarce. In one passage, Davis notes that "the building of a Ranch out at that remote place was quite expensive and laborious." Although "[c]edar posts were fairly easy to get," he added that ". . . all other fencing material was expensive and hard to get." Given the shortage of materials, Davis first fenced his land near Promontory "with smoothe [*sic*] wire, [as] this was before barb wire became in Vouge [*sic*]." As one might expect, this smooth wire was not up to the job. It "proved to be worthless, and rotten and brittle," and "the cattle would break it to pieces." To remedy this situation, Davis then used "lumber, and later barb wires," after which the ranch family "got on fairly well." To make ends meet, however, he also "did some teaming for the Rail Road Company, had some milk cows, and made a lot of butter to sell to rail road people." In the summer of 1886, the land was surveyed into the U.S. public domain and "placed in the market." Davis took a homestead of 160 acres in section 12—an even-numbered section. Of this 160 acres, "about half was bench land and above all water, and gravely and rocky." By contrast, most of his "hay land became [was surveyed into] an odd-numbered section," and "was called Rail Road land, and in time we would lose it." In about 1886, Davis noted, "the Rail Road Company sold all its lands that were embraced within the land grant to a company consisting of George Crocker, Captain Buford, and one John W. Taylor of San Francisco." About a year later, Thomas wrote that the "new company expressed a desire to purchase all the ranches . . . cattle and all . . . ." Because Davis believed that "so much of our hay land was within an Odd section" the family deemed it "advisable to sell, which we did." Still, after so much work, Davis and his family must have found this to be a difficult outcome. As he wrote, "I believe to this day that we made a mistake in disposing of that ranch, as It is in a good locality, and [experiences] short winters." From here, the Davis family moved to Idaho.[33]

Because most of the land in this area sloped down toward the railroad, trains of the Central Pacific were visible for a considerable distance. The parade of trains was a study in evolving railroad technology. When trains began running over Promontory Summit, the typical Central Pacific boxcar was 25 feet long and 15 tons in capacity. The cars were slightly larger and could carry heavier loads than most American boxcars at the time, which had a capacity of 10 tons. Central Pacific boxcars of this type had an interior space of 197 square feet and 1,158 cubic feet. They were about 8½ feet wide and had an interior height of 10½ feet. In the early 1870s, Central Pacific began to use somewhat larger boxcars measuring 28 feet in length. A standard feature of all such cars was the staff-mounted brake wheel found at one end of the car, reached by climbing up the car ends using metal rungs. Once atop the car, a man knelt on the roof walk or rooftop at the car's end, turning the brake handle clockwise or counter-clockwise to apply or release the car's brakes. This was a dangerous activity, and especially so when ice and snow fell on Promontory (fig. 5–9).

Southern Pacific freight car authority Anthony Thompson notes that "[i]mmediately upon completion of the transcontinental railroad in May, 1869, shipments of fruit commenced." Both Central Pacific and Union Pacific used special cars for this fruit traffic.[34] The ventilated boxcar and its cousin, the fruit car, were especially common in service over Promontory. Ventilated boxcars featured numerous, slatted vents in the car sides. As railroad historian John White Jr. noted, "Central Pacific became something of a patron of ventilated cars because it had so many on-line shippers requiring equipment of this type." Central Pacific soon built these cars in its Sacramento shops; the oldest of this type still in existence can be seen at the Nevada Railroad Museum in Carson City.[35] These cars were especially versatile in that they could carry fruit, grain, or ordinary freight. A freight car ventilated for such traffic is termed *fruit car*, but passenger trains used some special fruit cars to guarantee the fastest shipping. These cars rode on passenger trucks and had end platforms (fig. 5–10).

Central Pacific used the term *combination car* for boxcars with side vents that could be closed on the inside, and two types of side doors, solid wood plank and ventilated with slats. Depending on the type of

Braking in Hard Weather.

FIG. 5–9
As seen in this generic illustration titled
"Braking in Hard Weather," operating a train's
brakes using a brake wheel, always a dangerous
activity, became even more so when a train
rattled around curving lines like that over
Promontory—especially in ice and snow. From
The American Railway, 1888 edition.

service desired, the car could be either a regular closed boxcar or a
ventilated boxcar (fig. 5–11). These combination cars were found
wherever the railroads needed versatility in the car fleet. The typical
combination car might carry regular freight as a closed car on other
trips, in which case, the car would be sealed; horses on another trip; or
fruit on yet another. The last two examples would involve opened vents
and the ventilated doors positioned over the door openings to facilitate the flow of air.[36] These combination cars should not be confused
with combination passenger-baggage cars, which were of passenger car
design but had one windowless section (or end) of the car dedicated
to baggage storage.

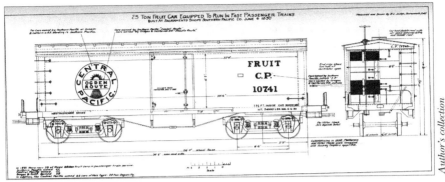

FIG. 5–10

Central Pacific Railroad plan showing a fruit car used in "fast passenger trains" built in the Central Pacific's Sacramento shops. Note the car's end platforms and passenger-car type trucks. See also Anthony Thompson, *Southern Pacific Freight Cars, Vol. 4, Box Cars* (2006).

Most of these freight cars were of wooden construction, strengthened by metal corner angle braces and truss rods that hung below the floor, which explains the expression *riding the rods* for the hoboes' risky method of free travel. Given the boxcar's versatility, they became the most common cars on many railroads. Most boxcars hauled a wide range of cargoes from furniture and canned goods to sacked wheat and flour. In 1871, the Central Pacific developed "an improved plan" for their boxcars—or "box freight cars" as the press called them. This involved building the body two feet taller and casing the car "inside and outside" to make it stronger and more weather-tight. This, naturally, increased the car's weight. At this time, the average weight of these new cars was about 20,000 pounds, or 10 tons.[37] Like everything else on the railroad, however, boxcars became larger over time.

To avoid mishaps and catastrophes, air brakes were added to Central Pacific's cars beginning in 1871. This was especially important for routes like the line over Promontory Summit, which had steep grades where it was easy for an engineer to lose control of his train descending into the lows on either side of Promontory Hill or Red Dome Pass. Designed and patented by the Westinghouse Air Brake Company in 1869, they were called "atmospheric brakes" and gave the engineer control of the train on such grades. These air brakes were relatively simple but ingenious. They required a compressor, a cylinder-shaped device, mounted on the locomotive. The compressor piped air to individual railroad cars in turn via hoses. Each car contained a hose connected to an air cylinder, which activated the handbrake chain when pressurized. When the brake lines were charged up, the brakes were applied. This was a real

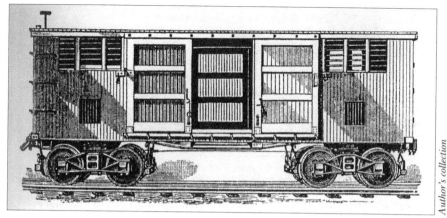

Author's collection

FIG. 5–11

A typical Central Pacific "combination" car of the early 1870s was an ingenious design: It could be sealed as tightly as a regular boxcar when the solid doors and louvers were shut or run as a ventilated car when louvers were opened and the grate-like door slid into place.

improvement over earlier direct (hand-powered) braking, but left much to be desired. Charging up the brake lines in a train required considerable time. Moreover, if the brake line separated anywhere in the train, there were no brakes. At such times, the crew did one of two things. They would likely scurry from car to car to apply firmly and quickly each car's hand brakes, hopefully slowing the train enough to avoid disaster. However, they might simply "join the birds" (jump off) to avoid being crushed to death when the train crashed, as all too often happened.[38] Despite these dire options, air brakes still represented some important gains in safety. Thus it was that at the very time the transcontinental railroad was completed, a series of developments took place that increased safety and simultaneously reduced labor costs and damage claims.

Long runs like the trip over Promontory Summit to and from California continued to stimulate improvements in passenger cars. Among these was the sleeping car, which provided passengers the opportunity to sleep in comfort and some privacy, as opposed to sleeping bolt upright in a coach. In June 1871, the Kimball Manufacturing Company of San Francisco unveiled a 67–foot-long passenger car with an interior "divided into four drawing-rooms and a rotunda at each end, with spacious halls passing around the rooms." The car's construction was unusual in that it featured long, unspliced timbers for support, and the wood of thirty-four different types of Pacific Coast trees, each highly polished, provided interior ornamentation. The car was mounted on two six-wheel trucks, each wheel being made of compressed rubber to soften or smooth the ride. In June, this car crossed Promontory Summit on its way east to be "exhibited in all the leading cities."³⁹ During that same summer, the Central Pacific began operating its first mail cars. Especially designed for this service, the car contained separate sections or "divisions for way mail for all points between San Francisco and Ogden, a department for through mail, and another, in the center of the car, for the convenience of the route agents—the whole car being devoted to mail service—whereas heretofore one car served for both mail and express." These new cars, the Sacramento *Daily Union* noted, "fill exactly the requirements of the postal business . . . ."⁴⁰

As things quieted down at Promontory after the big celebration, most of the commentary about the line related to rail passenger traffic. In June1870, for example, several Central Pacific officials traveled over the line on a "trip to Salt Lake."⁴¹ With increasing railroad traffic in Ogden, which was on the Pacific railroad as well as the Utah Central and the Utah Northern, the city needed a larger railroad station. On December 21, 1874, Loren Farr asked surveyor James H. Martineau "to assist in determining as to the arrangement of the grand depot at that place, of the Union Pacific, Utah Central and Utah Northern Railroads." On December 22, 1874, Martineau reported that he "consulted with Br. Reeves, agent U.C.RR. and Mr. Pratt, Div. Supt. Of C.P. RR. About the grounds, and it was determined that I should go to S. L. City to copy the C.P. map of the Depot grounds, Br. Farr going also." On December 23, Martineau "copied the map in Mr. Marshall's office," continuing on the project after Christmas. On December 28, Martineau diligently "worked on map of Ogden Depot."⁴² Upon completion, the "grand depot," as Martineau called it, was one of the Interior West's most important *Union Stations*—a term used for a large depot that could serve the needs of travelers using several railroads. This made travel on the Pacific railroad over Promontory easier, as it did for travelers from Salt Lake City and points in Idaho, who now "changed cars" in Ogden for San Francisco or Omaha.

Ogden figures in another aspect of the Promontory line. Not long after completion of the transcontinental railroad, two patterns in ridership became apparent. The first was *through travel*—that is, people traversing the line over Promontory as part of a long journey. The second, however, was quite different, and related to the distribution of towns along the Wasatch Front for what might be called "local" service. This local travel could be on the Central Pacific or the newly completed Union Pacific line to points north. On Friday, July 4, 1873, Martineau described riding a portion of the line from Corinne to Ogden. As he wrote in his diary, "An excursion went to Corinne today, by invitation of the Corinne people to celebrate, and have a rail road ride." Martineau added that "[t]here was [*sic*] about 200 persons on the train, which was nicely fitted up with evergreens and flags." Traveling with his wife, Susan J., Martineau added that "we had a pleasant ride over, and were met by the Corinne Brass Band." Later that afternoon after the community-railroad festivities, Martineau and Susan J. boarded the train, but "as we were about to start home at 4 pm while sitting in the car, Susan was suddenly seized with a very severe fainting spell, which continued more or less all the way home." By the next day, she had recovered but remained weak.[43] On numerous occasions, Martineau rode the Utah Northern from Cache County "to Corinne, thence by C. P. R. R. to Ogden" as on October 6, when Susan again experienced distress. As Martineau put it, "When near Ogden, she was again taken suddenly" and "very badly, but arrived safely at Ogden." The couple went to a hotel where, just after dinner, "she had a miscarriage of a little boy."[44]

The social and economic impact of the railroad on Utah was profound and can best be understood by observing how it encouraged the growth of the Mormon economy and non-Mormon enterprises. In 1864, five years *before* the completion of the transcontinental railroad, Henry Kendall, general secretary of the New School Presbyterian Church Board of Domestic Missions, visited Utah for a week. Kendall was investigating the feasibility of establishing a Protestant school in the middle of Mormon Country that would also attract Mormon students (that school ultimately became Westminster College of Salt Lake City). Bluntly put, Kendall hoped to encourage Protestant education to counter the dominance of Mormonism. During his visit, Kendall met with LDS Church President Brigham Young. To Kendall's surprise, Young informed him that he welcomed non-Mormon missionaries and invited Kendall to speak in the Mormon Tabernacle on Sunday! Tellingly, during this interview, "Young extolled the resources and prospects of Utah, particularly the anticipated completion of a transcontinental railroad that would link the territory with the two coasts."[45]

Five years later, with the opening of that railroad in 1869, Presbyterian minister/educator Sheldon Jackson arrived in Utah. Jackson summoned three ministers to towns on the Union Pacific. One of the towns, Corinne, was a booming community with a decidedly non-Mormon character and no religious institutions. Moreover, religion of any kind or denomination was simply not welcome here. In fact, when Melancthon Hughes attempted to establish a church in Corinne, he met strong opposition from "local rowdies who disrupted services and ridiculed the need for religion in a wide open town like Corinne."[46] Hughes left Corinne in less than two months and was replaced by Edward E. Bayliss, who reconstituted the church there after his arrival in April of 1870. If anything,

Bayliss was even more enthusiastic than his predecessor: he hoped to form the Rocky Mountain Female Academy in Corinne. Predictably, however, Bayliss never received the necessary support. Even the Presbyterian Church in Corinne faltered, eventually closing its doors.

Corinne was what historian Page Smith calls a "cumulative" community—that is, one founded solely on commerce and trade. Smith contrasts such cumulative towns with "covenanted" communities, like Salt Lake City and other Mormon towns, built on a covenant with God, and not on commerce.[47] Like most cumulative towns, Corinne thrived when commerce poured through its gates. However, the town's situation changed as soon as the transportation pattern in the vicinity developed. With the opening of the Utah Northern Railroad in the 1870s, Corinne's fortunes declined as the new Mormon-sponsored, narrow gauge line siphoned off Montana trade. Corinne's site—once strategically located north of Salt Lake at a point that could tap the northern trade—now became its curse. Although it was on the transcontinental line over Promontory Summit, Corinne began to change character as the railroads regularized operations. It did, however, ultimately become an important, and largely Mormon, farming town.

A beautiful bird's-eye view map of Corinne in 1875 (fig. 5–12) reveals that community's strategic, and changing, position as gateway to the north. Looking northward, the view shows a steamboat on the Bear River, which meanders through the scene from the mountains in the right distance. Steamboats once ran on the Great Salt Lake, connecting Corinne with points south, including Salt Lake City, in the days before the railroad. As seen in this map, the Central Pacific bisects and dominates the town of Corinne, which is platted in a checkerboard pattern. Corinne's main business streets—North Front, South Front, and Montana Street—parallel the railroad. Clustering in the area marked "depot" are a railroad station and other railroad-related buildings, including a freight station. Boxcars are lined up to be loaded or unloaded, and no fewer than five trains—three passenger trains, one freight, and one mixed train—are either arriving or departing. This likely was a result of artistic license rather than actual scheduling—a familiar technique of enthusiastic mapmakers of the time. Nevertheless, Corinne was now a rather bustling place—the location where a spur from the Utah Northern narrow gauge line joins the Central Pacific mainline. In the far left distance, Blue Creek is shown, behind which the "Promontory Range, 25 miles distant," looms. That Central Pacific freight train leaving Corinne will likely pick up a helper locomotive at Blue Creek to ascend the Promontory grade.[48]

To travelers, Corinne's location seemed both interesting and ominous. It marked, as *Leslie's Illustrated* put it in 1877—"the beginning of

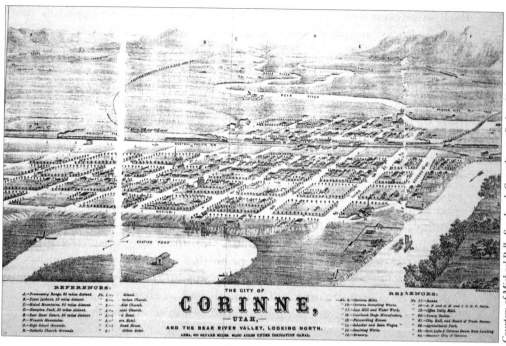

FIG. 5–12

A bird's-eye view map of the city of Corinne, Utah, 1875, reveals plenty of railroad activity, some of which may be the result of artistic license to illustrate as much rail traffic as possible. Nevertheless, this map is generally very accurate.

the Great American Desert." A panoramic lithograph (fig. 5–13) from the period reveals the impact of the Great Basin on the popular psyche. The train, telegraph poles, and distant town are the only marks of civilization, though the marsh land close to the lake is fairly luxuriant. Aside from this hundred-foot-wide strip, the rest of the scene is one of increasing desolation with each mile traveled westward—fascinating, of course, but frightening. Soon, for miles in all directions, the sagebrush-covered landscape will seem ready to devour the meager workings of humankind. This, as the accompanying magazine article warned, is "the Great Desert, that dreary waste so lately a *terra incognita* to tourists—the 'unexplored lands' of school atlases." To reach Corinne, travelers had to cross what one writer described as ". . . miles upon miles of alkaline tracts, looking like a badly frosted cake . . . ."[49] Another writer observed that one had to traverse "the dreary level of wet marsh, white with alkali, from whose shallow pools the yellow sunset strikes fire." Glancing westward, travelers could see "a distant glimmer of the Great Salt Lake and the ghostly Promontory Mountains beyond."

FIG. 5–13
Leaving Corinne behind them, the group of travelers heads westbound along the marshy shore of the Great Salt Lake in an open car that enables them to take in the scenery at "the beginning of the Great American Desert." Within about an hour, they will be climbing toward the summit of the Promontory Range. From *Frank Leslie's Illustrated Newspaper,* 1877.

After leaving Corinne, travelers came to "Promontory, famous in the history of the West as the meeting point of the two railroads—the spot where the last ties and the last rails were laid by Chinese workmen, the last spike driven, and the marriage of the Union Pacific with the Central Pacific declared in the presence of a thousand witnesses." Other than this destination, *Leslie's Illustrated* recognized Promontory as "[a]n insignificant little dot of a place," but nevertheless, one we must "take off our hats to . . . as we pass, and the long train roars its faint echo of the cheers that went up here nine years ago."[50] At not quite ten years of age, Promontory already seemed easy to overlook, except, of course, for the pivotal event that had occurred here in 1869. That is unfortunate, for during Promontory's long life, it had a number of other identities that had little to do with the joining of the rails ceremony, and much more to do with its position in the changing panorama of western railroading from the 1870s to around 1900.

Chapter 6

BIG TIME RAILROADING
(1875–1904)

So much has been written about Promontory as a unique place in 1869 that it has obscured the town's later role as one of many places along the railroad. During the period 1875 to about 1900, Promontory's character changed from a historical curiosity to another link in the chain of increasingly big-time railroading. This chapter covers Promontory as a location on a section of the mainline that ran through some of the most forbidding country in the American West.

In the 1870s, and 1880s, popular atlases often featured maps of Utah and Nevada as a single spread that spanned two full pages. Naturally, the transcontinental railroad was a major feature. One of the most beautiful of these maps was first published by Asher and Adams in 1873, with additional editions published for several more years (fig. 6–1). Its depiction of the section of the line from Ogden to the Nevada state line reveals just how isolated the countryside was along the right of way in the vicinity of Kelton, Terrace, and Lucin. On this map, the Great American Desert appears as an ominous gray stippled area. A hint of civilization is provided only eastward of Rozel, where the familiar rectangular survey gives a sense of order to the country from the Promontory Range to the Wasatch Front. Interestingly, a traveler, or would-be traveler, could use the mileages shown between communities—for example, $10^2/_{10}$ miles between Terrace and Matlin—to figure out how far he or she traveled. Typical Central Pacific public timetables of the period provided similar information.

At the same time that Asher and Adams published their map, *Gray's Atlas* featured a full-page map of Utah, showing the completed lines of

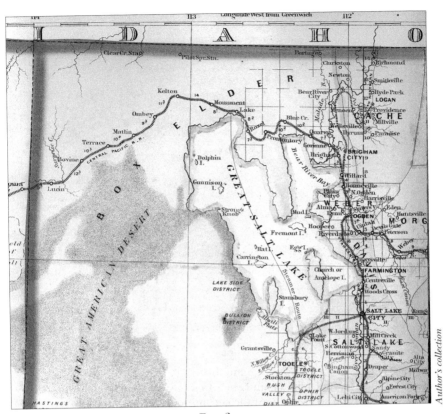

FIG. 6–1

Detail of the line over Promontory on Asher and Adams's beautiful map of Utah and Nevada, 1873, shows the Central Pacific line and its station stops fairly accurately.

the railroad. On this map (fig. 6–2), Promontory's location shows as a broad swale between two valleys—the Blue Spring Valley to the east and the Hansel Valley to the west. As was typical of the times, all of the stations along the route between Ogden and Lucin are shown. In some places, though, the topography is generalized and simplified. For example, on this map, the railroad appears to skirt the south end of the Red Dome Mountains on perfectly flat land, when, in fact, contour lines drawn at tighter intervals, for example one hundred or even twenty feet apart, would actually reveal this area to be rugged topography. By carefully consulting popular maps of the line over Promontory, we can observe a tendency to downplay the topography, and even straighten out the railroad's numerous curves in the area west of Rozel and Kelton. True, there are some long stretches of straight track here, and the Red Dome and Hogup mountains are not as imposing as the Promontory

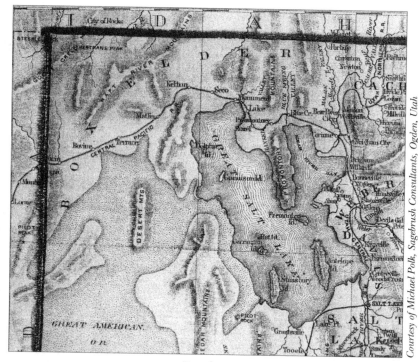

FIG. 6–2

Detail of the Utah map in *Gray's Atlas* (1873). Map of a portion
of the transcontinental railroad line over Promontory shows
most of the communities along the line but simplifies the
topography west of Kelton.

Range, but this map again simplifies the western portion of the line. It
is likely that the many verbal descriptions of how "monotonous" travel
was here, coupled with the name Great American Desert, tempted mapmakers to simplify this part of the route.

In the 1880s, much effort was spent in reconciling earlier land surveys with the most recent ones. The Surveyor General's office in Salt
Lake City was charged with showing the boundary "between old and
new" surveys and the work took them through Promontory. The 1885
map showing Township No. 10 North Range No. 6 West of the Salt
Lake Meridian focused on Promontory, which shows as a relatively flat
area where the "C.P.R.R" jogs slightly. The map's stylized town plan at
Promontory Summit indicates buildings lining both sides of the track
here, but other records confirm that most of them were north of the
tracks. Just south of town, the rugged Promontory Range (unnamed)
looms as a contorted cluster of hachures, with relatively level areas on
the mountainsides suggesting the level of ancient lake terraces. This

map reveals that even in Promontory's heyday, there was only a small community here surrounded by vast open spaces. The primary activity in the area adjacent to Promontory was ranching, and much of the stippled pattern on the map suggests the dominant sagebrush cover.[1]

Farther to the west, beyond Promontory Summit, the countryside was bleak indeed, and the railroad appeared to traverse an ancient and foreign land. West of Promontory, the popular guidebooks often made yet another common comparison to Utah as the Holy Land. To set the scene, an eastbound travelogue/guide writer noted, "We pass over, with a word of allusion, the stations of Rozel, elevation 4588 feet; Lake, and Monument, 4226 feet, where the air is impregnated with alkaline and saline odours from the Salt Lake. Monument Point is a grassy promontory, stretching far out into the waters of the Dead Sea of the West."[2] This country was probably the most evocative on the entire line, for it conjured up images of the wilderness described in the Bible.

Along the line west of Promontory, there were small, seemingly forlorn communities. Some were larger than others, and some were little more than stations around which a few buildings huddled. However, they all had one thing in common—to travelers, they all seemed desolate. Not all tourist guidebooks agreed on the importance of individual stations, and official railroad records contradict some guides. For example, in the 1880s, Rozel was the place where eastbound Central Pacific freight trains stopped to add helper locomotives. The water here came from Antelope Springs, which is located in the Raft River Mountains. Being a California railroad, the Central Pacific tended to use redwood for many things, including posts, beams, and siding for structures. A redwood pipeline built in 1874 originally conveyed Rozel's water but was replaced by a 3–inch-diameter pipe in 1883. The railroad's wooden water tower here was also built of redwood; its tank was 18 feet in diameter x 14 feet tall in a 23–foot-square housing.[3] Generally, despite these facilities, tank towns like Rozel did not impress travel writers. In 1879, *The Pacific Tourist* observed that Rozel was "an unimportant station, where trains meet and pass; but passenger trains do not stop unless signaled." Contributing to the bleakness of the site was the low, scrubby vegetation. As *The Pacific Tourist* put it, between Rozel and Lake, the train was "still crossing a sage brush plain, with occasional alkali patches, closing in upon the shore at times." For all its barrenness, however, Rozel did have one thing in its favor: the view was fantastic and "the lake can now be seen for a long distance, and in [*sic*] a clear day, with a good glass, the view is magnificent."[4]

As the train continued along the sweeping curve that followed the northern shoreline of the lake, it passed Monument, also called

Photo by author

FIG. 6–3
A marl formation, shaped like the head of an
elephant, stands near Monument Point (2005).

Monument Rock or Monument Point, one of the region's noteworthy,
and aptly named, landmarks. As *The Pacific Tourist* romantically described
it, "An isolated rock rises, like a monument, in the lake on the left, while
the hill on the right is crowned with turrets and projecting domes."[5]
Aside from Promontory Summit itself, this evocatively shaped rock was
one of the more commonly photographed scenes on the line. Nearby,
the marl rock in this desolate plain near the northern shore of the Great
Salt Lake contains oddly shaped topographic features, including eroded

spires and natural arches (fig. 6–3). Locomotive Springs, so-named at least five years before a train ever ran through the area, was also aptly titled, for "[o]n the west side of this hill are the Locomotive Springs which puff out steam at times, and which give them their name."[6]

To the west, between Kelton and Terrace, the railroad encountered relatively rugged topography, which provided some variety or relief from the brush-covered plains. Some travelers and travel writers were impressed with what they found here, but others were not. Of the Red Dome Mountains, *Crofutt's Trans-Continental Tourist* had little to say, except that "[h]ere these mountains—low sandstone ridges—are nearer the track, breaking the general monotony of the scene."[7] Nevertheless, the traveler in search of interesting scenery could find some here. As a more enthusiastic publication, *The Pacific Tourist*, observed, when one left Kelton westbound, the train encountered a "heavy grade," along which "you will notice a ledge of rocks on the left [i.e., south] side of the track, the lower end of which has been tunneled by the wind, forming a natural aperture like an open arch." Travelers often commented on the geological features defined in hard rock—such as the "beautiful conical dome [which] rises up, as a grim sentinel to guard the way." Red Dome contrasted with the flatness of "extensive salt plains, which in the sun glisten like burnished silver," which contrasted with "the green waters of this inland sea," as writers often characterized the Great Salt Lake.[8]

The scenery here was both terrible and sublime, and it left some of the most vivid impressions on transcontinental travelers aboard the trains of the Central Pacific. Virtually every travel guide and map called this area the Great American Desert. In 1877, the country west of Promontory was described in *Leslie's Illustrated* under moonlight, which "shining upon ghostly white alkali, gives the desert the aspect of a stagnant sea." To keep the oceanic metaphor going as the train moved across this area, the writer noted that "[l]ittle wooly tufts of sagebrush dot it everywhere," and "[w]aves of naked brown rock or arid land—we cannot tell which it may be—roll away in long swells against the horizon." The train "crossed the face of a forsaken land" here, while just sixty miles to the east, the Mormons had transformed the desert to "orchards and young grain where the dry alkali dust used to drift to and fro."[9]

As might be suspected, any settlement in this desolate area was worthy of at least some comment. In 1879, *The Pacific Tourist* characterized Terrace as "a railroad town on the edge of the Great American Desert." Located on a flat site—a low bench overlooking the western end of the Great Salt Lake—Terrace is appropriately named. The *Pacific Tourist*'s description of the railroad town was generic enough, as Terrace was the site of engine-servicing facilities and a substantial railroad yard (fig.

Courtesy of Utah State Historical Society Archives, Salt Lake City

FIG. 6-4

The Central Pacific station, rail yards, and commercial district are busy in the ca. 1880s scene of Terrace, Utah, a major railroad town on the line over Promontory Summit.

6-4). As a guide described it, "Here is a ten-stall roundhouse, and the machine and repair shops of the Salt Lake Division of the Central Pacific Railroad." The town was home to "about 300 people, which includes not only the railroad men and their families, but those who are here for the purpose of trade and traffic with them." It was also the railroad station stop for the mines in the Newfoundland District (eighteen miles south) and the Rosebud mines (ten miles north). Surrounding Terrace was "the desert with its dreary loneliness—a barren waste . . . ."

Given its location and the presence of the engine-servicing and repair shops here, Terrace naturally featured a water tank, which was "supplied with water brought through pipes from the springs in the mountains."[10] In this regard, Terrace was similar to the other spring-fed, aqueduct-dependent towns on this part of the Central Pacific, which had built its line through the arid, desolate lowlands sandwiched between the Great Salt Lake to the south, and the well watered mountain ranges, like the Raft River Range, looming to the north. The redwood pipelines or aqueducts that funneled water down from these mountains into places like Terrace, Kelton, and Rozel, were the veritable lifelines of the communities and railroad here.

The tracks ran in a northeast-southwest line through Terrace, which was the largest railroad town on the line between Ogden and Nevada. In the early to mid-1880s, an official Central Pacific station plan (fig. 6-5) reveals that there were several passing sidings, a 26½ x 76.4 foot, two-story depot, and two 24-foot-diameter water tanks here. Other

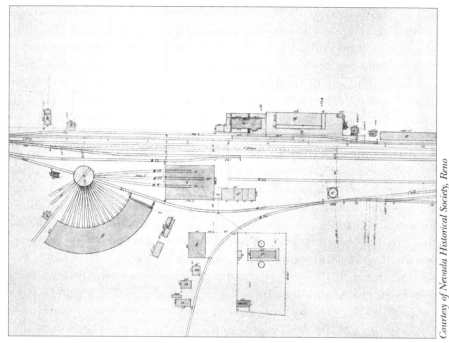

FIG. 6–5

An official Central Pacific Railroad station plan of Terrace, Utah, in the mid-1880s shows its numerous railroad-related buildings lining the mainline (upper center to *right*), turntable and large fifteen-stall roundhouse (*left*), three-track railroad shops (*just left of center*) and numerous railroad buildings along the spur track (*lower center*) near which the Terrace Atheneum and park were located.

facilities, however, assured Terrace's status as *the* railroad town along the line. These included a large roundhouse with fifteen stalls that were 62 feet in length. The turntable was 42 feet long—just long enough to hold the 4–4–0 and 4–6–0 locomotives of the period. Prominent in Terrace was the six-track machine shop, a large (82 x 120 foot) building for machining parts and making repairs. Behind the machine shop was a 17½ x 84 foot building containing an engine room, storeroom, office, and paint shop. There was also a 40 x 60 foot blacksmith shop adjacent to the spur track, which curved to the south and was flanked by an iron rack, and two storehouses. A large (62 x 312 foot) coal shed was built in October of 1883.

These facilities made Terrace a gritty workingman's community. However, despite the town's location in the middle of nowhere, Terrace was not a cultural wasteland—not if the railroad had a say in such matters. In addition to the 30 x 116 foot hotel built just north of the station in July 1883, Terrace also had a cultural amenity that few towns could claim: the Terrace Athenaeum located across the spur track from the blacksmith shop contained a 16 x 63 foot reading room surrounded by a veranda or porch, two ponds, and a series of contemplative, curving trails that ran through a landscaped, half-acre (121 x 200 foot) garden space.[11] The cultural facilities at Terrace represented the well-intentioned paternalism of the railroad companies at a time when unionization gained a stronger footing among American railroad workers.

At the time that Terrace grew into an important railroad town of several hundred European American workers in the 1880s, the Native American population along the Promontory route continued to decline. Despite the progress that the railroad brought to the area, conditions were difficult for the Native Americans who remained dependent on the physical environment. Adolph Reeder recalled that "[s]everal Indians lived in the mountains around Promontory." They were, evidently, drawn to the new town to trade hand-made items, including "buckskin gloves and belts for sheep pelts and grain."[12] These Indians typified the enterprising survivors in the Great Basin, who found new opportunities in the railroads (and the mines). At just about this time, though, most Indians moved onto reservations. The coming of the railroad, then, caused a redistribution of the human population here. Whereas before about 1820, people lived in widely dispersed families or bands, they now concentrated in clusters along a single line that demarcated the railroad.

Most of the Anglo-Americans who traveled through the area at this time commented on the scarcity of plants and animals. In traveling through the eastern Great Basin in 1876, the enterprising entrepreneur Don Maguire observed that large animals were fairly scarce in mountain ranges that "do not rise to high altitude, and hence do not afford streams in summer that supply the desert with water for wild animals." Maguire noted that "the only animals the Indians could use are the jackrabbit, mountain rats, mice, grasshoppers, crickets, horned toads and snakes." Summing up the vegetable products of this area, Maguire observed that "[t]he seeds of certain desert plants and pine nuts obtained in the stunted pine groves of the low mountains are the only plant foods."[13] The Promontory Range was one of the low mountains that Maguire may have had in mind, for he had traveled west of Ogden in search of horses for an expedition into the Great Basin, and thence to Arizona from 1876 to 1879. Rather than traveling over the Pacific Railroad, however, Maguire's route went farther south to the mining camps west of Salt Lake City and into central Nevada, Still, when Maguire drew a sketch map to illustrate his travels, he included the railroad route over

Promontory Summit. The reason, of course, was that the line had now become a major regional landmark.

The American map industry helped put the transcontinental railway, and the country adjacent to Promontory, on the map. Now it helped to keep it there. At this time, Rand McNally of Chicago emerged as a major player in the industry, frequently publishing maps for the railroads. For other railroads connecting with the Central Pacific, this line was a major draw because traffic could be routed to it over adjoining lines. A map by the Burlington & Missouri River Railroad showing the route of the transcontinental railroad in a solid black line flanked by a wider swath that highlights the Union Pacific-Central Pacific route is typical of this arrangement. On it, white dots indicate the location of communities, namely Lucin, Bovine, Terrace, Matlin, Ornbey, Kelton, Seco, Monument, Lake, Rozel, Promontory, Blue Creek, Quarry, and Corinne, with the more important transfer point of Ogden in larger letters. North from Kelton, a narrower black line heads north through Idaho; this is a stage line connecting important mining communities with the Central Pacific Railroad. West of the GREAT SALT LAKE (in capital letters) is the GREAT AMERICAN DESERT.[14] That evocative term suggests a huge, singular, forbidding region fixed in time, but that is not the case. The term *Great American Desert* had been used as early as the 1820s for the western Great Plains. Now, sixty years later, with that grassland being settled, the concept migrated westward to the area just west of Promontory, where a bleak landscape of salt flats—which Utahns call the West Desert—remains, to this day, one of the least populated places in the western United States.

Williams' map of the transcontinental railroad positions Promontory in a national context (fig. 6–6) and is typical of the cartographic products used by travel writers. It is interesting to note that all communities on such maps are represented as simple dots of equal size spaced more or less evenly along the railroad. These maps are what cartographic historian Kit Goodwin calls "designed maps" in that their information varies from what is actually found on site.[15] Although these maps give the impression that the area is equally settled and under control, in reality, it is anything but. Along the Central Pacific, at or near Promontory, the small towns are virtually the only communities here.

A map that accompanied A. Pendarves Vivian's popular *Wanderings in the Western Land* (1879) provided a colorful representation of the geology in this area. Its "Explanation of Colours" legend claimed that the line over Promontory consisted of Cambrian and Silurian strata. The numerous rock cuts excavated by the railroad[s] here (fig. 6–7), were of considerable interest to travelers then, and continue to be of

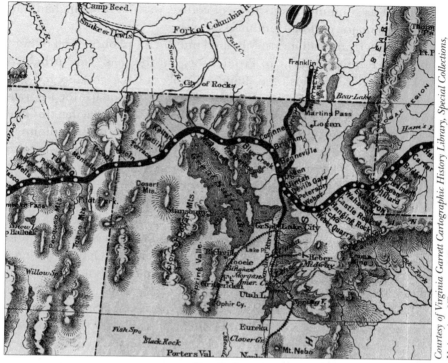

FIG. 6–6

The portion of *Williams Transcontinental Railroad Map* (1876) along the route over Promontory reveals it to be a "designed map"—that is, one that suggests the station stops are of equal size and spaced equally, creating the misconception that the countryside along the railroad was evenly settled.

interest to people visiting the site today. Vivian noted that the area west of Promontory consisted of alluvium of more recent age; on his map, he depicts the volcanic rocks to the north in bright red. Tellingly, however, the cranky Vivian made no comment about the railroad line in the text, simply noting that he boarded, in Ogden, a Silver Palace Car that "appears to be nothing more than a modification of a Pullman, and [has] the same comfortable berths, which we soon turned into." Like many travelers, Vivian crossed over Promontory Summit at night, and that may explain his failure to mention it.[16]

With the completion of the transcontinental railroad, freight traffic boomed. California produce could now be shipped east in a fraction of the time it used to take. Coinciding with this development was the invention of the refrigerator car. There were several types of refrigerated rail cars, or "reefers," as they came to be known. Most of the early reefers were insulated boxcars with tightly sealed doors and ice

FIG. 6–7
Rock cuts along the Promontory grade offered a cross section of the geology here—a subject that was often briefly discussed in the guidebooks of the 1870s and 1880s.

bunkers into which ice could be placed. One type of car built for the Central Pacific by George B. Dave of San Francisco in 1870 had ". . . double sides, ends, top and bottom, with sawdust filled in between the inner and outer boards." Ice, which was stored in boxes suspended by iron bands, was loaded through hatches in the roof. The cold air then drained down into the car, keeping fruit and vegetables fresh on their trip east.[17] The Central Pacific shops in Sacramento also built a car, called Booth's Refrigerating Car. It was "lined inside and out, like the fruit called of his design, and has in either end iron boxes as receptacles for ice, large enough to hold a quantity sufficient to last during a trip to the East." This car also had "two revolving fans in the roof, which are kept in motion by the momentum of the train" to "avoid the dampness which might otherwise arise from the ice." The enthusiastic writer reported that when this car was successfully tested in July of 1870 it "worked admirably."[18] With its ice bunkers at the ends of the car and fans to circulate air, this type of car soon dominated the refrigerator car fleet that Central Pacific, and later Southern Pacific, enlisted for shipping perishables from California to the Middle West and East. Typically, these cars were painted a distinctive mustard yellow color to distinguish them from the dark reddish brown boxcars.

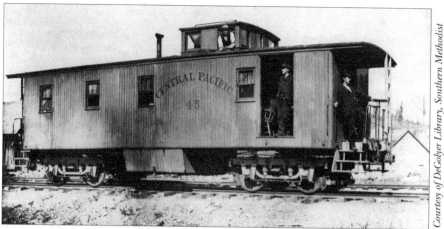

FIG. 6–8

Home away from home. A Central Pacific caboose from the 1870s resembles a short passenger car. It rides on wood beam trucks, was likely painted a yellowish color (perhaps to increase its visibility), and has the characteristic cupola from which the train cars ahead can be observed.

Later that year, the Sacramento newspapers reported that considerable work was being done at the Central Pacific Railroad shops, which were engaged in building cabooses and stockcars. The typical caboose of this era (fig. 6–8) rode on passenger car trucks, had passenger car-type platforms and upholstered seats, as well as fold-up berths "for the accommodation of the conductor and train hands." Behind this compartment was the conductor's office, over which rose a cupola, or "raised skylight with sliding windows on every side." Gazing out from this cupola in his elevated seat, the conductor "is enabled to watch his train as effectually while seated in his office as if standing of top of the car." Central Pacific cabooses were somewhat distinctive in that windows on both ends of the cupola featured a place to exhibit indicators (i.e., train numbers) so that trainmen would know which train was passing. Some cabooses were relatively simple affairs made from boxcars (fig. 6–9), but they served much the same purpose—a home away from home and an office on wheels.

The caboose was a specialized car designated for the official conducting of train-related business. In one sense, it was a non-revenue car in that it earned no direct income for the railroad. Other cars, however, had specific purposes. Despite the name, the new stock cars were quite versatile. Their sides consisted of a series of wooden slats separated by open space that naturally ventilated the cars. They were constructed to

Courtesy of DeGolyer Library, Southern Methodist University, Dallas

FIG. 6–9

Central Pacific caboose *No. 136*, which had "blind" ends (i.e., no platforms), was converted from a boxcar in 1901. Painted in the red color common by the late nineteenth century, it reflects the railroad's re-use of earlier equipment.

be more comfortable for animals being shipped and could be "transformed into ordinary box cars for freight purposes" when the side gratings were provided with doors that could be closed tightly. That these and other cars might not always stay on the track was evidenced by a third type of car described—the wrecking car. This was 36 feet long, 9 feet wide and "three or four times stronger than an ordinary car." It featured "a huge derrick twenty-two inches in diameter, and capable of hoisting about ten tons" and would "enable the company's workmen to clear up a wreck very expeditiously."[19]

In 1882, the Union Pacific issued a timetable for the *Union and Central Pacific Railroad Line via Omaha or Kansas City to San Francisco.* Billing the line as "The Great Shortline" and "the Old Reliable" because it was "the Shortest Route from the Principal Eastern and Western Cities to San Francisco by from 250 to 538 miles," the timetable shows two passenger trains each way per day. Running westward, train No. 6, the "Emigr'nt" [*sic*], and train No. 2, the "Express," arrived at Promontory at 6:25 p.m. and 8:30 p.m., respectively. Eastbound, train No. 5, the "Emigr'nt," and No. 1, the "Express," arrived at 4:00 a.m. and 6:15 a.m., respectively. At that time, both trains stopped at all the communities on the line, including Corinne, Blue Creek, Promontory, Rozel, Lake, Monument, Seco, Kelton, Ombey, Matlin, Terrace, Bovine, and Lucin. Describing opportunities in Utah in glowing terms, the timetable noted, "The topography of the territory is varied, comprising broad lakes, long rivers, mountains, salt deserts and marshy sinks." It added, "The valleys are farmed, more or less, and the terraces and foothills are famous stock ranges." Leaving no stone unturned, the Union Pacific and Central Pacific railroads also claimed that their entire "Old Reliable" route now featured "Well Balasted Road-Bed. Courteous Employees Pullman and Silver Palace Day and Sleeping Coaches. Emigrant Sleepers. Air Brakes. All Modern Improvements. Excellent Equipment. Picturesque Landscapes."[20]

For travelers on the line over Promontory Summit, the wide-open spaces often received some comment, as did the finery of ornate sleeping cars and parlor cars. For the most part, though, most people grew accustomed to traveling across the Interior West by train. Some remarked on Promontory but most did not. Ironically, on his 1882 trip across the very region he helped survey in the summer and fall of 1868, James H. Martineau makes no reference at all to Promontory. Rather, he observes that he "obtained a ticket to San Francisco, Cal. 883 miles, at $26.50 and sleeping car ticket for same place $6.00." Martineau dutifully notes that he "left Ogden at 6:45 P.M.," but he must have slept over Promontory Summit, for he next relates, on Saturday, November 25, "Awoke this morning at Halleck, Nevada. Got a poor breakfast at Elko, dined at noon at Battle Mountain, 348 miles from Ogden, and stopped at Humboldt Station" due to a "wrecked freight train that blocked the way." Like most travelers, Martineau confirmed that "the journey through Nevada is *very* dreary, passing the whole distance through a desert."[21] On a trip two years later, Martineau did much the same thing. Leaving "Ogden at 6:15 P.M. (Pacific time) 7:25 [local] Ogden time on September 18th," he notes that he "awoke at Terrace," and reached "Elko about 10 P.M."[22] The sleeping car ensured added comfort, but it also increased the likelihood that passengers would be unconscious for a part of the trip, which, in the desert of Utah and Nevada, might be counted as a blessing. Martineau was not alone in his tendency to sleep on the trip over Promontory and into the desert beyond. As British traveler George Alfred Lawrence put it, the Great Basin was "a country that tempts the traveler to take his uttermost pennyworth out of the sleeping cars."[23]

Southern Pacific Company (Pacific System) Employee Time Table No. 23, effective May 1, 1892, shows ten regularly scheduled trains—five each way—over the line. Of these, four were passenger trains (the eastbounds were called the "Atlantic Express," and those bound for San Francisco, the "Pacific Express"). The six remaining trains (three each way) were freight only. At that time, it took the typical passenger train about five hours to travel the 145.5 miles between Lucin to Ogden—an average speed of about twenty-nine miles per hour. However, an indication of the rugged topography in places along the line, notably in the vicinity of Promontory, passenger trains took about thirty-five to forty minutes to travel the 11.4 miles between Blue Creek and Promontory Summit, or an average speed of only about eighteen miles per hour.

Freight trains, of course, were much slower. The typical freight train in the timetable took about ten and one-half to eleven hours to travel from Ogden to Lucin, an average speed of about thirteen miles per hour. Here, again, the Promontory grade slowed things down to a crawl, or rather a trot. From Blue Creek to Promontory Summit, a freight train required one hour and five minutes, averaging about nine miles per hour. Freight trains in 1870 were about ten to fifteen cars long, but by the 1880s, thirty-car trains were common. They were called "freight drags," no doubt due to their heavy weight and slow speed.

It was the passenger trains, though, that drew the most attention. In this era of limited trains, the railroads rapidly improved their passenger cars. By the turn of the century, most new passenger cars featured closed vestibules. This innovation made passage from one car to another much safer and more comfortable. Passengers no longer had to pass from one car to another and risk falling off, or under, the train or be exposed to smoke, dust, and temperature extremes. The closed vestibules also tended to give the entire train a connected or integrated look, as there was no visible space between the cars.

The Southern Pacific car shown here (fig. 6–10) represents the epitome of passenger car design when through trains last ran through Promontory. The car is 76½ feet long over the sills and fully 80 feet long including platforms—about 25 feet longer than the passenger cars of 1869. It was 10 feet ⅜ inches wide—just a bit wider than the early cars—and it was a bit taller, too, at 15 feet 1 9/16 inches compared to about 12 feet. The biggest difference, though, was in weight. This car weighs 128,000 pounds (64 tons) and has gas and electric lighting. Compared to the old wood (or coal) stoves in the 1869 cars, this represented a vast improvement in comfort and safety.[24]

The car's window spacing reveals how different it is from a coach or sleeping car. It is, in fact, a dining car, which is an interesting story, as it pertains to the ultimate fate of Promontory's eating house. As railroad historian John White Jr. notes, railroads were slow to adopt dining cars. Small wonder: a dining car like *No. 10017* was the heaviest, most expensive, and most labor-intensive car on any late nineteenth-century

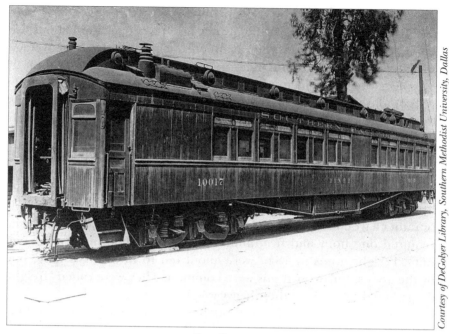

Courtesy of DeGolyer Library, Southern Methodist University, Dallas

FIG. 6–10

Southern Pacific dining car *No. 10017* represented the epitome of wooden car construction. Cars like it were seen on the express and limited trains over the range just after the turn of the century, signaling an end to eating houses like the one at Promontory.

passenger train. It was not until the 1890s that the Central Pacific (and Union Pacific) owned any dining cars—though the Pullman Company owned and operated some that, no doubt, traveled over Promontory Summit in the 1870s. However, dining cars were taken off trains and introduced—or rather, re-introduced—later. There was another reason for this: As White put it, "Central Pacific was known for the excellence of its eating houses, and it saw little reason to reverse this policy until the demands of faster schedules forced it to do so." That factor—speed— now demanded that passengers' time not be wasted in eating meals at places like Promontory when hours could be cut from the schedule by serving people on board a moving train.[25] Thus it was that the dining car became an important component of trains running over the Summit, especially those limited trains. Ironically, maintaining a rolling restaurant was never cost effective for the railroads, but rather a necessity to keep the train competitive by maintaining schedules faster than those of its competitors.

By the late nineteenth century, rail passengers expected speed, comfort, and even luxury. Consequently, passenger-car interiors became

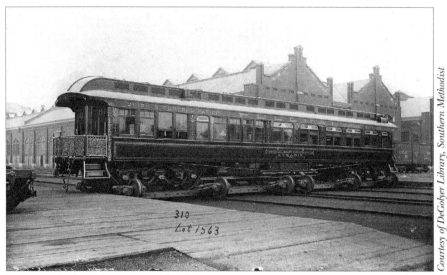

FIG. 6–11

Typically placed at the very end of a train, the beautiful Pullman observation-lounge car *Sybaris* featured a partially-closed vestibule (right end) and an ornate open platform (*left*) from which passengers could watch the receding track.

Courtesy of DeGolyer Library, Southern Methodist University, Dallas

increasingly elaborate by century's end. Inside and out, the Union-Central Pacific car *Sybaris* provides a case in point. Built in 1889, *Sybaris* represented the epitome of the builder's art. Its exterior (fig. 6–11) is a highly varnished dark green—that color would soon be known as "Pullman green" or a variant such as "coach green"— and most railroads would paint their own passenger equipment to match. *Sybaris* is ornately lettered and striped in gold. Its letter board features the bold name PULLMAN while in smaller letters, "Union & Central Pacific— Golden Gate Special," reveals its routing over Promontory Summit. An observation-lounge car, *Sybaris* featured an open observation platform surrounded by an ornate brass railing. Like its counterparts on other class-one railroads, *Sybaris* provided a glimpse of Victorian luxury with a partially open vestibule, wherein passengers walking from it to the other cars in the train passed through a narrow passage protected by doors on each side. Its plush interior (fig. 6–12) was a thing of beauty. Given Victorian tendencies toward lavish detailing, the inside of this car was, in a word, sumptuous. Decorated in exotic woods, its walls were papered with intricate designs. The windows of the clerestory roof, as well as those in the upper sashes of the side windows, were likely stained glass. Ornate gas lamps hung from the car's ceiling, their brass fixtures gleaming.

Fig. 6–12

Interior of the observation-lounge car *Sybaris* reveals the ornate
fixtures, carpeting, drapery, and trim of the Victorian period.

If the nineteenth century witnessed improvements in rail passenger travel, one of the most significant was the train schedule. In 1887, the Overland Flyer was inaugurated. This was a plush train, but an even plusher one was added for travel over Promontory Summit in December 1888 when the new Golden Gate Special was inaugurated. Billed as "the finest train in the world," a claim that just may have been true, the Golden Gate Special ran just once weekly. It was an extra-fare luxury train featuring ornate, highly decorated passenger cars. By the next year, however, Central Pacific decided to cancel the Golden Gate Special, replacing its service with an expanded version of the Overland Flyer, which was later named Overland Limited. In 1902, the "Overland," as it was popularly called, was upgraded. This included the distinction of being among the first trains to feature steel-framed cars and telephone service.[26] These improvements resulted from E. H. Harriman gaining control. That change in company leadership, though, ultimately signaled the beginning of the end for Promontory as Harriman was the outspoken advocate of another modernization project—the Lucin Cutoff across the Great Salt Lake.

Although much was said and written about passenger service on the Overland Route, freight had always been the most lucrative commodity on this line. The diversity of freight was impressive. In January 1876, for example, merchandise shipped through Ogden bound for Sacramento included, among many other items, "3 bundles copper bars, 45 sheets copper, 12 boxes candles, 2 barrels wire, 7 boxes hardware, 1 box jackscrews, 5 bars iron." Moreover, because the railroad cut the amount of time shipments took in crossing the Interior from months to days, cars in transit also included somewhat perishable merchandise, including "45 crates butter, 20 boxes and 20 kegs fish, 40 half boxes raisins, [and] 10 barrels currants."[27] Because the line over Promontory Summit now opened up eastern markets to California products, however, the flow of traffic continued to go eastward over Promontory Summit to middle-western and eastern states. As California markets built up during the period, eastern producers shipped their goods westward over Promontory.

By the 1880s, new boxcars were about 34 feet in length, though 28-foot cars were still being built. Most Central Pacific boxcars were of the standard closed-car configuration, but combination cars were still common. At this time, people at trackside along the mainline over Promontory Summit saw boxcars bearing the slogan "Southern Pacific Company Fast Freight Line" and "California Fast Freight Line" on their sides. These cars signified a joint effort between Southern Pacific and other railroads—notably Union Pacific, Chicago & Northwestern, Rock Island, and the Milwaukee Road—to expedite service between Chicago and San Francisco. These cars were most often found on fast freight trains.[28] The typical Central Pacific freight train would usually consist of cars of the home road, but a variety of cars from other railroads also went over the summit.

Essential to the shipment of perishables were ventilated cars and refrigerator cars. Although freight traffic was fairly heavy on this line, most of the cars were simply hauled through on trains bound for the east or west coasts. On occasion, however, a freight car would be set out at the siding or house track at one of the towns along the way. At this location, the car would be unloaded and its contents delivered to local customers. Where cars would be loaded directly from wagons, the term *team track* was used, presumably because teams of horses were used to drag the loads to and from cars that were set out on those siding tracks.

The line over Promontory Summit featured stations of numerous shapes and sizes. All appear to have been of wooden construction. Passengers could embark or disembark from those depots or stations, which represented the town's connection to the outside world. Promontory had its distinctive station and eating-house facility, but only the larger communities along the line, Terrace and Kelton, had substantial railroad stations. In keeping with its importance as a major railroad shop town, Terrace had the largest depot between Ogden and Nevada. It was an impressive two-story structure about 80 feet long. The depot at Kelton was one story and had a smaller footprint than Terrace's large station. One of the earliest structures on the line, Promontory Summit's depot was less conventional in appearance, housed in a multi-purpose building that was located on the south side of the tracks. In the smallest communities and water stops, such as Rozel and Matlin, railroad stations were simple affairs. Typically, a former boxcar would serve the purpose. In keeping with their freight-car origins, these were usually about 28 feet in length, about 8 feet wide, and were converted into stations by the addition of a smaller door and a few windows. Shorn of their trucks and wheels, such boxcar depots were usually placed parallel to the track on pilings to keep them level and free from rot. It is likely that these boxcar depots were made from some of the oldest cars on the railroad. Therefore, a lowly boxcar depot lasting into the 1920s or 1930s may have been upwards of sixty years old. Originally used in service hauling freight through Promontory on the mainline in the late 1860s and 1870s, these cars now served out their final years in non-revenue service, and in relative obscurity, along the dusty Promontory line.

Promontory Summit's railroad facilities kept pace with improvements in railroad technology. The station-plan maps of this section of the Central Pacific railroad are quite informative, for they help to

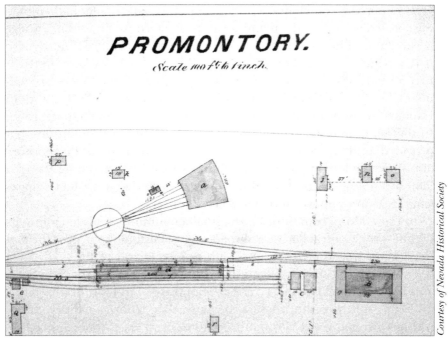

FIG. 6–13

Central Pacific station plan of Promontory in the mid-1880s reveals a turntable and three-stall roundhouse, coal dock (just below the turntable), railroad station and eating house (*lower right*), and numerous dwellings and section houses.

compensate for the lack of photographic coverage here in the 1880s and 1890s. By station plan, the railroad meant a relatively detailed map of all railroad track and buildings at a particular site. The Central Pacific Railroad's mid-1880s station plan for Promontory, as it was now called, depicts a 3–stall roundhouse served by a 54–foot-long turntable (fig. 6–13). If this plan is correct, that roundhouse would soon be either expanded into, or replaced by, a 5–stall brick structure. In recalling Promontory of the 1880s a half-century after the fact, numerous informants noted that several locomotives, perhaps six to eight, were based here in helper service. Promontory also had a hotel and telegraph office, which was 36 feet wide and stretched 78 feet along the right of way. Immediately to the west were two section houses (one 16 x 24 feet, the other 20 x 24 feet). Farther west, a coal shed 200 feet long sat adjacent to the mainline until it was removed in June of 1885. Still farther west, two car houses (one 14 feet square, the other 10 feet square) stood hard by the mainline. In these car houses, the track workers' handcars were stored.

The railroads' much-needed water supply, a tank 15 feet in diameter, was located alongside the mainline at the western passing siding, where a wooden tool house 8 x 10 feet square stood nearby. Promontory also had a "China section house" (where Chinese track workers lived). It had a road master's house, which was roughly 36 x 14 feet, an engineer's bunkhouse (which was finished on January 15, 1885), and an L-shaped section house, roughly 24 feet on a side, built October 1882. In that same month, a "new sand house" was built at Promontory that provided sand for locomotives. The official station plan for Promontory also showed a lodging house (for Simon Tooker) which was 24½ x 16½ feet, a dwelling house for John Henry that was 20 x 22 feet square, Charles Munn's house, and D. L. Davis' house.

In the 1880s, Promontory was a small community huddled along its lifeline—the Central Pacific Railroad. Most of its buildings were located on the north side of the tracks, with the exception of the coal dock, hotel, telegraph office, two section houses, and the houses of D. L. Davis and Jessie Brown. The pattern of development with most of the town's buildings north of the tracks appears to date from as early as 1869. Although small in size, Promontory now occupied a strategic position astride the mainline. According to the station plan, a new coal bin was constructed in June 1885. Railroad traffic continued with six passenger trains—three in each direction—passing through town daily.

At this time, Promontory had a somewhat unusual track layout. A long (1,944 feet) passing siding began east of the hotel and telegraph building, and ended at the coal dock—which was adjacent to the turntable and roundhouse. In a handwritten recollection about Promontory at around this time, Marion Woodward recalled that a snowplow was kept in the roundhouse, and that a sister, Katie, "had her finger cut off on the turntable, [and] I have a bad scar caused by stepping in a hot ash pit." Promontory could be a hazardous place for kids to explore, but it was a busy place for the railroad. Just west of the passing track that ended near the roundhouse, the mainline became a single track for several hundred feet until it reached another passing siding at the point where the track began to curve slightly to the south. At this point, another passing siding 1,765 feet long was located.[29] That single track at the top of the grade underscored Promontory's situation as a bottleneck on the line—though that appellation was normally given because the place lay at the top of a steep grade where gravity presented a perpetual obstacle to rail traffic.

Situated at the summit of a steep grade on a busy railroad, Promontory in 1900 was an important location. Reconstructing Promontory from the information in this chapter, we can envision its station alive with the click of the telegraph key and the air filled with coal smoke as a loco-motive or two simmered in the brick roundhouse with another taking a spin on the turntable. From time to time, double-headed trains chugged into town, their large Ten-Wheeler or Mastodon locomotives panting and emitting hisses of steam as if impatient to get underway again. A few passengers might be sauntering around the station platform as their trains took on coal at the spindly coaling station, or water from the dark red water tank. Though Promontory was not much of a town, it did have some services, including a school, hotel, and store. Lining the tracks, men who tended this section of the railroad occupied some railroad buildings. Though places like Promontory were the result of captains of industry, the railroad engineer was the real captain of the road—the conductor king—and the workforce of men required to keep trains running resembled a military engaged in noble but dangerous work. Responding to the conductor's watch, which was synchronized with the station's Regulator clock and the watch in the engineer's hand, the rail-road ran—if all went well—as smoothly as a well-oiled timepiece.

Even at this time, Promontory was also something of an archaeologi-cal site, as it possessed the ruins of activity dating from its early period. Consider, for example, vestiges of the early Chinese workers. By the early twentieth century, the "dugouts" had a number of Chinese work-ers occupied therein and are part of a widespread building tradition in the West, where lumber was scarce. In many cases, a dugout was exca-vated into a hillside so that the inside walls were simply what remained of the hillside; the excavated area served as living quarters (and some-times even commercial space). In other places, dugouts might be built into relatively flat ground. As Doris Larsen noted, the dugouts made by the Chinese laborers at Promontory ". . . were just big, big holes in the ground and then they'd usually have a canvas [roof] over the top." One entered such a dugout by descending steps or, as Ms. Larsen put it, an entry "[w]ith steps down" into it. She remembered these Chinese dug-outs at Promontory being located ". . . south of the railroad track and kind of west of the store."[30]

In addition to ruins here, other non-railroad buildings were note-worthy. Promontory was now an established service center for a large ranching area, so it had a school. W. A. Clay (born 1884) recalled that the schoolhouse was located "southeast of where the Golden Spike was driven." As opposed to many buildings in town, which "they didn't care whether they were painted or not," the schoolhouse was painted white. It had a belfry and faced south; one entered it by going up the steps.[31] Most old-timers remember the schoolhouse sitting rather high on a rock or stone foundation and recall that it was reached by front steps.

Fig. 6–14
A photograph purporting to be Promontory, ca. 1890, might indeed have been taken at the summit, as it shows a five-stall roundhouse, the existence of which was confirmed by archaelolologist Michael Polk.

Some also remember the school serving as a community church—in which case, the bell in the tower could have called students to school or townsfolk to worship—a distinct possibility in an age when there was less concern about maintaining the separation between church and state than there is today.

Unfortunately, Promontory was never the subject of a Sanborn fire atlas map, which would have shown in detail its buildings—by size and construction material. Nevertheless, Promontory's buildings can be reconstructed, so to speak, because they are mentioned so often in oral histories. Not all of the informants agree about specific details. For example, Marion Woodward also remembered the schoolhouse, but a bit differently than W. A. Clay did. She recalled "[a] little red school house where I and my sisters & brother attended school and in later years I taught school in the same building." Woodward recalled when the school burned down after a teacher dumped seemingly cold ashes next to it to fill a hole. This was, to Woodward's knowledge "the only fire in Promontory." After this fire, "[a] new school house was built a little larger than the first and also painted red."[32]

A photograph purporting to be Promontory taken about this time is of considerable interest and surrounded by some controversy (fig. 6–14). It shows a gently curving track running through a small settlement along the Central Pacific. Numerous features in the picture would appear to suggest that it was indeed taken in Promontory: It does, after all, have a 5–stall roundhouse, a number of buildings that could be

Promontory's as well as a general alignment of the track that seems to "fit." Even though the roundhouse appears a bit too close to the main track, the angle could be deceptive. Furthermore, although the track grading itself does not seem right (was the grading along the main track at Promontory ever so eroded?) It could be Promontory, as the curve appears to be the correct radius. But what about the background? Where are Promontory's characteristic hills to help us position the photograph? One explanation for their absence could be because the photo was taken on a hazy day. Overall, the photograph appears to be of Promontory, which is remarkable since there are so few images of any trains at the summit after the big day (May 10, 1869).

There is another caveat for researchers working with material bearing the name "Promontory" in archives. Documented plans and a specific name like Promontory does not mean a building was actually located at Promontory Summit. For example, a cold climate signal repair shed was reportedly erected at "Promontory" in December of 1903, and plans exist that illustrate it in detail. However, that date suggests a location on the new Lucin Cutoff rather than Promontory Summit, where railroad activity was actually winding down. In fact, the name "Promontory" is often used for Promontory Point; the Lucin Cutoff touched Promontory Point, not Promontory Summit, creating additional confusion.

Throughout this time when Promontory was on the mainline, the track was constantly upgraded to compensate for wear and tear and to accommodate heavier locomotives and rolling stock. Although most of the rails originally laid along this stretch were 50 pounds (per yard) Scranton, they were upgraded to 61½ pounds in 1893 and 76 pounds in 1898. The ties laid in 1883 were 6 x 8 inches x 8 feet Truckee Pine and were marked with a notch in one end (fig. 6–15) to differentiate them from the ordinary pine ties, because the railroad needed a way to determine when ties were laid because they had a limited service life. As the railroad's profile book noted, "All ties put in track during 1883 [were] marked by a chip taken off the upper east corner of tie, on right hand side of track going east." Conversely, "All ties put in track during 1884 [were] marked by a chip taken off the upper west corner of tie on right hand side of track going east."[33] Date nails were used beginning about a century ago, but it is worth noting that Central Pacific's tie-chipping technique worked well enough, though it became increasingly confusing with subsequent upgradings and replacements.

In 1886, the General Land Office published a map that revealed how problematical it was to represent Promontory (fig. 6–16). On the map, the town's site shows as two lines of buildings (square black rectangles), four on each side of the Central Pacific tracks. This map lacks the detail

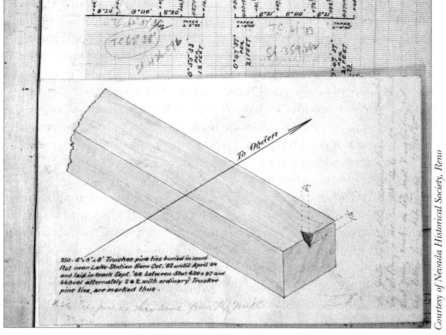

FIG. 6–15
Detail of date notching on railroad ties, from Central Pacific
Plans Book, Vol. 5, *Lucin to Ogden* 1883.

we would need to accurately reconstruct the town's layout at the time—
after all, Promontory consisted of two types of buildings, those on railroad land that served the railroad's needs and those off railroad land
that were owned by private individuals. Nevertheless, the map does suggest that the town was oriented to the railroad, and that was the case.
Perhaps the most revealing aspect of this map, though, is that it shows
the town to be situated in a fairly level site dotted with scrub-like vegetation, no doubt sagebrush.

In 1899, the United States Geological Survey published its *Map of
Utah*, which uses contour lines to depict the topography (fig. 6–17).
Contour lines are drawn at 1,000–foot intervals. As opposed to hachures,
they involve increased sophistication in showing features such as mountains, for they are based on surveys using advanced measurements that
accurately identify points above sea level. By connecting the dots, so
to speak, the mapmakers now depicted mountains according to equal
lines of elevation. The word *contour* is from the Italian *contorno* (to
round off or to turn around)—an apt term for lines that ultimately find
their way around mountains or hills. Note that the Promontory Range,
which is unnamed, rises about three thousand feet above the level of

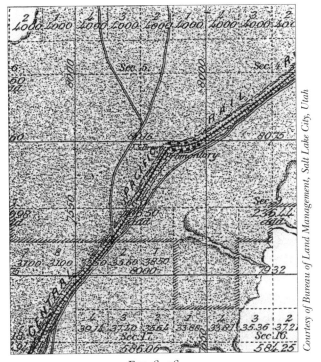

Courtesy of Bureau of Land Management, Salt Lake City, Utah

FIG. 6–16
Detail of Promontory and vicinity on the
General Land Office survey plat of T1ON
R 6W (1886) reveals a stylized depiction
of the town's layout.

the Great Salt Lake. This map is noteworthy because it also shows the railroad and selected station stops, depicting Willard, Corinne, and Kelton as the largest communities on the line. Had the railroad workers in Terrace studied this map, they would have seen a glimpse of the future. Developments in boardrooms as far away as San Francisco and New York were about to reshape the geography of this part of the West and the line over Promontory Summit.

This map shows Promontory at a critical moment in its history, its high point as a railroad-oriented town. By 1900, the United States Census information for the Promontory Precinct reveals five telegraphers, fifteen laborers, thirteen section hands, two section foremen, two engineers, three firemen, eighteen dry farmers, and four stock and cattle merchants. From these, we can see that serving the railroad was still a major occupation but that the rural economy was also becoming increasingly important. The majority (eighty-eight) had been born in Utah, but seven were from the British Isles, thirteen from Europe

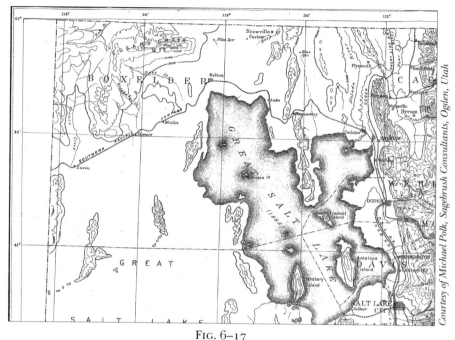

FIG. 6–17

A 1899 topographic map showing the line over Promontory reveals a tendency to simplify the topography, even on a scientific map, when contours are drawn far apart—for example, the thousand-feet elevation contours shown here.

(including nine Italians) and six from China. As in many places along the railroad, the Chinese and Italians were most likely to be railroad workers while the farmers and ranchers were from Utah, the British Isles, and northern Europe.[34]

From time to time, a miner or two had appeared on the census roles in the Promontory area. For example, in 1894, A. H. Snow reported, "Messrs. Toombs and Hickman, says the Brigham *Bugler*, have been quietly developing a valuable onyx quarry situated on Promontory [peninsula], twelve miles south of the station on the S.P. Ry. in Box Elder County by that name." The report went on to note that "[t]hey have taken out some beautiful samples, varying from very dark to white" and that "[f]ine specimens of marble are also found in the vicinity." It was further claimed that representatives of an eastern business found the material of such interest that they "organized a company called the Western Onyx and Marble Company, at Eau Clere [*sic*] Wis., where they will erect a new plant purposely to work the precious stones from this place." Mr. Toombs expected to hire "eight or nine men to work on the quarries . . ."; it was also noted that "[t]his find may mean thousands for our county."[35] Alas, like most extractive industries, this enterprise did not last very long.

Promontory's main claim to fame, and reason for existence, was the Central Pacific Railroad. Later in the nineteenth century, the name Central Pacific became increasingly rare as the Southern Pacific assumed control. At this time, *both* names, Central Pacific and Southern Pacific, were used more or less interchangeably to characterize the railroad here. The process by which the Central Pacific became part of the Southern Pacific was evolutionary and took place in several steps. The change was complex but was generally a result of limitations imposed on Central Pacific by early legislation. Railroad historian Ed Workman notes that "as a separate company, the Southern Pacific Railroad was not restricted by any terms of the Pacific Railway Act and so could incur indebtedness, construct, buy, [and] control other railroads and qualify for its own additional land grants." Workman also observed that the creation of the Southern Pacific was ". . . done almost entirely to protect the Central Pacific," but, by the last decade of the nineteenth century, ". . . the Central Pacific of the Big Four had changed from the operation of the SP lines to a creature of Huntington's SP."[36]

With Southern Pacific status came aggressive standardization of physical and plant equipment and rolling stock. Under the SP banner, the line over Promontory Summit became part of the "Ogden Route"—the popular nickname for the line from Ogden westward to California. This line was now, in fact, part of the Salt Lake Division of the Southern Pacific, which was the West's largest railroad. Southern Pacific's other two major routes (Sunset and Shasta) served as a reminder that this was a three-pronged system based out of San Francisco and reaching to Portland (Oregon), New Orleans, and Ogden. Southern Pacific's standardization was apparent in the large circular logo painted on boxcars of the various routes. All of these logos looked essentially the same, the main difference being the words (or name) for each route. A boxcar or refrigerator car, for example, would be easy to identify as an SP car from some distance—they were all pretty much of the same dimension. Only when one got closer could one tell if the car belonged to one of the various routes. These routes were larger than divisions. In fact, each of Southern Pacific's individual routes was larger than most railroads.

As Southern Pacific and Union Pacific inched closer to a possible merger under the genius of E. H. Harriman just after the turn of the century, both railroads—once fierce competitors—began to look increasingly like each other. With Harriman's takeover of SP in 1901, the vision of a huge railroad serving much of the West became a reality—until the United States Supreme Court stepped in to undo the vision. In the court's judgment, the Southern Pacific-Union Pacific alliance represented more of a monopoly than the operation of public corporations.

The buildup to the merger had repercussions across the West, including Promontory. In 1900, when the transcontinental Overland Route passenger trains still traveled over Promontory Summit, the railroads' publications usually commented on the signature event that had made this part of the line famous. The booklet *Souvenir and Views of the Union Pacific, "The Overland Route"* noted that, upon leaving Ogden westbound, "The train soon passes Promontory, which was originally intended to be the point of junction of the two lines forming the transcontinental route, namely the Union Pacific and Central Pacific railroads," but quickly added that "[l]ater, Ogden was decided upon as a compromise." More to the point, though, the booklet notes that "The traveler over the Union Pacific sees very few things aside from the physical features and general topography of the place to remind him of the scenes which occurred at Promontory, Utah, on Monday, May 10, 1869." In an interesting if subtle reminder that Harriman had brought both railroads under one banner—or rather, shield—the booklet used Promontory as metaphor: "It was here," the booklet observed "that the last rail was laid and the golden spike driven which united the Union and Central Pacific roads, and completed a work whose chief significance was that thereafter the Great East and the Great West were indeed but a single country, 'one and indivisible.'"[37] No strangers to metaphors, Harriman's advertising department knew how to equate the unification of the merger with the patriotism of a unified nation.

In 1901, a pamphlet titled *Sights and Scenes from the Car Windows of the World's Pictorial Line* was prepared to educate passengers about what they could see along "the Overland Route" of the Union Pacific. The pamphlet described Rozel as a place "where passenger trains only stop on signal." It also noted, "Between Rozel and Lake there is a signboard close to the track, showing the western limit of the ten miles of a track laid in one day." Of Kelton, it noted that there was a stage "daily except Sunday, at 6.00 [*sic*] A.M. for Bridge, 35 miles, $2; Conant, 48 miles $3 [and] Albion, 60 miles, $4." On Wednesdays and Saturdays, the stages left at 1:00 p.m. for Park Valley and other locations, while on those same days, stages left at 8 a.m. for Stone, Idaho. Of Promontory, the pamphlet featured a sepia tone photograph of the driving of the last spike, adding, "This place is celebrated for being the point where the connection between the Union Pacific and Central Pacific roads were made on the 10th of May, 1869."[38]

As travelers rode trains over Promontory Summit in the late nineteenth century, the place itself became more and more of a headache for the railroad. The fact was that Promontory's location was a function of the late 1860s, and the Southern Pacific Railroad now resurrected the Central Pacific idea of building a line straight across the Great Salt Lake from Ogden to Lucin. This line would be called the Lucin Cutoff after the name of that small community far to the west of Promontory. At the time the Lucin Cutoff was built, the line over Promontory Summit was experiencing a substantial amount of rail traffic annually—6 million tons worth, in fact—which amounted to ten trains daily, each consisting of thirty-three cars that carried 50 tons each. The 2.2 percent grade over Promontory Summit necessitated three locomotives per train to move each of these 1,650-ton trains. By this time, locomotives were becoming more powerful and larger. The Central Pacific now only rarely used 4–4–0 American-type locomotives. Larger engines, such as 4–6–0 (Ten-Wheeler) types on passenger trains, and 2–8–0 (Consolidation) and 4–8–0 (Mastodon) wheel arrangements for freight trains were common on Promontory by about 1900. In contrast to the 4–4–0 American-type locomotives that originally opened the line, the new locomotives now weighed twice as much—50 versus 25 tons. Their longer wheelbases necessitated longer frames, which reduced their ability to operate on tight curves.

As locomotives became larger, so did their tenders, which carried fuel and water. The latter was always an issue on the line over Promontory Summit. From around 1850 to about 1885, "tender size seemed pretty well frozen at 2,000 gallons [water] and 2 tons of fuel." Most of these tenders had two, four-wheel trucks (that is, a total of eight wheels), though "Southern Pacific . . . built a number of high capacity twelve-wheel tenders." The latter were a sign of things to come, because by the twentieth century, six-wheel trucks were common on large tenders. By the late 1880s, tenders often carried 3,000 gallons of water and 5 tons of coal. By the late 1890s, when Promontory Summit was still the scene of big-time railroading, tenders of large engineers like 2–8–0 Consolidations often carried 4,000 gallons of water.[39] These increasing sizes of motive power, in turn, necessitated strengthening bridges, and, in some cases, "straightening out" (decreasing the curvature of) trackage. These developments increasingly pointed a spotlight on Promontory Summit, which was branded as a "bottleneck" that restricted the traffic flow over the entire Overland Route due to its steep grades and tight curves. Ideally, those newer, larger locomotives could haul longer trains faster. That, however, assumed minimal grades and straight track—both of which were in short supply on the line over Promontory Summit.

The introduction of improved air brakes on trains made railroading over summits like Promontory easier and safer. The system consisted of a series of air cylinders that maintained air pressure while the train was in operation, but the release of pressure—say from an accidental uncoupling—would automatically apply the brakes. In addition to giving the engineer greater control of the train during normal operation, air brakes helped eliminate, or greatly reduce, the likelihood of a runaway if the train's cars became uncoupled. When this happened, air brakes went into the emergency braking position automatically. Air brakes also greatly reduced the number of men who had to ride the roofs of the cars to operate the hand brakes on each car.

In 1893, when the United States Railway Safety Appliance Act made air brakes mandatory, *Harper's Weekly* observed that railroading had lost some of its dangers and character since "the Heroic Age of the brakeman." A brakeman in action was a sight to behold. In keeping a train under control, ". . . he swung himself and twisted those brake wheels till it seemed as if they must come up by their iron roots." "Today's brakemen," the humorous and nostalgic article went on to observe, were not made of the same tough stuff as their predecessors. A modern brakeman, as *Harpers Weekly* put it, "could no more twist a brake till the chain creaked and the sparks shot out from the car wheels than he could go into Wall Street and twist a railroad 'til the stockholders creaked and the dollars shot from their pockets."[40] This made things sound a bit easier than they really were. Despite the use of air brakes, railroaders still had to be sure the brakes on all cars were charged before proceeding downhill. Nevertheless, Westinghouse safety air brakes were nothing short of revolutionary.

We know most about Promontory from railroad records and the recollections of rail travelers. However, one surprising source of information on the line over Promontory Summit just after the turn of the century came from an early day motorist. On his pioneer automobile jaunt across the United States in a brand-new 1903 Oldsmobile, John Hammond and his fellow driver Lester Whitman crossed from Nevada into Utah and entered what they called "The Great American Desert." Their trip across Nevada, of which they hoped they would "never set foot inside the cussed state again," had been tough going. Now across the state line, they hoped Utah would "treat man and machine more kindly than did Nevada's unbelievable desolation." This, however, was not to be. The first forty miles of road in Utah, which ran parallel to the Central Pacific line, "was a nightmare, full of sand and badly ditched by washouts from recent cloudbursts." Driving, or rather maneuvering, over this road required crossing gulches "varying from 3 to 10 feet deep with sheer sides looking like miniature Grand Canyons." Hammond and Whitman dug their way through some of these, plodding along at a snail's pace in the hot desert sun. Amazingly, they conducted this effort within sight of the transcontinental railroad line. As Hammond recalled, in what is probably the best description ever written of big-time railroad over the line across Promontory: "When the overland express trains thundered past us, their locomotive engineers would blow their shrill whistles and wave their arms in greeting. The passengers waved, too, and we felt comforted by all the momentary attention out on these remote, bleak barrens."[41]

By the time Hammond and Whitman arrived at "the small railroad town of Terrace," as they called it, they were bone tired. After dinner, they "began to forage for gasoline" but could not find a drop because the railroad used coal for both cooking and heating. However, they did learn that the Central Pacific railroad had "a supply of distillate at the engine house." When approaching the man in charge, who refused to sell them any because that was against company rules, they suggested he "look the other way"—which he did while they acquired several gallons. The Oldsmobile, which "would drink anything," ran fine on the distillate so they continued on toward Kelton. But before they reached Kelton, they found that they were low on water and tried to find some at a nearby ranch—to no avail. In the salt flats at the north edge of the Great Salt Lake, Hammond described passing "many bleached skulls and carcasses of cattle and sheep alongside our trail for several miles." Arriving at Kelton at 8 p.m., they found a small hotel after a long day in which they had driven seventy-five miles.

The next day, Hammond and Whitman drove across the salt flats, where they saw "teams of horses pulling scrapers, plowing up layers of salt to be shipped in vast quantities by rail to market." After "a most desolate ride," they arrived at Lake Station, where they saw the ruts left by wagons that had traveled along the "old emigrant's trail." Heading uphill under a hot sun, Hammond and Whitman arrived at Promontory at noon, where they visited the general store to pick up a five-gallon gasoline can they had ordered by telegram. However, when they asked about the gas can, the proprietor told them, "Well, it's gone." To their dismay, the storekeeper had recently sold it to "two fellows in a big auto" who needed it. Those fellows, as it turned out, were also trying to cross the continent in record time. The owner apologized for assuming the first motorists who arrived were the ones who had ordered the can. And why not? The storekeeper admitted, "That was the first auto I ever saw in these parts and I didn't figure there was another coming!"

Hammond says this incident occurred at Promontory, but then added that he and Whitman continued uphill for several miles more, "then downhill some," when he arrived at "Promontory on the

Painting by author

FIG. 6–18

As seen in this conjectural painting, the 1903 Oldsmobile has topped the Promontory Summit and is heading toward the Wasatch Mountains as a Southern Pacific passenger train ascends the grade on the east face of the Promontory Range.

Southern Pacific railroad." Their diary appears to confirm that there was a small spot in the road east of Lake called Promontory, but this was not the famed Promontory Summit.[42] Here, at Promontory Summit, they "stopped long enough to see that historic monument which marks the spot where, on May 10, 1869, just 34 years ago, those gold and silver spikes were driven." After dinner at Promontory, they continued east to the hill from which they could see "a large expanse of civilization in the distance." This greenery was located along the Bear River at Corinne where they encountered verdant green pastures the "like of which we had not seen for the last two weeks in the desert wilderness." They evidently did not photograph this scene, but it was described well enough to suggest that they were close to the railroad grade crossing. Perhaps they were lucky enough to witness a Southern Pacific train ascending the summit as illustrated in a painting done expressly for this book (fig. 6–18).

In recollecting this trip over Promontory Summit, Hammond added a note of irony: "Without the help of this railroad, the fledgling horseless carriages at the turn of the century might have been delayed for a few years in their attempts at successfully crossing the continent."[43] Could he have imagined that the automobile they had just driven through the Great Basin and over Promontory to New York in such discomfort would begin, within a generation, to threaten rail traffic itself? If he did imagine such a scenario, Hammond left no record of it. To him, in 1903, the railroad was king—even though Promontory was about to be dethroned in favor of the new railroad route that ran, much like freeways would later run, on a relatively level route directly across the Great Salt Lake.

Chapter 7

A Regional Branchline
(1904–1942)

After the Lucin Cutoff diverted almost all of the railroad traffic away from the original line over the summit, telegrapher Earl Harmon recalled that, "There wasn't much said about Promontory in them days." This statement beautifully captures how Promontory declined in the early decades of the twentieth century. Born in 1901, Harmon witnessed the era when Promontory found itself off the mainline and became just another place on a branchline. The year 1904 was crucial for the line over Promontory Summit. In that year, the Southern Pacific formally opened its new, more direct line across a portion of the Great Salt Lake from Umbria to Ogden. Umbria was located just west of the small station stop called Lucin, which was soon called Lucin Junction after the SP mainline diverged here to run straight across the Great Salt Lake on a trestle. The railroad had planned this new routing for some time. In 1901, with traffic volumes increasing and Harriman in control, the line over Promontory Summit was slated to be superseded using the soundest of principles that any railroad engineer could appreciate: the best way for a railroad to run between two points is not only in a straight line, but over a line that is gradeless or essentially flat. Anyone looking at a map could see that the line over Promontory Summit—with its grades and curves— was less than ideal. It was, in effect, a place where traffic slowed as the railroad fought gravity and friction.

Of course, building a railroad line across the Great Salt Lake presented obstacles of its own as deep pilings were necessary. It is one thing to build a perfectly straight and level railroad on flat land, but quite another to construct a veritable bridge or causeway for thirty miles. Although building a line across lake and salt flats would not be easy, that is exactly what the railroad did. One might ask, why replace an already existing line, regardless of how twisting or hilly, with a straight one at considerable cost? The answer was the connection of time to money. The new railroad cutoff would save hours between Lucin/Umbria Junction and Ogden—reducing the time from ten hours to about two. That was important because the Western Pacific's proposed line across the Great Basin, conceived around 1900 and completed in 1909, would run in a fairly straight line along the southern edge of the Great Salt Lake west of Salt Lake City. The developing plans of that newcomer thus presented a clear challenge to Southern Pacific's ability to move traffic competitively across the Great Basin to California. A straight and level line would also greatly reduce Southern Pacific's long-term operating costs. In addition to paying less in wages due to the reduced time needed to haul passengers and freight via the original line, the railroad would spend far less on fuel. Then, too, the railroad would eliminate the need for helper engines and crews. In other words, the high cost of building the new cutoff would be amortized in a decade or two by reducing labor and equipment costs. What made the Lucin Cutoff irresistible, though, was the impact it would have on both the Southern Pacific and the Union Pacific. Harriman did not conceive the cutoff as a way of helping only Southern Pacific, but rather to ensure that his new, consolidated (Union) Pacific system would be without peer in moving traffic to the Pacific Coast from the Middle West.

A booklet titled *Going to Sea by Rail—Great Salt Lake Cut-off Primer* was part of the "Union Pacific-Southern Pacific Series" that helped clarify Harriman's goals. In answering, "Why was the Great Salt Lake Cutoff built?" the booklet stated, succinctly: "To save the greater grades and curves and distance of the old line." The booklet reminded readers that "the old line runs around the north end of Great Salt Lake over Promontory mountain" and then added some striking statistics. It noted that the curves on the old line "would turn a train around eleven times" and that the grades required enough power to "lift an average man eight thousand, five hundred miles." As if this were not astronomical or mind boggling enough, the booklet stated that the power (that is, energy) saved by the new line could "carry a man four hundred times between New York and San Francisco." A map on the booklet's back cover substantiated the claim made earlier that, "The Cut-Off is as straight as the crow flies." This map was reproduced in several versions of the booklet, including the updated *Great Salt Lake Cut-off 30 Miles from Shore to Shore* (fig. 7–1). All versions achieved the same

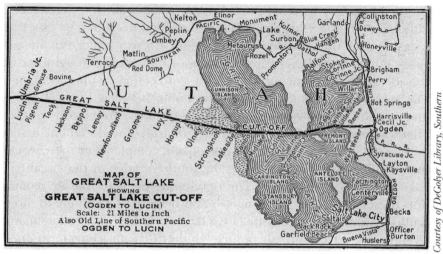

FIG. 7–1
Map of Great Salt Lake showing the "Great Salt Lake Cut-Off,"
also known as the "Lucin Cut-Off," supported the Southern Pacific
Railroad's claims that it saved considerable mileage.

purpose. By showing the contorted route of the original line, the map
confirmed Harriman's assessment. Tellingly, the route over Promontory
Summit was now shown as a thin line while the Lucin Cut-Off appears
in the bold, thick style reserved for mainlines. Even though it signals
the decline of the line over Promontory Summit, that map is valuable
for the historian: In its effort to make the old line seem congested and
complicated, it shows the major stations and even depicts some of the
streams along the old route over Promontory.[1]

Southern Pacific made frequent use of a comparative profile diagram (fig. 7–2) that showed just how much troublesome topography
the Lucin Cutoff had eliminated. For our purposes, though, the diagram reveals the hilly/mountainous nature of the Promontory Summit
line, where the tracks essentially ran across the grain of a portion of the
mountainous basin and range province. Note that the run from Kelton
to Ombey was the counterpart to the steep section from Blue Creek to
Promontory. Those were the highest portions of the line—the two lowest portions being the areas around Corinne and Monument/Kelton.

After the completion of the Lucin Cutoff on November 26, 1903,
some traffic was diverted off the Promontory line. On December 4,
1903, the Ogden newspapers reported that "the S.P. Pay car will reach
Ogden for the first time over the Cutoff, this evening."[2] By early 1904,
the townsfolk in Terrace no doubt realized their community's heyday
was nearing an end. Nevertheless, the old line could serve in the event

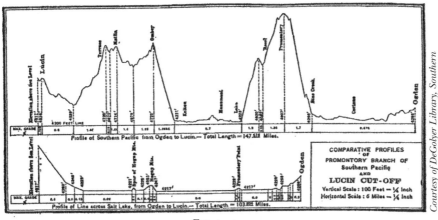

FIG. 7–2

Comparative profiles of the line over Promontory Summit (upper portion of illustration) with the Lucin Cut-Off (lower) graphically justified construction of the new line to stockholders and customers.

of problems on the new line. As if to remind everyone involved that railroading is hazardous business and that two options are better than one, a massive explosion shook Terrace with earthquake-like force on February 14, 1904. The source of that blast was a head-on train wreck on the recently completed Lucin Cutoff at Jackson, thirteen miles southeast of Terrace, but it seemed much closer. The wreck and subsequent explosion killed twenty-nine railroad laborers, who were living in outfit cars parked on a siding nearby.[3] At times like this, when man-made or natural catastrophe strikes the mainline, a railroad seeks a temporary alternate route. Still intact and serviceable, the line over Promontory Summit would serve as a bypass from time to time. Doris Larsen recalled that sometimes the Lucin line (i.e., Lucin Cutoff) "sank" and required repair. "That is when the line over Promontory again experienced 'long trains' that were quite a thing to see."[4] Nevertheless, by the fall of 1904, the cutoff was handling virtually all of the mainline traffic that had run through Promontory. This change occurred in two increments. After the cutoff's completion in late 1903, several months passed before regularly scheduled trains started using it in the spring of 1904. According to railroad historian David Myrick, "freight trains began crossing the lake on March 8th, while passenger trains took the old route via Promontory and Kelton (forty-three miles longer) until September eighteenth of that year."[5]

One of the truly stunning maps showing the line over Promontory Summit was actually prepared to show the Lucin Cutoff. Called *Line Across Great Salt Lake—Lucin to Ogden,* (fig. 7–3) the map was traced in

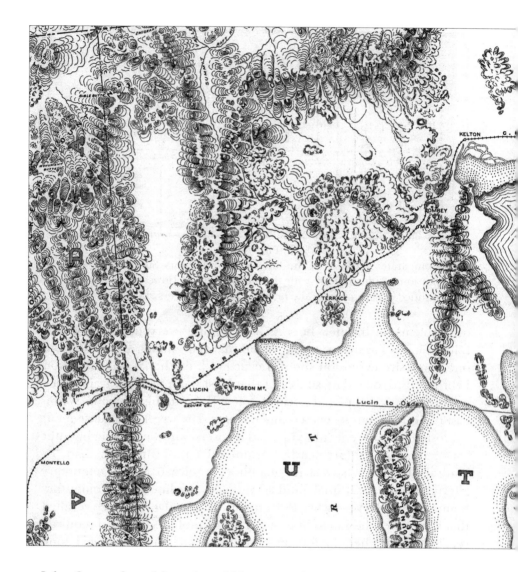

July of 1913 from blueprints. Using a combination of techniques that suggest both hachuring and contours, it shows both the Promontory Mountains and Hogup Mountains as obstacles around which the railroad weaves. It also shows the marshy areas adjacent to Great Salt Lake. Interestingly, this map, which was prepared ten years after the construction of the Lucin Cutoff, only shows the railroad crossing the lake as a thin black line, while all other railroads, including the line over Promontory [Summit], are shown using the bold line with crosstie pattern that was now a standard symbol for a railroad.[6]

A map featured in lantern-slide presentations in the period 1910–1920 shows the Promontory Summit branch of the Southern Pacific running

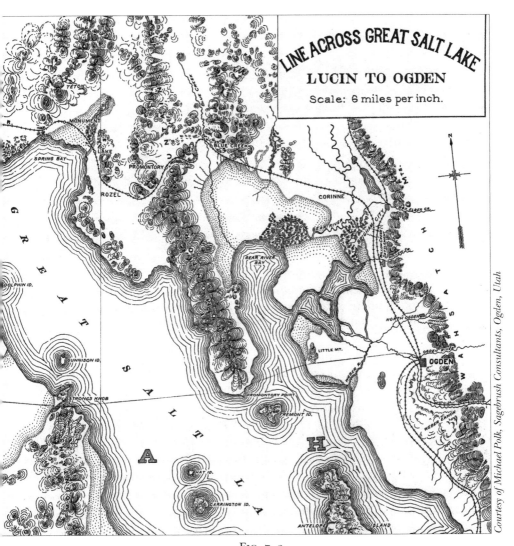

FIG. 7–3

Drawn from railroad blueprints in 1913, this map showing the *Line Across Great Salt Lake* oddly uses a lighter line for the cutoff than the darker crosstie-hatched old line over Promontory Summit.

around the north end of the Great Salt Lake, while the Lucin Cutoff stands out as an arrow-straight line across the lake. Interestingly, slides showing the stages of construction of the Lucin Cutoff drew considerable attention. The feat was, after all, Herculean. The sight of the trestle taking shape as steamboats and pile drivers laid trails of smoke across the lake awed audiences. Ironically, one of the vessels involved in putting nails in the Promontory Summit line's coffin here was called *Promontory*![7]

Courtesy of Utah State Historical Society Archives, Salt Lake City, Photo No. 763

FIG. 7–4
Straight as an arrow and level as a billiard table. In 1906, Southern Pacific's *Fast Mail* train is seen at Midlake on the Lucin Cutoff, where a passing siding was located. Two years earlier, this train would have crossed over Promontory Summit.

Without doubt, the building of the Lucin Cutoff was one of the most publicized events in railroad construction history. A stunning series of photographs in the California State Railroad Museum in Sacramento documents the construction, as does David Peterson's book *Tale of the Lucin: A Boat, A Railroad and the Great Salt Lake* (2001).[8] After its completion, too, the Lucin Cutoff was undoubtedly the most photographed portion of any railroad in the entire Intermountain West. Portraits of trains running over the cutoff (fig. 7–4) made great railroad publicity. The completion of the cutoff also coincided with the rise of picture postcards in about 1904. Tellingly, while no postcards of trains running over Promontory Summit during its glory days (ca. 1900) have been located, postcards of trains on the cutoff became common after about 1908. Simply put, the cutoff now served the American technological imagination in ways that the construction of the line over Promontory Summit had two generations earlier.

The route change left Promontory off the mainline, but local traffic still required telegraphers like Earl Harmon. Interestingly, Harmon came from a long line of railroad telegraphers. In fact, he remembered that his uncle Frank Davis was "one of the old-time telegraphers, and he was the first telegrapher they used out here at Promontory." Harmon believed that his uncle ". . . was the man that sent the message that it was finished" in 1869. That claim, if true, would mean that Frank Davis sent that message telegraphed around the world on May 10, 1869. However, most sources, including David Bain, claim that Central Pacific's Louis Jacobs and Union Pacific's Watson N. Shilling were the operators, with the latter credited with signaling, "done."[9] Despite Harmon's memories, Promontory declined during Harmon's lifetime: Of course, 1869 would be a difficult act to follow, though the railroad continued its operations there first as the mainline (1869–1904) and thereafter as a branchline. Harmon recalled, on his first visit there that ". . . it was just sagebrush. There was nothing there."[10]

Promontory Summit's fall from glory occurred quickly as the original railroad line was replaced by the Lucin Cutoff. Comparing activity at Promontory in the 1910s with that of, say 1875, reveals a story as different as night and day. That is because Promontory was now no longer where the urgent express trains roared through along the Overland Route from distant city to distant city, their smoke clearing long enough for another plume to appear on the horizon and the telegraph key in the depot rarely silent. But after 1904, Promontory found itself relegated to a secondary line much like a branch line. In fact, it began to be called the Promontory Branch at about this time. Now the rails might bask in the sun for many hours, even a full day, before the next train appeared. The telegraph key remained mostly silent except for a crescendo of activity close to train time. It was precisely during this period that Promontory began to fall off the map. Its major claim to fame was an event in 1869 that, however momentous at the time, now became an increasingly distant memory.

Even though Promontory was no longer on the mainline, excitement could and did occur from time to time. Promontory's folklore includes reference to a train robbery that is said to have occurred in the early twentieth century, probably 1908. According to one source, it supposedly took place when a local passenger train, evidently eastbound, was waylaid "over on the hill coming up where it is the steepest place" and the train was easiest to stop due to its slow speed. The robbers were apprehended "over at Monument, and they didn't have the money with them." They had hidden it "somewhere between there and over, well maybe it's Kelton, somewhere over on the other side of . . . [the west side of the Promontory Mountains]." Many locals, including Merlin Larsen's father, looked for the lost treasure.[11] This story is more-or-less confirmed by Isaac W. Finn, who related a variation of it. Finn was present when, after a passenger train finished taking on water at the Rozel water tank, "somebody started yelling 'Holdup!'" Finn wondered what was happening but quickly realized that the person meant train robbery. While the train was stopped, three robbers evidently held up the express car. This was apparently not a wise idea as a sheriff was also present in Rozel to supervise the loading of cattle into stockcars nearby to "see that there was no strays amongst 'em." Upon hearing that cry about the "holdup," the sheriff quickly yelled, "[C]ome on boys" and an informal posse set out on the trail of the train robbers. After some careful tracking, the posse neared the train robbers, who started firing at their pursuers. All three robbers were reportedly killed in the resulting shootout near Monument, but the money was nowhere to be found. As one might imagine, this piqued local curiosity and interest. Looking for the booty became a "weekend vacation for people," as Mr. Finn recalled, "I don't know how long people would go out there. Some of them would go out there and stay overnight." Although searching for that treasure became a major pastime, participants only got exercise and fresh air. Finn concluded: ". . . to this day, nobody's found that money."[12]

After the driving of the golden spike in 1869, the countryside near the railroad began to change. In the Promontory area, for example, ranching soon became an important activity. Local historian Bernice Anderson noted that the country "was covered with bunch grass" and considered fair enough grazing lands to encourage the creation of the Golden Spike Land and Cattle Company, which brought in about 75,000 head of cattle in the 1880s.[13] The Crocker family owned the ranch, but Captain Bufford ran it. Most of the grazing lands were to the north of Promontory, and on this sprawling spread there once stood a large ranch house. Called the "Big House," it stood about 1½ miles north and a bit west of Promontory Summit. That huge house, standing in a treeless, grass- and sagebrush-covered landscape, symbolized the concentration of wealth, but confirmed how broadly scattered the resources were that would require others to make a living here.

In some ways, dependence on ranching was also a factor in the area's declining health. Although much of the area looked unpromising, it was in fact rangeland. Those grasses in the area, especially in the middle elevations away from the lake, were the basis of the ranching economy. An old-timer named Pappy Clay, who called himself the "Sage of the Sagebrush," confirms that Promontory became a ranching area by the 1880s. Wild mustangs ranged here, but ranching changed the area's ecology. The house that Crocker built became the center of ranching operations. Called the "Big Money House" by locals, presumably after the Big Money Springs where the house was located, it became the headquarters of the Promontory Land and Livestock Company's ranching operations in the area. Given the "invigorating desert mountain air" of its setting, it served the "Pacific Coast elite" around 1895. The hard winters of 1888 and 1889, however, decimated the "thousands of

Hereford cattle" that the Promontory Land and Livestock Company had brought here. Such large numbers of livestock effectively overgrazed the vegetation.[14]

The area was also home to many smaller ranching enterprises, and the construction of the Lucin Cutoff benefited them in an odd way. As John Whitaker (born 1911) recalled, he and his father had used a lot of old timber for construction. Its source? "Dad and I went down on the lakeshore and picked up [old lumber] which had drifted off from the cutoff, you know, planks and poles, and we'd haul them up with horses." This lumber was used for buildings in the area, including a barn.[15] Those buildings represented the livelihood of people attempting to make a living off the land. Among these were dozens of ranch families raising stock, who were naturally dependent on the railroad for transportation.

By the early twentieth century, ranchers and farmers in the Promontory area noted an increase in the rabbit population—perhaps in part because gardens were becoming more common. Rabbit Drives were conducted to rid the area of these pests. These, Lorna Larsen Phillips recalled, involved men, boys, and some girls, who would gather where rabbits were numerous, usually "where there was a large cover of sage brush, or rabbit brush, which was different from sage brush; and they'd surround a large area and drive the rabbits, making noise and yelling and hollering, and into a corral that had wings . . . so that the rabbits would be gathered into the corral . . . ." Mrs. Phillips remembered hating the sound of the rabbits being clubbed to death, but these drives resulted in "rabbit meat [that] was used for food."[16] In this endeavor, the new settlers may have been re-enacting a much older Native American ritual: With the possible exception of the materials that the "corral" wings were constructed of, this is a close continuation of the rabbit drives Shoshones had held in this region. John Bidwell noted seeing the wings of such a Shoshone rabbit-drive corral in 1841 north of the Great Salt Lake. Now, however, the goal was eradication of the rabbits as pests that compromised agriculture. To meet hunters' demands and perhaps further encourage agricultural prospects here, the Southern Pacific at times ran a local train for the convenience of hunters in pursuit of wild fowl. The special train would stop at promising locations, drop off groups of the hunters, and then return later at an agreed-upon time. The railroad's operations also dovetailed with the seasonal demands of local enterprises. The line over Promontory Summit featured a number of stock pens where animals were placed aboard stock cars. Cattle were loaded at Kelton and a number of other stations adjacent to the ranches.

Courtesy of the National Park Service

FIG. 7–5
This view of Promontory, ca 1930, shows the Golden Spike
Monument and the few remaining buildings.

Normally, railroad historians rely in part on photographs to help decipher the story. However, railroad operations over the Promontory line
in the period 1880–1942 were not well documented, especially during
the early twentieth century. One wonders why railroad-oriented photographers avoided the Promontory line at this time, especially since
a stone monument, reportedly erected here in 1916 by Wilson Wright
of the Southern Pacific Company, became a landmark to travelers and
those exploring the backcountry (fig. 7–5). That obelisk-shaped monument contained a rectangular metal plate commemorating the driving
of the last spike. The selection of an obelisk shape for the marker built
on the century-old American tendency to copy objects from ancient
history, in this case the venerable Egyptians. As early as the War of
1812, Americans searching for the best design to commemorate events
debated which design would best serve that purpose. A statue of an individual might work, but that personalizes the event rather than making
it represent a broader, national effort. As the ancient Egyptians discovered several thousand years earlier, the obelisk was both ethereal and
simple. To the Americans, the obelisk's abstract quality made it perfect
for commemorating anything of importance. As cultural historian Neil
Harris observed, this stunning simplicity of the obelisk, coupled with
its association with permanence, made obelisks the logical choice for
monuments nationwide.[17]

Up until this time, a simple wooden sign had marked the location
where the rails had been joined. That sign (fig. 7–6) served well enough

Courtesy of the National Park Service

FIG. 7–6
The sign commemorating the driving of the
last spike at Promontory in a scene dating
from about 1930.

for decades, but it had a flimsy, temporary quality that seemed inappropriate for permanent commemoration. And yet, because the sign was easier to read and something was also needed on the other side of the track to inform passengers seated on the side opposite the obelisk, this wooden sign persisted into the 1930s. Interestingly, the concrete marker was erected at just the time that the automobile was revolutionizing transportation. That concrete pyramid, then, symbolizes the railroad—at least in American terms—as an ancient work worthy of permanent recognition.

Many people assumed that the line over Promontory Summit was abandoned immediately after the Lucin Cutoff was built, or that trains stopped running long before the rails were taken up in 1942. Even today, many old-timers believe(d) that trains only ran as far west as Promontory, the remainder of the line to Lucin being torn up at an early date. These impressions, though not correct, likely began or persisted because the line was now so marginal that relatively few people visited, much less used it. One might assume that Southern Pacific would simply abandon the line, but as we will see, its potential as a dry farming wheat bonanza line kept that from happening. Although the main line now bypassed the area around Promontory, it continued to witness considerable investment and interest by developers. And by keeping the line intact, Southern Pacific had an ace in the hole, so to speak. This old line could be—and was—used on occasion when the new cutoff needed extensive repairs. Every so often, when a wreck or maintenance on the new line dictated, Southern Pacific ran its mainline trains over the summit. The railroad ultimately learned, at great expense, that lake levels could rise in wet periods, necessitating new construction that, in effect, raised the level of trestles and causeways across the lake.

The Lucin Cutoff not only affected traffic volume over Promontory Summit, but also resulted in operating changes at the east end of the line. After the cutoff was completed, travelers found themselves taking a new route that paralleled the old line from Corinne to Ogden. Had they looked carefully at the old trackage, they would have noticed it deteriorating in the period from 1904 to World War I. By January 12, 1918, a portion of the original line at Corinne had fallen into such disrepair that, as an Interstate Commerce Commission evaluation report put it, "from MP 803.23 to the end of the valuation section . . . . This line is not in use; [and] a number of the bridges are burned or washed out."[18] This deterioration had actually begun more than a decade earlier. When the Lucin Cutoff rerouted traffic in 1904, Southern Pacific essentially abandoned that portion of its line from Corinne Junction to Cecil Junction, near Ogden. Since 1904, then, the Southern Pacific had shared trackage rights with the Oregon Short Line (Union Pacific) between these two communities. There is a note of irony here as that portion of the line that the Central Pacific had fought so hard to claim in 1869—namely, the trackage in the rich Utah farmlands along the Wasatch Front— was now in the hands of a former competitor that had become a partner under the Union Pacific shield. That, of course, would change on December 2, 1912, when a "momentous decision" by the United States Supreme Court declared the Harriman scheme monopolistic.[19]

That decision traumatized both railroads, but they still inherited many cost savings from the Harriman era and its standardization. This indirectly affected the line over Promontory Summit in several ways and was timed perfectly. The development of dry farmed wheat lands in the area adjacent to Promontory coincided with the standardization and modernization of boxcars perfectly suited to grain traffic. These boxcars were hallmarks of the Harriman period. First ordered in 1902, there were soon two thousand of them in operation on the Southern Pacific and Union Pacific lines by the fall of 1904. Southern Pacific received about 700 cars and Union Pacific about 1,300 cars. These cars had pressed steel underframes, and thus no longer used the truss rod system. They were 40 feet long, 50–ton capacity cars with 2,730 cubic feet of interior space. They appear in photographs of the Promontory line during the period when wheat was loaded into boxcars at numerous stations, including Promontory, Lampo and Rozel. A photo of one being loaded from a wagon, ca. 1920, captures a typical vignette along the Promontory line (fig. 7–7). Through the teens and twenties, these cars were joined by post-Harriman cars of various types.

Courtesy of Special Collections, Utah State University, Logan

Fig. 7–7
A Harriman-style boxcar being loaded at an unknown location along the Promontory line reflects the improving agricultural picture here in about 1920.

In a sense, the line over Promontory Summit became a technological relic in the twentieth century. With a new line now bypassing the original, Southern Pacific elected to hold off making improvements that would have been required on a mainline. In addition to resulting in lower speed limits and shorter trains over Promontory than those now rushing across the Lucin Cutoff, this had the effect of limiting the kind of equipment that could operate over the old line. This became apparent as Southern Pacific purchased or built new locomotives such as 4–8–2s, 2–10–2s and articulated engines like the huge 2–8–8–2s and 4–8–8–2s. As locomotives and railroad cars became longer and larger, the curves and grades on the line over Promontory Summit became increasingly problematical. The branch was limited to the smaller locomotives such as 4–6–0s and 2–8–0s. The fact that locomotives with no trailing trucks tended to derail when running backward at brisk speeds, especially on curving trackage, may help explain the persistence of turntables at certain locations on the Promontory line. The premise here is that it is easier to turn a locomotive around using a turntable than pull one out of a ditch using a wrecking crane. At any rate, the use of smaller locomotives on the Promontory Branch certainly helped this line retain a 1900–era quality for decades into the twentieth century. Similarly, newer passenger cars of steel construction, which became common after 1910, apparently never ran over Promontory with any frequency. For the remainder of its life, the branch over Promontory Summit witnessed traditional steam-powered short trains. The few available photos reveal that mixed trains with wooden passenger cars were common up until the end of service.

Passenger service on the Promontory Branch appears to have relied on the Common Standard wood sixty-foot coaches and chair cars. These

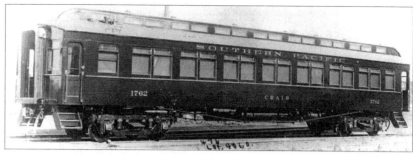

ACF Photo, G. E. Votava Collection

FIG. 7–8
Built in 1906, this Southern Pacific wooden chair car *No. 1762* is typical of the "coaches" that carried passengers on the Promontory line during its declining years.

dated from May 1905, which almost perfectly coincided with the beginning of the line's branchline status. These cars featured wood truss weight-bearing construction on their sides with metal truss rods. Four-wheel trucks were common, and the cars had closed vestibules. Each car had a toilet at opposite ends of the car—one for men and one for women. Clerestory roofs and side windows with transoms above them were a standard feature. Chair cars usually sat fifty-eight passengers and coaches seventy passengers.[20] Day coaches had more seats and less legroom but were otherwise very similar in appearance to chair cars. The common paint scheme at this time was dark green with gold lettering, which was much more somber than the brightly colored (often yellow) and elaborately lettered cars of the period 1870–1885 (fig. 7–8). In addition to these wooden, early twentieth-century cars, it is possible that steel, arched roof coaches of the Harriman lines traversed the Promontory Branch on mixed trains from time to time, but no photographs confirming this have so far been located.

The Promontory line became something of a museum, where small, turn-of-the-century-type locomotives hauled their consists over an increasingly archaic—but still operating—physical plant. There was simply no place for modern steam power here. This, coupled with the relatively light population density and marginal economic activity, ensured a slower pace of railroad operations. There is considerable debate about how often trains ran over the Promontory line on a regular basis after 1904. One resident of the area, Mayme Wells Lower, had good reason to remember the train schedule to and from Promontory: She worked for the U.S. Post Office (Postal Service) and delivered the mail three times a week for "a little over thirty years." She delivered mail to the Promontory Station "before they took the rails out . . . ."[21]

Lower recalled that the train ". . . would go from Ogden out to Lucin and back" on a regular schedule "[t]hree times a week. The same as the mail goes."[22]

Lower's statement reveals that the railroad still had a contract to deliver mail to this remote area. That contract, and the arrival of prospective wheat farmers, gave the railroad some cause for guarded optimism. Certainly, passenger traffic was light enough to justify downgrading service. Operations on the Promontory line now consisted of mixed trains carrying both passengers and freight cars in the same consist. Lower recalled that the mixed train hauled "[m]ail and some freight, but it would haul the grain when they'd start harvesting up top"—that is, on the broad slopes at the base of the Promontory Mountains where wheat farming was developing. Lower did not recall any storage bins for the grain at Promontory, adding that "[i]t just came straight down from the harvest to the train" where "they'd shovel it off into the car[s], [which were] grain cars, and they had what you'd call grain doors." Lower was referring to the openings on the sides of boxcars, through which grain was loaded as the larger doors were kept shut and sealed so the grain would not spill out. She also recalled the cattle corrals at Promontory, which were located "behind the house, behind the store," on the east side of the railroad tracks.[23] Those helped the railroad generate additional traffic as ranchers brought cattle for shipment to market.

An interview conducted in 1974 with Taro Yagi confirmed that the westbound train ran across Promontory Summit three times a week. Most of the grain was loaded at Blue Creek and Lampo. When the mixed train running west had a heavy load of eight or ten cars, those freight cars would be spotted (temporarily left) at Kelton. Yagi then described how the crews battled to move heavy traffic westward from Kelton. As many as three extra locomotives were required to pull the wheat trains "over what we'd call Red Dome hill" which, Yagi speculated, "must be the steepest, the highest in [the] route going to Lucin . . . ." To move this westbound traffic, Yari noted:

> they'd have these extra engines and they'd load up all these cars, I mean put on all these cars at Kelton and go on out and each engine pulling those hills would have probably maximum power with maybe eight or ten cars so they would double up and then there's a number of times when they would take these cars and leave them at the bottom of this hill before they got to Watercress and they'd leave it there and they'd pull what they could and then the three engines or the three extra engines would come back and pull the rest of them up and over.[24]

Taro Yagi's almost breathless run-on sentence reveals how much effort and skill it took to move traffic over this line and how exciting this process was to those witnessing it. Of course, at this time, the line over Promontory Summit was only a secondary branch line, but Yagi's statement also reveals why this line was such a bottleneck to Southern Pacific's transcontinental traffic until it was bypassed in 1904.

Leona Yates Anderson recalled riding on the passenger cars to Promontory. As she put it, "they had lovely passenger cars all plush, red plush." By this, she meant the double seats in the passenger cars were red—"[s]ort of a wine-velvet effect." When asked if the interior was really plush, Anderson replied, "Oh, yes. It was plush. It was sort of dirty." She also recalled the car's interior lighting, and the "stove in it with a fire and windows that slid up and down." From this description, Anderson appears to be describing the older wooden coaches or chair cars so common on branch lines during the 1910s and 1920s. She did, however, "remember when the main line train went through and they had sleepers and everything," adding "[w]hen I was a kid, we went down there and rode on them and yes, they had sleepers."[25]

Mayme Wells Lower recalled riding the train from Corinne to Promontory on a number of occasions in about 1918 or 1919 when she was a child of about five or six. The trip took about three or four hours and "would get there about 12 o'clock [noon]." Although she did not ride the train after that time, she recalled seeing it operate. When asked by the interviewers if the train needed a helper engine to get up the hill, she replied: "Sometimes, up over this side, for grasshoppers, I understand." This likely refers to the possibility that large numbers of grasshoppers or locusts could cause the locomotive to lose traction as it crushed the insects beneath the wheels, slickening the rails. She also noted that "if you had an outfit, uh, a train that was bringing some cars in for wheat, why, they'd have to have a helper [engine]."[26] Taro Yagi recalled that the trains he rode from Brigham City to Kelton via Promontory Summit had a helper engine "[a] number of times" from Blue Creek westbound when "[t]hey'd pick up a tremendous amount of wheat, more sox [sacks?] than anything, wheat and cattle."[27] Yagi added, "Most of the wheat went west" to California via Montello, Nevada.

According to Lower, the mixed train did not have a passenger car, though she did recall seeing some: "Oh, maybe once in a while they might have one of these cars on, but very seldom." However, Yagi, who rode the train on occasion using a pass provided by the railroad to his section foreman father, recalled that the train "had a passenger car and some freight cars."[28] Lower distinctly recalled that passengers rode in the caboose. As she put it, "[u]sually about all they had was a baggage car and a caboose." By baggage car, she might have meant a "combine," that is, a passenger car that only had a section devoted to passengers, with the rest of the car partitioned off into a closed baggage section. She recalled that the train carried a wide range of goods, including milk, and that many items—stoves, ironing boards, anything that was in the catalog—were shipped by mail.[29] This was called "lcl" (less-than-car-load) service, wherein smaller items or quantities that did not require a full car, were shipped as separate items.

It is likely that cabooses were used at times because many other old-timers also recall riding in them. As Evan Murray (born 1901) remembered catching the train in the morning: "The train, of course, was just a freight train with just a caboose attached to it." There was, as he put it, "[n]o passenger train there that late," so "[w]e got on the train and rode the caboose." Murray recalled the caboose being pretty comfortable, as it had "wooden benches," and "[t]here were other riders . . . four or five" on the train that day. All of them, like Murray, were teachers bound for a meeting. It is possible that Murray and his colleagues took a scheduled freight run that happened to have a caboose that could accommodate the passengers. Incidentally, Murray remembers that "at Promontory, you'd make a stop of some little time." Promontory made an impression on him. As he put it: "I still remember getting off the train at Promontory, walking back a few yards, going in the store, and buying some candy." He had the time because, as he recalled, "[w]ell, the train did whatever bit it had to do there, see that was a shipping point there, too." While walking around Promontory, Murray noted the water tower, warehouse, loading dock[s], tie section houses, the obelisk or pyramid-shaped monument, and the wye which "they used to use [to turn] a helper engine that went up there."[30]

Many old-timers rode the mixed train in the 1910s and 1920s, but they became more and more dependent on automobiles as time progressed. Mayme Wells Lower's last time riding the train, 1919, coincided with the family's purchase of an automobile—a Baby Overland—which she remembered as being "a pretty good little car." That Overland, an automobile that ironically bore the name of the famed overland pioneer wagon route that was replaced by the Southern Pacific's Overland Route line, now helped reduce the Southern Pacific's passenger revenues as more and more people traveled by automobile instead of trains. The automobile cut into mainline traffic but was especially hard on branch lines, where populations were smaller and more scattered. Rural folk always depended on mobility to get their goods to market, and the area served by the Promontory line was rural indeed. Located at the edge of two distinctively different types of environments—the well-watered irrigated oasis of Mormon farms and towns along the Wasatch Front near Brigham City and the sparsely populated ranching and dry farming area to the west that is typical of the Great Basin Desert—Promontory occupied a pivotal place in the West. As Lucius Beebe and Charles Clegg observed in their classic book *Central Pacific,* "West from Promontory, Everything is Nevada."[31] Like Nevada, the area experienced a minor boom as would-be wheat farmers plowed under sagebrush.

Some of these dry land wheat farmers came from Europe and Russia. A few sources state that Russian farmers settled west of Kelton. This is an interesting issue, as one of the placenames in this area—Russia Hill—may commemorate their presence here. Russians had evidently settled Russian Knoll, as old-timers called it, around 1915, but they were not successful. Evan Murray claimed it was because they were "down in the farthest side of the valley trying to dry farm, down on Duck Creek." This area at the lower reaches of the Curlew Valley is extremely dry. As Murray put it, "no water comes down there." Moreover, "the rainfall there is much more limited than in this area." As he concluded, "[y]ou don't get a lot of snow, a lot of wind, but not very much snow." Murray recalled hearing that there was a Russian cemetery, but little else, remaining in this forlorn area.[32] Although farmers did arrive to dry farm wheat here, there was no way of denying that much of the Promontory line ran through remote country indeed. Consider the life of a railroad family in this area such as the one Taro Yagi was born into. Yagi's father came from Japan in 1906 to work for the Southern Pacific as a section hand in Nevada. In about 1916, he began working in Utah, first as a section foreman at the west end of Great Salt Lake at Lakeside. Then, in late 1918, just five months after Taro was born, the family moved to Kelton. According to Taro, his father ". . . loved the hunting and fishing and wild game at that time [which] was in abundance out there." The fishing at Locomotive Springs, nine miles southeast of Kelton, "was real good. It was paradise as far as we were concerned because it was nothing for Dad to catch an eight or nin[e] pound trout." However, "[m]osquitoes would be so bad during the summer months at Locomotive [Springs] so we'd go up to cooler area[s]"—namely "those creeks up in Park Valley and Yost area . . . ."[33]

Yagi recalled that transportation at that time "was nil on most of the roads," which were especially muddy in the spring season and rutted throughout the year. In the winter, the roads were impassable by car because they were not plowed; therefore, sled transportation was the rule. Yagi recalled that people from the area would "come in after mail" by sled during the winter months. "The railroad was the only thing they had excepting sleighs [which] would go to points of Park Valley."[34] Yagi recalled riding the train from Kelton through the Promontory area and on to Brigham City on many occasions because "the railroad furnished a pass so it was free" for the Yagi family. At Promontory, Yagi remembered, Bernice Houghton would "always meet the train to bring the mail and we really got to know her when we were little[e] kids." Yagi was referring to the fact that certain railroad employees could ride free of charge using a pass that was about the size of a business card, and signed by a railroad official authorizing its use. He noted that Houghton was *always* there to meet the train, and probably "[n]ever had a sick day in her life because no matter when we'd come through I'd always see her." The Houghton store was seemingly stocked with many items and also served as a post office where mail would be put in individual boxes and sack(ed) mail would be provided to carriers servicing the rural routes. Like many others who grew up during this time, Taro Yagi recalled the Model A Fords that transformed the area by the late 1920s.[35]

Promontory in the 1920s was a bleak locale, and trees were rare. Those few trees that did grow here were artificially cultivated, for water had to be brought to the site. It is likely that trees were accidentally introduced here. Water was stored in cisterns and trees sprouted where water overflowed near the water trough. Old-timers recall a box elder tree at this location east of the depot. A large, old tree seen in the 1920s evidently began growing shortly after the town was founded and had died before 1928 or 1929. Taro Yagi remembered a younger but robust box elder tree near the cistern and water trough. It is unknown when Promontory's old wood-sided water tank house was removed. Yagi did not recall Promontory having an actual water tank, but some people claimed that it had a cylindrical wooden water tank mounted on a stilt-like support framework. A photograph reportedly taken at Promontory in 1942 shows one[36] (fig. 7–9). It may have been the same water tank mentioned in the earlier ICC valuation reports, but no evidence has been found to confirm this. Most of the buildings in town related to the railroad. The buildings included an engine house, station-hotel, pump house, and several section houses where section hands lived. These workers were called "gandydancers," and they helped maintain the track. The term *gandydancer* is of unknown origin. Some claimed it was from the Gandy Manufacturing Company of Chicago, but the trouble with this explanation is that there was no such company. The use of the term *gandydancer* was first recorded in 1918, though it may date from before then. Some say a gandy is a petty crook, or tramp, while it has also been used to define Italians, active socialites, and even womanizers.[37]

The term *section hand* was common at this time. As part of the Salt Lake Division, the line over Promontory Summit consisted of several

Courtesy of the National Park Service

FIG. 7–9
Photograph of a wooden water tank, reportedly taken at
Promontory Summit, 1942, reveals the declining condition
of the line at that time.

"sections," that is, portions of the line under the supervision of a section
foreman who supervised a crew of perhaps a dozen section hands. These
sections were usually about ten or twelve miles long. The main job of the
section crew was to keep the track inspected and in good shape. When
bridges needed work, B&B—short for bridges and buildings—workers
were sent out from Ogden. Typically, each section was headquartered
about midway on the section where both the homes of section foreman and the section hands were located. In recalling her husband's
job as a section worker who worked out of Kelton for twelve years in
the 1920s and early 1930s, Anderson recalled that the crew worked
in both directions out of Kelton: "They had their little sections up to
Ombey or Peplin or one of those little towns . . . ." In addition to section houses, one could usually find a hand-car shed and other buildings

housing supplies at these section points. Over the years, Lucin, Bovine, Watercress, Terrace, Kelton, Promontory, and Blue Creek (among others) served in such roles.[38]

As the son of a section foreman based out of Kelton, Taro Yagi was able to describe the section houses at Promontory in considerable detail. He remembered that there were five section houses, and that "the biggest share of them were tie houses with dirt roofs." When asked to elaborate, he added they were "clay roofed or dirt roofed." Some of the section houses had dirt floors, and "[s]ome of them had cruded [*sic*] plank[s] in there to keep the moisture away . . . ." Yagi noted that rooms were often small, about seven-by-seven feet, and had low ceilings "about six feet high." The section houses were very Spartan. According to Yagi, "those tie houses had no special designs" and were "simply made." Most of the houses had one large room where the occupants did "their cooking, and their eating." When needed, additional rooms could be added onto the houses using more railroad ties. As Yagi recalled, "[S]ome of these [tie houses] had small additions where their children had grown up[,] I guess to segregate the family, girls from the boys, I guess you'd say it that way." Like the earlier tents at Promontory, all of the section houses faced the railroad line; the majority of Promontory's section houses were located on the north side of the tracks, facing south. None of the section houses had electricity; illumination was provided by kerosene lamps. None of the houses had toilets; all used outhouses located "towards the back."[39]

In a 1974 interview, Bernice Anderson remembered the last remaining railroad section house in some detail. She recalled that it was painted "what you'd call a Southern Pacific yellow," adding that "[t]hey painted all their buildings that [color]." By this, she meant the characteristic creamy yellow color (with a light brown trim color resembling milk chocolate) that Southern Pacific used from about 1900 until the railroad merged with the Union Pacific in the 1990s. Anderson mentioned that she "scraped the yellow paint" off and found that this building had been painted a dull red underneath"—very likely its original color during Central Pacific days. In describing the fate of this building, which was in good condition when she first saw it, Anderson mentioned that it had burned down, probably as a result of lightning. This, she recalled, had happened "not too long ago," presumably in the 1950s or early 1960s.[40]

Mayme Wells Lower also remembered the section houses at Promontory, which "were made out of [railroad] ties . . . ." The outside of these section hand houses "was ties and chucked [chinked] and they were lined with floor boards as we call it . . . . Just like what they used to put the floor in the houses, you know." She recalled that these buildings had "dirt roofs," that gently sloped both ways. She had been in such houses many times, noting that "[i]t'd be just like walking into a little low house" with ceilings close enough to touch. Each of these buildings was heated by either a coal stove or a cook stove. Depending on the number of men who worked on a section or lived in the houses, "there'd be a kitchen and a dining room and a bedroom and maybe there'd be two to one room." Because water had to be hauled inside from a big red barrel, there was no sink. The water was provided via a cistern, which was filled via a windmill-driven pump.[41] These tie houses were also common on the Utah and Nevada portion of Southern Pacific's Overland Route, and are beautifully described by Frank Wendell Call in the book *Gandydancer's Children: A Railroad Memoir.*[42]

Chinese track workers were common, but after about 1910, Italians began to replace them on many section crews. In recalling life as a section hand, retired Southern Pacific section foreman Germano Pucci (born in Bazzone, Italy in 1898) noted that, in the 1920s, "practically all the people working for the Southern Pacific, they practically all from [the same] town, you know what I mean, close together there." Pucci worked mostly on the Lucin Cutoff but recalled that one of his compatriots—"that fellow Cocci [who] use[d] to be section foreman up at Promontory"—came from his hometown of Bazzone. Another Italian, Riamundo DiTorre (or Diatorri), was also a foreman at Promontory in about 1930. Pucci agreed with Bernice Houghton Gerristen, who had the store at Promontory: she responded, "Oh yes," when asked if there "were Italian section men out there" at Promontory. As Pucci put it, they "usually came on boat and they get together, that's the way it used to be." Like other track workers, Pucci recalled that "they used to have a section at a distance of about ten or twelve miles apart" and that in maintaining the track, "[y]ou had so many miles of track and the other man had so many miles and so on, you see." Pucci also noted that Mexican track workers were increasingly common after about 1920.[43] Very likely, these recently arrived Mexican Americans were refugees of the Mexican Revolution (ca. 1910–1920), a conflict that wreaked havoc on their homeland and helped change the demographics of the American West.

In describing life in one of these Southern Pacific section houses at Promontory in the early 1920s, Pablo Baltazar (born in Guanajuato, Mexico, in 1896) noted that "[t]he company furnished everything right there, coal in the winter, coal oil. You know, no got electrical [*sic*] right here." At this time, Promontory had no electricity. Baltazar noted that section hands slept in bunks, used coal stoves, and went to the larger boarding house to eat dinner. The meals were free, or as Baltazar put it, ". . . the railroad pay, I no pay nothing. The railroad paid everything."

The food, Baltazar remembered was "good." When asked if the woman cooking ever made "any Mexican food for you," Baltazar replied, "no, no"—a reminder that assimilation and economy, not accommodation to ethnicity, was stressed by the railroad.[44] This assimilation, of course, only went so far: Interestingly, Baltazar called Promontory by its name in Spanish—"Promontorio."

Being the son of a section foreman who operated out of Kelton, Taro Yagi was also familiar with dwellings occupied by the track bosses. At Promontory, he recalled that the section foreman lived in a larger home than the track workers' section houses. He also stated that this section foreman's house had been built later than the section houses. It "was what you'd call a two story"—actually more like a story and a-half—with "a bedroom up in the attic . . . ." Although Yagi never saw the upstairs of this house, he recalled the first floor layout in some detail. It had three rooms—"a living room, a kitchen, and a bedroom." The rooms were "fairly small" and the occupants had to obtain water from "a storage tank or cistern, whatever you want to call it."[45] Sam Nagata confirms Earl Harmon's account of Promontory by the 1930s. In an interview, he stated that, except for the white monument, "there was nothing there then . . . [n]othing at all," adding that "[i]t was a desolate place."[46] Nagata observed that out of about ten local Japanese families, only one—the Yagis—worked for the Southern Pacific Railroad.[47]

In 1904, in his popular book, *Over the Range to the Golden Gate*, Stanley Wood summarized the importance of this rather forlorn location:

PROMONTORY. A Point of Historical Interest

A small station surrounded by country covered with sage brush, and only worthy of mention for its history. At this point, on Monday, May 10, 1869, the Union Pacific Railroad, building west, and the Central Pacific Railroad, building east, met.[48]

The original edition of Wood's book a decade earlier (1894) contained much the same information. Wood was quite correct in his characterizing Promontory as "only worthy of mention for its history," for that was its only real claim to fame. Truth be told, Promontory was now little more than a historical curiosity, the place where the two railroads had once met. The fact that the meeting of the rails had taken place well within the recollection of many people tended to diminish its significance. Only when those people began to age, and then pass on, did commemoration of the event begin to become an issue. That, however, was still about a decade in the future.

In the meantime, people living along the Promontory line now faced reduced service. The drop off in rail traffic over the summit was immediately apparent, as revealed by the timetables of the period. In the January 1906 issue of the *Travelers Railway Guide Western Section*, the Southern Pacific lists ten daily passenger trains on the "Ogden Route." Two years earlier, all those named trains, plus about ten freight trains, would have gone over the summit at Promontory. Now the tracks were idle for many hours, sometimes most of the day. Although all now traveled over the Lucin Cutoff past "Promontory Point," there is a cryptic box titled "Salt Lake Div." that shows an unnamed "daily, except Sunday" train leaving Ogden at 8:15 a.m. and arriving in Montello, Nevada, at 3:50 p.m. Its counterpart left Montello at 6:30 a.m. and arrived in Ogden at 3:50 p.m. This was evidently the train on the line over Promontory Summit, for it took most of the day—about 7½ hours to travel just 166 miles.[49] The difference in eastbound and westbound times are likely the result of the train crossing the time zone at the Utah-Nevada border.

Ironically, the map reproduced in this 1906 *Travelers Railway Guide Western Section* is apparently older/dated, as it does not even show the Lucin Cutoff![50] One can only imagine the occasional bewildered passenger looking at the map showing the line going through Blue Creek and Kelton (Promontory is unnamed) only to gaze out the window at the surface of the Great Salt Lake! By the 1910s, everyone knew about the Lucin Cutoff. One could sense the nostalgia developing for the better days when Promontory had been on the mainline. Guidebooks frequently give it the mention normally reserved for obituaries. The United States Geological Survey's *Guidebook of the Western United States, part B, The Overland Route* (1915) was one such book. Published as a way of keeping travelers informed about sights (and sites) along the Overland Route, this guidebook made only one brief reference to Promontory when it tersely noted that, "The old transcontinental railroad line of the Central Pacific went west from Brigham [City] over Promontory Range and around the north end of Great Salt Lake" but "[i]t is little used now, for the trains go from Ogden straight across the lake."[51]

The automobile dealt a double blow to passenger service on the line over Promontory Summit. On *Clason's Guide Map* [of] *Utah* ca. 1918 (fig. 7–10), the major road taking motorists west out of northern Utah is the "Pike's Overland Peak Ocean to Ocean Highway." However, a secondary route generally parallels the old railroad line over Promontory Summit. This is, in part, the road blazed by early motorists like Lester Whitman, who had chugged over Promontory Summit in his 1903 Oldsmobile a generation earlier.

By the 1920s, passenger service over Promontory Summit continued to decline. This, it should be noted, occurred despite the fact that
Promontory's population was fluctuating. From 1900, when it had a
population of 148, Promontory lost about twenty people by 1910, but
then rose to 266 in 1920. In 1923, *The Official Guide* included timetable 19A, which covered "Corinne-Kelton-Montello." Train Number
181 left Corinne at 9:40 a.m. on Monday, Thursday, and Saturday, arriving in Promontory at 11:10 a.m., Rozel at 11:30 a.m., and Kelton at
12:50 p.m. Its eastbound counterpart, Train Number 182, left Kelton at
12:01 p.m., Tuesday, Friday, and Saturday, arriving in Rozel at 1:37 p.m.,
Promontory at 1:57 p.m., and Corinne at 5:25 p.m. This meant that service was not continuous but rather used Kelton as a stopping, and train
re-numbering, point.

Service from Kelton to Montello via Lucin was provided by Train
Number 205 on Monday and Thursday. A slow train in the classic sense,
Train Number 205 left Kelton at 1:20 p.m., reached Lucin at 4:35 p.m.,
and arrived in Montello at 5:30 p.m. This train's eastbound counterpart,
Number 206, left Montello on Tuesday and Friday at 8:00 a.m., reached
Lucin at 8:50 a.m., and arrived in Kelton at 11:40 a.m.[52] The schedule was
timed to enable a through trip over the line most days—even though the
train numbers changed at Kelton for reasons known only to the railroad.
One thing was certain. The service was no longer daily except Sunday, for
one could not travel through to Lucin (or Montello) on Saturday; nor
could one travel over the line except on particular days of the week. In
response to this reduction in both the frequency and speed of rail service,
locals in the area humorously called their train the "Alkali Flyer." Certainly
no match for the transcontinental trains that now rolled across the Lucin
Cutoff, saving hours, the Alkali Flyer averaged about twenty-two miles per
hour on its leisurely journey over the Promontory Summit line.

In one of the truly idyllic references to the Promontory Branch line's
passenger train, Lorna Larsen Phillips (born ca. 1906) recalls seeing
it from her family's farm on the south side of the Promontory Range.
The train was typically short and worked hard to get up the mountains;
Phillips remembered it "[g]oing up the grade, one little old engine puffing away with a lot of smoke trailing it and maybe two or three cars. We
knew the time of day by when that train came . . . . And if it was late we
were bothered about it. We waited to see it."[53] Despite the informality of
railroading on the Promontory Branch, the railroad was evidently serious enough about operations to run that train on a regular schedule.
For local people, too, the mixed train over Promontory became part of
the timing of life's activities. Still, fewer and fewer people rode it as the
twentieth century wore on.

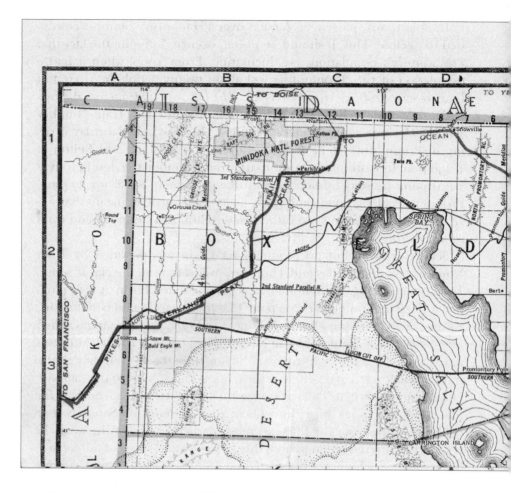

During its long downhill slide, Promontory became Mecca to Western history buffs. The town's most avid student, perhaps, was the late Bernice Anderson. Still affectionately referred to as "Bernice" by old-timers, she is immortalized as a guardian of the Promontory line's history. Born in Colorado in 1900, Anderson moved to Kaysville, Utah, when she was six months old. Her stepfather owned a ranch in Black Pine Canyon with two brothers, and they drove the cattle over Promontory Summit in the summer. Accompanying her mother in a buggy in 1905, she got her first look at Promontory. Being a curious youngster, Anderson later remembered that she had ". . . heard about Promontory even then from the cowboys that collected in our home and herded the cattle and took them out to the range."[54] The cowboys told her stories about the Irish and Chinese workers blowing each other up with sticks of dynamite until the "fun," as she put it, was stopped by mutual consent, and mutual necessity.[55] This supposed

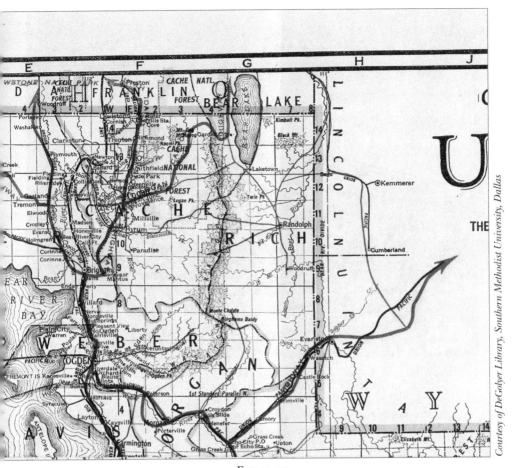

FIG. 7–10

Portion of *Clason's Guide Map [of] Utah* ca. 1918, shows the railroad
line over Promontory as well as the roads in the area, including the
marginal road over the summit, and the "Ocean to Ocean" highway
running farther north around the end of the Great Salt Lake.

Courtesy of DeGolyer Library, Southern Methodist University, Dallas

conflict between the varied ethnic workers here is not confirmed, but
it certainly did occur elsewhere in the West.

Because she was fascinated by what she heard about Promontory,
her grandmother took her to the railroad station here. Over the years,
Anderson watched the old railroad station, once the scene of so much
activity in the nineteenth century, become an empty shell (fig. 7–11).
She recalled that there was a water tank there as well as "several box
elder trees, big box elder trees," that were probably "watered some way
from the tank . . . ."[56] The water tank was filled by a water train that
hauled water up from the Bear River at Corinne in tank cars. The tank
was needed to provide water to road locomotives and helper engines

FIG. 7–11

The station at Promontory stands empty and forlorn in about
1930. To see how much railroad service had declined from
Promontory's heyday, compare this photograph with Fig. 5–7,
which was taken about half a century earlier.

powering local trains up the steep east side of the Promontory grade.
She also remembered the post office as a section house where she
thought a man lived with his family. This was Promontory after it had
been bypassed by the Lucin Cutoff, and it was a rather quiet place. As
she put it, "[t]here were no trains there at the time I was there."[57] By
this, we can assume that they were still running, but that Anderson had
not seen any on the occasions she visited the site. The lack of trains did
not cool her ardor, and may have actually fueled it. After all, there is
something captivating about a ghost railroad, or one near that status.
A 1927 photograph of Promontory reveals it as a forlorn location with
a few buildings including the Houghton store. A close-up photo of the
store's abandoned façade and overgrown surroundings (fig. 7–12) confirms Promontory's ghost-town setting.

Along with the railroad station, the general store was one of
Promontory's most important buildings. The store was apparently owned
by a Mr. Brown before Mr. Houghton purchased it and appears to have

Courtesy of Special Collections, Utah State University, Logan

FIG. 7–12
The long-abandoned Houghton store at Promontory, ca. 1930,
was one of the town's landmarks.

been built about 1890. Although rather modest in style—seemingly more like a house than a commercial building in design—its façade did face Promontory's main street and had a few flourishes of classical trim, namely its window lintels. Given its design and the fact that the proprietor and his family lived in a part of the store, it appeared to be both a commercial and residential building. This was apparent in its surroundings. John Whitaker (born 1911) recalled stories about goings-on in and around the store, which featured a hitching post and was adjacent to a small corral and livery stable. The store also featured some pea vines, which grew nearby. One fixture, a fifty-gallon barrel was part of the scene when Brown owned the property. Located near the hitching rail, this barrel figured in the folklore when a sheepherder took someone up on a $50 bet that his dog could not remove a particularly nasty badger from it. According to Whitaker, "[s]o this little sheepherder, he walked around and . . . went over and picked his dog up and threw his dog in the barrel." The outcome? "The badger grabbed the dog and the dog jumped out and drug the badger out." The sheepherder won the

$50 bet, though one wonders if the dog was as delighted as its owner.[58] Interestingly, although the store is long gone, as are all involved in the story, badgers are still common in and around Promontory Summit. Whitaker's tale is a reminder that sheepherding was an important activity in the hills surrounding Promontory.

The Houghton Store was a landmark, and several people remembered it in later years—the 1920s and 1930s—being painted yellow similar in color to the railroad section houses. Some, however, remember it as light green. It was one of Promontory's more verdant spots: Della Owens recalled that "[a]ll around the store there were trees, and of course . . . that vine. He [Houghton] had this vine that went all around . . . a fence around his store and grounds, and this vine went all the way around."[59] Some also remember Houghton's wife being in charge of the store. According to Grace N. Brough (born 1885), "Mrs. Houghton's store" seemed quite large when she was a girl. Like most old-timers, Brough recalled it being a frame building but was especially impressed by the fact that "[i]t had these bushes that growed all around there." She also remembered "a big, old tree" near the store, but what impressed her most was "a lot of these old bushes, I forget what they call them now." Even at that time, though the store—like Promontory itself— had seen better days. Brough remarked, "I guess it was quite a store at one time when the railroad, when they had a . . . major presence here, including the roundhouse, at Promontory."[60] Incidentally, the vines so common in Promontory and vicinity are called "pea vines" by some, "tea vines" by others, and even "Martha Washington vines" by a few. They could almost completely cover fences and low buildings.[61]

In 1974, Leona Yates Anderson (born 1895) recalled that the Houghton store at Promontory Station was "just a country store. It had everything." Although "[t]he main line didn't run through at that time, you understand," the store "had groceries and candy and everything that a farmer would need—nails, straps. Well, anything you would need." Anderson recalled the store as being small, but what impressed her most about it was Mrs. Houghton, who "was the nicest little lady" and who had an English accent that was both appealing and interesting. According to Anderson, "Mrs. Houghton ran the store," and at this time it served people from the surrounding area: "There were dry farms all around, and they raised a lot of wheat, [and] barley."[62]

By the 1930s and early 1940s, Promontory was haunted by its early status as *the place* where the rails met, and where almost nothing was happening now. In 1930, the population held at 132 souls, but by 1940, only 46 lived here.[63] In order to imagine life in Promontory during the twentieth century, we need to consult as many information sources as possible. At interviews, old-timers are asked questions and their answers are recorded on tapes and later transcribed. This, of course, makes us reliant on their words. What would happen, though, if one of these interviewees actually drew a map of Promontory as he or she remembered it or was assisted in doing so by a researcher? That is exactly what John Whitaker did when Ellis J. LeFevre interviewed him. The last page of Whitaker's interview indicates, "MAP STAPLED AT BACK OF TYPED HARD COPY (as of 20 Nov. 1995) . . . hard copy located in File 103–Cla, which is located 'in the archives.'" In the NPS Archives at Promontory, the researcher finds a simple white sheet of paper on which is a real treasure—a hand-drawn map summarizing Whitaker's recollections (fig. 7–13). On this map, which is oriented west (west is at the top of the page), the railroad shows as four parallel lines evidently drawn with a ruler. Crossing the railroad at an angle is a sinuous road that evidently postdates Promontory's heyday as it cuts through the former location of the turntable and roundhouse. Just to the right (east) of the crossing, where the symbol "RXR" is drawn, is a large tree. Left of the crossing is the "Spike Site." Below (south of) the tracks, a rectangle indicates the "store," which stands near a smaller tree and a line indicating the "hitching rail." Farther down the road, another larger rectangle indicates the "corral & livery stable," beyond which the road curves near a "well," which is shown as a circle symbol. Presumably, researcher LeFevre and old-timer John Whitaker worked together on this map, which joins the others in this book as part of the fragmentary, but essential, cartographic record of Promontory.

Oral histories are important and informative, but for the most definitive information on the railroad-related features along Promontory Branch in the early twentieth century, we must turn to the records of the Interstate Commerce Commission (ICC). The ICC conducted a thorough valuation of the property from Corinne (MP 820.78) to Lucin (MP 578.3) inventorying the trackwork, bridges, buildings/structures, and other related property. The valuations were conducted under the direction of E. Z. Kinnear. Beginning at Corinne in the early summer of 1917, a team of two inspectors (Kinnear and L. W. Clark) inventoried all the structures along the nearly 140 miles of branch line. By then, the roundhouse at Promontory, which existed from the 1870s until about 1913,[64] was gone—a reminder that this line was called the Promontory Branch with good reason.

When the ICC Division of Valuation (Pacific District) conducted an inventory along the line on June 16, 1917, R. E. Towne noted that the railroad's schedule affected his ability to obtain information: "owing to the fact that Terrace is off the main line of the Southern Pacific

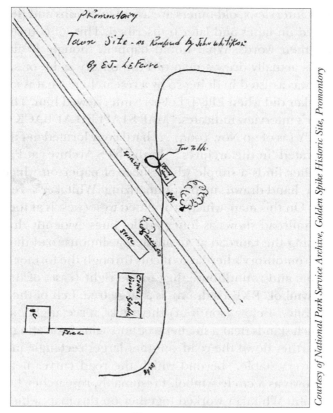

FIG. 7–13
A hand-drawn map showing Promontory, ca. 1910, was recently drawn from the recollections of old-timer John Whitaker and reveals the location of the turntable, the general store, and several other features.

Railroad, and can be reached by train only on Tuesday of each week, the return trip being made the following Wednesday, a statement of original cost and condition of this property by carrier was accepted in lieu of actual inspection, as such inspection would have entitled the loss of a weeks[*sic*] time for both I.C.C. representative and pilot for this small amount of property."[65] If a railroad inspector had trouble getting from place to place along the line, we can only imagine the difficulty Southern Pacific's fragmented schedule now posed for local travelers here.

Nevertheless, the inspectors documented a tremendous amount of information. From Lucin to Lake Station, for example, the rails were sixty and sixty-two pounds per yard. From Lake Station eastward over

Promontory, however, the rail was heavier—seventy-five and seventy-six pounds per yard. "There are," as a representative of the railroad put it, "some little variations in that—a little short piece of one or the other here and there." Another indication that this branch line was not up to main line standards was revealed in the types of railroad ties used for replacements. In responding to a query about this, a Southern Pacific official admitted that, "In the past years, most of the ties placed there were old ties." The official added that they were "second-hand ties" taken from some other place on the system. Moreover, the replacement rails on the Promontory line were "taken up [from] some of the old sidings, and we have drawn upon such supplies as that for our relaying in the case of a broken rail or a rail taken out of service for any cause." As the official finally concluded after interrogation: "There is no new rail on the Promontory Branch."[66] And, yet, that track did serve trains, including the railroad's own supply trains. A January 1918 valuation report on track in the Ogden yard notes, "From MP 821.05 to MP 825.5 (Sta. 1389 +08) the ballast is hauled from the Promontory Pit at Mile 770 on the old Central Pacific Railway around Great Salt Lake. The gravel is small and has a small amount of fine sand mixed with it."[67] Whether the irony of this—the Promontory line's activities helping to support the railroad's mainlines elsewhere—went unnoticed or not is unknown.

At just the time that traffic on the Promontory Branch dwindled, it was also dwindling on many other branch lines. Accordingly, Southern Pacific experimented with, and adopted, new ways to serve the public without having to offer trains pulled by locomotives. These alternatives included self-propelled rail cars like the gasoline-powered McKeen Cars (which Union Pacific Superintendent of Motive Power and Machinery, William McKeen had developed in 1904) and gasoline-electric cars produced thereafter by other manufacturers. Although these types of self-propelled railcars operated on many Southern Pacific branch lines from around 1908 to the 1930s, saving the company considerable expense, there is no evidence that they ever operated on the Promontory line. Similarly, there is no record that a diesel-electric locomotive ever ran on the Promontory line. Although the diesel-electric locomotive was pioneered in the 1930s and began to show up in switching service on Southern Pacific by the late 1930s, some railroad historians note that Southern Pacific was somewhat slow to dieselize—perhaps because it successfully built many of its own steam locomotives at its venerable Sacramento shops. The Promontory line, then, appears to be quintessential steam railroad territory from start (1869) to finish (1942).

The Promontory Branch operated at a slow pace during the 1930s, though nature provided some excitement at times. At 8:05 a.m. on March 12, 1934, an earthquake registering 6.6 on the Richter scale shook the area near Monument Point. The Hansel Valley earthquake resulted in four cracks crossing a road bordering the mud flats near Monument Point, and "one crack crossed and bent tracks of the Central Pacific Railroad." This did not pose a serious problem as rail traffic was light, especially at this time of year, and the damage was quickly repaired.

In oral history interviews, Pappy Clay recalls that after the Lucin Cutoff was built, and service further declined, "the old Central Pacific (now Southern Pacific) line over Promontory Summit was only running a jerk train a week as far as Kelton so most of the section houses between Corinne and Kelton had been abandoned."[68] Still the line over Promontory hung on, appearing more like a museum than an operating rail line. Train service was infrequent, and the physical plant was deteriorating. Given its forlorn status and quaint appearance it is surprising that more railroad enthusiasts did not seek out the old railroad line. Their absence here helps explain the paucity of photographs. Those that we do have, however, confirm the marginal nature of operations here at the margins of the Great American Desert.

Chapter 8

A CHANGING COUNTRYSIDE
& LANDSCAPE
(1904–1942)

By the early twentieth century, speculators eyed the Central Pacific lands, which on a map appeared to be part of a huge checkerboard pattern awaiting development (figs. 8–1a and b). The major activity in this area was ranching, and it would soon face competition from farming. Consider, for example, the fate of the Promontory Ranch Company, or PRC, as it was often called. According to its articles of incorporation filed in San Francisco on November 30, 1897, the Promontory Ranch Company was created for the purpose of engaging in and carrying on "the business of raising, buying, selling, exchanging and generally dealing in all kinds of live-stock;" and also "to buy, sell, hire, lease, let, hold, mortgage and improve all kinds of real property . . . ."[1] That broad charter would seem to offer nearly unlimited possibilities. And yet, PRC was formally dissolved on December 28, 1921.

The demise of the Promontory Ranch Company was part of a broader trend in land use and ownership in northwestern Utah. Great Basin historian Leonard Arrington noted that the Central Pacific was given alternative, odd-numbered sections of land from Corinne to Kelton, of which 400,000 acres eventually "became the personal property of Charles Crocker" whose large house soon became a landmark. Upon Crocker's death in 1888, two companies—the Promontory Ranch Company and the Curlew Ranch Company—were created. The main purpose for creating these enterprises was "to handle the vast

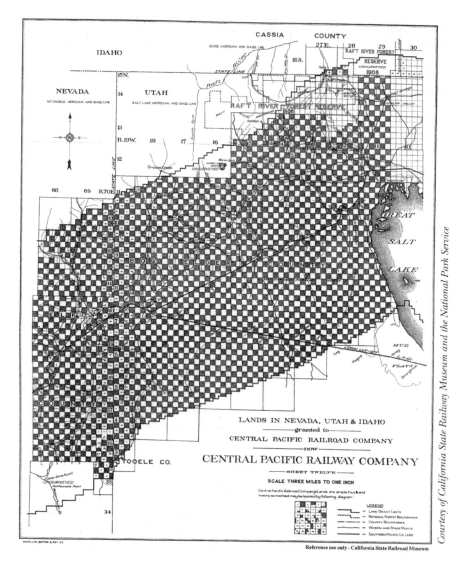

Courtesy of California State Railway Museum and the National Park Service

stock ranches then operating on the tract." Crocker's holdings had most of the water sources, making it virtually impossible for those who owned land in the even-numbered sections to subsist in this arid area. Crocker interests were unwilling to sell small parcels, in effect stifling development in much of the area adjacent to the railroad. That began to change in 1908, when Utah Congressman Joseph Howell and David Eccles proposed to buy all of Crocker's holdings in Utah and Idaho. Formed in 1909, the Promontory-Curlew Land Company purchased all 400,000 acres—about 625 square miles—of the former Crocker land. This, by considerable stretch of the imagination, was easy land

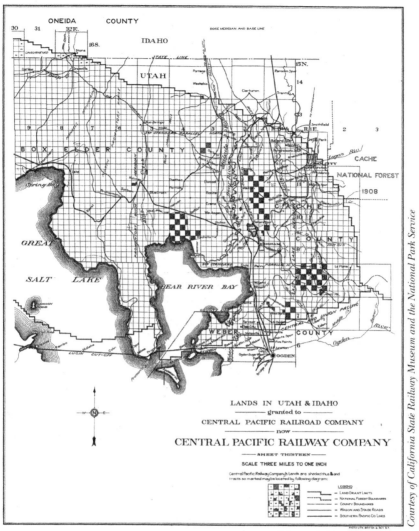

FIGS. 8–1A AND B
Map showing the land ownership of the area through which the
Promontory Summit line of the Central Pacific Railroad ran
reveals the checkerboard pattern of alternate railroad/private
ownership west of Promontory and the largely non-railroad
private holdings eastward.

on which to subsist. One observer candidly called it "this world of griz-
zled sage," but others saw real promise in it. In 1910, the Promontory-
Curlew Land Company's holdings were valued at \$1,651,472; of this,
the new town site of Howell was worth \$41,275, irrigated land was

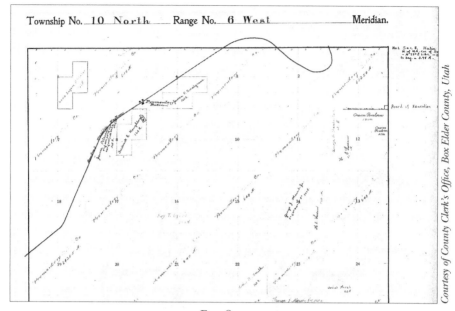

Township No. 10 North   Range No. 6 West   Meridian.

Courtesy of County Clerk's Office, Box Elder County, Utah

FIG. 8–2

Map of a portion of township no. 10 north and range no. 6 west
in about 1918 shows the area adjacent to Promontory as being
owned by the large Promontory-Curlew Land Company, but three
individuals also own land here.

estimated at $135,000, and the largest portion, dry farming land, was
valued at $1,475,197.[2]

A map (fig. 8–2) located in the Box Elder County Courthouse shows a
portion of township no. 10 north and range no. 6 west, revealing the area
surrounding Promontory Station to be owned for the most part by the
"Promontory C[urlew] L[and] Co" and three other owners: Frederick E.
Houghton owned 160 acres just southwest of the station; to the northeast, James P. Snodgrass also had a staggered parcel of 160 acres; so, too,
did Lewis Eugene Whitaker about a mile northwest of the railroad. On
this map, which is not dated but apparently reflects the situation around
1910, Promontory shows as a cluster of three buildings. The one south of
the tracks is evidently the Central Pacific station, and the two other buildings, possibly houses, lie just north of (and parallel to) the Central Pacific
tracks. This map is tantalizing, both for what it shows—and even more so
for what it does not show: where, we should ask, are the approximately
ten other buildings, which existed according to other descriptions, actually located? How is the town laid out in regards to roadways? These, alas,
are not shown, but from this map, we get a good idea of the dominance
of the new Promontory-Curlew Land Company in local affairs.

The political machinations in the formation of this company involved a close partnership between the private and public sectors. Much of the land in the Promontory Summit area was sagebrush-covered ranchland held in large parcels by individuals associated with the Central Pacific Railroad until the early twentieth century. When the honorable Joseph Howell, Utah's Congressional representative from Logan, met with Crocker interests in Washington, D.C., to begin developing the area into dry farms in 1909, it was part of an exciting experiment. Dry farming is the process by which plowed land in semi-arid areas is opened for cultivation. In many cases, seemingly marginal land can yield good crops of grain without irrigation—providing conditions are right. Successful dry farming requires knowledge of the climate, soils, slope of land, and other factors. Although practiced for millennia in varied parts of the world, Utah first pioneered American dry farming in 1865. When early settlers developed methods by which certain crops, especially grains like wheat and oats, could be grown on land that was otherwise only used for ranching, they expanded the definition of agriculturally productive land.

In dry farming, the objective is to utilize the moisture in the soils. This moisture is usually most plentiful in the late winter and rapidly evaporates as the spring progresses. However, by selecting crops such as winter wheat that can thrive in these conditions, farmers can raise a crop before the withering high temperatures of summer damages it. Summer fallow (that is, letting the land rest between plantings) further helps reduce the evaporation of soil moisture. Given its relatively deep soils, tendency to receive at least some winter precipitation, generally semi-arid climate, and varied slope patterns, the area around Promontory Summit proved suitable for dry farming. Normally, in this part of the West, crops of wheat can be harvested about three years out of five. This means about a 60% chance of success. With good luck, a farmer can harvest five years in a row. With bad luck, however, only one year in five, or even fewer, might be profitable. This makes dry farming a gamble with acceptable odds—at least for those willing to take the risks.

In 1910, when the Promontory-Curlew Land Company purchased much of the area to the north of Promontory Summit, including Promontory Station, it seemed to suggest that a new era was at hand. The company's letterhead presented a grand view of the future—a verdant, well-cultivated landscape through which a train chuffed confidently (fig. 8–3). The letterhead also noted "370,000 acres in Box Elder County, Utah, and Cassia and Oneida Counties, Idaho."[3] As part of their operations, the Promontory-Curlew Land Company offered large tracts of land in the Blue Creek Valley and the Curlew Valley, creating the town of Howell close to the "Big House" of Charles Crocker, which

FIG. 8–3

Letterhead of the Promontory-Curlew Land Company (1911) includes a well-ordered landscape traversed by a railroad line—an idealized version of the company's location adjacent to the Southern Pacific.

had been moved there in 1908.[4] Despite its new location, people still called it the "Big House" (or sometimes "Big Blue House"), but it symbolized the transition from ranching to dry farming. Photographs in the Promontory-Curlew Land Company's brochures (fig. 8–4) showed farmers contemplating the removal of huge tracts of sagebrush at a scale that would require environmental impact statements today. At that time, however, environmental concerns were in the future. Nature represented so much land to be reconfigured and so much brush to be removed before farming could work. The big questions back in the 1910s and 1920s were: would this new development work, and would it, in turn, stimulate the moribund rail line here?

It is tempting to think everyone believed that the line over Promontory Summit was doomed when the Lucin Cutoff was constructed. However, many investors thought otherwise. On the mainline or not, the Promontory area seemed to have good prospects as wheat farming country. The opening up of the lands to wheat here followed an early twentieth-century trend in dry farming in other parts of the American West. Developments north of the railroad line also prompted the Promontory-Curlew Land Company to lobby for an extension of track north into the more promising agricultural land of the Blue Creek Valley in the vicinity of the aptly-named, new town of Howell. As revealed in company records, the board of directors approached the Southern Pacific about this issue in 1910.[5] This may have seemed like so much overzealous speculation, but a handwritten note on the ICC valuation maps reveals that in effect, the proposed branch would begin at Blue Creek and run northward into the valley. If the line had been completed, it would have been something of an oddity—a branchline off a branchline. More

Courtesy of Special Collections, Utah State University, Logan

FIG. 8–4

Farmers contemplate transforming a sagebrush-covered landscape into wheat fields in an undated brochure produced by the Promontory-Curlew Land Company, ca. 1913.

specifically, it would have been a new branchline off an otherwise atrophying secondary line whose future was less than certain.

Four hundred thousand acres of the Promontory-Curlew Land Company consisted of only the odd-numbered sections in townships 6 to 15 north, ranges 4 to 10 west, Salt Lake Meridian in Box Elder County, Utah, as well as township 16 south, ranges 29 and 30 East Boise Meridian in Oneida County, Idaho. Although Howell's initiative led to the creation of the company by mid-1909, the actual sale of property to individuals took well over a decade. Ideally, the huge property would be divided into smaller parcels, and if all went as planned, sold off to farmers. The vision represented something like the Homestead Act (1862) in that it was meant to open up land to farmers. However, goals here were profit for the Promontory-Curlew Land Company and success for individual farmers. Congressman Howell is listed as the company's president, an action that was common enough before concerns about public-private conflicts of interest surfaced with the famous Teapot Dome oil lands in Wyoming about fifteen years later (1924). To his credit, it should be noted that Howell's ultimate goal was stimulating northwestern Utah's agricultural production and strengthening the local and regional economy. With the creation of the Promontory-Curlew Land Company, the area was set to boom—at least according to the hopes and visions of the company's boosters.

The company was dedicated to opening the area to individual farmers; before it could do so, however, it had to address the issue of the land's potential for crops. On June 19, 1913, the company's secretary sent a letter to Mr. John Q. Critchlow outlining the results of soil tests of Curlew Valley. The report revealed the concentrations of alkali to be .006% in areas where only sagebrush grew, .0068% where sage and shadscale grew together, and fully .0085% where only shadscale grew. The letter also noted that the "most successful" dry farming appeared to be practiced where alkali concentrations of .005 to .011 were found.[6] In other words, the lower, alkali-rich areas near the lake would be far less productive, while the higher sloping land far above the lake was best. The results, then, showed most of the company's lands to be well within that range. Being located at the moderate to high elevations, the company's lands were well drained and potentially productive.

Nevertheless, increased demand was needed to make the company's plans successful. By about 1915, the company found just the ticket to claim increasing demand—a world war. In a startling flyer prepared during World War I, the Promontory-Curlew Land Company claimed that "America Must Prepare to Feed the Old World, which has forsaken its Ploughshares and Pruning Hooks for Implements of War and Destruction." It claimed that the "European War will Make Wheat Raisers Millionaires." Noting that "non-irrigated lands are yielding from TWENTY TO FORTY BUSHELS OF WHEAT TO THE ACRE," the flyer also claimed, "THE SOIL is deep, rich and productive . . . THE CLIMATE is similar to that in the Salt Lake, Bear River and Cache Valleys . . . WATER for culinary purposes and truck gardens may be secured by drilling wells." Moreover, the flyer noted that "THE S.P. RAILROAD to Kelton crosses Promontory-Curlew Lands, thus affording ample facilities for marketing crops and securing necessities and luxuries not provided naturally in this section." The flyer concluded that "THE TOWNS of Snowville, Howell, [and] Promontory . . . are adjacent to the company's holdings" and that "[e]ach boasts first-class schools and good general stores." A map produced as part of the flyer reveals—in bright orange—the huge holdings of the Promontory-Curlew Land Company., A caption below noted that "Promontory Station, which Lincoln chose as the meeting point of the U.P. and C.P. Railroads, where the golden spike was driven, completing the first transcontinental railroad connecting the East with the West, is shown."[7] The use of President Lincoln's name here was gratuitous at best, for he had been dead for several years before Promontory was selected as the site. Nevertheless, the claim made a good impression despite its inaccuracy. The point here was that farmers could now join part of a national effort to prosper as a result of peace at home and war abroad. Posters prepared by the company during the war in Europe offered lurid details about how the world needed food as the countries participated in the conflict. As might be expected, the posters predicted a boom in demand for wheat and other crops that would be shipped long distances.

Coincidentally, these were just the types of crops that could be produced by enterprising farmers in Utah, or so the posters and brochures claimed. War, in fact, added to an already growing economy in the 1910s.

The solid economic picture, as well as war and rumors of war, resulted in talk of extending the railroad from Kolmar farther north into the bucolic Blue Creek Valley in 1913–1914. Actually, the Promontory-Curlew Land Company had begun to lobby for additional railroad lines several years earlier, to no avail. Now, however, the time seemed right and the company made a formal request. W. R. Scott of the Southern Pacific responded by noting that the railroad would indeed consider building a line into the northern Blue Creek Valley—provided that the company "furnish right of way, build grade and deed it to us if we complete the line and operate it." If those conditions were met, the railroad would offer limited service. Scott envisioned "service each way daily except Sunday, and perhaps less than that, unless business would warrant it." The service would be by a "mixed train," that is, one that carried freight cars and at least one car for passengers. Recognizing his advantage here, Scott noted that he would not specify anything other than this minimal service.[8] However, nothing ever came of this as Scott's words—and conditions—must have been sobering to the company's directors and to the farmers with whom he corresponded. Despite this lobbying for expanded rail service, then, the existing railroad infrastructure along the Promontory line would have to suffice for the Promontory-Curlew Land Company—at least for the present.

A brochure titled "A Winning Combination" describes the Promontory-Curlew-area lands using several maps. On the inside front cover, a Utah map containing a small United States map features Utah and Idaho in a shaded pattern; to accentuate their actual location, an arrow directs the reader's eye to the area north of the Great Salt Lake on the map of northern Utah. This map's adjoining text claims that these lands offer the "Greatest Dry Farm Opportunity in the West Today!" It also lists the advantage of the "Trans-continental Railroad through the property," along with "good schools, churches, and prosperous towns."

In addition to glowing text, the brochure includes photographs of the lands under development and transportation facilities. The photo of a "Central Pacific Railroad Train at Monument Utah" (fig. 8–5) offers a glimpse of a mixed train stopped at the station, which appears to be little more than a freight-loading platform and an old caboose body. That caboose appears to be a 1900 vintage wooden car with blind ends (i.e., it has no end platforms) and a cupola. Given the scarcity of photographs taken along the line, we are fortunate to have this vignette. Moreover, the brochure features other photographs promoting the

FIG. 8–5

Illustrated under the topic of "Markets and Transportation" in a Promontory-Curlew Land Company brochure, a Southern Pacific mixed train pauses at Monument on the Promontory Branch in about 1915. Note the old caboose body, possibly serving as a station.

company's lands, and agricultural equipment helping to reap bumper crops of wheat.

The tour de force of the brochure, though, is the large centerfold map showing Promontory-Curlew Land Company property in Utah and Idaho (fig. 8–6). The entire area around Promontory is shown in a checkerboard pattern with the section numbers circled. A stippled pattern indicates "land sold," while a blank or white square indicates "land available." As can be seen, the best land—that is, the better-watered upland with richer soils—went first. Note, too, that a web of "proposed railroads" suggests that the company planned additional railroad service for farmers on the western slope of the Promontory Range and then north into Idaho. The position of this proposed railroad seems to anticipate the closure of the line over Promontory, for if that eventuality occurred, the railroad would run from near Promontory Point on the new Lucin Cutoff and avoid all topographic obstacles as it meandered along the western edge of the Promontory-Curlew Land Company's holdings.[9]

Although new settlers were attracted here, the farming was difficult. Sagebrush-covered lands seemed to offer great hope but cutting down the tall plants required hard work. It was, in effect, like pulling up small trees. The Great Basin's Indians have an expression about sagebrush—that when the world experiences catastrophe and turns upside down, one should hold onto a sagebrush because its roots will keep one from falling off.[10] Sagebrush was everywhere, served many purposes, and lingered for a long time in the memory of these early twentieth century dry-farming pioneers. In Howell Valley history, Luella Douglas recalled that "[f]or firewood we burned sagebrush." In fact, as Douglas quickly added, "[m]ost of the farm was in sagebrush when we first saw it and had to be cleared and grubbed off." Douglas was

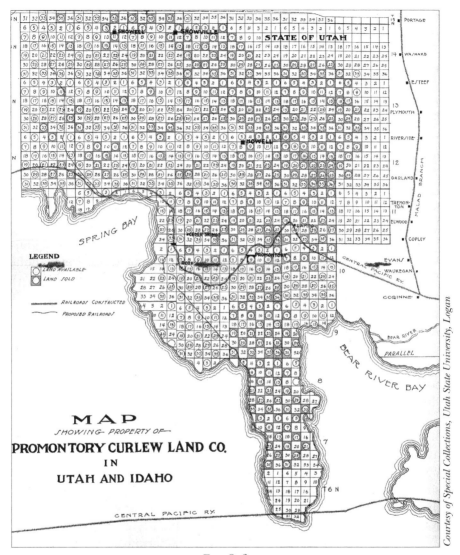

FIG. 8–6
On this map showing available parcels of land, the Promontory-Curlew Land Company shows not only the existing Central Pacific line over Promontory (and the Lucin Cutoff), but also two projected rail lines—one from Monument Point, and one north into Idaho from a point near Spring Bay.

nearly overwhelmed by this plant; "I can still smell the sage burning. It was . . ." as she put it, "a sweet sickening smell." The family kept the sage in "a big woodbox by the stove," but "[y]ou could never get the sage into the stove without spilling it all over the floor and it would only burn for a few minutes, then it was out and you had to start all over again."[11]

All of the commercial literature seemed to suggest good prospects for railroad development here. Although Promontory had been bypassed by the Lucin Cutoff, the land adjacent to the tracks took on added importance as prospective development promised to stimulate the area's economy. To learn about how the land was used—and what potential it had—we can again turn to maps prepared by the railroad. In 1916, Southern Pacific Company prepared a series of *Right of Way and Track Maps* at a scale of 1 inch = 400 feet. These were, in effect, valuation maps that coincided with the ICC valuation report. The Promontory Branch, as it was now officially called, required thirty-five separate maps in Box Elder County, which comprised Valuation Section 2. About ninety miles in length, this section ran from Lucin (Map V2–1) to Bonneville (Map V2–35). The last map in the series (V2–36) detailed the track about four miles into Weber County. From there to Ogden, a new series (V3) consisting of three maps covered the line. At Ogden, the series featured several highly detailed maps including the yards and engine terminal. At this time, the Southern Pacific had a 100–foot turntable, a 30–stall roundhouse, and large car shops and mainline shops as well as a yard consisting of eighteen tracks. Ogden was the hub of Southern Pacific's Salt Lake Division and locomotives. While most of the activity was over the Lucin Cutoff, locomotives used on the Promontory Branch were also serviced here.

For our purposes, several sections of the Promontory Branch are worth a closer look because they reveal so much about both the railroad and the countryside through which it ran. From Ogden to Corinne, the line is single track running in the center of a strip of land 400 feet wide. What makes these original maps at the National Archives of even greater interest, though, is the written commentary on them. The adjacent land was evidently interesting enough to note as "good farm land" and "fair farm land" near Bonneville and Brigham City. Owners of adjacent properties are named in a box on the map. Just east of the river and Corinne, the maps feature some additional notations. "Good pasture land—[and] a little farmland" and "very fine spot" are mentioned, as is "low pasture good land (soil)" along the east side of the Bear River. Those maps are also an excellent source of information about railroad facilities. Corinne has a passing siding and small yard, with a connection to the OSL (Oregon Short Line), as recorded in detail on Station Map S32–60935. At Corinne, the map shows a cluster of railroad buildings, (including a tool house, cook house, and coal house) and a stockyard east of the "SP Co Warehouse" which is located between the yard track and passing siding.

West of Corinne, the penciled-in marginal comments about land quality become even more detailed. Just west of town, the land is noted to be "level [and] mostly irrigated" while other areas where "portions are in pasture and sage brush" represent good land with considerable agricultural potential. As the comments noted, "A drainage district has been formed," "[t]he land is bonded for 17.50 [dollars] an acre," and "When reclaimed it will produce good crops." With the "water right[s] worth 50.00 per acre," these drainage district lands are now valued at $67.50 per acre. Several miles west of Corinne, however, the situation changes. Although there is some "fair grazing land," increasing mention is made of "alkali wast[e] land" along the stretch of track toward Blue Creek. At Blue Creek, the situation improves, with "Dry farms at a distance from track" noted. A wye for turning helper locomotives was also found here at Blue Creek, the turntable having been replaced some years earlier.

As revised in 1924, the Lampo detail on the sheet map (V2–27) shows a grain elevator, stockyards, warehouses, scales, and other indications of a thriving agricultural economy. An inset on the map also shows the railroad's 3–inch pipeline running from numerous springs to Lampo and Blue Creek (V2–27). At the sweeping curve just north of Lampo, notations show "Dry farms below R[ight] of W[ay] . . ." while alongside the rugged Promontory grade, "some side hill grazing" was reported near Surbon (Map V2–26). Between there and Promontory, "side hill grazing land" yields to "bench land at top of grade," which is "partly dry farmed." At Promontory (fig. 8–7), the comments record several buildings, namely a "store and 3 houses" (Map V2–24). This map also shows the location of the numerous railroad-related buildings in the town at this time.

Just west of Promontory (V2–24) is "mostly level dry farm land about ⅓ to ½ [of which is] in grain. Balance in sage brush." This condition, it was noted, "applies to whole map." West of Promontory Summit, the maps show the single track line winding down the west side of Promontory on its 400–foot right of way to Lake, where another wye is located for helper engines (V2–20). A passing track was also shown, but as the commenter observed, there was "nothing here." West of Lake, the commenter noted one bright spot: "Part of land farmed on this [south] side" of the railroad tracks. Near Kosmo, things became a bit bleaker: "Level dry farm land—small crops" and "Level dry farm land— poor" and "sage brush . . . ." West of Monument, which featured a passing track parallel to the curving main line, the land was characterized as "generally level but some of it rolling. Suitable for winter sheep grazing only." (Map V2–18) Similarly, near Nella,[12] the "land throughout this map (V2–17) was characterized as "sagebrush [*sic*] desert generally

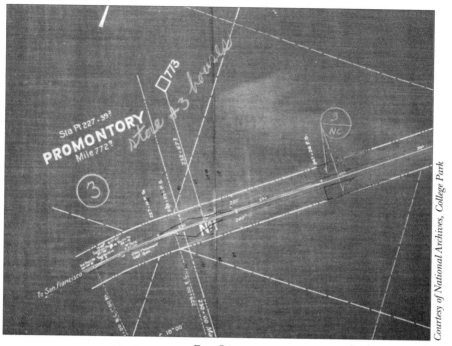

FIG. 8–7

On Southern Pacific blueprint map No. V2–24, Promontory's railroad buildings cluster along the right of way, while a comment written on the map notes that a "store and 3 houses" are found there in 1924.

flat but some of it rolling country suitable only for winter sheep grazing." Much of the same was written for the next two maps (V2–16 and V2–17). The latter included Kelton, which was noted as "a shipping point for some grain[.] trains run from here to Brigham [City]." At Kelton was a double-ended yard track and passing siding, a passenger and freight depot stockyard, sand house, pump house, and square water tank, as well as a 27 x 30 foot section house, bunk house, ice-house, cook house, and cellar. A hotel and seven houses were also mentioned north of the tracks (V2–17). Kelton, it will be recalled, was the place where the only through train over the line changed numbers and ran on varying days.

South and west of Kelton, the same notation of sagebrush desert land that was generally level to rolling and only suitable for winter sheep grazing continued for several maps. At Peplin, the commenter noted that there was "no town." Similarly at Ombey, he noted, "nothing here." However, Ombey did have a wye, passing siding, and a spur track. Matlin had almost exactly the same minimal arrangement—a wye for turning locomotives, passing siding, and a spur track (V2–9). At Terrace, the

Photo by author,

Fig. 8–8

At the site of Terrace today, there are virtually no above-ground features. Note, however, that the long-abandoned turntable pit shows as a depression in the landscape with portions of the early turntable strewn about. The Red Dome Mountains are seen in the distance.

commenter noted only "an old brick building about 28 or 30' by 70 or 80'" was standing. That building shows on the map as a "machine shop," and it was evidently the only aboveground feature left there. The commenter must have been amazed by how things had changed from the time when Terrace was a major railroad town! Aware of Terrace's history, he wrote about its heyday in some detail. "There was a small town here at one time," he began. Noting of the former improvements that "[t]he townsite was largely graded with cinders," he added that "[t]here was a roundhouse here at one time" (fig. 8–8). The site he visited was forlorn. As he put it, "[t]here are no houses here now." Nevertheless, at that time, he still could report that "[t]here is a siding and there is a small amount of freight shipped from here." As he put it, though, Terrace had no future. "All outside of 200' R of W [on each side of the tracks] should be classed as N.C. No station grounds necessary here." The meaning of N.C. is not given, but it likely meant nonconducive for agriculture.

A few miles farther west, at Watercress, that same notation about the land only being good for winter sheep grazing is found. Watercress did have a passing siding, two corrals, two tie houses, a water tank and an old railroad car body, which likely served as a storage shed (fig. 8–9).

Photo by author

FIG. 8–9

At Watercress, the concrete footings of the long-abandoned water tower remain visible in the desert landscape.

At Bovine, the commenter found "no town," though there was a passing siding, water tank, car house (presumably a house made from a railroad car, but also possibly a handcar shed), and section house. At Lucin, the commenter evidently found little except the connection of the Promontory Branch with the much shinier rails of the mainline. The map shows a wye here. It also notes that the original line that joined the mainline at an acute angle had been "abandoned." Replacing that junction was a reverse curve that took the Promontory Branch into the mainline as one leg of a wye. The commenter did, however, summarize the area's landscape in almost exactly the same way on every map from Kelton to Lucin: "The land extending throughout this map is all sagebrush desert generally level but some of it rolling, only suitable for winter grazing for sheep." He did, however, add one additional note to what had evidently become a mantra. The "entire zone," as he put it, was "of [the] same general character." (V2–1)[13]

The population figures, however, began to reveal a change in the character of the area. By 1910, farmers outnumbered all others in the Promontory precinct, including railroad workers. Of the two hundred residents counted in the census, forty-six listed their occupations: Twenty-eight were farmers, fifteen were railroaders, and the remaining three were a miner, a blacksmith, and a road commissioner.[14] The 1910s were an interesting time in this area as there was substantial interest in agriculture. With increasing tensions in Europe, the prospects for agriculture brightened considerably.

If 1919 was a banner year for Promontory, that was only because it marked the fiftieth anniversary of the joining of the rails. Ironically, though, virtually all of the celebratory activities were centered on Ogden, where the Golden Jubilee ceremony was held on May 10. The weather just before the ceremony brought intense rain, but the sun soon appeared and the parade traversed the city's streets. One of the unique floats featured "a replica of the ancient engine Jupiter." Reportedly, the original engineer, George Lashus, was on the pilot of this replica. This, of course, does not square with historians who claim that George Booth operated the *Jupiter* in 1869. Could Lashus have been the fireman of the *Jupiter*? Given the paucity of official records, we may never know. At any rate, the other dignitaries on hand in Ogden in 1919 included William H. Hood, who was in "charge of more railroad construction work than any other man in the world." Another float—a daughter of the West with the beaus of the East—showed the advantage obtained from the union of the rails. Mostly, though, the Golden Jubilee provided the opportunity to tout the progress that had been made rather than to portray history accurately. A special air show, for example, featured planes buzzing in formation. To that end, a float depicting the Lucin Cutoff was also highly visible. Despite the emphasis on progress, others compiled lists of engineers on the various locomotives in May 1869. The conflict over the identity of *Jupiter*'s engineer notwithstanding, this list might prove invaluable to future researchers.[15]

One should not overlook the commercial motivation for the 1919 Jubilee celebration. A 1919 advertisement for West Ogden Milling and Elevator Company in *The Ogden Examiner* asks, "Why Not Try the Golden Spike Flour?" The illustration with this advertisement, evidently the flour's beautiful label, shows two dignitaries pounding in the golden spike at Promontory Summit on May 10, 1869. No doubt, this brand originated with the flurry of activity surrounding the big celebration for the 50th anniversary of the Golden Spike on May 10, 1919. Meanwhile, Promontory Summit persisted in relative isolation, though many of its agricultural products, including wheat, found their way east to Ogden via the rails of the branchline.

In the period 1910–1930, farming became the major economic activity along the Promontory line. The 1920 census for Promontory precinct reveals only ten railroaders (eight Italian section laborers, one engineer, and one section foreman), thirty-two farmers, two farm laborers, nine stock farmers, one U.S. Army stockman, one cowboy, and seven sheepherders (mostly Mexican). Thirty-three were potash laborers, and one was a potash "Kemist" (chemist). This suggests that mining of potash was important for a brief time.[16] That was typical of life in the area of Promontory, which was sustained by agriculture and periodically hosted, with only limited success, extractive industry.

A specially published map of the State of Utah showing "lands designated as non-irrigable by the Department of the Interior under the Provisions of the Enlarged Homestead Acts" (1920) shows lands qualifying under the "general provisions" in red, and under "non-residence provisions" (Section 6) in blue. With the exception of a few small areas, most of the area in Box Elder County consists of blue squares, and most of these lie to the north of the Promontory Branch, with the important exception of land south of Promontory and Rozel.[17] Under the Enlarged Homestead Acts, individuals and families could settle on, and claim, up to 640 acres of land, a huge increase from the 160 acres under the original Homestead Act. The checkerboard pattern around the Promontory Branch reveals the private ownership that resulted when the railroad was given land in alternating sections as a provision of the Pacific Railroad Act. Now, with the expansion of the Homestead Act and the rise of dry farming, the area near the Promontory Branch was being offered to souls brave enough to try their hand at agriculture.

Dry farming always suggests risk, but it can also cause potential problems by removing the natural vegetation and exposing the soil to erosion by wind and water. With that risk in mind, perhaps, the U. S. Bureau of Agricultural Economy (BAE) prepared a series of maps from 1934 to 1937 showing the "Problem Areas" of Utah. Using a base map originally compiled by cartographer A. S. Hasson, in 1921 and 1922, the BAE identified areas such as eroded range land, irrigated farmland, and dry farm land. On one map (fig. 8–10), apparently prepared in 1934, a pattern of diagonal lines indicates areas that potentially could be dry farmed, but also shows areas in yellow that evidently were dry farmed. Note that much of the arable area of northwestern Utah (including western portions of the Curlew Valley) is not indicated as being dry farmed, but that much of the area near Promontory Summit is. The area near Howell and Blue Creek shows as a swath of dry farming, with an area of irrigated farming close to Howell. The "tongue" of dry-farmed land extending in a north-south direction sweeps to the west of Promontory, reaching almost to the Great Salt Lake near Monument Point. From Promontory Summit and extending southward, a smaller tongue of dry farming is also found.

The map indicates a very large area of "eroded range land farther west of Promontory, in the area west and south of Kelton. This, evidently, was a result of overgrazing in the very fragile desert ecosystem—a legacy of

Courtesy of Cartographic and Architectural Records Section, National Archives, College Park

Fig. 8–10

A map showing "Problem Areas" of Utah by the United States Bureau of Agricultural Economy shows the area in the vicinity of the Promontory Branch (ca. 1934) as eroded range land (turquoise color), dry farmed land (yellow), and potentially dry-farmed land (diagonal stripes).

the late nineteenth century. Tellingly, this is the same area where the comments were found about land "only suitable for the winter grazing of sheep" on the Southern Pacific Company's *Right of Way and Track Maps* of the Promontory Branch in the mid-1920s. Now, in the 1930s, with the realization that overgrazing was irreparably damaging the land, measures were taken to stop, or at least slow, the erosion. It should be noted here that although all grazing has an affect on the land, some grazing animals have a greater negative impact than others. Sheep are notoriously hard on land as they graze the grasses and other vegetation down to, or at least very close to, the roots. Even if sheep could graze the grasses here in winter, the hot, dry summers would take their toll on the vegetation, with consequent soil erosion following. With the passage of the Taylor Grazing Act in 1934, there was a steady improvement in the range. Even today, however, the area near Terrace is still recovering long after years of overgrazing followed by repeated droughts. Minimal vegetation and gullying are common.

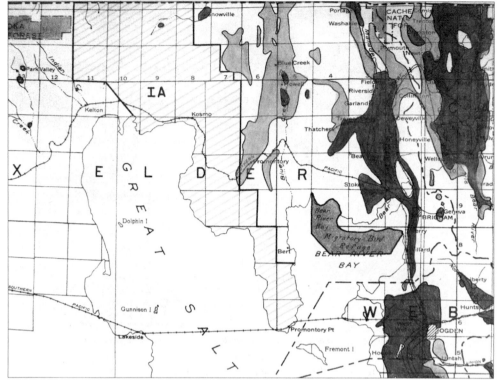

FIG. 8–11

When the Bureau of Agricultural Economy prepared this map showing "Land Use Adjustment" in 1934, dry farmed areas (orange) were in good condition, but a large area (pale yellow stripped) is shown as "problem dry farmed land."

Dry farming, too, could have a negative impact, especially in those marginal areas where low precipitation is normal and droughts occur with regularity. To that end, the BAE also prepared another problem area map showing "Land Use Adjustment" (Preliminary) (fig. 8–11). Note that there are two types of dry farming shown on this map. The dry-farmed areas near Promontory, and toward Blue Creek and Howell (shown in orange), are healthy enough. However, a very large dry-farmed area, colored a pale yellow, stretches all the way from Idaho southward to Promontory Point and is shown as "problem dry farmed land." This assessment was based on the impact of dry farming on the land here. Coupled with the fact that crop failure was far more common here than in the more well-watered, deeper soils near Promontory and Howell, the best advice to farmers was to avoid dry farming in the area altogether.

On yet another *Preliminary Land Use Adjustment Map,* this one dated 1937 and presumably still in final draft form, the dry farm land area remains much the same. However, the "problem dry farmed land" on the other map is now replaced by the term *submarginal dryfarm land.* The meaning, however, is much the same: dry farming is not a wise idea here. West of Kelton, a new category appears: "Railroad Land—Every other sec[tion] Desert Quality." This, of course, means the land may not be utilized for any use—at least not on a long-term basis. With these three maps, we see that the Promontory Branch ran through varied country that was changing due to both the *experience* that people had acquired over the years, and the increasing *regulation* of land use by governmental bodies. That rise of government was in part a result of the Great Depression which created "alphabet agencies" (like the BAE, WPA, and so on) to help private industry get back on its feet and individuals find work.[18]

As land was fenced, and wheat planted, the countryside's appearance and character changed. One aspect almost overlooked during this transition is that it tamed the land, so to speak. In the period 1910–1920, as ranch life began to be eclipsed by dry farming, wild horses became scarcer. Isaac W. Finn (born 1886) recalled that these horses were called "Promontory Mustangs" and that they were "mighty good horses." Finn recalled breaking "more than you can count on all your fingers," and that they were shipped from Rozel, where he loaded them "for $2.50 a head." According to Finn, Hereford cattle dominated the range. There were "stockcars here and the chutes running right up into the cars" which made it easier for the wranglers to "drive the cattle right up the chutes and into the cars."[19]

In 1920, the Promontory-Curlew Land Company began to explore the possibility that the area held significant reserves of oil. Ten years later (1930), petroleum geologist S. Goring Vidler prepared a report for the company on its "lands lying in Box Elder County, Utah and Oneida County, Idaho." He began by noting that these lands "lie just West [*sic*] of what is known as the promontory which extends into the Great Salt Lake, making a physical protuberance which is well recognized." This protuberance was, of course, the Promontory Range. Vidler continued that "[t]he lands are a rolling terrain for the most part covered by sage brush which in itself is indicative of fertile soil, and where cultivated land produces excellent crops of wheat, etc." Of the geology, Vidler noted that under the land's surface, at a depth of approximately 1,300 feet were "black carbonaceous shales of the basic Pennsylvania[n] and upper Mississippi[an]." The material above these shales was dense enough to trap oil, forming as Vidler called it, a "natural reservoir . . . ." After providing what he called "a short dissertation on the genesis of oil," Vidler

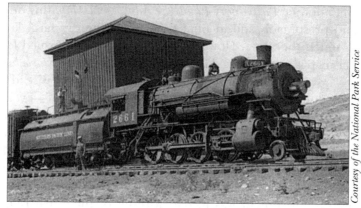

FIG. 8–12

An oil-burning Southern Pacific 2–8–0 locomotive with a whaleback tender takes water at the Blue Creek tank house, ca. 1935. Although small by Southern Pacific mainline standards, Consolidation-type locomotives like this were the largest and heaviest power that normally operated on the Promontory Branch.

concluded that "there are four possible horizons from which oil could be produced on this property, all above 4,000 feet [below the surface] . . . ." Vidler's assessment was glowing, to put it mildly. He noted that "during my twenty odd years in the profession as a geologist and having had seven [oil] fields already to my credit, I wish to say that from the geological and geophysical evidence here, this should be one of the greatest potential oil fields that has yet been discovered on the North American continent." Vidler's recommendation, of course, was "that drilling be started immediately . . . ."[20] Having made favorable prognostications about the value of resources themselves, the management of the Promontory-Curlew Land Company was evidently cautious about undertaking extensive—and expensive—drilling. Nevertheless, oil was an enticing prospect.

By this time, most of Southern Pacific's steam locomotives were fueled by oil, as was the developing automobile and trucking industry, but alas, the area did not become an oil producer despite Vidler's grand prediction. This was ironic, for Southern Pacific's Ogden facility now featured a huge oil tank that stored bunker C locomotive fuel, a thick oil that required heating before it would flow into the firebox. Locomotives on the Promontory line now burned this fuel oil, as evidenced by their semi-cylindrical whaleback and Vanderbilt tenders (fig. 8–12). The relatively small Consolidation (2–8–0) locomotives like No. 2661 featuring these oil tenders were the largest power used on the line.

Courtesy of the National Park Service and Utah State Historical Society, Salt Lake City

FIG. 8–13

The outside braced boxcars in this scene at Lampo, ca. 1930, typify the largest freight cars used on the line, normally hauling grain from dry-farmed areas near Promontory to distant markets.

In addition to Ogden, oil facilities on the Promontory Summit line were located at Kelton. Leona Yates Anderson's husband was based out of Kelton for about twelve years. She recalls that Kelton had "a pit, a big pit that they kept the oil in." This lined pit was covered, but one could still smell the oil in it when the wind was right. The pit was filled with locomotive fuel oil when "[t]hey'd bring an oil tank [car in] and hot it up to the pit and leave it on the high line [an elevated track] and it would go down [i.e., drain by gravity] into the pit." To get the oil into the locomotive tenders, "they'd pump it out and pump it in to the engine." As Anderson noted, that "heavy, black" oil—"kind of like a tar oil . . . . That's what run the engine."[21] This type of oil pit was common on the Southern Pacific at this time, and the remains of the one at Kelton are still visible.

Photographs taken at Lampo (fig. 8–13) and Blue Creek (fig. 8–14) beautifully reveal the Promontory Branch in the 1920s and 1930s. The large, outside-braced boxcars hauled grain and other materials at this time and were the largest freight cars on the line. Most boxcars now were forty feet in length, while some were fifty feet long—twice the length and nearly twice the weight, of the first boxcars used on the line in 1869. Remarkably, the Blue Creek water tank house was still standing at this time, after about sixty years of service, which was listed as the serviceable lifetime of such water tanks when the ICC valuators visited the area in 1916–1917, and the tank was evidently making good on that

Courtesy of the National Park Service

FIG. 8–14
In this photograph of the
Blue Creek water tank
house taken in about 1930,
a Southern Pacific boxcar
stands on the siding.

promise. This water tank house was among the last of the nineteenth-century structures standing and serviceable on the Promontory Branch. To the SP, though, economics—not historic sentiment—was the order of the day. That old water tank house represented just one more item that would soon need replacement. In a 1974 interview, Joseph Nicholas (born 1907) fondly remembered the water tank at Blue Creek in the 1920s. The "big tank," as he called it, was "I'd say close to sixteen feet high and at least twenty feet across." In winter, because "the tank leaked a little bit," ice would form "chunks [that seemed to be] as big as this room . . . and being damp in there like that, why it'd stay in there until July." As Nicholas recalled, in early summer, "sometimes we'd go to town and stop in and get a drink of water and bust off a chunk of ice and take it home and make ice cream."[22]

As Promontory matured, which is to say declined, the commemoration of the golden spike became an issue as people drove over the back roads in increasing numbers. As noted earlier, there was still some interest in the big event that had occurred in 1869, though it was a distant memory to old-timers. The people who did travel here took notice of the white, concrete obelisk-shaped marker put up in 1916 to commemorate events nearly fifty years earlier. That concrete marker suggested a kind of permanence, as well as antiquity, and it became a landmark at the site. The 1917 valuation maps show the marker as originally placed on the south side of the tracks as close as possible (or known) to where the original golden spike was hammered home. By the 1920s and 1930s, then, the passage of time had begun to increase Promontory's allure. The Golden Spike Monument was isolated and associated with a grand event in the Victorian West, and it drew an increasing number of history-seeking adventurers willing to tackle trails and rugged roads of the West on foot or in automobiles.

Many people traveling through the back roads here found themselves at the obelisk-shaped marker and posed for photographs in front of it. An old family photograph shows a radiant Ella Stokes flanked by beaming travel companions John Chugg and Ferman Westergard in about 1931 (fig. 8–15). Their tall, laced boots and jodhpurs suggest that they are prepared for adventure, and the monument almost appears archaeological—an obelisk commemorating the great works of the ancients of Egypt. To give that scene a touch of more modern archaeological drama, an old building (possibly, the Houghton store) is visible in the background. Promontory at this time had attained the status of ghost town—a forlorn place that even though not entirely abandoned, had seen much better days. Now, more than a half-century after the big event, Promontory represented a fragment of a vanished West marked by memories of wood-burning locomotives, ornate passenger cars, and obligatory station stops.

At just this time (namely the 1920s and 1930s), an interest in the history of Promontory began to grow, but the railroad contemplated abandoning it. After all, carloads were relatively few compared to many other areas, and passenger traffic was virtually nil. Besides, the state (and federal) government increasingly built roads, so that trucks might just as easily handle the traffic here. In other words, the railroad viewed abandonment as a way of reducing red ink. It was no secret that the Promontory Branch cost far more to operate and maintain than it earned in income. Not surprisingly, then, abandonment increasingly seemed like the only way out in the 1930s. As the ICC valuation report showed, the railroad line here was now a second-class line at best. In April of 1933, Southern Pacific sought permission from the Interstate Commerce Commission to abandon the 55–mile section of the Promontory Branch from Lucin to Kelton. This section was the most forlorn, and lightly used, on the line. Still, though, the ICC refused Southern Pacific's request.[23] The line hung on into the early 1940s. However, by the beginning of World War II, with calls for scrap metal to assist the war effort, the time seemed right. Accordingly, in early spring of 1942, the railroad applied for abandonment of the entire line from Corinne to Lucin.

Abandonment hearings are usually intense affairs, and this one was no exception. At a formal meeting in Salt Lake City on May 2, 1942, the

Courtesy of Wendy Simmons Johnson, Sagebrush Consultants, Ogden, Utah

FIG. 8–15
In about 1931, a beaming Ella Stokes is flanked by travel companions John Chugg and Ferman Westergard as they pose in front of the obelisk-shaped marker commemorating the driving of the golden spike here.

official "Abandonment Proceedings" convened. Among the testimony received was that from W. H. Barnard, a farmer from Hansel Valley. When asked for more details about his occupation, Barnard stated, "My principal crop is wheat. I am what they call a dry-land farmer." In response to other questions, Barnard noted that he was located close to the point on the Southern Pacific line called Kosmo, which was located southwest of Hansel Valley. When asked how many acres in the roughly five-square-mile valley was planted in dry-farmed wheat, Barnard stated "practically all of it . . . approximately twenty thousand acres of land, of wheat land." That amounted to "around two hundred thousand bushels" of wheat. Barnard noted that the distance to the Union Pacific Railroad at Tremonton was about thirty-eight or forty miles, over a divide.[24] By contrast, it was a gradual slope—"a natural down-grade"—to Kosmo, and that Tremonton took considerable time and effort to reach. Barnard noted that he and about fourteen other farmers had "put up our own loading facilities" at Kosmo at a cost of "between fifteen hundred and two thousand dollars."[25]

The subject of sheep and cattle ranchers also came up, at which time D. H. Adams of Layton recounted the names of those licensed to run stock in the area, including "the Browning people [who] have a license for four thousand . . . on the old Promontory." Barnard specifically noted just west of the old Promontory station "the Ellisons and many others from there down to the Salt Wells Valley and around Monument and around that country . . . is set aside for cattle only, and I am satisfied there are fifteen thousand cattle in there, between there and the Nevada line in the winter time." Adams concluded that abandonment of "this branch line from Corinne to Lucin," as the hearing examiner called it, "would have a serious effect on all of those that are licensed to stay in there."[26]

Yet, when pushed to state where the livestock were sent to railhead, Adams had to concede that most were "loaded over at Burley, Idaho" and at Oakley. "There are," he admitted, "not any of them loaded on the old line here"—although he added, "there are a few loaded down at Lucin on the main line, but that is all."[27] The examiner then asked an interesting question: Is it "a fact that if the railroad was maintained to Kelton, that you would have a fair degree of security–[?]" Adams answered, "No—no, because of the fact that from the north end and from Ombey, Matlin and Watercress, you would be so far from Kelton that it would be impossible for your horses to pull a load through there." Another examiner asked Adams about the number of individuals who graze their sheep in the territory "from Promontory west to Lucin," and Adams guessed about 125. Of these, Adams stated that anyone "building up an outfit, I would say, whether it would be a dry farm or a ranch" would be adversely affected by the railroad's closure. As Adams put it, "because he wouldn't want a ranch or a sheep outfit or a cattle outfit out in the desert some place where he couldn't get feed if it was necessary, and your railroad facilities make a nice setup." Adams concluded, "without the railroad I would feel that my investments wouldn't be worth what they are at the present time with the railroad."[28]

Not all the complainants were farmers or ranchers. For example, J. C. Wood represented the Quaker Crystal Salt Company at Monument. Wood, who also owned a ranch "on this old line," noted that the "salt company leased land from the Southern Pacific to the beaches of Great Salt

Lake." The Quaker Crystal Salt Company began operations about 1939 and was developing canals and roads to expand its current operation of "about 85 acres of salt gardens." Wood noted the importance of the rail-road, but was forced to admit that Quaker Crystal had not yet shipped any salt on the Southern Pacific, as the rates were too high. When the subject of shipping salt northward out of the area to Highway 30 came up, Wood noted that was not feasible because the roads were so poor.[29]

Given his farming interests, the examiners then asked Wood about shipping wheat by truck. Wood, who noted that "at this time I am load-ing from Promontory and Lampo; [but] not loading anything from Kosmo," stated that he would have trouble because "I can't move my crop unless I can get some tires"—which was unlikely given the ration-ing of rubber during World War II. Wood confirmed that people devel-oped farms near Howell precisely because the railroad ran nearby at Blue Creek. Wood agreed that "with the loading point at Lampo," farm-ers had "a ready and easy means to get their crop onto the railroad." Wood stated that "we loaded out 47 carloads last year—15 or 16 hun-dred bushels to the car." Returning to the issue of salt production, Wood concluded that if the railroad was abandoned, the Quaker Crystal Salt Company would have to close down.[30]

The hearings continued with others testifying as to the railroads' importance. John P. Holmgren of Bear River City, a "farmer, livestock grower" and "businessman too" was also president of the Box Elder County Cattle and Horse Growers' Association. Holmgren stated that "we located, as cattlemen and ranchers, all the way from Tremonton to Lucin, expecting the railroad to remain there, and we have built accord-ingly, and if the railroad is taken away we have thousands of acres that will be reduced in value for saleable purposes." Holmgren also predicted that Box Elder County "will have a big reduction in income from taxes from the Railroad Company . . . ."[31] Despite this statement, Holmgren admitted that he personally had not used the railroad to ship stock from his ranching land near Monument. Upon learning this, Holmgren was asked why he hoped the railroad would not be abandoned: "What, in your opinion, is the necessity of having this branch line and maintain-ing it around north of the Lake, west to Kelton and Lucin?" Holmgren quickly responded, "There are occasional severe winters, when that rail-road has been very serviceable to the cattlemen and farmers in the west, to import cottonseed cake and corn and baled hay at certain seasons of the year, when severe winters come along." Holmgren continued that about thirty livestock growers from the area west of Promontory stated at a meeting that "the loss to them in range values would be consider-able if this railroad were abandoned." Moreover, that under the "present crisis"—by which he meant the war—truck shipments were difficult, so that even farmers would be hard put. He speculated that "a dry-land farm will decrease in value I will say five dollars an acre" and that "I think the sheepmen and the cattlemen will suffer a good deal for the necessities of that railroad in bad seasons" if the railroad were abandoned.[32]

Later in the hearing, W. S. Young, an employee of Farmers' Grain Co-operative of Ogden, reported on the importance of grain to the branch line. The co-op, which had been in business since 1938, averaged 75,000 to 100,000 bushels of grain per year from the Kosmo District. Young estimated that this was about half of what was grown there. Moreover, he cited some impressive figures from the Southern Pacific that he made into "exhibits." Over a five-year period, 901 cars of wheat had been shipped of which 51 were from Kelton. The 850 cars from east of Promontory carried more than 1 million bushels of wheat. The average number of bushels from the Lampo area was 560,000, but only 62,750 originated from Promontory. Additionally 200,000 bushels were grown in the vicinity of Kosmo. The total for the entire area shipped by rail was 1,340,767 bushels, but 4,113,750 bushels were shipped out by all types of transport. Young estimated that "only one car by rail for every three" trucks was the norm—meaning that trucks were *normally* the more economical way to ship. However, his figures for the last year revealed an increase in rail traffic. This, according to Young, "definitely indicates that the movement is back toward the rails." The reason? Evidently, because "truck tires are wearing out."[33]

The Rosette Asphalt Company of Rozel also weighed in on the proceedings. According to a Mr. Janssen, their business had shipped two carloads in 1937 and one each in 1938, 1939, and 1940—but four cars in 1941. Moreover, during the first four months of 1942, they had shipped one car per month! Buoyed by increasing orders for asphalt, the company planned to ship 2.5 to 3 million pounds of asphalt in drums. One problem with current shipments by rail was that Southern Pacific would not handle any lcl (less-than-carload) freight from a point marked in red on the map used at the hearings. That point was "on the east side of the lake," so Rosette Asphalt had to ship their product by truck. Janssen noted that the bad condition of the road over Promontory made it difficult to ship by truck to Brigham City. Moreover, there was another problem. In noting the distance to Brigham City on a map, the mileage showed as 39; however, the mileage on several cars [that is, automobiles] showed it to be 50.[34] This is yet another example of a problem with a map, only this time it came at the very end of the life of the Promontory line. But this shipper made a critical point: "Where our product goes we will have priorities. All our stuff goes into Defense, in other words." Interestingly during the hearing, it was stated that sugar beet traffic accounted for 75 percent of the volume of the line. This was technically true, but virtually all of that traffic was derived from the very eastern end near Corinne and Brigham City.

Toward the end of the hearing, it became apparent that this was a complicated case. Southern Pacific revealed that it had already entered into discussions about divesting itself of the property—that is, selling it. Then, too, it was stated that the Navy Department proposed to requisition the property if the railroad could not sell it outright. The issue of salvage value of the "sixty-two pound rail from Kelton to Lucin" also came up, as one applicant was interested in that. The day's hearing concluded with the presentation of expense figures on the portion of the line from Corinne to Dathol or Stokes, which totaled $5,288. In itemizing this figure, the costs for station employees ($2,056), wages of train engineers ($550), trainmen ($754), and fuel oil ($221) were also given. As these figures were contrasted with income, the handwriting on the wall became clearer.[35]

The effective date of certification of abandonment, June 11, 1942, was extended to September 10, 1942, but that was merely a stay of execution, and a technicality. In "cases disposed of without printed report," a terse listing is found: F.D. No. 13655 Central Pacific Railway Company Et Al Abandonment, Decided June 11, 1942." The certificate permitted "abandonment by the Central Pacific Railway Company of the part of its Promontory branch between Lucin and Corinne, Utah; and (2) abandonment of operation by the Southern Pacific Company (a) over the Promontory branch between Lucin and Corinne Junction, and (b) over the Oregon Short Line Railroad between Corinne Junction and Ogden, in Box Elder and Weber Counties, Utah. Condition prescribed."[36]

Leading up to this, an order of the ICC, held at its office in Washington, D.C., on July 10 that "the Central Pacific Company was permitted to abandon, and the Southern Pacific Company, lessee, to abandon operation of, inter alia [among other things], the line of railroad extending from a point near Lucin to a point near Corinne, approximately 120.78 miles . . . on the condition that the carrier first named shall sell the segment of the line between Dathol and Corinne to the Oregon Short Line Railroad Company or the Union Pacific Railroad Company at a price equal to the fair net salvage value thereof . . . ." The document went on to state that "*It further appearing*, that negotiations are in progress between the applicants, the Navy Department, which has requisitioned the line, and representatives of the Oregon Short Line Railroad Company or the Union Pacific Railroad Company for continued operation of the portion of said line extending from Dathol to Corinne, approximately 4.8 miles . . . ."[37]

Courtesy of the National Park Service

FIG. 8–16
On September 8, 1942, two contemporary steam locomotives participated in the "undriving" of the spike that signaled abandonment of the Promontory Branch after seventy-three years of service.

The actual abandonment of the Promontory line was apparently unlike any other abandonment in western railroad history. Just as a ceremony marked the completion of the line in 1869, so, too, was the *removal* of a spike that signaled the demise of the line. More than two hundred people attended the event, which took place on September 8, 1942. As in 1869, two steam locomotives faced each other, speeches given, music played, and news was again made (fig. 8–16). The steam locomotives, however, were relatively modern and more typical of the power that was used on the line at the present time. Their somber black paint was a reminder of just how much railroading had changed from the days of Jupiter and *No. 119*. This event, too, was far more somber. Whereas the golden spike driven in 1869 symbolized Promontory's place in the future, the removal of a simulated golden spike at the event in 1942 symbolized the end of Promontory's rail connection to the outside world. The removal of the spike also signified another sacrifice, as the steel rails were scheduled to go to the nationwide metal drive necessitated by the war industry. In this case, the rails would go to the Navy's Clearfield supply depot and other locales. Significantly, at almost exactly this time, the Geneva Steel Mill in Provo opened, and it required huge amounts of iron ore and scrap. It is unknown whether any of the Promontory line's 123 miles of removed rail went there. Most sources suggest that the rails were in good enough shape for reuse as trackage in various naval depots, and therefore not actually scrapped. Most people present felt the removal of the line was for a good cause, but a few questioned whether the quantity of steel removed really justified the dismantling of this important piece of railroad history. It should be recalled that at this crucial time in history, other historic objects made of metal, including historic automobiles and locomotives, were sometimes scrapped.

At any rate, Promontory was about to lose its railroad but would not go out quietly. In anticipation of the line's dismantling, the large ceremony was a carefully orchestrated event. Ogden *Standard-Examiner* columnist Frank Frances was master of ceremonies and officials present included Utah Governor Herbert Maw, officials L. P. Hopkins[38] of the Southern Pacific and E. C. Schmidt of the Union Pacific, and Everett Michael of Hyman-Michael Company. In contrast to the 1869 event, LDS Apostle George Albert Smith provided the invocation, after which officials made speeches. Confirming that this event was a team effort, each official "undrove" the spike about an inch until it was free. Interestingly, only one person was present at both this ceremony and the joining of the rails seventy-three years earlier: Mary Ipsen had served as a waitress on the mess car in 1869.[39]

Removal of the line was still fresh in the mind of Merlin Larsen in 2005. Larsen, it will be recalled, lived along the line most of his life. In 1942, at about twenty-five years of age, he was part of the crew that removed the rails for the Southern Pacific. The railroad contracted this crew, likely due to labor shortages during the war. Larsen's job was to pull out all but three spikes so that the rails could then be easily slipped out. To do so, Larsen recalls, "I had a big clamp, like an ice clamp, hooked onto the rail, [which] tipped over the rail, so it could slide out over [the] spikes." With this done, the crew "lifted it with a pulley, then shoved it onto a flat car." The train removing the line had three or four flat cars, and they were brought to Lucin "to hook up with another" that evidently carried the rails off.

Larsen recalled that the removal crew "started at Lampo, [and] went west to Rozel" and he confirmed that the work did not proceed without incident. He noted that "the sharpest bend on the whole railroad was near Rozel, and as they pulled the spikes, the last three wouldn't hold—the rail moved and the locomotive 'dropped' onto the ties. It took several hours to jack up the locomotive and jack the rails underneath it." The locomotive on the work train was typical. Larsen recalled that it had six drive wheels—probably a Mogul (2–6–0) or Ten-Wheeler (4–6–0)—though Consolidation (2–8–0) locomotives were often used

Photo by author

FIG. 8–17
Promontory's ranching and dry-farming past is suggested by what locals call the "old school house" and a broken windmill, which are located just east of the former community and which survived the town's abandonment.

on the line, too. The entire project of removing the track was rather more difficult for other reasons. Some of the men were bitten by rattlesnakes, others suffered heatstroke in the late summer sun, and the work had to be suspended briefly as a brushfire of unknown origin burned the tinder-dry vegetation along the line.

As a lasting tribute to the early construction of the railroad, Merlin Larsen noted that many of the ties (4½ x 4½ inches by about 8 feet in length) were in good enough shape to be reused as fence posts by farmers. Larsen and his brother "pulled down the telegraph line from Corinne to the other side of Locomotive Springs." At the golden spike site itself, Larsen recalled that there were about six poles, driven so deep that we busted them off." These redwood telegraph poles were still sturdy enough for use as billboard posts—another testimony to the durability of the California redwood brought in by the Central Pacific railroad.

At Promontory itself, the few buildings that remained had developed the patina of abandonment. A reminder of the town's ranching and farming days was seen in the old windmill and what locals call the "old school," whose pine boards have been burnished to a bronze color by the sun, rain, snow, and wind (fig. 8–17). Like the railroad itself, the

Photo by author

Fig. 8–18

With the abandonment of the line over Promontory Summit in 1942, rails were removed for the war effort, leaving the Promontory line one of Utah's many ghost railroads. This picture at Lucin Junction looks westward from the old roadbed of the Promontory line which is marked by the leaning poles (*right*) to a point where it intersected with the Southern Pacific main line (*left*).

fabric of the community was time-worn but tenacious. Both, however, were living on borrowed time.

The line over Promontory did not surrender easily, but by fall of 1942, it was added to the many miles of ghost railroad trackage in Utah. Travelers on the mainline just west of the Great Salt Lake could gaze northward at Lucin Junction to see the remains of the old line to Promontory, which was now only an abandoned roadbed with all track removed (fig. 8–18). The old line to Promontory stretched off into the distance in a northeasterly direction while the mainline headed straight for, and across, the lake. In 1942, during the early days of World War II, a traveler heading to San Francisco recalls that mention was made of the old line to Promontory at this point as she rushed westward in her Southern Pacific passenger train.[40] Promontory had been well established as both a fact and a legend at this time. With the abandonment of the old line to Promontory, an era spanning more than three quarters of a century had ended, but another had already begun.

Chapter 9

REMEMBERING PROMONTORY
(1942–Present)

The removal of the spike at Promontory in 1942 had special significance to the movie-going public, who had seen the golden spike
ceremony of 1869 re-enacted in the recent Cecil B. DeMille film *Union
Pacific* (1939). It was one thing to read about the events of 1869 at
Promontory, but quite another to see them recreated on film, that per-
suasive medium so capable of shaping, even manipulating, popular
beliefs. *Union Pacific* was a celebration of the railroad as a shaper of history. In order to depict the building of the transcontinental railroad,
DeMille had to find other locomotives as stand-ins. Despite their fame
in 1869, the Union Pacific No. 119 and Central Pacific Jupiter had
been scrapped in the early twentieth century. That, however, did not
stop their reincarnation in pageants and in motion pictures. A show
at the San Francisco Panama-Pacific Exposition in 1915, for example,
depicted the joining of the rails at Promontory. Similarly, in the late
1930s, other events featured replicas of the two locomotives. In one
case, two Nevada Central steam locomotives, numbers 5 and 6, were
cosmetically altered to appear more like their prototypes. Number
5 became the Jupiter, with its large bonnet-shaped smokestack, and
number 6 was transformed into Union Pacific No. 119 with its straight
stack. Along with their passenger train consists, these locomotives and
cars made brave, if somewhat strained, stand-ins—the biggest inconsis-
tency being the fact that they were narrow gauge equipment![1]

This faux equipment was widely viewed in San Francisco, but films also
presented Promontory to the American public. *The Iron Horse* directed
by John Ford was released in 1924, and the 1939 film *Union Pacific* made

FIG. 9–1

In 1939, the Cecil B. DeMille epic *Union Pacific* featured a clamorous
re-enactment of the joining of the rails at Promontory in 1869.

two more locomotives—in this case, standard gauge from the Virginia &
Truckee Railroad in Nevada—even more famous. As portrayed on cel-
luloid by DeMille, the trains and scenes of Promontory, or approxima-
tions of them and the event, became icons for yet another generation.
Union Pacific celebrated the winning of the West, a potent theme to a
nation just digging itself out of the Great Depression (ca. 1929–1939).
DeMille reportedly pondered whether to portray the Union Pacific or
the Santa Fe railroad in this film, and tossed a coin to decide. Union
Pacific was the winner, and the rest is cinematic history. Naturally, a film
about the Union Pacific just had to feature the driving of the golden
spike at Promontory—a challenge that DeMille relished as it was the
kind of spectacle he loved to film.

Union Pacific was an important late-1930s, early-1940s era Western
film as it marked the beginning of a Renaissance in the genre. Its simple
plot of good triumphing over evil, and things ending happily, was typical DeMille. However, through its use of wide-open landscapes and its
seemingly authentic depiction of railroading, DeMille's film gave the
events on-screen a larger than life quality that would become a hallmark
of later Western films. Its cinematography by Victor Milner and Dewey
Wrigley, though filmed in black and white, gave audiences prolonged

views of western scenery and railroad activity (fig. 9–1). *Union Pacific* ran over two hours in length (133 minutes) at a time when most Westerns were an hour or an hour and a-half in length, and was by all accounts an epic. Naturally, the plot of construction overseer (Joel McCrea) versus gambler (Brian Donlevy) and the presence of Barbara Stanwyck as "athletic heroine, leaping on and off boxcars with the best of them" are contrived.[2] However, the box-office success of *Union Pacific* worked to help unify the nation and venerate the past. Ironically, although *Union Pacific*'s final scenes could have been filmed at Promontory, which still had its railroad at this time, they were not. The real Promontory was remote and not quite as photogenic as the Nevada locations that DeMille selected. After long film careers, the two locomotives used in *Union Pacific* can still be seen today, "UP 119" is on display at Old Tucson, while the "Jupiter" is exhibited at the Nevada State Railroad Museum in Carson City.

With the romantic action of the driving of the golden spike immortalized on film, celebrations at Promontory did not end in 1942. By the mid- to late twentieth century, events celebrating the joining of the rails here became an institution—first drawing people locally, then nationally. In an interview on December 9, 2005, Delone B. Glover (born 1924) of Brigham City fondly recalled Promontory celebrations. Her first was in 1947. Then, in 1951, a few people visited the site for a "makeshift re-enactment. The men put on false beards and dressed in period clothing. The women donned dresses." This commemorative event on May 10, 1951, was, in fact, the first *annual* golden spike commemoration. The Brigham City Chamber of Commerce initiated these yearly events, which were carried on thereafter by the Box Elder Golden Spike Association, of which Bernice Anderson served as president. Glover recalled being part of the annual events for several years when, "in 1957, we got the status of a Golden Spike Monument." To help fund the ceremonies, the group sold gold-painted 3–inch mine spikes and printed programs for 25 cents. Ms. Glover recalled that J. D. Harris of Tremonton "gave us a hundred dollars to put his ad[vertisement] on our programs for many years." Noting that she has saved all of the programs from those events, Glover recalled how rewarding it felt when "in 1965, we were designated a historic site."[3]

These ceremonies in the early 1950s became bigger and bigger annual events that brought local communities together (fig. 9–2). The only time Ms. Glover recalled missing the ceremony was when the date fell on a Sunday, which she would not attend for religious reasons. Consequently, the event took place on Saturday. However, as she put it, "so many people came on Sunday that they held a ceremony then,

FIG. 9–2

From the 1950s onward, Golden Spike celebrations at Promontory became popular anniversary events on May 10th, such as this one in 1959. At this time, the concrete obelisk-shaped marker was the focal point.

too—twice in one year!" Glover remembered that one time it was so windy that the wind blew the fake whiskers off the men! She recalled that the ceremonies went on regardless of weather—"rain, dirt, dust, [and] wind."[4]

On May 10, 1958, at one of the annual re-enactments of the driving of the golden spike at Promontory, something seemed to be missing. Although several hundred people were present, as one observer put it, "they noted that nothing but a small cement monument and a short strip of rail remained at the historic site." In his speech to the crowd, Horace A. Sorensen stated that "something ought to be done" to rectify the situation. Sorensen and his wife contacted members of Congress as well as the National Park Service, which had begun to take an interest in the site. At that time, the National Park Service was becoming more actively involved in interpreting and preserving historic sites of national importance, and Promontory definitely qualified. The Sorensens' visit to Washington, D.C. certainly paid off, and upon returning to Utah, they interested the Union Pacific in helping to immortalize the "age of steam railroading at Corinne. Here, on the strip of land between the railroad and US Highway 30, Union Pacific installed trackage and donated rolling stock and a steam locomotive. As the second actor in the original golden-spike ceremony, Southern Pacific also donated a steam locomotive as well as a section worker's handcar. With the support of the National Park Service and the Sons of Utah Pioneers, the project moved ahead rapidly. A railroad station was moved to Corinne from Honeyville, and an 80–foot stage erected for the re-enactment. As backdrops, replicas of the original engines in the 1869 joining of the rails were built. The "railroad village," as it was called, was dedicated about a year later. On May 9, 1959, a re-enactment marked the 90th anniversary of the joining of the rails. This, however, was considered "only the beginning," as a working relationship with the National Park Service had now been established.[5]

On May 10, 1960, the Golden Spike Association of Box Elder County and the Box Elder County Commission sponsored a re-enactment at Promontory Summit. After speeches, band music, and the "Advance of the National Colors," National Park Service officials, state dignitaries, railroad officials, and special guests were welcomed. The pageant itself—the Driving of the Golden Spike—was directed by L. D. Wilde at 12:47 p.m. Judge Lewis Jones introduced and discussed "Stalwarts of the Golden Spike Era" after which a memorial wreath was laid, with one minute of silence for "Taps." Officials of the Golden Spike Association included President Bernice Gibbs Anderson, Vice President Dean Coombs, and Secretary-Treasurer Delone Glover.[6]

By the mid-1960s, plans were well underway for the big event—the centennial celebration—just four years in the future. This event represented a partnership between various levels of government and the private sector. On July 30, 1965, the Golden Spike National Historic Site was created to commemorate the completion of the first transcontinental railroad across the United States. Also in 1965, Horace A. Sorensen wrote an article in the *Sons of Utah Pioneers News,* stating that "Utah's Next big centennial will be observed in 1969, and will commemorate the completion of the first transcontinental railroad—the joining of the Union Pacific and Central Pacific at Promontory Point [*sic*] in northern Utah in 1869." Sorensen wrote that the "historic incident," as he called it, "has been recorded by western historians as one of the ten greatest events in the history of America." He also noted that the state of Utah had

Photo by author

FIG. 9–3
At Corinne, a portion of the original station stands just
south of the railroad track.

appointed a committee to make sure that the railroad centennial event was not treated as shabbily as the centennial of the Pony Express, "in which Utah did very little outside of selecting a queen and putting on the regular musical play 'Annie Get your Gun' which was a great show but had nothing to do with the Pony Express!" Sorensen's statement is revealing, for it reflects a growing interest in historical accuracy and authenticity. Noting that real expertise, or "know how" as he called it, was necessary to pull off a major event, Sorensen observed that a *national* committee had helped make the commemoration of the Pony Express successful. That kind of broad cooperation was necessary, and Sorensen said that kind of effort "should prove helpful in the Golden Spike observation."[7]

Even though she was far too young to recall the Promontory line's heyday, Delone Glover remembered that one of the buildings at Promontory—a frame building—was moved from a farm in the Fielding area northeast of Tremonton. Another building that Glover was quite familiar with—the old station at Corinne, which was later used as a museum in the 1960s and 1970s—figures prominently in the history of this line (fig. 9–3). Ms. Glover recalled that people brought in artifacts from all over the area to add to the museum's growing collection. Given

Photo by author

FIG. 9–4
Unbeknownst to most people traveling through Corinne, Utah, the
modern market and gas station incorporates a section of the original
Corinne Station into the rear section.

his unflagging interest in bringing Promontory's history to life, Horace
Sorenson helped finance the facility. He donated a train car, which stood
south of the building. When the depot was sold, however, Glover recalled
that the railroad car and all the artifacts were taken out and removed by
train. The trains themselves, she believed, went to Heber City.[8] The station building at Corinne was cut into sections; one part is now (2008)
the busy general store and gas station just north of the highway and railroad right of way, while the other portion rests on wooden supports just
south of the railroad tracks across the highway from the gas station and
store. This building (or rather buildings) is noteworthy, for it is the line's
only known Central Pacific building in existence (fig. 9–4).

In the 1960s, artists frequently depicted images of the transcontinental railroad. For example, the completion of the railroad at Promontory
Summit was one of numerous themes used by the Church of Jesus Christ
of Latter-day Saints in the Mormon Pavilion at the New York World's Fair
in 1964–65.[9] In integrating the joining of the rails with other themes in
Utah history, including the development of irrigation canals that enabled
the state of Utah to develop, the Mormons successfully wedded their history to that of the railroads (fig. 9–5). And why not? As the historical
record reveals, the church was an important player in railroad-related
developments in the 1860s and 1870s. The composition of the Mormon

Courtesy of Nate Kogan, Fort Worth, and the LDS Archives, Salt Lake City

FIG. 9–5
At the 1964–65 New York World's Fair, a section of the large mural
in the Mormon Pavilion recounted one of the West's most important
events, the joining of the rails at Promontory in 1869.

mural of early Mormons developing an irrigation canal in 1847 and the painting of the Golden Spike Ceremony of 1869 is quite revealing. Note that both seminal acts of western history are conflated and seem to be simultaneous. Rather than the traditional, horizontal side view depicting both locomotives meeting, this painting is kinetic in that it emphasizes action. By featuring a locomotive that, at first glance, appears to be moving toward the viewer, it suggests there is more to come up ahead. Like the irrigation ditch just to the left of the locomotive, which is under construction by a group of animated workers, the scene invites the viewer in and encourages the action to leap off the canvas, or rather wall, into the viewer's consciousness. The locomotive painted is evidently the *Jupiter*, the bonnet smokestack tells us as much, its bright red trim and gold accents complimenting the rich golden yellows of the fields. Note, too, that the poses of the dignitaries at the joining of the rails suggest reverence for what is occurring: It is as if God wills both the railroad and irrigation to transform the West. At just this time, the mid-1960s, Utahns were cognizant of a centennial event that was taking shape for 1969—the one-hundredth anniversary of the driving of the golden spike.

In 1968, people in the area were working actively to make the centennial a memorable event. In preparation for events at the Golden

Spike National Historic Site, the eleven-foot-tall concrete obelisk commemorating the joining of the rails was moved by a 100–ton crane on September 10, 1968, so that it could be closer to the visitor center which now became the hub of activity. The monument had been erected in 1916, the brainchild of Wilson Wright, an engineer for the Southern Pacific. When originally constructed, the large obelisk-shaped monument was built to last—or remain in one place—for it was anchored fully 6½ feet into the ground. Word went out that the celebration would be special and crowds of people prepared to visit the site on May 10, 1969—despite the fact that there were no locomotives present.

As the centennial drew near, and public interest increased, miniaturizing the event into souvenirs gained marketing appeal. Among the items in the collections at the National Park Service's Golden Spike National Historic Site is a liquor-bottle replica of the *Jupiter*. Now empty, that bottle evidently contained spirits potent enough to bring back memories of those that flowed on May 10, 1869. The bottom of this bottle notes that it is a "Commemorative Edition," created by B. Harness for McCormick. Interestingly, the liquor was dispensed through the smokestack![10] This artifact is a reminder that the centennial of the golden spike in 1969 reached the public in various ways, some educational and some recreational.

By the time the Golden Spike Centennial Celebration took place, model railroading had become a popular hobby. As might be expected, the centennial was marked by the production of numerous models of both the Central Pacific *Jupiter* and the Union Pacific *No. 119*. Of these the HO scale Centennial Set made by Atlas Industries in Japan and imported by Pacific Fast Mail (PFM), represented state-of-the-art, brass scale models. Similarly, Balboa Scale Models produced an HO scale Commemorative Set of both locomotives, as illustrated in an advertisement that ran as late as the September 1970 issue of *Model Railroader* magazine. These brass models became collector's items, but considerably less expensive, plastic versions of the *Jupiter* (fig. 9–6) and the *No. 119* marketed by Bachmann in both HO scale and N scale enabled modelers to own a piece of history. The models of the two locomotives present at Promontory continue to be produced in 2008, and remain perennial favorites. Originally, all the Central Pacific *Jupiter* models featured the same incorrect red-colored tender that historians had assumed existed, but more recently, that has been corrected to feature the startling blue color of the actual *Jupiter*. These HO scale locomotive models are realistic enough that readers will do a double take, for we have digitally placed the model locomotives into an actual photograph taken at Promontory in 2005. The realism of these model locomotives is all the

FIG. 9–6

Through the magic of digitization, the Bachmann HO-scale locomotive models are positioned into the modern-day landscape at Promontory—making it hard to tell that these are miniatures (less than a foot long each).

more apparent when compared to the *Jupiter* and the *No. 119* used in commemorating the Golden Spike today (fig. 9–7).

The passenger cars present on May 10, 1869, have also been produced as scale models. In 1969, the Westwood model company of Fort Wayne, Indiana, produced two, accurate HO-scale sets of the railroad cars at Promontory Summit, one for Union Pacific and one for Central Pacific. The Central Pacific set features kits of the commissary car and President Stanford's private car (fig. 9–8). When assembled, these cars are highly detailed versions of the prototype built for the centennial celebration. As part of Westwood's marketing, and to emphasize the rarity (and enhance the collectability) of these "Limited Run" models, "only 1,869 kits (year prototype built)" were released.

As a tribute to the centennial of the golden spike, *Railroad Model Craftsman* magazine featured an article by E. L. Moore in its May 1969

FIG. 9–7

In this 2005 photograph, the *Jupiter* (*left*) and *No. 119* (*right*) move closer to each other to commemorate the driving of the golden spike in 1869. Compare with Fig. 9–6.

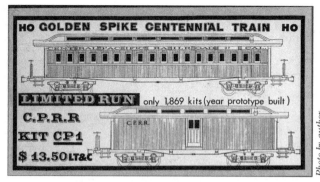

Fig. 9–8
As noted on the label of the Golden Spike
Centennial Train box (*above*) only 1,869 kits
were produced—a marketing technique that
simultaneously calls attention to the year
1869 and assures the kits' "collector" status.

issue. Well known for his sense of humor and appreciation of the absurd,
Moore did not disappoint. His six-page article began with a poem about
"what was it the Engines said" patterned after "Bret Harte, more or less."
As with his prose, Moore's photographs are humorous. To commemorate the centennial of 1869–1969, Moore constructed a miniature
scene featuring trains similar to the Central Pacific *Jupiter* and Union
Pacific *No. 119*, festooning them with dozens of miniature human figures, including Indians, miners, track workers, and, of course, the railroad's top brass. Moore's sense of humor dictated that he place a few
inebriated individuals leaning at odd angles, a scenario that in fact
occurred at the original ceremony, when champagne and other spirits were liberally consumed by many in the crowd. Moore's alter ego,
his fictitious great-grandfather, Lucifer Penroddy Snooks, was supposedly present for the real event's miniaturized hijinks. Moore's stated
goal, however, was to give readers "a gander at the low level people who
really turned up the sod (and many of them, their toes) and spiked the
rails" at Promontory. In this spirit, his model scene of the event generally reproduces Russell's, Hart's, and Savage's photographs, but one
big banner proclaims, "The Irish Done it!" while the slogan near the
Central Pacific locomotive apparently, or at least allegedly, says much
the same thing, only about the Chinese workers in Chinese characters.
An American flag flies above the entire miniature scene, parodying the
joining of the rails.[11]

These simulated re-enactments elsewhere, however, could not com-
pete with the concept of Promontory as the real place where history

occurred. In recognition of the site's importance to national history, the National Park Service had become a partner in this process by showcasing history at the Golden Spike Historical Site. The acquisition of the site by the National Park Service/Department of the Interior coincided with the rise of historic preservation and a growing demand for authenticity and accuracy. This occurred at the same time that an increasing number of people became interested in experiencing history firsthand. Whereas *any* old steam engine might once serve to symbolize the Central Pacific or Union Pacific engines originally involved, as had occurred in 1942, people now became more demanding. They wanted engines that looked like the originals from 1869.

Similar concerns arose with regard to structures at Promontory. In 1969, National Park Service staff hoped to erect tents for the centennial ceremony. However, time and cost restrictions prevented this from occurring. With the nation's bicentennial (1776–1976) celebration looming in 1974, tents again sprang up on the site of Promontory. These included eleven replica tents and one Indian teepee. Exhibits included the questionable but stereotypically "old time" activities of blacksmithing and baking bread in wood-fired stoves. This enthusiasm was understandable, for the goal was to encourage visitors to experience the past with all his or her senses. Expressing concern about such well-meaning efforts, National Park Service historian Robert Utley noted that certain activities might be "correspondingly distractive [*sic*] if not actually subversive." Living history was acceptable, even encouraged, provided that it met standards of "honesty as well as accuracy," as the National Park Service *Interpretive Guidelines* (NPS-6) of 1980 put it. Activities at the site from the late 1960s to early 1970s fell short of newer, increasingly strict standards. By the late 1970s, the existing tents were modified, and interpretive activities improved, all in an effort to improve accuracy.

The concept of accuracy was all the more important because the National Park Service was about to embark on improvements at the Golden Spike Historic Site as well as the construction of two superb replicas of the locomotives that stood, pilot to pilot, on May 10, 1869. In spring 1979, *Great World of Model Railroading* magazine published a "Transcontinental 110th Anniversary Special Issue." In addition to describing the HO-scale locomotives available, this issue highlighted the production of DeMille's *Union Pacific* and the 1939 celebration of the golden spike in Omaha, Nebraska. As the earlier celebration in Ogden (1919), the event in Omaha brought many people together. One source noted that "[t]he entire civic, business and labor interests of the community have joined hands with other towns to make the occasion the most outstanding in the history of Omaha and the motion picture

Photo by author

FIG. 9–9

A Work in Progress: Following recent research, the full-scale operating replica of Central Pacific locomotive *Jupiter* was repainted to feature the more accurate blue (rather than red) color scheme worn by the original.

industry." Indians from several tribes were also represented. The *Great World of Model Railroading* article notes that "[a] solid downtown block of store front buildings, covered with false fronts to resemble a street of 1869 . . ." was the centerpiece of the event.[12] The magazine also featured an article on the "Full-Size Models of the Promontory Engines" which were under construction in 1979 and beginning to attract considerable attention. These, of course, are the stunning replicas that run today—which author Bill Wright enthusiastically branded, "What may be the last two steam engines ever built."[13]

The construction of the two operating locomotives (fig. 9–9) and (fig. 9–10) is remarkable in that no plans of the original locomotives existed in the 1970s. With the original plans lost to history, these replicas had to be based on *photographic* evidence and written documents; they are so close to the originals that it is virtually impossible to tell them apart, even after carefully scrutinizing historical photos of their prototypes. They are painted as accurately as possible despite the fact that the colors of the original locomotives are not known with

Photo by author

FIG. 9–10

A Work of Art: Resplendent in the original paint scheme, this operating replica of Union Pacific *No. 119* is used in re-enactments of the joining of the rails at the Golden Spike National Historic Site, Promontory, Utah.

certainty. When the locomotives were constructed, their bright colors startled all observers. Victorian-era locomotives were simply stunning, especially given the way their colors stand out in the sage-covered landscape. Interestingly, portions of the *Jupiter* (especially its tender) were originally painted in red, as that seemed to be the most likely original color—until an article in an early Sacramento newspaper was recently discovered, revealing the color to be blue. Given the National Park Service's interest in accuracy, the color was quickly changed to the bright royal blue originally noted in the builders' general literature on locomotive paints.

One question that plagues those involved in the Golden Spike Historical Site is just how much of the original Promontory Summit should be reconstructed? Currently (2008), the interpretation focuses on the locomotives and the remainder left to interpretation in the visitor center. However, in the late 1970s, the interpretation of Promontory's "Hell on Wheels" period was achieved, at least in part, by the furnishing of the Union Pacific ticket office and the Red Cloud Saloon (fig. 9–11).

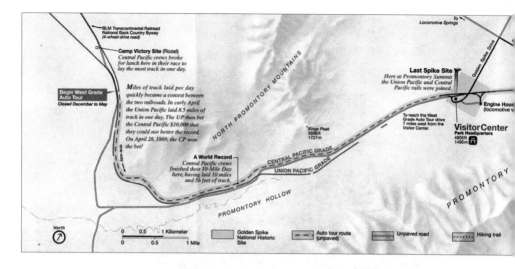

FIG. 9–11

For a time in the early 1980s, Promontory featured replicas of tents; these, however, were removed as they did not meet increasing standards of accuracy.

Even though these "were not as accurate as hoped, in scale, location or furnishing"—as a National Park Service historian diplomatically put it[14] —they were popular with visitors.

This search for accuracy is, and remains, a real concern. The National Park Service is constantly raising the bar in hopes of providing the visiting public with the most authentic, which is to say accurate, environment at Promontory. Of course, there are limits, only some of which pertain to accuracy. Imagine, for a moment, recreating Promontory as it was in 1869 for the public. Although early claims of its wildness (and violent nature) may have been exaggerated by travelers then, consider

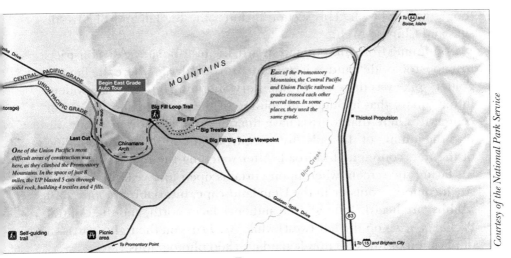

FIG. 9–12

This map of the Golden Spike National Historic Site identifies key features interpreted by the National Park Service.

the impact of offering the public "the meanest breakfast any one ever sat down to: sour bread, sour hash, and sour hot cakes without syrup"— as a reporter for the Elko *Independent* described food at Promontory in 1869.[15] Better (or worse) yet, envision a re-enactment of "a motley crew of rowdies, blackguards, gamblers, and abandoned women, [who] made [the] night hideous with their drunken orgies"—as the British traveler Frederick Whymper described a sleepless layover at Promontory in his essay "From Ocean to Ocean—The Pacific Railroad" at about the time the rails were to be joined.[16]

To ensure that Promontory was appreciated in its geographic context, the right of way on both sides of the Golden Spike National Historic Site was also included. Thus, the site is a sinuous strip of land along which several larger rectangular areas cluster (fig. 9–12). Beginning at the base of the Promontory Mountains at Blue Creek, the 200–foot-wide strip follows the railroad grade uphill along the east face of the Promontory Range. In the area of spectacular cuts and fills, the strip widens into a pattern of interlocking rectangles. This, of course, was contested ground between Central Pacific and Union Pacific crews who probably performed the most extensive, and expensive, of the duplicative work anywhere along the entire transcontinental railroad here. The sites here are featured on the National Park Service's informative brochure titled *Golden Spike National Historic Site, Utah, National Park Service, United States Department of the Interior.* An automobile tour of sites on the East Grade is part of the historic site, though it can be experienced on foot as well as by car. This section includes the Big Fill and Big Trestle sites and Chinese Arch.

Continuing from this point westward, the historic site again constricts to a 200–foot-wide band as it runs into the broad vale where the famous golden spike was driven at Promontory Summit. Here, the site widens into a square that includes the joining of the rails site and the visitor center. It is here that tourists have the opportunity to dramatically witness the joining of the rails after viewing a film outlining the building of the transcontinental railroad. After watching the movie, the group sits facing the screen, whereupon curtains open to reveal the two full-size locomotives outside in the Utah landscape. Invariably, "Ooohs" and "Aahhs" are heard. Tellingly, the audience faces north, and the Central Pacific *Jupiter* is on the left (west) while *No. 119* is on the right (east)—a duplication of Russell's now-legendary 1869 photographs.

At the visitor center and nearby, the question becomes: which time period is to be represented? 1869? If so, the visitor center itself becomes an issue, as it was located with little reference to the period when the golden spike was driven. For example, the location where the ceremony is re-enacted appears to be some distance—possibly several hundred feet—from the original location. However, the construction activity about thirty years ago at the visitor center resulted in considerable alteration of the site. This is problematical today because the emphasis is on accuracy (as well as correct artifact provenience). The ambitious construction, however, removed many traces of the original alignments as well as foundation locations of buildings. Similarly, the presence of the obelisk-shaped marker (fig. 9–13), which was moved about 150 feet to the visitor center represents a conundrum. True, it is located in a convenient place for those entering the center to experience it, but the marker has been separated from its original setting. The problem is all the more apparent when one realizes that the marker dates from 1916—about fifty years after the *original* ceremony, which is depicted here daily during the summer months.

The challenge, then, is to reconstruct Promontory using as much evidence as possible. Just as deconstructing photographs can help us understand the Promontory of 1869, images can be used to help in the reconstruction. Given the presence of maps depicting the site at various time periods, along with historical photographs, it may be possible to reconstruct vignettes of Promontory at different time periods using carefully coordinated photogrammetry and GIS rubber-sheeting techniques. Still, the construction at the visitor center has compromised a third possibility—the anchoring of those images to actual traces of material elements such as foundation corners or old roadbeds.

Photo by author

FIG. 9–13
Promontory's original obelisk-shaped marker dating from about 1916
was moved to the visitor center, as shown in this 2006 photograph.

From the visitor center at Promontory Summit westward, the strip again narrows to 200 feet, occupying the Central Pacific right of way through Promontory Hollow. The old Union Pacific grade lies south of the Central Pacific grade here. Continuing westward on the old Central Pacific grade, which is a gravel automobile road, the historic site snakes northwestward downgrade over the roadbed along which Central Pacific crews laid a record ten miles of track in one day (April 28, 1869). A replica of that historic sign is located here. The Golden Spike Historic Site ends about a mile from Victory Camp, where Central Pacific crews had lunch on that noteworthy day when they laid the ten miles of track.

From there westward, a four-wheel drive road following the old Central Pacific grade becomes part of the Bureau of Land Management

Photo by author

FIG. 9–14
Remains of old railroad culverts and short trestles can be found along the right of way, as noted in this scene between Terrace and Watercress. The view is eastward.

(BLM) Transcontinental Railroad Back Country Byway.[17] Whereas the Golden Spike National Historic Site offers the most easily accessible portions of the old railway grades, and also features the major interpretive facilities, exploring elsewhere along the old railway grades on BLM land is more difficult, involving considerable care and planning. However, a number of the locales, for example, Seco, are well marked with BLM signs outlining the site's history. Moreover, the roadbed, though eroded and impassable in several places, has been the focus of BLM's efforts to create an interpretive trail for the serious history-oriented hiker. The trail is only interpreted using a small one-page brochure now, but could be expanded to include a more in depth natural and cultural history component involving both Native peoples and later arrivals. The geology and vegetation of the area, so important to the line over the range, could also be interpreted. A good place to start is with BLM's 1994 report called *Rails East to Promontory: the Utah Stations.*[18] This trail currently begins at Rozel, but could be expanded to start in the vicinity of the Bear River Bay along which the old right of way is still visible, continue over Promontory Summit, and then run to Lucin. Along the current BLM portion west of Rozel may be seen the remains of old railroad culverts and short trestles (fig. 9–14) as well as classic Utah ghost town

Photo by author

FIG. 9–15
The old Central Pacific right of way west of Promontory is strewn
with remains of the railroad. At Kelton, in 2005, the long abandoned
supports of a bumper at the end of a siding rise out of the landscape.

sites such as Terrace and Kelton (fig. 9–15). The area along the marshy
shore of the Great Salt Lake from near Corinne to Blue Creek, however,
is also rich in both natural and cultural history features.

The crown jewel—the current Golden Spike National Historic Site—
would be the centerpiece of the new trail. Over the range and into
the vast BLM lands west of the Promontory Mountains, serious hikers
can experience the dusty trail to Kelton, of which little above ground
remains but about which so much could be presented. From Kelton,
the trail could extend southwestward to the fabled Red Dome Pass and
Matlin, along some of the most rugged and remote topography traversed by the railroad. The trail could then continue to Terrace, where
the present modest signage could be expanded to include maps/station
plans of communities there and along the old route to Lucin.

Hikers using the entire trail from near Corinne to Lucin would
need good maps to better comprehend the nature of the countryside.
Fortunately, the entire area is covered by USGS topographic maps at a
scale of 1:24,000, though some are still primitive in that they include
only photographic overlays and not detailed contour mapping. Oddly,
the abandoned Central Pacific line here is not indicated on some of

these maps and would have to be added. For interpretive purposes, these new topographic maps could be compared to copies of the actual railroad survey maps. If this "Pacific Railroad Hiking Trail" were to ever materialize, however, there would have to be caveats not unlike the warnings on the maps of early wagon roads. West of Promontory, especially from Rozel to Lucin, the trail is often miles away from well-traveled roads. This is hazardous, rough country intended for only the more serious and experienced of hikers and trail bike riders. One serious misstep or miscalculation here could bring disaster, for although the lights of cities across the Great Salt Lake are clearly visible from many places, that distance is not traversable. The Great Salt Lake is still a major obstacle, and the surrounding desert here is still as unforgiving as any in the North America. The trail, though, enables those who experience it to more fully understand the challenges faced by the early survey teams and roadbed graders of the Pacific Railroad.

One more caveat is in order about exploring the old Promontory line. The task of seriously interpreting the physical remains of the railroad here is threatened by well meaning, but overly enthusiastic, collectors. In the book *Right-of-Way: A Guide to Abandoned Railroads in the United States*, Waldo Nielsen asks: "Who knows what treasure can be found along the right-of-way or in the vicinity of abandoned stations?" Adding that "[t]his book should be useful to the insulator collector, the bottle collector and the treasure hunter," Nielsen gives a green light to those who would indiscriminately collect artifacts along old railroad grades. In the section on Utah, Nielsen identifies the Promontory line, listing the section length from Lucin to Dathol as 122 miles and from Corinne to Ogden as 25 miles, both sections abandoned between 1937 and 1944.[19] Although it appears impossible to stop overzealous collectors, one hopes that they can be educated to respect the sites and artifacts, for an artifact removed without any indication as to its context becomes little more than an interesting curiosity now unable to answer the most important questions about the site and the people who lived along and traveled over it. This is true for both public and private lands, including that important six-mile-long section of the line from Corinne to Stinking Springs at the northeastern edge of the Great Salt Lake now owned by the Golden Spike Heritage Foundation.

The event at Promontory Summit lives in both the interpretation/re-enactments at the Golden Spike National Historic Site and on the screen—both large and small. In 2005, the TNT television miniseries "Into the West" portrayed the drama of the West's settlement from about 1830 to 1890. One crucial aspect of that drama, naturally, was the building and opening of the transcontinental railroad. The first appearance of the railroad theme was portrayed in episode 3, "Hell on Wheels" (on July 8–10, 2005), which covered the start of construction in Omaha and Sacramento, California. As roadbed grading begins in the Sierra foothills, a labor dispute with Irish workers leads a railroad official to suggest that the Chinese in San Francisco be used as track workers—to the chagrin of a racist construction foreman, who declares that he will not work with any Chinese. Like many dramatic TV shows of its time, "Into the West" featured several themes (such as Native American-settler and other social-ethnic conflicts) in one episode. As the Native Americans fight for their dwindling lands, the railroad development theme continues at strategic intervals. In "Into the West," the railroad serves as a metaphor for the relentless march of technology and civilization across the West. After part of the episode treats the Sand Creek Massacre, the construction of the Union Pacific railroad at "North Platte, 300 miles west of Omaha October 1866" is shown as the pivotal location where construction is marching westward on the Great Plains. At North Platte, a young man says that there won't be much left of the West after the railroad tames it. Although "Into the West" presupposes that the railroad would eliminate the Indians through conflict (and conflict did indeed occur on the Union Pacific), it is a popular misconception that the Indians were annihilated.

Generally, for each Union Pacific scene, "Into the West" features a Central Pacific counterpart. The next railroad scene at "Cape Horn, Northern California" portrays Chinese workers defying the ramparts of the Sierra Nevada as they help blast a right of way across the mountains. After another segue to Crazy Horse's elimination of soldiers in Wyoming, the action at "Donner Summit, 7000 feet above sea level 1867" is portrayed. Immediately, the Union Pacific at North Platte, Nebraska, appears, and the viewer senses that both railroads are edging closer together. A 4–4–0 locomotive and bunk/work car at North Platte provides a view of the type of equipment the Union Pacific used on construction trains. The next scene features the successful completion of a tunnel in the Sierra Nevada. After Indians sign a treaty on the Plains, the Union Pacific is again featured at North Platte, where an interpersonal drama between a young man, his angry father, and a young woman occurs. Cheyenne, Wyoming—reportedly about halfway on the route—appears next as the Union Pacific work train moves west. The competition between Central Pacific and Union Pacific becomes apparent at "Humboldt Sink, Great Basin Nevada 1868" as Donovan must keep the Chinese workers building the line despite increasing strife. Meanwhile, in Wyoming, tensions mount as Indians seek to expand back to their former territories.

As the conclusion of this episode nears after the railroads have frantically built toward each other, a man announces that the rails will meet "at Promontory." Another man observes, "That's Mormon Country, and they say brother Brigham approves of the railroad." The two railroad lines finally meet at the site that a title proclaims to be "Promontory Point [*sic*], Utah, May 10, 1869." Naturally, the union of the rails provides an opportunity for "Into the West" to offer some pithy social commentary. For example, it highlights the new type of westerner who will transform the region; not the hard-driving pioneer or track layer, but rather the urbanite who knows how to provide people with the goods and services they need. As the pompous speeches proclaim, "We are a great people," who have been able to bridge the continent. "Into the West" gives the victory a worker's voice: As the railroad brass take the credit, a half white/half Indian track worker picks a splinter of wood out of a crosstie, hands it to a Chinese worker, and adds a concluding line that at least *we* know who *really* built the railroad.

That, of course, is the message that has always resonated at Promontory Summit. It was a celebration of capitalism and western progress, but even observers at the time noted the accomplishments of the workers, Chinese and white alike. They also know that the railroad, and all it represented, will further affect Native Americans. Similarly, the challenge then as now is to tell the story as fairly as possible—a balance not always easy to achieve.

In the 2007 film, *Night at the Museum,* one of the dioramas that come to life after hours is a construction scene on the Pacific Railroad. Two locomotives are shown; one is the *No. 119,* and the other appears to be the *Jupiter* (or a similar bonnet-stacked 4-4-0). The railroad under construction is a single track line through desolate country, and the scene includes a brigade of Chinese workers grading roadbed and laying track. This diorama is titled "Wild West," and it is part of what the diorama's lead character (a miniaturized cowboy played by Owen Wilson) calls "Manifest Destiny." This movie is a spoof on the stodgy world of the museum, but it is telling that the scene depicting the Wild West features the feverish railroad construction that put Promontory on the map in 1869. In our collective memory as Americans, Promontory signifies an event that both expanded the nation and unified people living on both coasts.

Promontory's story is not only about people and technology but about the *place* itself. Like the people here, and the technology of railroading, the place has changed considerably over the more than 160 years. Perhaps the most evocative way to observe this is from the air.

As noted at the beginning of this book, travelers today on flights over Promontory Summit can look down at the area from around 35,000 feet. There, visible in a single glance, the forlorn north-south-trending Promontory Mountains jut into the Great Salt Lake. At the eastern edge of this view, along the Wasatch Front, are oasis-like benches densely settled with farms and communities. Farther to the west, but east of Promontory, a large industrial facility grabs one's attention. This is the Thiokol Company's plant, and it has an interesting recent history.

In 1956, after considering several sites in Utah, Thiokol selected the area near Blue Creek to build solid fuel rocket motors. Thiokol chose this site because it was a considerably safe distance from urban areas, and "because raw materials were close at hand from the Intermountain West, the labor market was advantageous, and railroad transportation was available."[20] Although Thiokol would use a portion of the Central/ Southern Pacific line west of Brigham City, Union Pacific now operated that line; ironically, the railroad was a visible player in luring Thiokol to Utah. Most people involved in the deliberations recognized the symbolism of the plant's location, as one observer put it, "across the road from an old railroad facility, Lampo Junction, built to service the railroad that formed the original transcontinental railroad completed in 1869 at nearby Promontory Summit."[21] This meant that the Promontory line was again front and center in a transportation race, this one ultimately culminating in getting men to the moon in 1969—almost exactly a century after the completion of the transcontinental railroad. Like that earlier venture, the Promontory plant site offered a number of advantages that placed it ahead of other locales in Utah. Interestingly, although Thiokol's presence was reduced after the end of the Cold War in 1991, a recent decision (2005) to launch a second manned mission to the moon ensures that the Thiokol Promontory plant will see renewed activity. This means that the soulful wail of the whistles of *Jupiter* and *No. 119* will continue to be interrupted by the thunderous roar of rocket engines being tested at nearby Thiokol.

Continuing to look westward from the Thiokol plant, an air traveler glimpses the stark Promontory Range looming out of Great Salt Lake and stretching northward to a saddle between what are, in effect, two mountain ranges in one. It is here at this saddle that history was made on May 10, 1869. It is amazing to contemplate just how little of the original infrastructure along the railroad can be seen from this high altitude. However, there below, one can glimpse—if barely—the scars of the abandoned rights of way. Of Promontory Summit, little or nothing can be seen from this high altitude except a gentle cleft in mountains where the railroad originally crossed over the range to the bleak, alkali-riddled

Photo by author

FIG. 9–16
Lucin Cutoff, now also known as the Salt Lake Causeway,
remains a marvel of railroad engineering, and the cause
of Promontory's decline.

land to the west. Away from the nearly imaginary line where the railroad once ran, into the higher country at the base of the Raft River Range, the large gridiron-patterned mosaic of Curlew Valley's wheat fields in an otherwise desert-like land give some order to the chaotic wilderness. They are a reminder that this railroad helped shape the local economy and landscape as well as connected distant places.

To the south, as if drawn with a straightedge, the modern line of the Union Pacific railroad cuts across the Great Salt Lake on a bee-line course from Ogden on the east to the desert wilds where Utah meets Nevada. That straight line is, of course, the Lucin Cutoff, now also known as the Salt Lake Causeway (fig. 9–16). More than a century old now, it looks surprisingly modern. However, the cutoff is occasionally threatened with abandonment in favor of other routes less vulnerable to the expensive temperamental challenges posed by the Great Salt Lake. Therefore, even though that straight-line causeway is a more recent artifact on the land than the old railroad grades at Promontory, it too, is part of the story and a reminder that railroads maximize profits as they minimize obstructions. The Lucin Cutoff, then, is actually no less significant an artifact than Promontory Summit, for its presence signifies the beginning of the end of the original line. That line, although

Photo by author

FIG. 9–17
Slow freight trains still traverse the right of way east of
Corinne, as seen in this photograph of a Union Pacific
train headed from Corinne to Brigham City.

long gone, still has a hold on the popular imagination. It also continues
to raise questions about both the people and places it shaped.

For its part, the early Promontory Summit line of the Pacific Railroad
is a ghost railroad, but one small portion of it still sees (2008) some
sporadic railroad activity. The active rails reach westward from Brigham
City to Corinne, which is today the literal end of the line. Westward from
Corinne, with the exception of the recreated trackage at the Golden
Spike National Historic Site, only abandoned roadbeds mark the rights
of way. East of Corinne, though, slow-way freight trains can be seen wad-
ing along the weed-flanked right of way as they serve some of the industries in the Corinne to Brigham City area (fig. 9–17). Significantly, the
locomotives hauling these trains bear the familiar Union Pacific colors
and lettering—a reminder of that railroad's ultimate victory in the corporate battle that began in the early 1860s and lasted until almost the
end of the twentieth century.

Today, the site at Promontory Summit is miles from any railroad connection to the outside world. The fact that Promontory still resonates with
the public is clear from the symbolism on Utah's new 25–cent piece (fig.
9–18). Released in October 2007, the Utah quarter might have featured
sites associated with the state's fabled Mormon history—the beehive, Salt

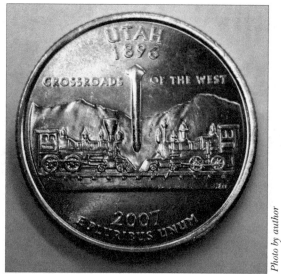

Fig. 9–18
On Utah's commemorative state quarter, which was issued in October 2007, the joining of the rails remains the signature event in state history.

Lake Temple, seagulls, and the like. Instead, the committee selecting the imagery chose the meeting of the rails as *the* singular event in the state's history. Not surprisingly, then, Promontory lives on as the quintessential symbol of union or unification. The fact that the original ceremony took place in the Victorian West may add to its charm but does not restrict the event and place to the past. Promontory Summit is still relevant to people in the twenty-first century—the enduring question being which part of Promontory's long history we choose to remember, and portray.

As evidence of this, consider the May 10, 2008 ceremony held at the 139th anniversary of the big event in 1869. To rectify the absence of Chinese people in the 1869 photograph, NPS deliberately staged a photo opportunity involving representatives of the Utah Organization of Chinese Americans and their guests from China. Under a brilliant blue sky, as the locomotives' pilots nearly touched and re-enactors in period dress posed, so too did Chinese Americans and their guests (fig. 9–19). When compared to the 1869 photograph, the basic armature of people and machines is in place. Now, however, the centerpiece is the brightly dressed Chinese, proudly posing for their place in the new— but really old—history.

FIG. 9–19
Under a brilliant blue sky, the May 10, 2008, re-enactment of the joining of the rails exactly 139 years earlier rectified an oversight in the original photos as members of the Utah Organization of Chinese Americans and their guests from China now proudly posed for the camera.

Epilogue

FULL CIRCLE

In describing the recent (2004) completion of Australia's first trans-continental railway through the desert heart of that huge country, historian Geoffrey Blainey observed that, "there's something symbolic about a railway." Blainey noted that, "a railway is created in one grand gesture" as opposed to a road, which usually develops in stages along the route of earlier trails. Uniting Adelaide with Darwin was, to the Australians, much like uniting New York and San Francisco to Americans almost a century and a-half ago. Both railroads were exercises in "nation-building," as Prime Minister John Howard characterized the Australian project in 2004. In 1869, the completion of the Pacific Railroad promised to bring two disparate parts of the country together, and it delivered on that promise. Like the first American trans-continental railroad, Australia's new railroad drew considerable attention for both its practical and symbolic value. As Blainey concluded: "We're a visual people, and a line drawn across the map, almost dead center, captures the imagination." Americans, too, are a visual people, and the line of their transcontinental railroad drawn across the Great American Desert in 1869 captured their imagination. Like Australia's new railroad, ours traversed the most desolate country imaginable, but did so in the spirit of national unity. The route over the Promontory Range was, and is, part of our nation's rich heritage. It was once the future, and now our past. Hopefully, readers of *Over the Range* can now better visualize that railroad as a line drawn across our collective mental map of the American West.[1]

Notes

Introduction

1. Stanley Wood and C. E. Hooper, *Over the Range; a complete tourist's guide to Colorado, New Mexico, Utah, Nevada, California, Oregon, Puget Sound, and the great Northwest* (Chicago, Ill.: R. R. Donnelley, 1904). Interestingly, this book was published in many editions and originally appeared as *Crest of the Continent*; both were actually guidebooks for the Denver & Rio Grande Railroad, but their coverage of the Pacific Railroad over Promontory Summit is noteworthy.

2. David Haward Bain, *Empire Express: Building the First Transcontinental Railroad* (New York, N.Y.: Viking, 1999).

3. Andrew M. Modelski, *Railroad Maps of North America: The First Hundred Years* (Washington, D.C.: Library of Congress, 1975).

Chapter One

1. Richard Francaviglia and Jimmy Bryan, Jr., "'Are We Chimerical in this Opinion?'—Visions of a Pacific Railroad and Westward Expansion Before 1845" *Pacific Historical Review* 71, no. 2 (2002): pp. 179–202.

2. *Picturesque America, or, the Land We Live In: a delineation by Pen and Pencil of the Mountains, Rivers, Lakes, Forests, Water-Falls, Shores . . . .* vol. 2 (New York, N.Y., ca. 1872–74), p. 161.

3. See Frank L. DeCourten, *The Broken Land: Adventures in Great Basin Geology* (Salt Lake City: University of Utah Press, 2003), p. 181; and Bill Fiero, *Geology of the Great Basin* (Reno: University of Nevada Press, 1986), pp. 117–40.

4. Howard Stansbury, *Exploration of the Valley of the Great Salt Lake,* (Washington, D.C.: Smithsonian Institution Press, 1988), p. 103.

5. Hellmut H. Doelling, *Geology and Mineral Resources of Box Elder County* (Salt Lake City: Utah Geological and Mineral Survey, 1980), p. 46.

6. Ibid., p.70.

7. David M. Miller and Holly Langrock, *Interior Geologic Map of the Monument Point Quadrangle, Box Elder County, Utah. With a Booklet on the Geology of eastern Curley Valley, Box Elder County, Utah.* Open-File Report 348, Utah Geological Survey, p. 15.

8. Stansbury, *Exploration,* pp. 103–4.

9. Stansbury, *Exploration,* pp. 202–3.

10. Michael Polk, *Cultural Resources Overview and Preservation Recommendations Promontory Route—Corinne to Promontory, Utah* (Ogden, Utah: Sagebrush Consultants, 1998), p. 22.

11. Ibid., pp. 3–5.

12. *Map of the Utah Superintendency Showing the Location of Different Bands of Indians therein and the Boundaries of the Land of Each as Claimed by Them,* ca. 1861,. [map #372], tube 338, National Archives, College Park, Md. (hereafter National Archives).

13. The term *discovered* here needs to be used advisedly, however, for the Indians knew a great deal about the plant life here. Discovered, then, simply means new to science.

14. S. August Mitchell, *Description of Oregon and California: Embracing an Account of the Gold Regions . . . .* (Philadelphia, Pa.: Thomas Cowperthwait, 1849), p. 34.

15. John C. Frémont, *The Exploring Party to the Rocky Mountains and to Oregon and North California* (Washington, D.C.: Government Printing Office, 1845), pp. 61–65.

16. Lansford W. Hastings, *The Emigrant's Guide to Oregon and California* (Princeton, N.J.: Princeton University Press, 1932), pp. 70–71.

17. Franklin Langworthy, *Scenery of The Plains, Mountains and Mines: A Diary Kept Upon the Overland Route to California by Way of the Great Salt Lake: Travels in the Cities, Mines, and Agricultural Districts—Embracing the Return by the Pacific Ocean and Central America, in the Years 1850, '51, '52, and '53* (Ogdensburgh, N.Y.: by J. C. Sprague, Book-Seller, Hitchcock & Tillotson, Printers, 1855), pp. 99–100.

CHAPTER TWO

1. *Map of United States* in Asa Whitney, *A Project for a Railroad to the Pacific* (New York: George W. Wood, 1849).

2. "Explorations and Surveys for Rail Road Routes from the Mississippi River to the Pacific Ocean, War Department, Profiles of the Main Routes Surveyed, Compiled in 1855, by Lieutenants G. K. Warren & H. L. Abbot, Corps Top[GL.] Engineers: with Revisions and Additional compilations, by Lieutenants J. C. Ives, Corps Top[GL.] Engineers, from the Results of Subsequent Examinations and Surveys Prepared in the Office of Pacific Rail Road Explorations and Surveys, Captain A. A. Humphreys, Corps Top[GL.] Engineers in Charge by Direction of the Hon. Jefferson Davis Secretary of War," 1856.

3. *Map Of The Territory Of The United States From The Mississippi River To The Pacific Ocean.* Originally prepared to accompany the "Reports of the Explorations For A Pacific Railroad Route . . . Compiled from authorized explorations and other reliable data by Lieut. G. K. Warren, Top'l. Eng'rs. In the Office of Pacific R.R. Surveys, War Dept. under the direction of Bvt. Maj. W. H. Emory, Top'l. Eng'rs.," 1854. Capt. A. A. Humphreys, Top'l. Eng'rs. in 1854–58. Partly recompiled and redrawn under the direction of the Engineer Bureau in 1865–66–67. Engineer Bureau, War Department. Engraved on stone by Julius Bien, New York.

4. *Sketch Exhibiting the Routes between Fort Laramie and the Great Salt Lake,* From "Explorations by J. C. Frémont, H. Stansbury, Capts Corps of Top. Engrs., F. G. Beckwith, Lieut 3 Art., F. T. Bryan, Lieut. Top Engrs. And F. W. Lander Chf. Engr. Sth Pass. Pacific Wagon Road, War Dept. Office Explorations & Surveys. Drawn by E. Freyhold," Jan. 1858. 2nd edition, Apr. 15, 1858, with Corrections & additions from map prepared by Maj. F. J. Porter, USA. Scale 1:1,000,000 or 16 miles to one inch.

5. Explorations and Surveys For a Rail Road Route From the Mississippi River to the Pacific Ocean. War Department. Route Near the 41st Parallel, map. No. 1, *From the Valley of the Green River to the Great Salt Lake,* from "Explorations and Surveys made under the direction of the Hon. Jefferson Davis, Secretary of War by Capt. E. G. Beckwith, 3rd Artillery, F. W. Egloffstein, Topographer for the Route," 1855. Scale 1:760320 or 12 miles to one inch.

6. Ibid.

7. Ibid., map no. 2, *From Great Salt Lake to the Humboldt Mountains.*

8. Skeleton Map Exhibiting the Route Explored by Capt. J. W. Gunnison USA 38 Parallel of North Latitude (1853) and also that of the 41 Parallel Explored by Lieutenant E. G. Beckwith 3rd Art. (1854). Drawn by J. W. Egloffstein. Scale 50 miles to one inch. G. K. Warren, Lt. Topographical Engineers.

9. "Territory and Military Department of Utah," Compiled in the Bureau of Topographical Engineers of the War Department, Chiefly for Military Purposes under the authority of Hon. J. B. Floyd, Sec. of War, 1860. Courtesy of Michael Polk, Sagebrush Consultants, Ogden, Utah.

10. Telegram to Brigham Young, Aug. 27, 1861, CR 1234 reel 59, box 45, folder 23, Church of Jesus Christ of Latter-day Saints Archives, Salt Lake City, Utah (hereafter LDS Archives).

11. H. W. Carpenter to Brigham Young, telegraph, 6 p.m., Oct. 24, 1861, CR 1234, reel 59, box 45, folder 23, LDS Archives.

12. Message to Salt Lake City, [Oct.] 24, 1861, signed H. W. C[arpenter], CR 1234, 1, reel 59, box 45, folder 23, LDS Archives.

13. Heber C. Kimball and Samuel H. Weber, Great Salt Lake City, to Mr. [E] Creighton, Chicago, Illinois, Sept. 24(?) 1862, , CR 1234, 1, reel 59, box 45, folder 23, LDS Archives.

14. Wallace D. Farnham, "The Pacific Railroad Act of 1862," *Nebraska History* 43, no. 3 (Sept. 1962): pp. 166–67 [pp. 141–67].

15. See Lucius Beebe, *Central Pacific and Southern Pacific Railroads* (Berkeley, Calif.: Howell-North, 1963) and Maury Klein, *Union Pacific* (Garden City, N.Y.: Doubleday, 1987).

16. Telegram from D. N. Barney to Brigham Young, Sept. 10, 1863, CR 1234, reel 59, box 45, folder 23, LDS Archives.

17. Telegram from Omaha to Brigham Young, n.d., , CR 1234, 1, reel 59, box 45, folder 23, LDS Archives.

18. *Deseret Evening News*, May 21, 1868 In UP-Mormon Contract file, LDS Journal History, Union Pacific Archives, Council Bluffs, Iowa (hereafter UP Archives).

19. Brigham Young letter to Franklin D. Richards, May 23, 1868, *Millennial Star*, vol. 30, p. 427. LDS Journal History, UP Archives.

20. G. Reynolds to G. F. Gibbs, Salt Lake City, June 4, 1868, *Millennial Star*, XXX 28, 443–44.

21. "Copy of Instructions to S. B. Reed from the Engineer's Office Union Pacific Rail Road, to Samuel B. Reed for Peter A. Dey, Apr. 25, 1964, 3-4-39-36, Levi O. Leonard Railroad Collection, University of Iowa Special Collections, Iowa City, Iowa (hereafter Leonard Collection).

22. Mel Thurman, "Warren, Dodge and Later Nineteenth-Century Army Maps of the West." In *Mapline: A Quarterly Newsletter*, Issue no 53 (Mar. 1989): pp. 1–3.

23. Attachment to Grenville Dodge letter to Mr. E. R. Harlan, Des Moines, Iowa, June 4, 1915 (86-92362), Newberry Library, Chicago, Ill..

24. James Akerman, *Mapline: A Quarterly Newsletter*, Issue no 53 (Mar. 1989): p. 2.

25. See *Map of the Military District, Kansas and the Territories*, Maj[or] G. M. Dodge, Commanding 1866 [which was] Executed under the Direction of Geo. T. Robinson, Chf. Engr. [and] Drawn by T. H. Williams, ms map 6F.G4050 1866D6, Newberry Library.

26. Charles Lubrecht and R. Rosa, *The American Continent Topographical and Railroad Map of the United States, British Possessions, West Indies, Mexico and Central America.* (New York, N.Y.: Ch. Lubrecht & Co.),1864.

27. "The Union Pacific Railroad," *The Pittsburgh Gazette*, Saturday, Dec. 9, 1865, in Union Pacific Railroad History Construction 1865–1869 file, MsC 159, box 32, Leonard Collection.

28. Samuel Bowles, *Across the Continent: A Summer's Journey to the Rocky Mountain, the Mormons and the Pacific States* (Springfield, Mass.: Samuel Bowles & Co., 1865).

29. Ayer MS 300, box 2, map 2, Newberry Library.

30. W. K. Keeler, *National Map of the Territory of the United States*, 1867, Ayer MS 3008, map 2, Newberry Library. See also Graff Collection, £ 2281.

31. Route around Salt Lake. GMD to J. Blickensderfer, Mar. 30, 1868 (W), box 337, GMD Papers, UP Archives.

32. Don Strack, *Ogden Rails: A History of Railroads in Ogden Utah from 1869 to Today* (Ogden, Utah: Golden Spike Chapter, Railway & Locomotive Historical Society, 1997), p. 7.

33. Telegram from Brigham Young to all the Bishops south of the City, Sept. 5, 1868, CR 1234, reel 59, box 45, folder 23, LDS Archives.

34. Samuel B. Reed to wife Jennie, Echo, June 14, 1868 (H), box 154, GMD Papers, UP Archives.

CHAPTER THREE

1. "Huntington to Friend Crocker," New York, Jan. 1, 1868, Huntington letters, UP Archives.

2. Huntington to Charles Crocker, NewYork, Jan. 26, 1868, Huntington letters, UP Archives.

3. Eng. Office, J. E. House to GMD; Omaha, Jan. 16, 1868, box 153, GMD Papers, UP Archives.

4. U.P. w of Salt Lake. Leonard Collection 1:3:33, GMD to Crane; Washington, May 11, 1868 (H). UP Archives.

5. Wallace Farnham, "Shadow from the Gilded Age: Pacific Railwaymen and the Race to Promontory—or Ogden?" in David Miller, ed., *The Golden Spike* (Salt Lake City: University of Utah Press, 1973), p. 11 [pp. 1–22].

6. Map 10A, tube 112, record group 49, Cartographic Records Section, National Archives.

7. 1000th Mile U.P.R.R., map 16, tube 58, Recd from Secty of Interior, Apr. 28, 1869; Recd in Secretary's Office, December 14, 1868, National Archives.

8. Stanford-Hopkins Correspondence, UP-CP and the Mormons: Stanford to Hopkins, SLC, June 9, 1868.

9. *Deseret Evening News*, July 11, 1868, Adolphus H. Noon to editor, June 28, 1868, Journal History, LDS Archives.

10. Thomas A. Davis. Handwritten ms., 9 pp., Utah Historical Society.

11. "Moroni Stone Says Men had Splendid Wage in Early Days," *The Ogden Standard*, May 10, 1919.

12. Martineau Diary, July 8, 1868, p. 267, box 1 (8), Huntington Library, San Marino, California (hereafter Huntington Library).

13. Martineau Diary, p. 271, box 1 (9), Huntington Library.

14. Song on pp. 273–74 of Martineau's Diary.

15. Martineau Diary, Aug. 14, 1868, p. 274, Huntington Library.

16. Letter, GMD to TCD, Red Dome Pass, Aug. 27, 1868 (H), I:3:35, Leonard Collection.

17. Martineau Diary, Aug. 28, 1868, p. 275, Huntington Library.

18. Martineau Diary, Aug. 28 and 29, 1868, p. 275, ibid.

19. James H. Martineau, "An Engineer's Tribulations," *The Contributor* 12, no. 8 (June 1891): p. 320 [pp. 317–20].
20. Martineau Diary, pp. 277–78, box 1, Huntington Library.
21. Letter from Grenville Dodge to TCD, Sept. 2, 1868, UP Archives.
22. Dodge to B. Reed, Sept. 5, 1868.
23. Martineau Diary, p. 278.
24. Letter, Huntington to Hopkins; NY, Sept. 14, 1868. Huntington letters, UP Archives.
25. Martineau Diary, p. 278, Huntington Library.
26. Martineau Diary, pp. 278–79, Huntington Library.
27. James H. Martineau, "An Engineer's Tribulations," *The Contributor* 12, no. 8 (June 1891), p. 318 [pp. 317–20].
28. Huntington to Stanford, Oct. 9, 1868, Huntington letters, UP Archives.
29. Gray to Stanford letter, Oct. 9, 1868, Stanford-Hopkins Correspondence, UP Archives.
30. George E. Gray to Stanford, Oct. 11, 1868. Stanford-Hopkins Correspondence, UP Archives.
31. M. A. Carter to George Gray, Oct. 12, 1868, Stanford-Hopkins Correspondence, UP Archives.
32. Stanford to Hopkins, Nov. 9, 1868 (H), Stanford-Hopkins Correspondence, UP Archives.
33. Martineau Diary, p. 282, Huntington Library.
34. Ibid, p. 283.
35. Ibid.
36. Ibid., p. 285.
37. Ibid., pp. 285–86.
38. Ibid., p. 287.
39. S. B. Reed to TCD, Feb. 16, 1868 [*sic*; should be 1869] III:4:11, Levi O. Leonard Collection. University of Iowa.
40. Salt Lake City *Telegraph*, Apr. 13, 1869.
41. Robert Spude, "Promontory Summit, May 10, 1869, A History of the Site Where the Central Pacific and Union Pacific Railroads Joined to Form the First Transcontinental Railroad . . . ," unpublished report (Cultural Resources Management, Intermountain Region, National Park Service, 2005): p. 11.
42. Personal telephone communication, Michael Polk, Sagebrush Consultants, Ogden, Utah, with author, June 9, 2007.
43. *Map Showing the Locations of Routes for the Pacific Railroad between Ogden City & Bear River as made by the Union Pacific Railroad Company and the Central Pacific Railroad of California* . . . prepared by the Special pacific R.R. Commission, Official W. K. Warren, Chv. Special PR Comm., May 14, 1869, map 1, tube 60, National Archives.
44. *Map Showing the Locations of Routes for the Pacific Railroad between Bear River & Summit of Promontory* as made by the Union Pacific Railroad Company and the Central Pacific Railroad of California . . ., Jan. 14, 1869, map 2, tube 60, National Archives.
45. See, for example, John Signor, *Southern Pacific's Salt Lake Division* (Wilton and Berkeley, Calif.: Signature Press, 2007), pp. 31–36.
46. *Map showing the Locations of Routes for the Pacific Railroad between Summit of Promontory & Monument Point*, map 3, tube 59, National Archives.
47. *Map showing the Locations of Routes for the Pacific Railroad between Monument Point & Red Dome Pass*, map 4, tube 60, National Archives.

48. Strack, *Ogden Rails*, pp. 6–7.
49. Union Pacific Location Survey, Private Copy of Grenville Dodge, UP Archives.
50. Jesse H. Jameson, "The Last Fourteen Miles," *Sons of the Utah Pioneer News* (Mar.-Apr. 1959): pp. 17–18.

CHAPTER FOUR

1. *Montana Post*, Helena, May, 14, 1869.
2. *The Deseret News*, Salt Lake City, Utah, May 19, 1869.
3. The golden spikes from California were alloys—mostly gold, hardened for strength with a mixture of copper.
4. See J. N. Bowman, "Driving the Last Spike at Promontory, 1869," *Utah Historical Quarterly* 37, no. 1 (Winter 1969): pp. 78–79.
5. Isaac Morris, *Railroad Commissioner Report, May 28, 1869*, 44th Cong., 1 sess., House Executive Document 180, 44th Congress, 1st Session. By "combs," he apparently meant something like the ridge of a roof, resembling the comb or fleshy crest, on the head of a domestic fowl.
6. Letter to "Dear Olive" from unknown, July 7, 1869, UP Archives.
7. "Letter from the Front," May 10 1869, in Stan Garner, *Capitol Life: Sacramento California August 19, 1868 to January 20, 1876* (Grand Junction CO: Monte Vista Publishing, 2005), p. 9.
8. *Crofutt's Trans-Continental Tourist*, (Chicago: Geo. A. Croffut & Co., 1871), p. 91.
9. Ibid., p. 94.
10. *The Daily Bee*, Letter From the Front, Thursday, May 13, 1869, in Garner, *Capitol Life*, p. 8.
11. The third type of device for turning a train is a balloon track, which consists of a track that loops a full 180 degrees. These require considerable space, and were used at relatively few locations—usually terminals.
12. Ames letter to Dillon and Duff, Apr. 29, 1869 in Grenville Dodge, *A brief biographical sketch of the life of Major-General Grenville M. Dodge* (New York: Press of Styles & Cash, 1893: reprint, New York: Arno Press, 1981). "Autobiography."
13. Spude, "Promontory Summit," pp. 35–39.
14. Albert D. Richardson, "Through to the Pacific" letters to the *New York Herald*, May-June, 1869, in Abby Richardson, *Garnered Sheaves* (Hartford, Conn.: Columbian Book Company, 1871).
15. Henry Austin Diary, Aug. 1869, file, Golden Spike National Historic Site, Promontory, Utah (hereafter Golden Spike Historic Site).
16. Elko *Independent*, Oct. 13, 1869.
17. Isaac Morris, Railroad Commissioner Report, May 28, 1869.
18. W. W. Foote, *Omaha Herald*, May 15, 1869.
19. Ibid., May 20, 1869.
20. Grenville Dodge, as interviewed by the *Omaha Herald*.
21. See Spude, "Promontory Summit," p. 35.
22. M, J. W., *The Cincinnati excursion to California: its origin, progress, incidents, and results : history of a railway journey of six thousand miles— complete newspaper correspondence . . .* (Cincinnati, 1870), p. 39.
23. Ibid.
24. Letter, Montague to Dodge, June 7, 1869; and letter, Dodge to Morris, July 15, 1869, in Dodge, "Autobiography."
25. See Spude, "Promontory Summit," pp. 42–43.

26. The *Reporter*, Aug. 4, 1869, as noted in Spude, 2005.
27. Hammond to Ames, Oct. 25, 1869, Hammond letters, Union Pacific Collection, Nebraska Historical Society, Lincoln.
28. For a more detailed account of locomotive design, see John White, Jr., *A History of the American Locomotive: 1830–1880* (New York, N.Y.: Dover Publications, 1979).
29. Jim Wilke, "Victorian Splendor at Promontory," *Locomotive & Railway Preservation*, issue 49, (Sept.-Oct., 1994): pp. 32–41.
30. Ibid., p. 35.
31. John White, Jr., "Jupiter and 119," *Trains* 29, no. 7 (May 1969): pp. 49–50.
32. Wilke, "Victorian Splendor," p. 38.
33. Personal telephone communication, Kyle Wyatt, California State Railroad Museum, with author, Aug. 10, 2007.
34. Garner, *Capitol Life*, p. 3.
35. *The Daily Bee*, Oct. 9, 1868, in Garner, *Capitol Life*, p. 3.
36. See Fred Kniffen, "American Architecture's Debt to Transportation," *Geographical Review* 47 (1957): pp. 582-583.
37. "Elaborate Cars," *The Daily Bee*, May 12, 1869, in Garner, p. 8.
38. Copy of the handbill at the Brigham City Historical Depot, Dec. 2, 2005.
39. "The Railway Dining Cars" in the Local News section of *The Daily Bee*, June 18, 1869, in Garner, *Capitol Life*, pp. 12–13.
40. From *Profile of Central Pacific Railroad*, vol. 4, *Battle Mtn. To Lucin*; and vol. 5, *Lucin to Ogden*, Nevada Historical Society, Reno.
41. See Strack, *Ogden Rails*.
42. H. T. Williams, ed., *The Pacific Tourist: An Illustrated Guide to Pacific R. R. [and] California, Pleasure Resorts Across the Continent* (New York, N.Y.: Adams & Bishop, Publisher, 1879), pp. 163–64.
43. *The Deseret News*, vol. 18, May 12, 1869, pp. 163–64.
44. Williams, *Pacific Tourist*, p. 166.
45. See John White, Jr., *The American Railroad Freight Car* (Baltimore, Md.: John Hopkins Press, 1993).
46. S. G. Snively, "Salt Lake Division," *Southern Pacific Bulletin* 14, no. 9 (Sept. 1926): p. 17.
47. *Central P.R.R.—final location of the—from Wadsworth to Ogden from Maj. H. N. Roberts &c &c*, Copied from Latest Data Obtained from Central Pacific R.R. Co. Engineer Office, Military Division of the Pacific. San Francisco, Aug. 1869.
48. Historic American Engineering Record, Promontory Route Railroad Trestle complex, 11 miles west of Corinne, Corinne Vicinity, Box Elder County, Utah, HAER No. UT-64. (Denver, Colo.: National Park Service), pp. 14–15.
49. Adrienne B. Anderson, "Ancillary Construction on Promontory Summit, Utah: Those Domestic Structures Built by Railroad Workers," [n.d., n.p.], p. 227 [pp. 225–38].
50. Delone Glover, interview by author, Brigham City, Utah, Dec. 9, 2005.
51. Bain, *Empire Express*, p. 667.
52. David Lemon-Old Timer Fired Engine at Golden Spike Driving May 10, 1869; from *Union Pacific Magazine*, May, 1924, pp. 5–6. http://cprr.org/Museum/Lemon_Interview.html, accessed Apr. 4, 2007.
53. Although the particular library was not named, correspondence suggests it was the library at Stanford University, where numerous objects from the golden spike event were featured.
54. A. J. Russell, Joining of tracks, Promontory, Utah, photograph, 30-N-36-2994, National Archives.

55. Letters from T. Clapp to H. C. Cram, Eng. (on letterhead of Pontoosuc Woolen Manufacturing Company, Pittsfield, Mass., Aug. 24 and Aug. 26, 1869. In the John Todd file, box 31, Leonard Collection.

CHAPTER FIVE

1. *Map Showing U.P.R.R. Lands in the Salt Lake District,* Offices of the Union Pacific Railroad Company, Boston, Mass., Jan. 10, 1870, National Archives.
2. "Rules and Regulations for Employees," on verso of *Central Pacific Railroad Humboldt Divisions* [Timetable], no. 2, 1868.
3. See A. Dudley Gardner and Verla R. Flores, *Forgotten Frontier: A History of Wyoming Coal Mining* (Boulder, Colo.: Westview Press, 1989).
4. Arnold Hague and S. F. Emmons, "Descriptive Geology," in Clarence King *Report of the Geological Exploration of the Fortieth Parallel.* Professional Papers of the Engineering Department, U.S. Army 18 (Washington, D.C.: Government Printing Office, 1877), pp. 420–22.
5. *Crofutt's Trans-continental Tourist,* p. 91.
6. "Diagram of the Survey of the Third Standard Parallel North and Exterior Lines in Utah Territory," by Joseph Garlinski deputy surveyor under his contract No. 26, bearing [the] date the 20th day of November, 1871. Map courtesy of Michael Polk, Sagebrush Consultants, Ogden, Utah.
7. Twining noted that the Union Pacific Railroad accomplished from mile post (MP) 960 to 1,000 by Feb. 10, 1869; 1,000 to 1,020 by July 16; and MP 1,020 to 1,033.68 by Nov. 6. The Central Pacific road bonds were issued as follows: from 560 to 660 on Mar. 2, from 510 to 570 on Mar. 27, from 570 to 670 by May 27, 670 to 690.3 by July 15, from 690.3 to 757.5 by July 16—but that "$1,338,000 of this lot [was] delivered to Union Pacific Railroad Company." 44th Cong., 2d sess., House Executive Document 38, pp. 6–7.
8. Ibid., p. 13.
9. Ibid., p. 15.
10. Central Pacific later rebuilt this tank when it assumed control of this portion of the line.
11. Robert Spude, "Railroad Water Supply at Promontory Station: Suggestions for Research, Documentation and Resource Management," unpublished paper (Cultural Resources Management, Intermountain Region, National Park Service, 2005), p. 2 [19 pp].
12. Southern Pacific Company (Pacific System) Salt Lake Division Time Table No. 23, To take effect Sunday May 1, 1892 at 12:01 O'Clock, A.M.
13. *Map of the C.P.R.R. and Connecting Lines,* Southern Methodist University Special Collections, DeGolyer Library, Dallas (hereafter DeGolyer Library).
14. See James E. Ayres, Archaeological Survey of Golden Spike National Historic Site . . ., March 1982, pp. 83–85.
15. Contributed by Adolph Reeder, file, National Historic Site.
16. Doelling, *Geology and Mineral Resources,* pp 167–69.
17. Carol Brown Austin, "Thomas George Brown," *Sons of Utah Pioneers News,* Jan./Feb. 1961, pp. 11, 13.
18. Local News, *The Daily Bee,* May 24, 1869, in Garner, *Capitol Life,* p. 10.
19. Local News, *The Daily Bee,* June 4, 1869, inGarner, *Capitol Life,* pp. 10–11.
20. Ibid., p. 11.
21. "New Sleeper," *The Daily Union,* Dec. 11, 1869, in Garner, *Capitol Life,* p. 13.
22. "New Sleeper," *The Daily Union,* Tuesday, Feb. 22, 1870, in Garner, *Capitol Life,* p. 15.

23. Jules Verne, *Around the World in Eighty Days* (New York, N.Y: Viking, 1994), pp. 210–15.

24. John White, Jr., *The American Railroad Passenger Car*, vol. 2 (Baltimore, Md.: Johns Hopkins University Press, 1978), pp. 466–71.

25. Robert Louis Stevenson, *The Travels and Essays of Robert Louis Stevenson* [*The*] *The Amateur Emigrant; Across the Plains; The Silverado Squatters* (New York, N.Y.: Charles Schribner, 1901), pp. 15.

26. Ibid., pp. 134–42.

27. *The Daily Union*, November 4, 1871, in Garner, *Capitol Life*, p. 24.

28. *Crofutt's Trans-Continental Tourist*, pp. 88–89.

29. *The Central Pacific Railroad: A Trip Across the North American Continent from Ogden to San Francisco*, Nelson's Pictorial Guide Books (New York, N.Y.: T. Nelson and Sons, 1871), p. 8.

30. *Crofutt's Trans-Continental Tourist*, pp. 88–89.

31. Williams, *Pacific Tourist*, p. 163.

32. Thomas Davis, England to US-Mormon Pioneer '63—farm boy. . . the 68-69 RR worker. Work of Promontory 69-87 cattle rancher. [Ranch] sold to R.R. people. Promontory Railroad file, Utah State Historical Society, Salt Lake City.

33. Anthony W. Thompson, *Southern Pacific Freight Cars*, vol. 4, *Box Cars* (Berkeley, Calif.: Signature Press, 2006), p. 55.

34. John White, Jr., *The American Railroad Freight Car*, pp. 29–30, 293–94.

35. See Anthony Thompson, *Southern Pacific Freight Cars*, pp. 31–54.

36. City Intelligence, *The Daily Union*, Mar. 14, 1873, in Garner, *Capitol Life*, p. 30.

37. Incidentally, "joining the birds" was not a foolproof method, as many railroaders were killed by the impact of landing on the ground or on objects along the railroad.

38. City Intelligence, *The Daily Union*, June 2, 1871, in Garner, *Capitol Life*, p. 21.

39. *The Daily Union*, Aug. 2, 1871, in Garner, *Capitol Life*, p. 23.

40. Garner, *Capitol Life*, p. 17.

41. Martineau Diary, pp. 343–44, FAC 1499, box 1, folder 10, Huntington Library.

42. Ibid., p. 309.

43. Ibid., p. 312, In Salt Lake City, Susan J. was diagnosed with heart problems, which worsened; she lingered in bad health for months, dying on Jan. 29, 1874.

44. R. Douglas Brackenridge, *Westminster College of Salt Lake City* (Logan: Utah State University Press, 1998), p. 28.

45. Ibid., p. 31.

46. Page Smith, *As a City Upon a Hill: The Town in American History* (New York, N.Y.: Knopf, 1966).

47. "The City of Corinne, Utah, and the Bear Valley, looking North." Birds-eye view map, Strobridge & Co., Lithographers, Cincinnati, Ohio, 1875.

48. Frederick Whymper, "From Ocean to Ocean—the Pacific Railroad," in H. W. Bates, Ed., *Illustrated Travels* (London; New York: Cassell, Petter, and Galpin, 1869–70).

49. *Frank Leslie's Illustrated Newspaper*, 1877, as quoted in Richard Reinhardt, *Out West on the Overland Train* (Secaucus, N.J.: Castle Books, 1967), p. 111.

Chapter Six

1. *Map of Township No. 10 North, Range No. 6 West of the Salt Lake Meridian*; sheet 147A; [map] is strictly conformable to the field notes of the survey thereof on file in this office, which have been examined and approved. Surveyor General's

Office, Salt Lake City, Utah, Oct. 21, 1885. Map courtesy of Michael Polk, Sagebrush Consultants, Ogden, Utah.

2. *Central Pacific Railroad*, p. 10.

3. Anan S. Raymond and Richard E. Fike, *Rails East to Promontory: The Utah Stations*, no. 8 (Cultural Resources Management, National Park Service): p. 97.

4. Williams, *Pacific Tourist*, p. 166.

5. Ibid., p. 167.

6. Ibid.

7. *Crofutt's Trans-Continental Tourist*, p. 98.

8. Williams, *Pacific Tourist*, p. 172.

9. *Frank Leslie's Illustrated Newspaper*, 1877, as quoted in Reinhardt, *Out West on the Overland Train* pp. 111–12.

10. Williams, *Pacific Tourist*, p. 172.

11. Station Plans, Central Pacific Railroad, Mill City to Ogden, n.d. (ca. 1885), p. 28, Nevada Historical Society, Reno.

12. Adolph Reeder, handwritten manuscript, file, Golden Spike Historic Site,.

13. Gary Topping, ed., *Gila Monsters and Red-Eyed Rattlesnakes: Don Maguire's Arizona Trading Expeditions, 1876–1879* (Salt Lake City: University of Utah Press, 1997), p. 14.

14. Map, 29986, Utah State Historical Society, Salt Lake City.

15. Kit Goodwin, "All Aboard! Railroad Maps in the Late Nineteenth Century," *Compass Rose.* 5, no. 2 (Fall, 1991).

16. A. Pendarvis Vivian, *Wanderings in the Western Land* (London: Sampson Low, Marston, Searle & Rivington, 1879), p. 329.

17. "New Refrigeration Car," *The Daily Union*, July 1, 1870, in Garner, *Capitol Life*, p. 17.

18. "Booth's Refrigerating Car," *The Daily Union*, July 22,1870, in Garner, *Capitol Life*, p. 18.

19. City Intelligence, *The Daily Union*, Dec. 29, 1870, in Garner, *Capitol Life*, pp. 18–19.

20. *Union and Central Pacific Railroad Line via Omaha or Kansas City to San Francisco* [timetable] (Omaha, J. W. Morse, Gen'l Pass'r Agent: Union Pacific Railway, p. 2, p. 14, p. 64, DeGolyer Library.

21. Martineau Diary, FAC1499, Box 1, Folder 14, p. 500, Huntington Library.

22. Martineau Diary, p. 551, FAC1499, Box 1, Folder 16, Huntington Library.

23. George Alfred Lawrence, *Silverland* (London: Chapman and Hall, 1873), p. 95.

24. Southern Pacific No. 10017 Dining Car, Wooden 72-D class, built by Pullman Co.,1909, photo, n.p., Southern Methodist University, DeGolyer Library.

25. John H. White, Jr., *The American Railroad Passenger Car, Part 1* (Baltimore, Md.: John Hopkins University Press, 1978), p. 320.

26. Brian Solomon, *Southern Pacific Railroad* (Osceola, Wisconsin: MBI Publishing, 1999), pp. 52–54.

27. City Intelligence, *The Daily Union*, Jan. 20, 1876, in Garner, *Capitol Life*.

28. See Thompson, *Southern Pacific Freight Cars,*, p. 45.

29. Station Plans Central Pacific Railroad, Mill City to Ogden, n.d. (ca. 1885), pp. 32–33, Nevada Historical Society, Reno.

30. Doris Larsen, "Growing up at Promontory, Utah," interview by Robert C. Sidford, June 4, 2003, p. 35, Golden Spike Oral History Project, Mountain West Center for Regional Studies, Utah State University, Logan (hereafter Golden Spike Oral History), p. 35.

31. W. A. Clay, interview by Greg Thompson and Phil Notarianni, Sept. 3, 1974, Ethnic Oral History Program, American West Center, University of Utah, Salt Lake City (hereafter Ethnic Oral History), pp. 8–12.

32. Marion Woodward, "This is Promontory as I remember it," written recollections, Utah Historical Society, Salt Lake City.

33. *Profile of Central Pacific Railroad*, vol. 5, *Lucin to Ogden*, p. 1, p. 36.

34. Draft, Promontory Station and Maintenance of the Transcontinental Railroad, n.d., n.p., p. 5.

35. *The Resources and Attractions of Utah as they Exist Today* (Salt Lake City, Utah: Geo. Q. Cannon & Sons, 1894), p. 57, Utah Ephemera Collection, DeGolyer Library.

36. Ed Workman, "Common Standard Freight Cars—Part 1," *The Streamliner* 11, no. 4, [1997]: pp. 19–20 [pp. 18–31].

37. *En Route to California—Souvenir and Views of the Union Pacific, "The Overland Route," World's Pictorial Line*, 5th ed. (Omaha, Neb.: E. L. Lomax General Passenger and Ticket Agent, Union Pacific Railroad, 1901), p. 64 [76 pp].

38. *Sights and Scenes From the Car Windows of the World's Pictorial Line* (Omaha, Neb.: E. L. Lomax General Passenger and Ticket Agent, Union Pacific Railroad, 1901, pp. 62–63 [108 pp.].

39. John H. White, Jr., *American Locomotives: An Engineering History, 1830–1880*, rev. ed., (Baltimore, Md.: Johns Hopkins University Press, 1997), p. 529, note to p. 233.

40. "An Instance of Degeneration," *Harper's Weekly*, July 15, 1893. See also Reinhardt, *Workin' on the Railroad*, pp. 102–6.

41. Hammond, *From Sea to Sea*.

42. When interviewing old-timers in 1974, historian Greg Thompson astutely noted that "… as we've talked to people several times I've gotten the impression that they were talking about two different locations." Thompson thought that one place was called Promontory Station, where the Houghton store was located, but that "Promontory Summit would be further west of there, would it not?" The person he was interviewing, Della Owens, replied: "No, it is the same spot." Clearly, though, several accounts, including Hammond's, suggest that there was a place called Promontory on the road farther west of Promontory Station/Summit. See Della Owens, Corinne, Utah, August 22, 1974, Ethnic Oral History, pp. 5–6.

43. Hammond, *From Sea to Sea*, pp. 75–78.

CHAPTER SEVEN

1. *Going to Sea by Rail, Great Salt Lake Cut-off Primer, Union Pacific Southern Pacific Series* (n.d., n.p.) pp. 1-2 [22 pp.].

2. Minutes and Notes from the Ogden Library Club, 1903, p. 109, LDS Archives.

3. David Myrick, *Railroads of Nevada and Eastern California*, vol. 1, *the Northern Roads*, Berkeley CA: Howell North, 1962),p. 37.

4. Doris Larsen and Merlin Larsen, interview by author, Dec. 10, 2005.

5. David F. Myrick, "Refinancing and Rebuilding the Central Pacific: 1899–1910" in David Miller, ed., *The Golden Spike* (Salt Lake City: Utah State Historical Society and University of Utah Press, 1973), p. 116 [pp. 85–117].

6. "Line Across Great Salt Lake–Lucin to Ogden, Scale 6 miles to one inch, traced from blueline print—July 8, 1913—W.H.D.," Map courtesy of Michael Polk, Sagebrush Consultants, Ogden, Utah.

7. Lantern Slides of the Great Salt Lake, PH 4879, box 1 [see also box 2], LDS Archives.

8. David Peterson, *Tale of the Lucin: A Boat, A Railroad and The Great Salt Lake* (Trinidad: Calif.: Old Waterfront Publishing, 2001).

9. Bain, *Empire Express*, pp. 664, 665–66.

10. Earl Harmon, interview, Ethnic Oral History, p. 8.

11. Merlin Larsen, interview by Deloy Spencer, Oct. 17, 1995, file, Golden Spike Historic Site.

12. Isaac W. Finn, interview by Greg Thompson and Phil Notarianni, Salt Lake City, Aug. 21, 1974, Ethnic Oral History.

13. Bernice Anderson, interview, Ethnic Oral History, p. 6.

14. Pappy Clay, "Wild Horses and Wild Parties," Jan. 29, 1969, interview, http://www.nps.gov/gosp/research/pappy_clay1.html, p. 2 of 4, accessed June 22, 2004.

15. John Whitaker, interview by Ellis J. LeFevre, file, n.d. [Nov. 20, 1995?] Golden Spike Historic Site.

16. Lorna Larsen Phillips, interview, Salt Lake City, Aug. 28, 1974, GS-12. Golden Spike Oral History Project, American West Center, University of Utah, pp. 5–6.

17. Neil Harris, *The Artist in American Society, 1790–1860* (New York, N.Y.: George Braziller, 1966), pp. 192–99.

18. Interstate Commerce Commission Division of Valuation Pacific District Close Out Report Roadway, C.P. Ry. Utah 2, Jan. 12, 1918, signed H. J. Friedman, Asst. Field Engr.

19. Don L. Hofsommer, *The Southern Pacific, 1901–1985* (College Station, Tex.: Texas A&M University Press, 1986), p. 52.

20. *Southern Pacific Passenger Cars, Vol. 1: Coaches and Chair Cars* (Pasadena, Calif.: Southern Pacific Historical & Technical Society, 2003), pp. 14–15.

21. Mayme Wells Lower, interview, Aug. 8, 1974. Golden Spike Oral History Project, American West Center, University of Utah, Ethnic Oral History, p. 17.

22. Ibid., p. 9.

23. Ibid., p. 9.

24. Taro Yagi, interview, September 4, 1974, Ethnic Oral History, pp. 14–15.

25. Leona Yates Anderson, interview by Phil Notarianni and Greg Thompson, Brigham City, Utah, Aug. 29, 1974, Ethnic Oral History, , pp. 11–12.

26. Mayme Wells Lower, interview, Aug. 8, 1974, p. 22.

27. Taro Yagi, interview, Sept. 4, 1974, p. 14.

28. Ibid., p. 14.

29. Mayme Wells Lower, interview, Aug. 8, 1974, p. 22.

30. Evan Murray, interview by Phil Notarianni and Greg Thompson, Logan, Utah, Aug. 29, 1974, Ethnic Oral History, pp. 5–10.

31. Lucius Beebe and Charles Clegg, *Central Pacific* (Berkeley, CA: Howell-North Pubs, 1963), pp. 111–233.

32. Evan Murray, interview, Aug. 29, 1974, pp. 20–21.

33. Taro Yagi, interview, Sept. 4, 1974, pp. 5–6.

34. Ibid., p. 5.

35. Ibid., p. 9.

36. Ibid., p. 13.

37. See WorldWideWords by Michael Quinion, http://www.worldwidewords.org/ga/ga-gan1.htm.,accessed Aug. 24, 2007.

38. Leona Yates Anderson, interview by Phil Notarianni and Greg Thompson, Ogden, Utah, Sept. 4, 1974, Ethnic Oral History, pp. 8–9, 19–22.

39. Taro Yagi, interview, Sept. 4, 1974, pp. 10–11.

40. Bernice Anderson, interview, August 9, 1974, Ethnic Oral History, p. 2.

41. Mayme Wells Lower, interview, Aug. 8, 1974, pp. 10–12.

42. Frank Wendell Call, *Gandydancer's Children: A Railroad Memoir* (Reno: University of Nevada Press, 2000).

43. Germano Pucci, interview by Phil Notarianni and Greg Thompson, Brigham City, Utah, Aug. 29, 1974, Ethnic Oral History, pp. 13–14.

44. Pablo Baltazar, interview by Phil Notarianni and Greg Thompson, Corrine, Utah, Aug. 15, 1974, Utah Minorities Number S-120, Ethnic Oral History, pp. 30–31.

45. Taro Yagi, interview, Sept. 4, 1974, pp. 11–12.

46. Sam Nagata, interview by Greg Thompson and Phil Notorianni, part of interview with Mrs. Suzuko Nagata, Corinne, Utah, Aug. 22, 1974, p. 7.

47. Ibid., pp. 10, 13.

48. Stanley Wood, *Over the Range to the Golden Gate: A Complete Tourist's Guide to Colorado, New Mexico, Utah, Nevada, California, Oregon, Puget Sound, and the Great Northwest* (Chicago, Ill.: R. R. Donnelley & Sons, 1904), p. 145.

49. *Travelers Railway Guide—Western Section With Through Time Tables to all Principal Points* (Chicago, Ill.: American Railway Guide Company, January 1906), p. 139.

50. Ibid.,

51. Willis T. Lee, Ralph Wistone, Hoyt S. Gale, et.al., *Guidebook of the Western United States: part B, the Overland Route*, Bulletin 612, U.S. Geological Survey, Department of the Interior (Washington, D.C.: Government Printing Office, 1915), p. 107.

52. *The Official Guide of Railways . . .* (New York, N.Y.: National Railway Publication Co., Oct., 1923), p. 797.

53. Lorna Larsen Phillips, interview, Salt Lake City, Utah, Aug. 28, 1974, GS-12, Golden Spike Oral History, p. 12.

54. Bernice Gibbs Anderson, interview by Phil Notarianni and Greg Thompson, Corinne, Utah, Aug. 9, 1974, Ethnic Oral History, p. 1.

55. Ibid., p. 3.

56. Ibid., p. 1.

57. Ibid., p. 2.

58. John Whitaker, interview by Ellis J. LeFevre, n.d. [Nov. 20, 1995], n.p. .

59. Della Owens, interview by Phil Notarianni and Greg Thompson, Corinne, Utah, Aug. 22, 1974, Ethnic Oral History, pp. 11-12.

60. Grace N. Brough, interview by Phil Notarianni and Greg Thompson, Thornton, Utah, Sept. 5, 1974, Golden Spike Oral History, pp. 15–18, p. 31.

61. Joseph Nicholas, interview by Phil Notarianni and Greg Thompson, Murray, Utah, Sept. 6, 1974, Ethnic Oral History, p. 14.

62. Leona Yates Anderson, interview, Aug. 29, 1974, Ethnic Oral History, pp. 7–8.

63. U.S. Census, Promontory Precinct.

64. Michael Polk, personal conversation, Ogden, Utah, Aug. 1, 2006.

65. Interstate Commerce Commission, Division of Valuation, Pacific District. Closeout Report—Mechanical & Electrical. Carrier Central Pacific Railway Co. Terrace, Utah, June 16, 1917. Forms PM-125, Feb. 8, 1917 [one page].

66. Before the Interstate Commerce Commission, Finance Docket No. 13655, In the Matter of the Application of Central Pacific Railway Company and Southern Pacific Company for permission to the former to abandon a portion of the Promontory branch in Utah, Salt Lake City, Utah, Friday, May 1, 1942, pp. 23–24, Collection of Michael Polk, Sagebrush Consultants, Ogden, Utah.

67. Account 11—Ballast ICC Division of Valuation 1-22-18 Central Pacific Ry. Utah 3, [one page].

68. Pappy Clay, "Wild Horses and Wild Parties," interview, Jan. 29, 1969, p. 2 of 4, http://www.nps.gov/gosp/research/pappy_clay1.html, accessed June 22, 2004.

CHAPTER EIGHT

1.   "In the Superior Court of the State of California, in and for the City and County of San Francisco. In the matter of the Application of Promontory Ranch Company, a corporation, for a Judgment of Dissolution. No. 121266, Dept. No. 13, *Decree of Dissolution.* (last three pages; original incorporation documents, pp. 1–3).

2.   Leonard J. Arrington, *David Eccles: Pioneer Western Industrialist* (Logan: Utah State University Press, 1975), pp. 263–65.

3.   Letter from Promontory-Curlew Land Company to S. A. Langton, Blue Creek, Utah, Feb. 9, 1911.

4.   Craig L. Torbenson, "The Promontory-Curlew Land Company: Promontory Dry Farming In Utah," *Utah Historical Quarterly* 66.1, 1998, p. 11.

5.   Board of Directors Report, Promontory-Curlew Land Company, March, 1910, Special Collections, Utah State University, Logan.

6.   Outgoing correspondence, June 19, 1913, Mr. John Q. Critchlow, Ogden, Utah, from Secretary of the Promontory-Curlew Land Company, Outgoing 1911–1919, Special Collections, Merrill-Cazier Library, Utah State University, Logan, Utah (hereafter Merrill-Cazier Library).

7.   European War Will Make Wheat Raisers Millionaires, P-C Land Co., ca. 1915, DeGolyer Library.

8.   Promontory-Curlew Land Company records, MSS 178, folder. 4, box 3, pp. 149–50, Merrill-Cazier Library.

9.   "A Winning Combination," brochure, Promontory-Curlew Land Company, n.p., n.d.[1917], Merrill-Cazier Library.

10. Richard Francaviglia, *Believing in Place: A Spiritual Geography of the Great Basin* (Reno: University of Nevada Press, 2003), pp. 4–5.

11. *Howell Valley History*, 1900–1975, n.d., n.p.

12. The name Nella appears to be new, a result of early twentieth-century agriculture; it does not appear on early Central Pacific maps or timetables.

13. *Right of Way and Track Map Part of Promontory Branch From Lucin to Beginning of Leased Line West of Cecil Junction. Central Pacific Railway Company Operated by Southern Pacific Company. Salt Lake Division. Box Elder County, Utah.* Scale 1 inch to 400 feet. June 30, 1916. Office of Chief Engineer, San Francisco, California, National Archives.

14. Draft, Promontory Station . . . ., p. 6.

15. From the *Ogden Standard* and other local newspapers, May 9 and May 10, 1919, files, National Historic Site.

16. Draft, Promontory Station . . . ., p. 7.

17. State of Utah Lands Designated as non-irrigable by the Secretary of the Interior under the Provisions of the Enlarged Homestead Acts—Includes Patented as well as Vacant Land. Edition of June 30, 1920,. no. 57, Utah Sheet B, National Archives.

18. 1) *Problem Area Map. State of Utah,* showing Dry Farm Land, Irrigated Farm Land, Ungrazed Areas [and] Problem Areas: Dry Farm Land, Eroded Range Land, Pumping, Irrigated Farm Land, [and] Water-Shed areas, n.d. (ca. 1934), n.p. 2); *Land Use Adjustment Map, State of Utah*—Preliminary Map Showing areas Where Land Retirement is suggested; also showing Forest Reserves, Indian

Reservations, National Parks & Bird Refuges, Land Use Adjustment Projects, Irrigated Land, Dryfarm Land, Railroad Land Every Other Sec. Desert Quality, [and] Problem Areas Submarginial Dryfarm Land, Submarginal Irrigated Land [and] Stranded Agricultural Communities. 59-00.502.

19. Isaac W. Finn, interview, Aug. 21, 1974, Ethnic Oral History, pp. 14–15.

20. S. Goring Vidler, "Geological Report of Lands Lying in Box Elder County, Utah and Oneida County, Idaho, Los Angeles, California," Feb. 3, 1930, n.p. [3 pp.].

21. Leona Yates Anderson, interview, Aug. 29, 1974, , pp. 21–22.

22. Joseph Nicholas, interview, Sept. 6, 1974, Ethnic Oral History, p. 8.

23. Don Strack, *Ogden Rails: A History of Railroading at the Crossroads of the West* (Cheyenne, Wyo.: Union Pacific Historical Society, 2005), p. 113.

24. Central Pacific Railway Company, et.al. Abandonment Proceedings, May 2, 1942, pp. 200–202.

25. Ibid., pp. 200–201.

26. Ibid., pp. 209–210.

27. Ibid., p. 211.

28. Ibid., pp. 212–14.

29. Ibid., pp. 223–26.

30. Ibid., pp. 223(11)–23.

31. Ibid., pp. 27–28.

32. Ibid., pp. 30–34.

33. Ibid., pp. 40–42.

34. Ibid., pp. 57–59.

35. Ibid., pp. 88–90.

36. ICC Cases Disposed without Printed Report, p. 805, Collection of Michael Polk, Sagebrush Consultants, Ogden, Utah.

37. Order at a session of the Interstate Commerce Commission, Division 4, held at its office in Washington, D.C., on the 10th day of July, A.D. 1942.

38. The L. P. Hopkins mentioned here naturally begs the question: Was he a descendent of Mark Hopkins of "The Big Four"? Although Mark Hopkins and his wife, Mary, did not have any children, following Mark Hopkins's death, Mary adopted Timothy Nolan, who later worked for the Central Pacific Railroad's general office at Fourth and Townsend Streets. From 1883 to 1892 Timothy was assistant treasurer, then a director and treasurer of the company. When the Southern Pacific Company was organized in 1885, he served as its first treasurer and as a director, positions which he held until 1892. Timothy married Mary's niece, Mary Kellogg Crittenden. but they had only one child—a daughter, Lydia Hopkins. The information here was obtained from http://dgmweb.net/genealogy/FGS/H/HopkinsMark-MaryFrancesSherwood.shtml and http://dgmweb.net/genealogy/FGS/N/NolanHopkinsTimothyN-MaryKelloggCrittenden.shtml.

39. David Mann, "The Undriving of the Golden Spike" *Utah Historical Quarterly* 37, No. 1 (Spring 1969): pp. 132–34

40. As recalled by Mrs. Virginia Garrett of Forth Worth, Texas, in a conversation with the author, Oct. 2005. Mrs. Garrett was a new bride accompanying her husband to his new job in San Francisco where he worked for the FBI.

CHAPTER NINE

1. David Myrick, *The Railroads of Nevada and Eastern California*, vol. 1, *The Northern Roads* (Berkeley, Calif.: Howell North, 1962), pp. 74–75.

2. See Phil Hardy, *The Western* (New York, N.Y.: William Morrow and Company, 1983), pp. 99–100.

3. Delone Glover, interview , Dec. 9, 2005.

4. Ibid.

5. *Golden Spike 90th Anniversary, 1869–1959, Railroad Museum Dedication, May 9, 1959*, Special Publication, Sons of the Utah Pioneers, no. 4–5 (Apr./May 1959): pp. 1–2.

6. "8th Annual Golden Spike Ceremony, May 10, 1960," *Sons of the Utah Pioneers News*, (Mar./Apr. 1960): p. 10.

7. Horace A. Sorensen, "Time to prepare for 'Spike' Event," *Sons of the Utah Pioneers News*, (Nov./Dec. 1965): p. 16.

8. Delone Glover, interview, Dec. 9, 2005.

9. Nate Kogan, "The Mormon Pavilion: The Church of Jesus Christ of Latter-day Saints' Development of Proselytizing and Emergence into Mainstream America," senior thesis in American History, Columbia University, Apr. 15, 2004; and Brent L. Top, "Legacy of the Mormon Pavilion," *Ensign* 22, no. 10 (Oct. 1989): pp. 22–28.

10. Information provided by the staff at the Golden Spike National Historic Site, Aug. 13, 2007.

11. See E. L. Moore, "The Centennial Celebration of the Golden Spike Laying at Promontory Point, Utah, May 10, 1869," *Railroad Model Craftsman* (May 1969): pp. 34–39.

12. Robert Schleicher, "The 110-Year Celebration of the Transcontinental," *Great World of Model Railroading* 6, no. 2 (Spring 1979): pp. 4–9.

13. Bill Wright, "Locomotive Reincarnation," *Great World of Model Railroading*, Vol. 6, No. 2, Spring 1979, pp. 10–13.

14. Spude, "Promontory Summit," p. 100.

15. Elko, Nevada, *Independent*, Dec. 15, 1869.

16. Frederick Whymper, "From Ocean to Ocean—The Pacific Railroad" in Henry Walter Bates, *Illustrated Travels: A Record of Discovery, Geography and Adventure* (London and New York: Cassell, Petter, and Galpin, 1869), pp. 63–69.

17. *BLM Utah Transcontinental Railroad National Back Country Byway* (Box Elder County Tourism Council, Golden Spike Empire Travel Region, Bonneville Bicycle Touring Club, Thiokol Corporation: 2 sided 1 page brochure, nd.)

18. Anan S. Raymond and Richard E. Fike, *Rails East to Promontory: the Utah Station.* Cultural Resource Series No. 8. (Livingston, Texas: Pioneer Enterprises, 1997).

19. Waldo Nielsen, *Right-of-Way: A Guide to Abandoned Railroads in the United States* (Bend, Ore.: Old Bottle Magazine, 1974), p. 7, p. 101.

20. Eric G. Swedin, "Thiokol in Utah," *Utah Historical Quarterly* 75, no. 1 (Winter 2007): p. 66.

21. Ibid.,p. 68.

EPILOGUE

1. Simon Worrall, "Full Speed Ahead: A Railroad, finally, Crosses Australia's Vast Interior . . .," *Smithsonian* 36, no. 10 (Jan. 2006): p. 93 [pp. 90–100].

Index

188, 196, 207, 218, 229, 235, 240,
260, 270, 275; interest in the history
of, 267; removal of spike in 1942,
277
Promontory Branch, 215, 221, 254, 260,
266
Promontory Hill, UT, 165
Promontory Land and Livestock Co.,
216–17
Promontory line, 92, 227, 303; abandonment of, 267–76; railroad stations on,
110, 192, 235
Promontory Mountains, UT, 1,10, 11,
12, 13, 16,17–21, 23–24, 28–29, 32,
33, 43, 51, 64, 66, 71, 79, 80, 82–83,
88–89, 94, 100, 104, 105–6, 131, 141,
147–48, 151, 170, 172, 174, 215, 252,
293, 301
Promontory Pit, 241
Promontory Point, UT, 11–13, 46, 64,
71, 79, 151, 197, 232, 262, 300
Promontory Precinct (U.S. Census),
154, 199, 258
Promontory Ranch Co., 243
Promontory station, 125, 236, 269
Promontory Summit, UT, 1, 12, 33,
50–51, 64, 71–72, 78, 84–85, 88,
96–98, 105–6, 109–12, 116, 125–26,
128, 141–42, 145, 147, 151, 157–58,
163, 166, 169, 175–76, 192, 202, 204,
206, 208, 210, 212, 219, 221, 223–24,
260, 301, 304; abandonment of line
over in 1942, 276; "Hell on Wheels"
period interpretation, 291; land ownership, 245; railroad facilities at, 192;
visitor center, 295
Promontory-Curlew Land Co., 244–47,
248, 249–52, 263
Pucci, Germano, 230
Pullman cars, 157, 189

Quaker Crystal Salt Co., 269–70
Quarry, UT, 161
quartz miners, 156

rabbits, 83, 217
Raft River Mountains, UT-ID, 22, 33, 72,
175, 178, 302
Railroad Model Craftsman, 286
railroad surveys, 38–48
railroad: tie houses, 162; ties, 162

rails, 197; conditions of, 241
Rails East to Promontory: the Utah Stations
(1994), 296
ranching, 162, 175, 216–17, 269
Rand McNally Co. of Chicago, 181
Red Cloud Saloon at Promontory, 291
Red Dome, UT, 13, 97, 128
Red Dome Hill, UT, 223
Red Dome Mountains, UT, 46, 73, 88,
140, 173, 177
Red Dome Pass, UT, 78–80, 165
Red Dome Summit, UT, 73, 142
redwood, 275
Reed, Samuel, 61, 65, 77, 81–82
Reeder, Adolph, 155–56, 180
refrigerated rail cars, 182–83
removal of line, 274
Right of Way and Track Maps of
Promontory Branch, 254, 261
*Right-of-Way: A Guide to Abandoned
Railroads in the United States*, 298
roads, 270
rock cuts, 183
Rocky Mountain Female Academy, 169
Rogers Locomotive Works, 120
Rosette Asphalt Co. of Rozel, 271
roundhouse, 108, 154–55, 178–79,
193–95
roundhouse, five-stall, at Promontory,
196
Rozel, UT, 116, 150, 156, 163, 173–75,
178, 186, 192, 202, 216, 220, 233, 260,
274, 296, 298
Rozel Flats, UT, 100
"Rules and Regulations for Employees,"
143
Rumsey, David, 3
Russell, Andrew J., 102, 109–10, 122, 139
Russian cemetery, 226
Russian farmers, 226
Russian Hill, 226

Sacramento Daily Union, 123, 167
Sacramento, CA, 96, 157
sagebrush (*Artemisia tridentata*), 28–29,
32–33, 105, 175, 198, 248, 249, 250,
252, 255
salt, 269–70
Salt Creek Marsh, UT, 24
Salt Lake Causeway, 302. *See also* Lucin
Cutoff